ASP.NET Core Application Development: Building an application in four sprints (Developer Reference)

James Chambers
David Paquette
Simon Timms

PUBLISHED BY
Microsoft Press
A division of Microsoft Corporation
One Microsoft Way
Redmond, Washington 98052-6399

Library of Congress Control Number: 2016958907
ISBN: 978-1-5093-0406-6

Printed and bound in the United States of America.

1   16

Microsoft Press books are available through booksellers and distributors worldwide. If you need support related to this book, email Microsoft Press Support at mspinput@microsoft.com. Please tell us what you think of this book at http://aka.ms/tellpress.

Acquisitions Editor: Laura Norman
Developmental Editor: Troy Mott
Editorial Production: Ellie Volckhausen
Technical Reviewer: Rachel Appel
Copyeditor: Rachel Jozsa
Indexer: Julie Grady
Cover: Chuti Prasertsith

I would like to dedicate this book to my loving wife. Thank you for your support and I look forward to spending more time outdoors with you once I finally emerge from this office.

—David Paquette

I would like to dedicate this book to my children who have been forced to play without me while I work feverishly pressing buttons in front of a glowing box and my wife who taught them to sing Cat's In The Cradle outside my office door. Without their support I would be but a quarter of a person. I love them more than I have words to express.

—Simon Timms

I dedicate this book to my incredible, intelligent and striking wife who has supported me for over twenty years while I chase dreams and sometimes our pet dog who gets out in the middle of the night. I dedicate it to my children that I love endlessly and completely. I can't wait to spend more time with them, even if they need more showers and should ask for rides less.

—James Chambers

Contents at a Glance

Table of Contents

What do you think of this book? We want to hear from you!

Microsoft is interested in hearing your feedback so we can improve our books and learning resources for you. To participate in a brief survey, please visit:

http://aka.ms/tellpress

What do you think of this book? We want to hear from you!

Microsoft is interested in hearing your feedback so we can improve our books and learning resources for you. To participate in a brief survey, please visit:

http://aka.ms/tellpress

Introduction

ASP.NET Core MVC is Microsoft's latest web framework for .NET developers. It is the next version of the now-familiar MVC Framework and aspires to cross boundaries by enabling cross-platform development and deployment. It leverages a wide assortment of open source libraries and is, itself built as open source software. ASP.NET Core MVC helps developers to separate concerns like business logic, routing, services, and views and provides new systems for configuration and extensibility. It uses the C# programming language and the Razor view engine. If you are an experienced .NET developer or a newcomer to the .NET platform, ASP.NET Core MVC is likely what your projects will be built from.

This book follows the first few sprints of an application being redeveloped by a team at a fictional company named Alpine Ski House. Each chapter contains a little bit of information about the challenges the team is facing and how they work to overcome them. Despite having a short story element to each chapter, the book dives deep to cover not only the features of ASP.NET Core MVC, but also the tooling around it that developers will use to build, maintain and deploy their applications.

In addition to its story elements and technical information around ASP.NET Core MVC, the book discusses the new version of Entity Framework, package management systems, and peripheral technologies that are used by modern web developers. Beyond the explanatory content, the book also comes with an accompanying project—the very same project that the developers at Alpine Ski House have built.

Who should read this book

The book takes a programmer through all the steps necessary to build a brand new application on ASP.NET Core and push it out so it is available on the Internet. There is still a great population of programmers who have yet to journey onto the web or have done so only using webforms, much less using the full gamut of tooling that is available today. This book will help put the skills and confidence needed in place to build modern applications on an emerging framework. It will help you explore application architecture, deployment and building applications that are designed for the cloud.

Assumptions

Readers should know how to program at an intermediate to senior level. Readers should be proficient in C#, have a background in web development, and understand fundamentals of working in Visual Studio. Experience with previous versions of MVC will be beneficial, but not required. Familiarity in working with a command line interface will be an asset. After completing this book you will be able to build a meaningful and relevant database-driven application and deploy it to a cloud-based infrastructure.

This book might not be for you if...

This book might not be for you if you are an advanced ASP.NET MVC developer who has been closely following or contributing to the development of ASP.NET Core MVC.

Organization of this book

This book offers the innovative approach of taking developers through individual sprints in the development of an application. It will cover not just the technology, but also the process of recovering from mistakes and adjusting to user feedback, starting from a blank canvas and ending with a real working product.

This book is divided into four sections:

- Part 1, "Alpine Ski House," Covers background information that sets up the example app and fictional characters in the story used throughout the book

- Part 2, "Sprint Retro: A Journey of 1000 Steps," focuses on the features required to get our application out the door, configuring the pipeline so that deployment happens on-the-fly in a way that the whole team understands.

- Part 3, "Sprint Retro: The Belly of the Beast," focuses on the core features needed to get the business running with our sample application. Here we introduce data access using the Entity Framework Core, creating views using Razor, Configuration and Logging, Security and User Management, and finally Dependency Injection.

- Part 4, "Sprint Retro 3: Home Stretch" covers JavaScript and dependency management, along with building on top of the previous foundations.

Postfix covers some important topics such as testing, refactoring and extensibility.

Finding your best starting point in this book

The different sections of ASP.NET Core Application Development: Building an application in four sprints cover a wide range of technologies associated with the ASP.NET Core framework. Depending on your needs, and your existing understanding of Microsoft's web stack, you may wish to focus on specific areas of the book. Use the following table to determine how best to proceed through the book.

If you are	Follow these steps
New to ASP.NET Core development, or an existing ASP.NET Core developer	Focus on Parts I, II and III, or read through the entire book in order.
Familiar with earlier releases of ASP. NET	Briefly skim Chapter 1 and Chapter 2 if you need a refresh on the core concepts. Read up on the new technologies throughout the renaminder of the book.
Interested in client side development	Read Chapters 15, 16 and 17 in Part IV. Skim the section on JavaScript services in Chapter 20.
Interested in cross-platform development	The entire book is applicable to cross platform developemnt but Chapter 8 and 9 are specifically deidcated to the topic.

Most of the book's chapters include hands-on samples that let you try out the concepts just learned. No matter which sections you choose to focus on, be sure to download and install the sample applications on your system.

Conventions and features in this book

This book presents information using conventions designed to make the information readable and easy to follow.

- The book includes samples for C# programmers and syntaxes such as HTML, CSS, SCSS and Razor.

- Boxed elements with labels such as "Note" provide additional information or alternative methods for completing a step successfully.

- A plus sign (+) between two key names means that you must press those keys at the same time. For example, "Press Alt+Tab" means that you hold down the Alt key while you press the Tab key.

- **A vertical bar** between two or more menu items (e.g. File | Close), means that you should select the first menu or menu item, then the next, and so on.

System requirements

You will need the following hardware and software to run the sample application accompanying this book:

- .NET Core 1.0 or newer, available cross platform from https://dot.net.

- Your code editor of choice. We use Visual Studio 2015 (any edition) or newer on Windows and Visual Studio Code on Windows, Mac and Ubuntu Linux.

- SQL Server LocalDB (included with Visual Studio 2015 or newer on Windows). Linux or Mac users will need access to a SQL Server database hosted either on a Windows machine or in Microsoft Azure.

- Computer that has a 1.6GHz or faster processor

- At least 1 GB of RAM

- 4 GB of available hard disk space

- Internet connection to download software and sample project

Depending on your Windows configuration, you might require Local Administrator rights to install or configure Visual Studio 2015.

Downloads: Sample Project

Most of the chapters in this book include snippets from the sample project. The sample project is available on GitHub:

https://github.com/AspNetMonsters/AlpineSkiHouse

Follow the instructions on the GitHub repository to download and run the sample project.

> **Note** In addition to the sample project, your system should have .NET Core 1.0 or newer installed.

Errata, updates, & book support

We've made every effort to ensure the accuracy of this book and its companion content. You can access updates to this book—in the form of a list of submitted errata and their related corrections—at:

>   *https://aka.ms/ASPCoreAppDev/errata*

If you discover an error that is not already listed, please submit it to us at the same page.

Get all code samples, including complete apps, at: *https://aka.ms/ASPCoreAppDev/downloads*.

   If you need additional support, email Microsoft Press Book Support at *mspinput@microsoft.com*.

   Please note that product support for Microsoft software and hardware is not offered through the previous addresses. For help with Microsoft software or hardware, go to *http://support.microsoft.com*.

Free ebooks from Microsoft Press

From technical overviews to in-depth information on special topics, the free ebooks from Microsoft Press cover a wide range of topics. These ebooks are available in PDF, EPUB, and Mobi for Kindle formats, ready for you to download at:

>   *http://aka.ms/mspressfree*

Check back often to see what is new!

We want to hear from you

At Microsoft Press, your satisfaction is our top priority, and your feedback our most valuable asset. Please tell us what you think of this book at:

>   *http://aka.ms/tellpress*

We know you're busy, so we've kept it short with just a few questions. Your answers go directly to the editors at Microsoft Press. (No personal information will be requested.) Thanks in advance for your input!

Stay in touch

Let's keep the conversation going! We're on Twitter: *http://twitter.com/MicrosoftPress*

Alpine Ski House

Here is some background information that introduces the fictional aspect covered in this book, including the fictional characters that are creating the Alpine Ski House application.

Even the most fervent riders had to admit it: the season was at an end. It hadn't been the best season in memory but nor had it been the worst. It had been, in every way, unremarkable. There had been moments, a power outage in late February had forced the dusting off of an emergency plan which had long been practiced but never used. There had been reports on the local news station about children trapped on gondolas for hours but with the balmy weather nobody had ever truly been in danger. A smattering of free passes was all that was required to keep the skiers and riders coming.

The spring was a time for the permanent staff to regroup and the seasonal staff to return to wherever it is that lefties go in the summer. A rumor among the permanent staff was that at least half of the seasonal staff were rounded up by immigration as soon as they stepped off the hill and sent back to Australia. Danielle couldn't imagine why the young seasonal staff would resist being sent back to Australia. One thing was for sure, it was much more exciting in Australia than in the sleepy mountain town that reemerged from hibernation each winter.

It was still too early to plan the next year and Danielle was looking forward to a month or two of down time before the cycle began anew. She had been the lone developer for Alpine Ski House for close to a decade and every year was about the same. Most of her time involved keeping legacy systems running and adjusting whatever small things were needed for the next year's activities. It wasn't the most exciting job in the world but over the winter months it was expected that everybody would sneak off for a couple of hours skiing on nice days and that was a perk she thoroughly enjoyed.

Opening the door to the low-rise that Alpine Ski House called home she was surprised to see that things were buzzing. People she wouldn't have expected to see in the office for a couple of hours were scattered about in huddles throughout the open plan office. Confused, Danielle dumped her bag and grabbed a coffee before looking for a huddle to join. The rest of the IT staff seemed to be orbiting Tim, the portly IT manager and her boss. Danielle headed over to join.

"Danielle! What do you think of the news, going to be an exciting time if you ask me," boomed Tim.

"What news is this?" asked Danielle.

"Where have you been?" asked Arjun, "We just bought out Thunder Valley and Mount Ballyhoo. They're merging operations and we're all going to lose our jobs!"

The two other ski areas were a few miles down the road. Thunder Valley was a small operation with only three lifts but a loyal following of ski bums. It was a favorite for the locals who wanted a break from the crowds of tourists in the winter months. It couldn't be more different from Mount Ballyhoo if it had been the output of Babbage's difference machine. Mount Ballyhoo was a huge ski hill spanning three mountains with countless lifts and enough on hill accommodation to house everybody in town twice over. Every weekend they had bands playing on the hill, and it was not uncommon to see famous people like Scott Gu and John Skeet there rubbing shoulders with the commoners.

"Now Arjun," said Tim, "nobody has said anything about layoffs or redundancies or anything of the sort. Why at times like this the workload for IT usually increases because management wants systems integrated right away. We're just going to have to wait and find out what the plans are."

Danielle had to sit down. She was years still from retirement and didn't want to find another job. How many jobs would there be for programmers in a seasonal town like this? "This is silly," she told herself, "there is no use planning a move back to the big city based on this sort of uncertainty. Things will shake out in the next couple of weeks."

As it turned out nobody was waiting a couple of weeks.

As soon as lunch, a dandelion and walnut salad, with balsamic sweet potato crisps, was over, Tim came knocking at her cubicle.

"We're gathering in the big conference room. It sounds like the programmers from Thunder and Ballyhoo are here."

Gulping down the rest of her goat's milk, Danielle grabbed a pen and a big yellow legal pad and hurried towards the conference room. The pad and paper were just for show; she hadn't taken notes at a meeting in years. It was easier to just engage people around the small office in person than plan things out way in advance on a notepad. Better to make a good impression right away with layoffs on the horizon.

The big conference room was rarely used outside of potlucks because there simply weren't enough people to fill it. But today it was, if not packed, at least well used. Five young hipster looking individuals sat at one end of the table sipping on all manner of exotic looking smoothies. Danielle wondered how one would even go about importing rambutan and what sort of carbon footprint it would have. Still it was better than that time she had hacked her way into a durian only to have to defenestrate the offensive fruit.

Clearly divided from the hipsters were a group guys who would have been called "suits" in the big city. Out here they looked like they had just stepped of a golf course. Somehow they were already tanned and relaxed looking.

Tim waited for everybody to settle and then addressed the room, "Good news, everybody, this is the team we're moving forward with. If you've made it to this room, then your job is safe and you can relax. I'm sure you all have questions about that and you can come see me individually after this meeting if you want to talk.

"Management has asked me to keep a larger number of programmers on staff after the merge because they have some exciting new initiatives that they want us to embark upon. Over the next few years we're going to be refreshing all the custom systems we have in place to run the hill. They recognize that this is a big undertaking and some of them have been reading CIO magazine and they've learned about agile and microservices. I can assure you that I've given instructions that all future copies of that magazine are to be burned before they reach management's hands but for now we're stuck with it."

Tim had always had a bit of a rocky relationship with management's great new ideas. He was the emergency brake on their crazy ideas. He continued on. "The first thing management want is a way for people to buy their lift tickets online. I'm told that it is 2016 and that we should have that in place already and that every other hill in the world has it." Tim seemed exasperated by management's generalizations; it must have been a fun discussion when these orders came down.

"Management wants to see a prototype in a month's time. I think I can buy another week if we can show that we're making progress."

A month's time! Danielle was beside herself. A month was how long Danielle liked to spend getting her head around a problem. She looked over at the hipster developers hoping they shared her ashen face. But the wheatgrass crew were nodding along happily.

Tim looked like he was coming to a conclusion and readying to step down from his soapbox. "Look guys, we need this to buy us some capital with management. I'll clear any roadblocks in your way. Use whatever technology you think is best buy whatever tools you need. I trust you to get this done."

## CHAPTER 1

How We Got Here

When Tim finished his speech, he and the golf course crew tumbled out of the room, leaving Danielle alone with the five hipster programmers. Of course, nobody had been put in charge of the new development team. Likely, Tim had read a bit of the CIO magazine he was throwing out, and had decided that the best team was a self-organizing team. Danielle figured that slipping a twenty to the mail carrier to lose the magazines in the future might save her at least that much in pain killers over the next year.

The hipsters all introduced themselves as Adrian, Chester, Candice, and the Marks: Marc and Mark. They had all come over from Mount Ballyhoo, which had decided just a few weeks earlier that it was going to cut its offshore development team and hire a full team internally. The hipsters had all worked together at a Silicon Valley startup and Mount Ballyhoo had hired them as a complete team, which Danielle agreed was a pretty great idea. They hadn't even been at Ballyhoo long enough to start on a project before they were bought out. They all seemed really friendly and excited.

"I love that management is letting us pick our own technologies," remarked Mark. "It shows that they trust us enough to get out of our way."

"Picking a technology is always my favorite part of a project," said Candice.

"There are a million great choices out there these days: Phoenix, Revel, Express, even Meteor. What's your bread and butter, Danielle?" asked Adrian.

Phoenix? Express? It sounded like web frameworks were being named after their author's favorite Chinese food restaurants. Danielle hadn't heard of any of these things. She was an ASP.NET developer through and through. She'd arrived there from writing Winforms applications and had only she been working the last year with ASP.NET MVC. Throwing caution to the wind, she replied "I usually use ASP.NET."

"Oh yeah!" shouted Marc. It seemed like the lack of a 'k' in his name resulted in every comment being delivered at 90 dB. "The team at Microsoft is doing some amazing things with ASP.NET Core. You should see the throughput numbers they are getting! It is lemonade!"

Danielle wasn't sure what "lemonade" meant in this context. It didn't seem like it was a bad thing, so she nodded along in agreement.

"Huh," said Candice. "I wasn't expecting ASP.NET to be on the table."

"It is new and cool ," said Marc. "Danielle, you have some history in ASP.NET. Can you walk us through how it got to where it is now?"

Web development is not all that new anymore. In the very early days, the web was just a static place with hyperlinks controlling navigation. The limitations of this approach quickly became apparent. It was difficult keeping a theme consistent on every page, and showing the same webpage to everybody was boring.

Web servers started supporting technologies that allowed webpages to appear differently depending on their inputs , because. Plenty of technologies have come and gone, like Server Side Includes, while others like Common Gateway Interface (CGI) scripts have remained in one form or another. The name Active Server Pages, or ASP, has remained for two decades, although the technology has changed dramatically. We are on the cusp of another big change in the technology behind the ASP name. Before we get too far into the new technology, let's take a look at how we got here.

Active Server Pages

In 1996, version 3 of Internet Information Services was released with support for the first version of ASP. ASP is built on top of the Active Scripting technology. The use of Active Scripting is not limited to ASP, because the technology is included as part of Internet Explorer, and Windows Script Host as well.

ASP allows scripts written in another language to be included and executed as part of serving a webpage. In theory, most languages are supported via the Component Object Model (COM) integration in Active Scripting. JScript and VBScript were the two well supported Microsoft languages competing in the space at the time. This was the mid-1990s, however, so languages such as Perl were popular too. Perl allowed for some degree of cross platform portability because it was supported on Linux and could run via the Apache CGI-gateway. Perl was one of the most popular languages at that time for creating interactive web applications to run on early versions of Apache and was the precursor to Apache's NCSA HTTPd.

Let's look at a sample file using VBScript as the scripting language. Let's make sure that the output uses modern HTML5-based tags. There is no reason that ASP cannot be used to build modern applications.

```
<%@ Language= "VBScript" %>

<html>
  <head>
  <title>Example 1</title>
</head>
<body>
 <header>
  <h1>Welcome to my Home Page</h1>
 </header>
  <section id="main">
    <%
    dim strDate
    dim strTime

    'Get the date and time.
    strDate  = Date()
    strTime = Time()

    'Display a different greeting depending on the time of day
    If "AM" = Right(strTime, 2) Then
```

```
        Response.Write "<span>Good Morning!</span>"
    Else
        Response.Write "<span>Good Afternoon!</span>"
    End If
    %>
    Today's date is <%=strDate %> and the time <%=strTime%>

    </section>
  </body>
</html>
```

In this sample you can see a number of different approaches for pushing data into the output. The first approach is to use the direct access to the response stream through `Response.Write`, which is done for the greeting. The second is to use the <%= %> directive, which is a short form to write out to the response stream. The approach here is very much like what you might see in other scripting languages, such as PHP. HTML tags are ignored by the compiler unless they are special tags that contain directives. These can be recognized by the sequence <%. The <%@ directive is a processing directive that gives the ASP compiler the information it needs to process the page. The example above uses a directive to set the language to be used as the primary language for the rest of the page. The plain <% directive denotes a simple code block.

Unlike PHP, Active Server Pages are able to share libraries through the COM. This allows for access to native components that can perform at high speed or access native functionality. It also allows you to compile component libraries that improve the ability to structure an application and promote code reuse.

In the late 1990s, Microsoft started developing its next generation development environment. At the time it was called Next Generation Windows Services, or NGWS. By late 2000 this had become the .NET framework. This framework included a reimagining of the popular Visual Basic language. This reimagining added object oriented programming to the language, which was a dramatic change. In many ways VB.NET, as it became known, was a totally different language from the previous version. .NET included a well architected base class library that provided a lot of common functionality. The Base Class Library (BCL) was heavily influenced by a similar library that underlies Java.

.NET introduced a brand new language called C#. Heavily influenced by Java, C# provided a more C-like syntax for those who had come from a C or Java background. Microsoft pushed C# quite hard and as a result it has become the most popular language on the .NET framework.

In conjunction with the new languages of C# and Visual Basic .NET, a new version of ASP was introduced. This version was called ASP.NET.

ASP.NET

Even in the late 1990s it was apparent that the World Wide Web was going to be more than a passing fad. Unfortunately, Microsoft had a problem. They had spent years building tools to allow for the creation of desktop applications through a drag and drop editor. Developers were used to building applications using that model, and companies were not likely to pay to retrain their entire workforce. Interaction with the controls was provided using an event handler model. A button on a form would take an event handler to perform some behind-the-scenes action and could then update the User Interface (UI). The developer community was comfortable with this approach and, what's more, was very productive. To this day there remains almost no tool as productive as the What You See Is What You Get (WYSIWYG) code generation found in Visual Basic, and later WinForms. It might not have been the most visually stunning interface, but if your product called for gray boxes on a gray background, you can do much worse than Visual Basic 6 or WinForms.

ASP.NET Web Forms was an attempt to bring this productive environment to the web. Similar drag and drop functionality existed for adding controls to a grid and interacting with them using compiled, server-side code.

Unfortunately, the postback model, in which interactions are posted back to the server, ignored the fundamental difference between web applications and desktop applications, which was that every call to post back data and perform an action on the server required an entire HTTP request and response trip over the Internet. Despite this flaw, ASP.NET Web Forms has become a hugely successful product that powers countless websites both internal to companies and on the greater World Wide Web.

Pages in Web Forms usually include two parts: A view and its code behind. The view, or display, portion is written in a special syntax that mixes HTML and either Visual Basic or C#. These files end with the .aspx extension and are passed through an ASP compiler. There is some debate about what these files should contain. They are very open ended so some people put all of their logic in the file, while others restrict the content to only display related logic. There have been successful projects using both approaches. The portions in the code behind are compiled into a DLL, which means that making changes on the fly isn't possible. The .aspx file are compiled on the fly, which means that it is possible, although highly unadvisable, to make changes on the server with just a text editor.

Each page is implemented as an HTML form. This allows Web Forms to easily capture state changes and react to them by capturing a post back of the form. If you ever use a site that reloads the entire page when you mouse away from a data entry field, it is likely a Web Forms application posting the page state back to the server so that it can make decisions about what to change on the page based on the input. This isn't a fantastic interaction model, and can be improved through the use of AJAX and Update Panels, which post back only portions of the page.

In order to maintain a consistent look and feel over a website, Web Forms use master pages. These pages can contain common look and feel components. You can then plug different sections in depending on the page being executed. This eliminates a lot of work, avoiding the need to update the look and feel in many places. An application can have many different master pages and the pages can even be nested. You might have a master page for logged out users, and a master page for logged in users. Being able to nest master pages also enabled some interesting scenarios where pages could be created like a nest of dolls with each master page adding just a bit more content to the page, as shown in Figure 1-1.

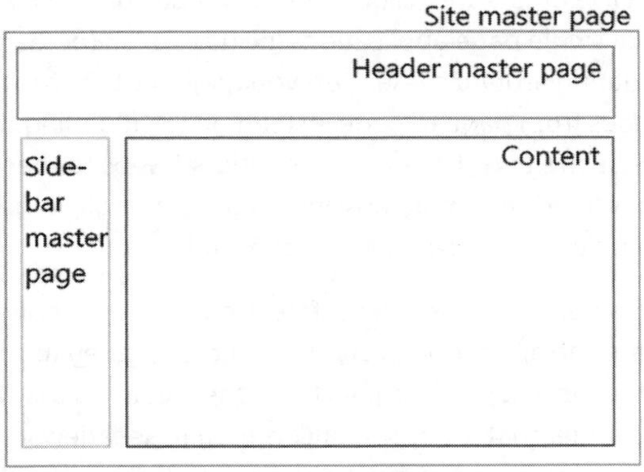

FIGURE 1-1 Nested master pages

User controls are another reuse mechanism. Typically located in .ascx files and an accompanying VB or C# code behind, a user control is like a tiny portable .aspx page that can be put inside of other pages. For example, if you need to have a drop-down for selecting a brand of car all over your site, all you need to do is build a user control containing the logic for selecting car brands. This control can then be embedded wherever it is needed. The logic and display code for a user control can be centralized ensuring that you don't feel the need to repeat yourself everywhere.

Building impressive user controls became a business model on which many a company was founded. Table controls, which were always mind-numbing to create, were especially popular and resulted in something of an arms race between component vendors building more expansive and feature-rich tables. No matter what your need, there is likely a vendor willing to sell you a collection of controls that meet your requirements. This is actually an incredible boon to productivity after you have learned to use these complex controls.

While productive, the user experience in Web Forms is perhaps not what users have come to expect of the modern web. The problem with building an abstraction to make the web programmable like the desktop is that the web isn't the desktop. Many of the shims that are needed make the interaction feel clunky. While the interaction model might be fine for intranet sites, there are likely very few major sites in operation that are built on the foundation of Web Forms. In many ways it is like trying to fit a round peg into a square hole, as shown in Figure 1-2. It fits but there are some gaps.

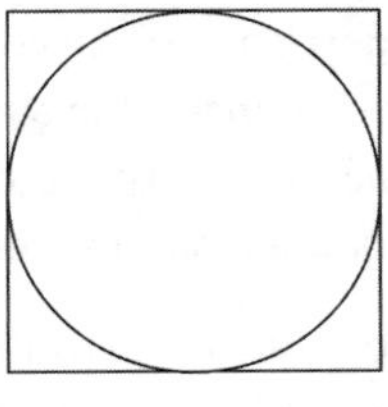

FIGURE 1-2 A round peg in a square hole

Single page applications (SPAs) are pages that live on the web client and do not perform full page refreshes during navigation. Fantastic examples of single page applications include Gmail (perhaps the first popular SPA), Trello, and Twitter. When navigating around these sites, you might notice that the reloaded data is limited to the content that changes from page to page instead of downloading the entire chrome of the site. The user experience for such sites is better than traditional websites because there is a feeling of continuity during navigation. While it might be possible to build a single page application using nothing but Web Forms, it would be very difficult and time consuming.

The state of a Web Form page is kept in a container known as a ViewState. Depending on how the site implements ViewState, the encoded ViewState can appear on every page and be passed around between the client and the server on every request. As you can imagine, this adds greatly to the weight of the page over the wire, especially when you consider that it was not uncommon to see ViewStates pushing several megabytes in size. In Internet scenarios, speed of transmission can affect everything from user satisfaction to search ranking. The problem is compounded by the prevalence of mobile devices. Bandwidth costs are non-trivial for many on mobile platform and the time to load a large page over a cellular network can be enough to drive users away.

To address some of the shortcomings of Web Forms, another change was made in 2007 with the release of ASP.NET MVC.

ASP.NET MVC

The teams inside Microsoft always make a great effort to maintain backward compatibility with previous versions of a product. While ASP.NET MVC is superior in many ways to Web Forms, it was never intended as a replacement so much as a second way of building a web application. To avoid the obvious argument, It should be said that Web Forms still have some advantages over ASP.NET MVC. ASP.NET MVC is closer to the wire than Web Forms, stripping away many of the abstractions that made Web Forms both heavy weight and easy to work with. You do not necessarily need to make a decision about which approach to take, because you can mix MVC and Web Forms together in a single project. Indeed, this is a fabulous way to start migrating an existing application from Web Forms to MVC, by replacing pages one at a time.

The first idea from Web Forms to be altered in MVC is having a code behind the model for each page. It was possible to build Web Forms applications with good separation of concerns. It was, however, just as easy, if not easier, to build an application that ignored the proper layering of responsibility. ASP.NET MVC built on top of the Model-View-Controller pattern, and encouraged isolating UI concerns in a view, behavior concerns in a controller, and storage and communication concerns in a model. The built in separation of concerns allows for better testability and promotes code reuse. This is just one of the ways that ASP.NET MVC encourages developers to fall into the unavoidable pit of success.

When a request arrives at an ASP.NET MVC site, one of the first things it encounters is the routing table, which directs the request to a destination that might be a file or it might be a chunk of code in a controller. This breaks the reliance on .aspx files existing on disk. The route table opens up a number of interesting possibilities. It enables custom URLs that are handy for giving users hints as to what is on the page as well as for search engine optimization. If you have a multi-tenant site, it is now trivial to make URLs that look like the following:

```
https://site.com/{ComapnyName}/User/Add
```

This is instead of the far less friendly version that is common:

```
https://site.com/User/Add?companyId=15
```

You can also add multiple routes for a single end point that can eliminate a lot of code duplication.

Routing usually maps a request to a controller. Controllers are simple objects that descend from the controller base class. Within the controller, public methods that return an ActionResult are candidates for routing. Action methods can take in the normal parameter types you might expect in a .NET method. MVC uses model binding to convert parameters found in the HTTP request into the .NET types. Model binding is amazingly powerful and makes development far easier. Custom model binders can be added to map complex objects; however, in most cases the default mapper does everything needed.

The method chosen by the framework is a function of the name of the controller, the method on the controller, and any annotations on the methods. For instance, it is possible to have two methods in a controller called Add, which vary only by the method signature. The method chosen can be hinted at by annotating the methods with [HttpGet] or [HttpPost] attributes.

```
[HttpGet]
public ActionResult Add(){
//perform some operation
return View();
}
[HttpPost]
public ActionResult Add(AddModel model){
    //validate model
    //save
    //redirect
}
```

A commonly used paradigm is that the GET action returns a form page and the POST action accepts the contents of that form, saves them, and then redirects to another action. There are a number of different ActionResults that can be returned from an action. You can return a redirect result to redirect the user to a different page or a file stream result to stream back a file. JSON results set the mimetype to application/json and return a serialized version of the action's results. View results pass the result of the action into the view engine responsible for converting the result of the action into HTML, which is what is passed back to the end user.

The views (that's the V in MVC) are the presentation layer and do most of what you would have done previously in an .aspx file. The view engine in MVC is pluggable, allowing for different syntaxes to be used. Early versions of MVC made use of the same view engine as Web Forms, but in more recent releases Razor has become the default view engine. Razor is a more modern view engine that mixes far more seamlessly with the HTML. The design goals for Razor included making it easy to learn and make you more productive. Those goals were certainly achieved and the experience is far better than using the old WebView syntax.

Razor syntax is closer to pure HTML than previous view engines. In organizations where web designers edit actual HTML, a practice that is becoming more common, there is a lower barrier to entry for designers with Razor than with the Web Forms engine.

The data passed to the view by the controller can take a couple of routes. The first approach is to add values to either the ViewBag or ViewData, which are collections available in the view and in the controller. ViewData is a dictionary of strings pointing to objects, while ViewBag is a dynamic object on which one can simply address properties. Obviously, both of these collections are loosely typed, which might require casting in the views introducing the potential for runtime errors.

The second, and generally better, approach is to use a strongly typed model to communicate between the view and controller. Models can enforce that the data in the model is what is expected and also that it is named correctly. The runtime errors in the ViewBag and ViewData approach are converted to compile time errors, which is almost always better.

A model is a plain old CLR object (POCO), which contains a collection of fields. MVC provides some features around the model that allow for validation. Using the annotations inside of the ComponentModel namespace fields can be marked as required, not null, restricted to a range, or a number of others. Custom validator can also be written allowing all sorts of complex validations like checking against the database or calling out to a third party validation service. The validations can be fired during the processing of the action in the controller by simply checking if the ModelState is valid.

One complaint about early versions of ASP.NET MVC was that it lacked the productivity of Web Forms. A particular challenge was that the power of user controls wasn't readily available in MVC. This was rectified through the creation of editor and view templates. This fantastic and underused feature allows you to assign a template to a field in a model. When Razor can encounter a directive to display an editor for that field, such as the ones shown here it examines the model to see if there is a special editor or view defined in the form of an HTML helper or partial view.:

```
@Html.DisplayFor(model => model.StartDate)
@Html.EditorFor(model => model.StartDate)
```

These directives can be defined by convention or by annotating a field in the model with a UI Hint annotation that determines which template to load. The helper templates are Razor files that can contain any specific display or editing logic needed to show the field. In the case of the StartDate shown in the previous example, the editor template could contain a control for editing dates. By spreading the annotation around to various models, you can centralize the displaying and editing of dates to a single place. If there is a change to the way dates are displayed, it only needs to be done in one file. This is an example of a cross cutting concern, where you apply the same logic to many different classes.

This is not the only cross cutting point in the MVC framework; there are also filters. A filter is applied with an annotation to either a whole controller or to individual action methods inside a controller. Filters can intercept and change any request adding data or mutating existing data, even changing the flow of the request. Security is often applied using filter annotations. Authorization attributes provide for a very simple way of applying complex authorization rules throughout the application.

Another example of centralizing logic in an MVC application is middleware. Middleware, built on the Open Web Interface for .NET (OWIN) standard, largely takes the place of the custom Internet Information Server (IIS) modules, which were once the only way to intercept all requests. In middleware you can perform all manner of generalized operations. For instance, if you want to add some logging information to every request, middleware could be used for entry and exit logging.

Cross cutting concerns don't necessarily need to be in the logic of the application. They can be in the user interface. Just as Web Forms support master pages, MVC supports layouts that work in pretty much the same way as master pages. One added feature is that a single view can fill in multiple sections in the layout, which allows you to put in, for example, content and the breadcrumbs leading to that content in one file.

MVC allows for greater control over the content on the wire and removes many of the incompatible abstractions from the Web Forms era. Applications built using MVC tend to be more testable, better architected, faster from the user's perspective, and easier to introduce to new developers.

Web API

The near-instant popularity of ASP.NET MVC inspired another new web property from the ASP.NET team: the Web API. Where ASP.NET MVC tried to take some of the mindshare of Web Forms, Web API attempted to do the same thing for Simple Object Access Protocol (SOAP) services created as .asmx files. The .asmx file extension was the first generation of remote method invocation over HTTP that Microsoft embarked upon. SOAP web services were a powerful paradigm, but rapidly became extremely complicated. Standards such as WS-Security and WS-BPEL were complex and poorly understood. To address these standards, Microsoft created Windows Communication Foundation (WCF) a runtime and set of APIs that took the complex standards of WS-* and ramped up the complexity to the point where no single human being could understand it.

A simpler method of communicating between services and between web clients and servers was required. Fortunately, Roy Fielding's thesis on representational state transfer (REST) was gaining popularity. REST is a simple method of communicating actions on a set of objects by using the HTTP verbs. In a SOAP web service you would create an end point named something like AddUser, which would take the parameters needed to create a user wrapped in a SOAP envelope. The envelope contains the message body and possibly some headers. The server would then return some response confirming that the user had indeed been added. A request might look like the following:

```
POST /User HTTP/1.1
Host: www.example.org
Content-Type: application/soap+xml; charset=utf-8
Content-Length: 299
SOAPAction: "http://www.w3.org/2003/05/soap-envelope"

<?xml version="1.0"?>
<soap:Envelope xmlns:soap="http://www.w3.org/2003/05/soap-envelope">
  <soap:Header>
  </soap:Header>
  <soap:Body>
```

```
      <m:AddUser xmlns:m="http://www.example.org/user">
        <m:FirstName>Glenn</m:FirstName >
        <m:LastName>Block</m:LastName >
      </m: AddUser >
    </soap:Body>
  </soap:Envelope>
```

As you can see, this is quite a complex message. If the server was able to process the request correctly, it would probably return an HTTP 200 result code. A RESTful message doing the same thing might look like:

```
POST /User HTTP/1.1
Host: www.example.org
Content-Type: application/json; charset=utf-8
Content-Length: 75

{ "FirstName": "Glenn", "LastName":"Block"}
```

What is more interesting than the stripped down payload is that the server would probably respond with a 201 status code. If you're not familiar with this code, it is the "Created" status code. REST attempts to strip out much of SOAP's noise by leveraging the conventions found in the HTTP specification. For instance, to delete an item, use the DELETE verb. To get information about an entity, you could use the GET verb.

WCF supported creating RESTful web services through the creation of their WCF Web API project. This was a much simplified version of WCF which set rational defaults for many of the settings available in WCF. This WCF Web API project eventually morphed into the vanilla Web API project, which was simpler again.

When first looking at a Web API project's code, a person could be forgiven for mistaking it for an MVC application. A Web API project contains a Controllers folder as well as a Models folder, much like a full MVC application. The Views folder, as well as others like Content and Scripts, are missing, but they contain resources used to render the UI, which doesn't exist in a Web API project.

Looking at a controller in a Web API project, you'll notice that the actions are named after the HTTP verbs they respond to. For instance, there could be a Post method, which is what would be executed in the event the controller received an HTTP POST request. The default scaffolding generates a Post method which looks like this:

```
public async Task<IHttpActionResult> Post(User user)
        {
            if (!ModelState.IsValid)
            {
                return BadRequest(ModelState);
            }

            // TODO: Add create logic here.

            // return Created(user);
            return StatusCode(HttpStatusCode.NotImplemented);
        }
```

You can see that it is indeed named after the verb it responds to.

WCF supports self-hosting, that is running outside of IIS and that heritage has flowed into Web API. This means that it is simple to spin up a quick Web API application that is bin deployable.

Perhaps the most interesting part of Web API is that it is one of the first open source projects from Microsoft. The source code for it was fully released and is now licensed under the Apache 2.0 license. The project is part of the non-profit .NET Foundation, an independent organization that aims to foster open development around the .NET ecosystem.

Most of the functionality of Web API is mirrored in vanilla ASP.NET MVC. There is some confusion about when to use a Web API controller and when to use an MVC controller as the MVC controller can be bent to preform pretty much as the Web API controller does for simple use cases. Web API and MVC can both be used in the same project.

ASP.NET Core

ASP.NET's evolution is ongoing and the next step is ASP.NET Core. You might have also heard it referred to as ASP.NET vNext, ASP.NET 5, or ASP.NET MVC6, which were all early names. The development of the next version of ASP.NET and ASP.NET MVC has been done in a very open fashion. While previous versions of ASP.NET MVC were open source, their development was still done behind closed doors. It was possible to submit code to the projects but to do so the process was quite involved. One might even say that contributions weren't encouraged. This meant that you were still at the mercy of Microsoft to include a feature that was very important to your project.

ASP.NET Core was developed on GitHub where anybody can make pull requests with suggestions for features or bug fixes. There have been significant community contributions and while the governance is still owned by Microsoft, the product is far better than it would have been had it been developed in-house.

If you're interested in contributing to ASP.NET, head over to *https://github.com/aspnet/home* and read how to contribute.

ASP.NET Core is a substantially different product from previous version of ASP.NET. It is a far reaching modernization effort designed to make ASP.NET highly competitive with the most powerful web frameworks of the day, such as those from the Node, Elixr, and Go communities.

ASP.NET Core goes hand in hand with the modernization efforts on the .NET runtime called .NET Core. This effort focuses on a number of improvements, perhaps the most important of which is that .NET Core is supported on operating systems other than Windows. This means that you can develop your application on macOS and deploy it via a Docker image to a collection of Linux machines running on the Azure cloud.

ASP.NET Core is a fabulous engineering effort and one that is arguably worthy of at least one book.

Summary

The Microsoft web stack supports a number of different server side technologies. The right choice of which technology to use is highly dependent on the requirements of the project. There are some places where Web Forms might still be the correct approach and others where more output fine tuning is required making MVC and Web API the better choices.

As the Microsoft stack has been evolving, so have other web development stacks. No matter how large and influential Microsoft might be, it cannot dictate the future of the web by itself. It is therefore important to also understand how ASP.NET fits into the greater web sphere and what has influenced it. We'll cover that in the next chapter.

## CHAPTER 2

Influencers

Danielle blinked; it seemed like she had been talking about ASP.NET for ages. Twenty years of ASP.NET history distilled into an hour and three whiteboards full of arrows and stick figures. Danielle had never really thought about the whole history of ASP.NET before. It was interesting to see how things had evolved.

"I don't know," Candice mused. "This sounds a lot like we're going to end up mired in some type of Microsoft-only technology stack. I'm not convinced that we're going to be doing things in the best way but rather just the Microsoft way."

Danielle knew that not everybody did things the same way as Microsoft, but their approach wasn't that different, was it? Everything was servers and web pages, right? Web Forms was a bit special, but MVC was very similar to everything else. Before she could voice her thoughts, Marc, of course, jumped in.

"Oh for sure that would have been the case a decade ago. Microsoft did some things back then. Anybody remember that thing in IE4 where you could use PowerPoint-style transitions between pages?"[1]

"But this latest ASP.NET Core really takes a lot of the best ideas from other frameworks and makes them their own. The default template comes with gulp, npm, and bower by default."

"Really?" asked Danielle. She hadn't been paying attention to what had been happening with the new framework.

"Yep!" said Marc, who was quickly becoming an advocate for ASP.NET Core. "Early versions of ASP.NET might have been built in a vacuum, but many other frameworks like Rails have been influential in shaping ASP.NET Core."

The island of Madagascar is just far enough away from mainland Africa that it is difficult for plants and animals to transfer between the two landmasses. The result of this is that Madagascar has some of the most interesting and wildly unique flora and fauna on earth. Most places don't benefit from this sort of isolation and plants and animals are heavily influenced by invaders from hundreds, or even thousands of miles away. ASP.NET long lived on one of these isolated islands. ASP.NET MVC was a more open version of ASP.NET that took some of its ideas from other popular frameworks, and ASP.NET Core ends this isolation altogether and is heavily influenced by other web frameworks and technologies. In this chapter we explore some of the reasons that the ASP.NET team made the design decisions they did and from what other projects they took some of their ideas.

---

1 *https://msdn.microsoft.com/en-us/library/ms532847(v=vs.85).aspx#Interpage_Transition*

Backward compatibility

It's said that ASP.NET Core is a dramatic departure from the way that ASP.NET worked before. This is the same complaint that was leveled against ASP.NET MVC when it was first released and likely at ASP.NET Web Forms when it entered a world dominated by plain Active Server Pages. It is certain that each one of these transitions was a departure from the previous generation of tooling. Each one of these changes, however, was an incremental change building on the previous generation. For instance, the HTTPRrequest object has been a fairly consistent object since the early 2000s.

Microsoft Windows is a phenomenal example of a product that strives to maintain backward compatibility. It's likely that applications originally written for Windows 95 will run, unmodified, on the latest version of Windows. Of course, this sort of backward compatibility does not come without a cost. Every change made to the Windows API has to be carefully examined to ensure that it doesn't break any existing applications. As you can imagine, this means that there is a tremendous testing load for even the smallest change. Continuing to evolve the operating system is hampered by the weight of these legacy support requirements.

Maintaining a sense of familiarity of names and concepts between products is a huge concern for the ASP.NET team. A great deal of energy is dedicated to ensuring that there is a path forward for all developers when moving to a new product. The primary influencer on ASP.NET Core is certainly previous versions of ASP.NET, and those who have worked with a previous version of ASP.NET MVC will likely find ASP.NET Core MVC familiar. The fundamental types—Models, Views, and Controllers—remain. Razor is still the default view engine, and actions on controllers still return the same named types. The changes that have been made have been done with a great deal of deliberation. Among the changes in ASP.NET Core MVC are updated best practices in the JavaScript space, as well as improved testability and first-class support for dependency injection.

Let's examine some of the framework's other influencers.

Rails

No discussion about Model View Controller (MVC) web frameworks should avoid mentioning Ruby on Rails. MVC is an old pattern dating back to the 1970s, so its eventual application to the web was inevitable. Ruby on Rails is an implementation of MVC using the Ruby programming language. Ruby on Rails, or simply Rails as it has become known, emerged from the company 37 Signals in the early 2000s. It was built to aid in the development of the Basecamp project management tool and was open sourced by its creators.

Web development at the time of Rails' release was something of a jumble. ASP.NET existed, but the only official way to work with it was through Web Forms. In the Java space, the Spring framework was emerging as a powerful tool that included some MVC tooling. Spring's MVC was largely a reaction to Jakarta Struts, a framework that built on top of the servlets that were the official Sun approach to server-side web programming. Of course, PHP was also popular at that time, as it remains today. Early versions of PHP were pretty rough around the edges. The frameworks at that time were limited to a small handful, that were largely organic in their design, meaning that they weren't easily testable or extensible.

Rails was a breath of fresh air into this space. It is a highly opinionated framework, meaning that it provided for the Ruby or the Rails way of doing things and deviating from that approach was quite difficult. Instead of allowing for complex configuration options and an infinitely configurable application framework, Rails favors using conventions. This can be seen permeating all facets of Rails. For instance, the directory structure for a Rails application, as shown in Figure 2-1, is generated by the Rails tool and is the same for almost every Rails project.

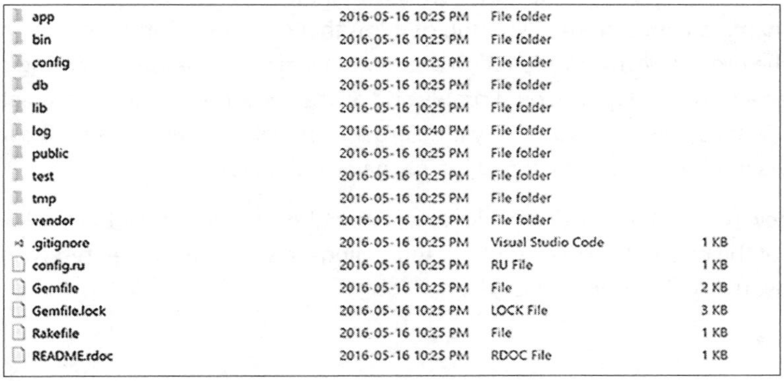

app	2016-05-16 10:25 PM	File folder	
bin	2016-05-16 10:25 PM	File folder	
config	2016-05-16 10:25 PM	File folder	
db	2016-05-16 10:25 PM	File folder	
lib	2016-05-16 10:25 PM	File folder	
log	2016-05-16 10:40 PM	File folder	
public	2016-05-16 10:25 PM	File folder	
test	2016-05-16 10:25 PM	File folder	
tmp	2016-05-16 10:25 PM	File folder	
vendor	2016-05-16 10:25 PM	File folder	
.gitignore	2016-05-16 10:25 PM	Visual Studio Code	1 KB
config.ru	2016-05-16 10:25 PM	RU File	1 KB
Gemfile	2016-05-16 10:25 PM	File	2 KB
Gemfile.lock	2016-05-16 10:25 PM	LOCK File	3 KB
Rakefile	2016-05-16 10:25 PM	File	1 KB
README.rdoc	2016-05-16 10:25 PM	RDOC File	1 KB

FIGURE 2-1 An example of the directory structure created by the Rails tool

Controllers are found in /app/controllers and are named with the _controller suffix. Views are found in /app/views. When adding a new entity, use the Rails command to generate not just the controller, but views, helpers, and even unit tests.

```
rails g controller menu

Running via Spring preloader in process 15584

        create   app/controllers/menu_controller.rb

        invoke   erb

        create   app/views/menu

        invoke   test_unit

        create   test/controllers/menu_controller_test.rb

        invoke   helper

        create   app/helpers/menu_helper.rb

        invoke   test_unit

        create   test/helpers/menu_helper_test.rb
```

```
invoke    assets

invoke    coffee

create    app/assets/javascripts/menu.js.coffee

invoke    scss

create    app/assets/stylesheets/menu.css.scss
```

This convention-based layout approach might look familiar because it was also used by the ASP.NET team during the creation of ASP.NET MVC. In the Web Forms world, there was no common directory structure and no implied naming conventions. The result of this is that each Web Forms application is unique. The structure of the project becomes a function of the whims of the developers working on the project. Too often, inexperienced developers would simply add all the .aspx files to the root directory, resulting in a directory with hundreds of files and very little organizational structure. This makes it very difficult for new developers to walk into a project and rapidly gain an understanding.

In ASP.NET MVC, the new project template came with a defined directory structure. Even within controllers, the influence of the convention over configuration mindset is obvious. When returning a view from an action, you would typically write this:

```
public ActionResult Index()
{
    return View();
}
```

A large number of conventions are at play here. The first is that any public method that returns an `ActionResult` is considered to be a public end point. Second, this method is called Index, which is a special name mapped to the root route of the containing controller. Next, the View method here takes no arguments. By convention, the cshtml file returned from this action is the one named Index.cshtml in the subdirectory of /Views, which matches the name of the controller.

If the ASP.NET team had instead decided to make all of these selections explicit, the same, simple-looking method would balloon to something like this:

```
[ActionMethod]
[Route("/Menu")]
public ActionResult Index()
{
    return View("~/Views/Menu/Index.cshtml");
}
```

This code is much more verbose. The drawback to relying heavily on conventions instead of configuration is that the learning curve for new developers is steep. This learning curve however, is one that must be climbed only once for ASP.NET MVC instead of learning a new project layout for each of the projects a developer might touch.

The conventions in both Rails and in ASP.NET MVC can be overridden with custom conventions should the need arise. This approach should be used sparingly and only for good reason because new developers on the project will be doubly confused by a technology that values convention over configuration being used in an unconventional fashion.

Another idea inherited from Rails is routing. In the Web Forms days, the web server would look for files on disk that matched the name of the file in the HTTP request. There were ways to intercept the requests and reroute them to other pages to handle scenarios where the file had been moved. Rewriting rules were not the norm however; it would be unusual to see the rewriting module used on a project. ASP.NET MVC introduced routing that was likely inspired by Rails. In the startup of the application, a set of rules are introduced that can map requests to either files on disk or actions inside a controller. Not every action in the application needs to be mapped explicitly: the routing table is another place where convention over configuration rules. Examine the following entry:

```
routes.MapRoute("Default", "{companyName}/{projectName}/{controller}/{action}/{id}",
            new { id = UrlParameter.Optional });
```

This entry creates a route in the application that maps a generic set of URLs to controllers and actions. This particular route also extracts variables for the company name and project name. These variables can then be used in the action instead of extracting them from the query string.

In addition to providing some pleasant conventions, routing allows for "friendly" looking URLs. You can write:

```
/AlpineSkiHouse/Rebrand/user/details/12
```

Or, instead, you can write:

```
/user/details?id=12&companyName=AlpineSkiHouse&projectName=Rebrand
```

Not only are these URLs easier for users to read, but they are better for search engine optimization.

Another design principle behind Rails is that you should not repeat yourself. An example of this is that the model is used all the way from the UI back through the controller to the database mapper, ActiveRecord. This same idea can be found in ASP.NET MVC in conjunction with Entity Framework.

Rails was, and still is, a popular framework, so it makes sense that the ASP.NET team would consume some of its good ideas. These ideas have made their way into ASP.NET MVC and also into many other frameworks and tools. The relationship between technologies like Rails and CoffeeScript has been largely symbiotic, with each one prompting the other's growth. The relationship between ASP.NET MVC and Rails is much the same.

Node.js

Popular blogger Jeff Atwood has coined what he calls Atwood's law: "Any application that can be written in JavaScript, will eventually be written in JavaScript." This rather comical law has proven itself true time and time again despite predating Node.js by several years. Node is an event-driven, multi-platform, single-threaded runtime for JavaScript. Node supports pretty much any functionality imaginable and has become especially popular in building web applications. If Rails was an impetus for the development of ASP.NET MVC, Node plays a similar role in the development of ASP.NET Core 1.0. The symbiotic relationship is even stronger between Node and ASP.NET Core MVC 1.0 because many of the tools used in the ASP.NET Core build process leverage the Node runtime.

Even before ASP.NET Core was developed, Node was influential in the development of ASP.NET's web socket implementation, SignalR. Node popularized the idea of server push and WebSockets for real-time communication between web browsers and web servers through the Socket.io package. Socket.io was revolutionary and highly influential in the development of SignalR. SignalR was originally an open-source implementation of a number of technologies, such as long polling, forever frame, and WebSockets. SignalR ended up becoming the official Microsoft implementation. Although not shipped as part of the first release of ASP.NET Core, SignalR is a high priority for subsequent releases.

A vast number of tools are built on top of Node.js. Web development tools such as Grunt, Gulp, and even TypeScript all run on top of Node.js. Even the open-source editor Visual Studio Code is based on a technology called Electron, which is based on Node.js. The flexibility of Node has allowed minimalist implementations. A simple web server can be built by using just a few lines of code:

```
var http = require('http');
http.createServer(function(req, res){
... res.writeHead(200, {'Content-Type': 'text/plain'});
... res.write('hello world');
... res.end();}).listen(5678);
```

Notice on the first line that the HTTP module is included. Node makes use of small, granular packages provided through the npm package manager. By not having an equivalent to the Base Class Library, Node has been able to grow rapidly with most of its functionality living in packages. When distributing an application, you include only the exact libraries needed. These granular modules were part of the inspiration for the modularization of the .NET runtime. The .NET Core relies heavily on the package manager NuGet. In previous versions NuGet could be used to pull in common libraries, such as Autofac and Newtonsoft's Json.NET. With the granularization of the .NET Base Class Library, NuGet has become something that every .NET developer needs to know.

The minimalist projects in the Node world also inspired the lightweight projects generated when creating a new .NET Core project. This approach should allow for smaller distributions and, in theory, faster applications. It also minimizes the surface area that needs to be tested and also the attack surface area should a security vulnerability be found. With highly modular applications, a vulnerability in one part of the .NET runtime is likely to require patching only applications that use that module directly rather than rereleasing every application built on top of .NET.

Node has been influential in the architecture of .NET Core as well as ASP.NET Core. The default ASP. NET Core build process also relies heavily on Node.js to compile resources and even manage client-side packages through bower (written in JavaScript and runs on Node.js). It's probably more accurate to compare Node.js with .NET Core, than to compare it with ASP.NET Core. What sets .NET Core apart is that it is more than just a single language runtime; it is also a collection of well-designed and production-hardened libraries. This is something that Node.js lacks, which leads to massive fragmentation in implementations of standard constructs.

Angular and React

JavaScript is a popular language. It has come a long way from a language whose primary purpose was to validate forms on a web page. Two of the most popular frameworks in the JavaScript space are Angular and React. Angular is a larger framework that takes more functionality under its wing than React. It includes a data binder, as well as a controller implementation, a router, and a dependency injection framework. React is basically just a view engine. Both of the frameworks support custom tags or declarations however. These custom tags allow you to create components that encapsulate markup, functionality, and even style information. If you have a website containing numerous instances of a control, the shared functionality can be extracted into a component. React and Angular are, themselves, building on the ideas of previous frameworks. Java supported a concept known as a Taglet back in the early 2000s and there might even be earlier examples.

Let's imagine a calendar drop-down, a common control on websites. It's a UI nicety to show the user a small calendar whenever she selects a date. HTML5 defines a date picker control that satisfies the functional requirements, but not every browser has support for this control, nor is the look and feel consistent across browsers. In most cases the best approach is to make use of a third-party calendar control. These third party controls tend to be feature-rich, often too feature-rich, and the list of configuration options reads like the obituary page(s) in a newspaper in *Game of Thrones*. Having to look up the configuration options each time a new instance is added to the site is painful, to say nothing of the Herculean task of updating all the instances any time an option is changed. It would be great to be able to extract this functionality into a common place.

Both React and Angular provide for this in a similar fashion with the aforementioned custom tags. Instead of writing the following:

```
<div class="calendar-container">
    <h4>Birth Date </h4>
    <input id="datepicker" style="background: blue" data-start-date="1904-01-01" data-end-
date="2012-01-01" data-allow-range="false" data-date-format="yyyy-MM-dd"/>
</div>
```

Since this contains a bunch of easily forgotten configuration information, you can simply write this instead:

```
<calendar name="birthDate" label="Birth Date"/>
```

Inside of the calendar component, you can centralize all of the configuration needed to ensure that the calendar control remains consistent all over the site. You could even take the componentization further by creating a control specific to birth dates:

```
<birth-date-calendar name="birthdate"/>
```

ASP.NET Core MVC has adopted this same idea of using custom HTML tags to denote a component. You can read much more about tag helpers in Chapter 19, "Reusable Components."

Ironically, these components bring ASP.NET Core MVC closer to the custom user control model that was popular in Web Forms. This was one of the reasons why Web Forms was such a productive environment. It was easy to throw a handful of controls onto a page and wire them up. Having this sort of functionality in a modern web framework brings you the best of both worlds: rapid application development and easy-to-build, standards-compliant components.

Open source

You cannot help but be amazed at the cultural shift inside the developer division at Microsoft in relation to adoption of open source. ASP.NET MVC's source code was released openly so that others could read it and learn from it. Having the code available has allowed developers to delve into the implementation to better understand and solve some particularly difficult problems.

ASP.NET Core MVC has taken the idea of open source inside Microsoft farther. Whereas the original ASP.NET MVC was simply released, fully open sourced, on CodePlex, the development of ASP.NET Core MVC has taken place on GitHub in open repositories and the various projects hosted in the open took pull requests from the community. This democratization has resulted in a much more impressive product than could have been written just by the ASP.NET team working internally. Some of the contributions have been very impressive. If you encounter some piece of functionality that is missing from ASP.NET or uncover a bug, instead of simply waiting around for the next release, you can become actively involved in the evolution of the project by submitting code. There is no guarantee that the team will take the contribution, but they will certainly engage in a conversation. The influence of countless open-source projects has changed the way in which ASP.NET is developed. Let's look at some of them.

OWIN

The Open Web Interface for .NET (OWIN) is a change that has been in the works for a number of years. The original ASP.NET defined fairly large objects for request and response, large enough to be deleterious to the process of unit testing. They were also highly coupled to IIS because the objects were filled in by the IIS request pipeline. OWIN defined an open interface that could be used between a web server and ASP.NET. Complying with this standard allowed for servers other than IIS to serve up ASP.NET pages. The OWIN project was originally a community initiative, but it was wholeheartedly adopted by the ASP.NET team.

As OWIN and ASP.NET matured, the synergy between the two increased to the point where a new project in Visual Studio would come with the OWIN libraries included. OWIN also became the official way to communicate between ASP.NET and whatever web server you might choose. The monoculture that was IIS has been broken. Kestrel, the libuv-based web server, is an example of a server gaining popularity in the ASP.NET Core world for its Linux support.

It is also important to note that OWIN is a standard rather than an implementation. There have been several implementations over the years, such as Katana and Freya. ASP.NET Core is one more implementation.

OWIN is described in its own section but it could just as easily have been included in the "Rails" section. The reason for this is that Rails embarked some years ago on a very similar effort to open up the interface between web servers and Rails. The result of this effort was Rack, which allows for great interoperability between web servers and various different Ruby web frameworks (of which Rails is just one example). This section could also have appeared in the "Node.js" section. Node has a middleware layer called connect from which many of the ideas of OWIN were taken.

Bringing together some of the best parts of a variety of technologies, as shown in Figure 2-2, is an impressive feat. Each of the ideas has been adapted to be more, for lack of another word, .NETty. The end result of this effort does not feel disjointed, and all the parts play well together. To do all of this in such short order is nothing short of amazing and should lead to a most interesting future.

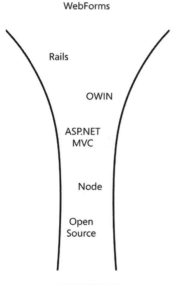

FIGURE 2-2 The influencers of ASP.NET Core

Summary

ASP.NET Core is ostensibly a completely new framework, however, it is easy to see the influence of many other technologies. The end result is a pleasant hybrid of best practices and familiar approaches. Those coming from almost any community will find something familiar in ASP.NET Core.

In the next chapter we'll explore some of the basic building blocks of ASP.NET Core MVC: the model, the view, and the controller.

## CHAPTER 3

Models, Views, and Controllers

It was a surprise when Adrian popped over to Danielle's cubicle. Maybe more surprising was the furrowed brow he was sporting. "Got a minute?" he asked in a hushed tone, and then walked away without waiting for an answer. She nodded a confused yes, mostly to herself, and slowly got up to follow him to a side room. She scanned around the development pit, but didn't see anyone watching, much less interested, and couldn't really get a read on why he was assuming the role of secret agent in this software docu-drama.

He closed the door behind her as she stepped into the room. "Look, I'm a CSS guy. I'm not going to sugar coat it. I know my way around jQuery well enough to troubleshoot, but I'm no programmer." He looked tense and Danielle wondered what he'd been thinking. "Everyone else seems to be buying into this shift over to Core or whatever it's called...but I'm...I mean, come on, I run Linux on my laptop and I don't even use Office." The room quickly drew silent.

"Are you still nervous, Adrian? Marc had mentioned that you were worried about the cuts." Danielle was nervous too, truth be told. She had lost some good friends herself when the merge went through, but she wasn't sure that was what he needed to hear at the moment.

"Well yeah, I guess," he replied. "But my knowledge of MVC is that it stands for Model-View-Controller, and I haven't taken a look any deeper than that. And you guys keep referring to it as a framework. If it's a framework, but you have to make your own models, views, and controllers, then the MVC part seems more than a little misleading, don't you think?"

He had a point. "Well, yeah, that's actually pretty true," said Danielle.

"I'm coming from a different view here; I just want to wrap my head around it. I want to learn, but I'm not sure I know where to start, either." Adrian pounded back the rest of his coffee like it was about to expire. "I know they said we're safe if we're still here, but I don't want to get caught with my feet standing still if they think there's still room to shrink the team."

"Okay, look," said Danielle, "I've got a bit of time right now, let's run through the basics and we'll learn together. We're all going to be fine."

The M, the V, and the C of it

Let's face it, the MVC Framework is a pretty boring name. The acronym used in the title is from the well-known Model-View-Controller pattern, and it helps to organize a project. If you're familiar with it, the name literally spells out some of the original intent to separate concerns, and moves away from the other common pattern at the time known as Page-Controller. The name can also be misleading. The framework is much more than just models, views and controllers. ASP.NET Core MVC has a growing set of tooling and libraries available to that help developers create great applications, worthy of the modern web world.

Let's do a quick recap on the aspects you should already understand, and then move into some more interesting aspects of the framework, officially known as ASP.NET Core MVC.

Diving into Models

First up is the letter M, so we'll start with Models. The model represents the data that we need to properly render an experience, or part of an experience, for a customer. Customers are navigating to a page in the application that is data-driven, and models are the data part. However, as far as intent goes, the model in question is actually what you'll be using to support the rendering of the view, and not the entity or entities in question in which you persist to the database.

Let's consider this example from Alpine Ski House's possible database design that deals with user account summaries, as shown in Figure 3-1. When you want to indicate to the user that she has a current season pass, you don't want to return the list of season passes to the view and iterate over the collection to see if one exists that has not yet expired.

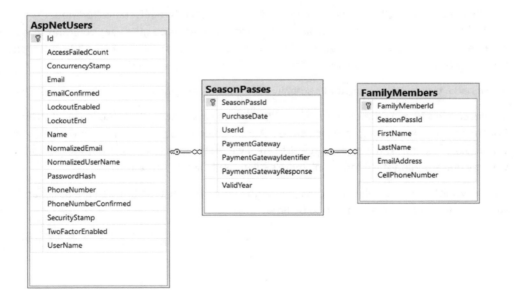

FIGURE 3-1 A screen shot showing a sampling of tables that might be used to model purchasing season passes

Returning all of this information to the view would be more than is required. Listing 3-1 contains a view model that might more closely approximate the information you would want to display to the user. As you can see, this is a POCO that sports the properties you can use to satisfy the view requirements without the view needing to make any decisions about what to display or any implementation of business logic. The view doesn't need to know what qualifies as a current season pass nor does it need to sift through any of the purchase details or iterate through child records in related tables to make sense of the data.

LISTING 3-1 The AccountSummaryViewModel Class

```
public class AccountSummaryViewModel
{
    public Guid UserId { get; set; }
    public int YearsOfMembership { get; set; }
    public bool IsCurrentSeasonPassHolder { get; set; }
    public List<string> IncludedFamilyMembers { get; set; }
}
```

The differentiation between what you craft for models on the front end, versus what you store in the database, is important not just for separating the concerns of the view and the business logic that supports it, but also for helping to prevent certain types of security issues. On the "write" side of things, when a view uses a database entity, the application becomes more likely to fall victim to overbinding bugs or attacks. Overbinding occurs when fields that weren't anticipated from an incoming request are present in form or querystring parameters. The model binder sees the properties, doesn't know that you hadn't intended for them to be there, and kindly fills in your data for you. As an example, consider the class representing some kind of a digital asset in Listing 3-2.

LISTING 3-2 The AccountSummaryViewModel Class

```
public class DigitalAsset
{
    public Guid AssetId { get; set; }
    public Guid AssetOwnerId { get; set; }
    public string Title { get; set; }
    public string Description { get; set; }
    public Uri AccessUri { get; set; }
}
```

This type of model can be used to display a list of resources made available to a user, and doing so is quite harmless. But, if you use the same object to receive edits for the record, a malicious user can exploit the fact that AssetOwnerId is a property and use that to take ownership of the asset. In fact, this is how Egor Homakov gained administrative privileges for the Ruby on Rails (RoR) repository on GitHub in 2012[1] (The technique in RoR is exploited through improperly checked models that make use of the

---

[1] GitHub reinstates Russian who hacked site to expose flaw, John Leyden, March 5, 2012, *http://www.theregister.co.uk*.

mass assignment feature, an analog to automatic model binding in ASP.NET Core MVC. Thankfully, Homakov's intentions were pure and no harm was done. We have learned from those binding conventions and habits of yore though. Today, we have many ways to protect ourselves, which we'll cover later in Chapter 13, "Identity, Security and Rights Management," but likely the easiest way is to make sure we're using models that are appropriate to the task at hand.

Most of the examples you find for view models will likely use an entity directly as the model type for the view; however, the approach does not facilitate other aspects of software development, such as testing, nor does it help with separating concerns in your controllers. Using the entity directly in a view means that you've achieved an undesirable level of coupling from the database all the way up to the view.

A model should be everything you need to render your page after you've taken care of business logic and often has a flattened view of a denormalized record from several tables in the database. For these reasons, and considering the intent of the object you're building up when you create a "model," you should likely think of it as the "view model" due to its close relationship and responsibility to the view.

Views

Here, the view in question happens to start with V and is indeed the view we're talking about in our new favorite acronym. Views in ASP.NET Core MVC are the files used to interleave parts of the model with the HTML needed in order to present the user with the intended user interface. If you create a new project from the default application template you will find all the views in the Views folder, or you can search Solution Explorer with the term ".cshtml," which is the extension used for Razor views.

Using the Razor view engine and syntax you've seen through the last few iterations of the MVC Framework, you can switch effortlessly between the syntax used to control flow or access our model or services, and the markup required to generate HTML.

In Listing 3-3 we have created an unordered list with values from the model's `IncludedFamily-Members` collection. Razor lets you use C# inline with the HTML and is pretty smart about how it interprets what you throw at it. A simple @ character is enough for the parser to know you're flipping into C#, and since angle brackets can't be used at the start of a valid C# statement, it can tell when you've switched back to HTML. We'll be covering Razor in greater detail in Chapter 11, "Razor Views."

LISTING 3-3 An example of mixing C# and HTML in Razor Syntax.

```
<ul>
    @foreach (var familyMember in Model.IncludedFamilyMembers)
    {
        <li>@familyMember</li>
    }
</ul>
```

Partial Views

Toolbars, authentication cues, shopping carts, parts of dashboards, and other similar components of your application often find themselves appearing on multiple pages, or even on all pages. In the name of Don't Repeat Yourself (DRY), you can create these components using a partial view, which can in turn be used repeatedly from any other page. You'll also see partial views referred to more simply as "partials." We'll use those terms interchangeably throughout the book.

Partials are not typically rendered on their own, but are used in composition of other views in your project. The first place you see this in any MVC application is likely to be in the _Layout.cshtml, where the view relies on partials to render the login status. Other common uses include using a partial view to render items in toolbars, shopping cart summaries like those you see at the top of an ecommerce site, or side bars with relevant data for the current page.

Child actions had to be rendered synchronously in previous versions of the MVC Framework, but the same ideas that made partials possible can now be used to construct view components and invoked asynchronously. We'll talk about View Components more in Chapter 18, "Reusable Components," which is important in certain scenarios to keep performance in check on the site. Complex generated views and partials that interact with services are examples of this, which we'll talk about later in this chapter.

Before users can get the output of a view, and in order for you to load any kind of model into the view engine, we must talk a little bit about Controllers in your project.

Controllers (...and Actions!)

Controllers are the traffic cops of MVC applications, ensuring the right types of bits travel to and from the correct places. Controllers typically inherit from the base `Controller` class, but if you don't need the functionality of the base class, you can also use the convention of ending your class name with "Controller," such as in `SeasonPassController`.

The default convention assumes that you are putting your controllers in a folder called "Controllers" in the root of the project. This is no longer required because Core MVC actually does an assembly scan using the naming and inheritance conventions, but it's still a recommended practice to organize your controllers in a recognized way. This helps other developers, including the future version of yourself, to easily manage and maintain the code base down the road.

As software developers, we use controllers as a container for related sets of handlers for incoming requests. These handlers are called actions and are implemented as methods in our controller class. Each method, or action, can accept zero or more parameters that are automatically filled in by the model binding step in the execution pipeline if they are presented by the incoming request.

As the authors of these "traffic cops," our goal is to code our controllers using some well-accepted practices. The primary responsibility of an action is to process a request, validating the incoming parameters and creating an appropriate response.

From time to time, this also requires creating or requesting an instance of a model class, or producing an appropriate HTTP status code based response. You should try to avoid having any business logic in your controller, which is the responsibility of your model or other components, as well as keeping data access or external calls out of your actions, which should be part of your application services. This is represented in a high level in Figure 3-2.

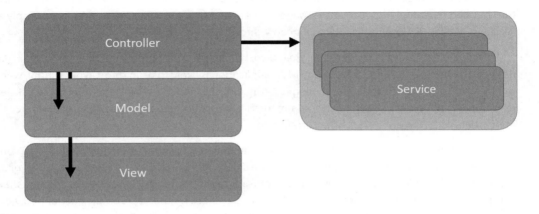

FIGURE 3-2 An illustration showing how controllers are responsible for invoking business logic that helps to generate an appropriate HTTP response

Keeping these services external might seem to make things more complex, or raise questions like, "Who will create these services for me?" This is a great question and one that we'll answer in the "Dependency Injection" section later in this chapter.

It's Not Just About MVC

As discussed earlier, there's actually a lot more going on than just the models, views and controllers themselves in your solution. We'll continue to explore these throughout the book, but here are some important ideas to have in the peripheral as you develop.

Middleware

Here is the secret about middleware in ASP.NET Core MVC: it's pretty much all middleware. All of it! During application start-up you have the opportunity to load your configuration, configure your services, and then configure the request pipeline, which is where the concept of middleware is called into play. You can see this in the Configure method of the Startup class in the default project template.

Often, the description of middleware and the interpretation by the reader overcomplicates a fairly simple premise. The purpose of middleware is to allow an application to say, "Have each request processed by the following components in the order that I specify." Middleware is a simplification over previous incarnations of similar functionality in ASP.NET, namely HTTP Modules and Handlers. Middleware replaces both with a common approach in a fashion that is easier to implement.

There are several pieces of middleware that ship publically to handle most scenarios that you need to cover during the execution of your application, both in lower level environments such as staging and QA, as well as in production:

- **Diagnostics:** Provides exception handling and runtime helpers like database error pages and technical details to developers.

- **Static files:** Allows a short-circuit of the request pipeline to return a file from disk.

- **Identity and Authentication:** Allows applications to protect end points and assets of an application.

- **Routing:** Resolves which controller and action should be executed based on the incoming path and parameters.

- **CORS:** Handles injecting the correct headers for cross-origin resource sharing.

- **MVC itself:** Usually at the end of the configured middleware pipeline as it consumes requests.

Each middleware component has the option to execute code before and after the next component in the chain, or to short-circuit the execution and return a response. The name middleware likely comes from the idea that you can execute a piece of software in the middle of something else, as shown in Figure 3.3. In this instance, you see a series of different requests that are handled by the various middleware components in the default project template. In some cases, the request is handled by the static files middleware, returning an asset in wwwroot. At other times, the request is allowed to pass all the way through to the MVC execution pipeline where your controller is created and you can return a view.

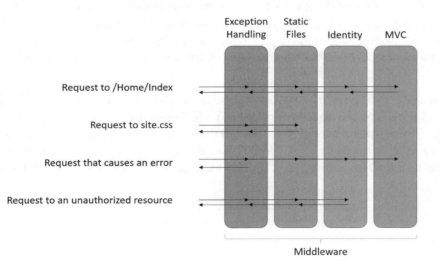

FIGURE 3-3 An illustration showing examples of different request types as handled by middleware

You can bring in other middleware from third parties, additional helpers that are provided by Microsoft, or you can write your own to handle cross-cutting concerns that are needed throughout your application. The middleware pipeline can also be branched based on paths or predicates to allow dynamic, flexible rules around processing requests.

Dependency Injection

There are many written volumes covering dependency injection, but we'll recap the basics here for completeness.

Generally speaking, it's likely going to be a good idea for your code to be obvious about the dependencies that it takes on. In C# you tend to do this by putting the components and services you need in your constructor, such that any creator of the class has to provide your dependencies for you.

Let's consider the constructor of the HomeController class in Listing 3-3. The class requires that any time it is being created an instance of an ILogger implementation would be provided for it.

LISTING 3-3 The HomeController Class Constructor

```
public class HomeController{
  ILogger _logger
  public HomeController (ILogger logger)
  {
    _logger = logger;
  }
}
```

HomeController doesn't need to know how to configure or create an ILogger, it doesn't need to know where to log to, or how it is to be done. But from any point after instantiation, HomeController is now able to add valuable information to your log files as required. This one simple parameter on the constructor explicitly defines your requirements and is referred to as the Explicit Dependencies Principle.

For this controller to be created by the pipeline, you need to have something in the runtime aware of how to resolve the ILogger requirement. You configure these services and components in a container, and then these types of dependencies are injected for you into the constructors at runtime. And voila, dependency injection! Being a broader topic, and also by virtue of ASP.NET Core MVC introducing some new ideas for Dependency I njection (DI), we're going to take a deeper look at the idea of inverting control in Chapter 14, "Dependency Injection," where we'll also explore what is required when replacing the default container.

Other Gems

ASP.NET Core MVC contains some great improvements over previous versions and we are going to explore them throughout the book.

- **Configuration and Logging:** Long considered afterthoughts in the .NET space, these critical application aspects have been revamped, simplified, and made into first-class citizens. Read more about these in Chapter 12, "Configuration and Logging."

- **Tag Helpers:** Along with a few other aspects of simplifying front end development, in Chapter 18, "Reusable Components," we'll examine Tag Helpers and how they more closely resemble the HTML we're trying to return to the client.

- **Identity:** A user is more than just a name and a password. In Chapter 13, "Identity, Security & Rights," we'll explore the new features, uses, and components around security and rights management in ASP.NET Core MVC.

Summary

Each iteration of the MVC Framework has helped shape part of what it's become today. Some lessons learned along the way have helped to bring better assets to developers and the models, views, and controllers we have at the heart of our applications today take up only a small part of our development efforts.

> Before they knew it, the morning had escaped them and Danielle had all but plastered the whiteboard with dry erase marker. Adrian flopped back in his chair and said, "Geez, Danielle. Someone should write a book on this."

## CHAPTER 4

Scoping the Project

Tim's inspirational speech seemed to be over now and he looked a little out of breath. Never one for running or even walking quickly, it was unusual to see him so energetic about anything. He was typically very measured and relaxed about most of the comings and goings at the office. He slumped into one of the chairs at the front of the room and gestured at a spry looking young man wearing a sports coat and a white v-necked shirt. "Balázs here will take you through what we're looking to achieve over the next few weeks."

Balázs bounded up to the front of the room, full of a nervous energy. He looked like he might have taken his fashion advice from a book called "Styles of Silicon Valley Entrepreneurs," probably from the chapter entitled "Default CTO Style." Danielle glanced at Tim who was mopping his brow. Even looking as spent has he did, she noticed that he'd somehow managed to snag a donut. She wasn't sure how he'd managed that, since the nearest box was on the other side of the room. Danielle dragged herself back from wondering if Tim was hiding some sort of a donut transporter technology to find that Balázs was already picking up a dry erase marker and heading for the whiteboard.

"Three years I spent looking at the problem of optimizing lift lines and ticket purchasing out East. I'm really excited to get to apply some of ideas here. The Imagineers are really the gold standard in dealing with large crowds and I think we can repurpose many of those ideas here. The first thing we have to deal with is buying passes. How do people buy passes right now?" Balázs paused slightly and glanced about the room. He spoke with a very slight Eastern European accent as if having moved from there in his early years.

Danielle hadn't purchased a pass in quite some time. All of the office employees got yearly passes for free. It was a management initiative to get them out of the office and onto the hill interacting with the skiers and the hills. How did people buy passes these days? She wasn't sure. Worried that she might be called upon, she tried to look distracted by something on the floor and averted eye contact with Balázs. As it turned out it didn't matter at all, Balázs, was steaming on without waiting for an answer from the room.

"I'll tell you how they buy them now. Inefficiently. I've looked over the numbers from the past year and we're doing over 98% of our sales on the hill the day-of. 98%, that's almost 100%! More than 80% of the people buying passes on the hill are doing so using credit cards and another 16% are using debit cards. Cash is almost dead and we had one person try to pay with a beaver animal pelt." Balázs chortled at his own joke and carried on. "With all these people using electronic payments, we have a chance to shift the purchase of passes earlier on. If we let them buy passes ahead of time from their computers and smart phones we could reduce the number of staff working in the ticket booths."

That sounded like a pretty good idea to Danielle. Nobody liked waiting in line and the audience on the hill was a pretty young one. They would likely have access to computers and certainly had smart phones. Balázs continued his analysis. "Problem is that we're still scanning people's passes on the hill using barcode portable readers. This is slow and error prone. What's worse is that we print out the passes on expensive ultra-durable paper and attach them to people's coats using zip ties. That's expensive to do. Simply producing a pass like that costs us almost a dollar in supplies and labor. We need to find a way to cut down on that. We can't just have people print their tickets at home because not everybody has a printer and nobody has printer paper that would survive a wipeout if it was attached to somebody's jacket."

"What we need is a new way for people to buy tickets and for us to manage tickets both on the hill and before getting to the hill. We need Project Parsley. Let me tell you all about my vision."

Project Parsley is the ongoing example application for this book. Almost every example is taken from some actual Project Parsley code and you can download the completed project from GitHub. We've attempted to make the development as realistic as possible, so you'll find issues in the GitHub repo, as well as code and a full commit history.

> **Note** You should be able to dig into the repository to see how our thinking has evolved as we ourselves move through the sprints outlined in this book. The repository is hosted at: https://github.com/AspNetMonsters/AlpineSkiHouse.

The application is split into a number of parts. First you're going to need a place for customers to come to enter their information and buy their passes. Next you're going to need some way of communicating back to the system that a pass has been used on the hill. Finally, you're going to need an administrative interface that allows the business to gather some metrics on how things are going on the hill and with ticket purchases. There will, of course, be some sort of a database to hold various sorts of information for customers and passes. We'll walk you through how we developed the application and our technology choices over the rest of the book, but for now we need to outline what the application should do rather than how it should be done.

For many developers, the File then New Project dialog is a siren song. "Click me and start a new project," it calls. "Don't worry you'll discover the business problem though code," goes the song. Oh, many a time have we been intoxicated by that song and wrecked ourselves upon the rocks of action before understanding. Being agile is all very well, but it's important that we have some understanding of the problem space before embarking on creating a new project. Let's lash ourselves to the mast and proceed past the siren call.

Ski Slopes

For those unfamiliar with ski hills let us start there. A ski hill consists of two major parts: a way up the hill and a way down the hill. Getting down the hill is largely handled by gravity and a little bit of skill on either skis or a snowboard. The trails down the hill all start at the offloading or uphill side of a ski lift. From there the trails diverge in every which way following the slopes of the mountain. The trails, or runs, are categorized by difficultly using icons: green circle (easy), blue square (medium), and black diamond (difficult), as shown in Figure 4-1. On some hills, there are also double black diamond runs which are the ultimate adventure. Many times these runs do not fall under the avalanche protection measures so skiing on them requires avalanche gear, such as a transmitter and shovel.

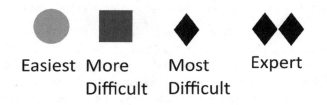

FIGURE 4-1 Difficulty ratings

Just as the runs diverge at the top of the hill, they again converge at the downhill terminus of the lift. This allows for a continuous loop of skiers, moving from lift to hill and again back to the lift. Most hills have more than a single lift with some of the largest having more than twenty lifts capable of bringing thousands of people an hour up the hill. There have been many different types of lifts over the years ranging from simple rope tows to the more expensive chair lifts.

Many ski hills provide lift tickets as pieces of paper that skiers attach to their jacket or pants. At the base of the lift, the passes are normally scanned by a person with a portable barcode scanner to verify their validity. Passes are typically valid for a single day, but you can also purchase half day passes, multi-day passes, and even yearly passes.

Passes are usually bought at a kiosk at the bottom of the hill. A day of skiing costs something like fifty US dollars. The investment in a day of skiing is not a small one. It is also a far less enjoyable experience than purchasing an additional 0.5 of a copy of this book, something we encourage you to do.

Customers come from far and wide to go skiing and they don't want to spend a lot of time in line waiting to purchase a pass. Thus, we need to provide a way to purchase passes online and get skiers on the hill.

Fortunately, the price of Radio Frequency Identification (RFID) chips has been dropping for many years. It is now economical to embed them in something like a ski card. RFIDs (pronounced 'are-fids') are small chips capable of being read at some small distance without physical contact. You might have made use of a similar technology, such as PayPass™ or PayWave™, embedded in major credit cards, or in security keycards used for entering office buildings or hotel rooms. Each card has a unique identifier tied to it allowing for the distinction of one card from its identical looking twin.

Scanners for RFID cards will take the place of the manual barcode scanners at the base of the chair-lifts. So long as skiers have the passes on their person, they should be able to pass through a gate allowing them access to the lift. If skiers do not have the passes on their person, the gate does not open. In addition, scanners are placed at the tops of some runs to give a good idea where riders are going. This information can be used to build heat maps which give an idea of where people ski the most. It also allows riders to view a log of their runs and how long it took them to get from the top to the bottom. The number of vertical feet skied in a day is a fun metric for those who like to ski hard.

The RFID card is mailed out to customers if they purchase their passes sufficiently in advance to ensure postal mail delivery. Should they purchase passes on the hill or with too little notice to ensure mail delivery, then the cards are also available on the hill. The cards are reusable so a single customer might use the same card for many visits across many seasons. While the initial investment in cards and mailings is higher than printing paper passes, a small discount encourages customers in possession of a pass to bring it back on future trips.

When logging into the site, first time users are prompted to set their login credentials as well as their shipping address. Next, users are asked to add a number of "customers" or "skiers" requesting a card. For each customer, you need only his name and age for determining the cost; kids rates are cheaper. Instead of storing the age, management would like to store a birth date so that the marketing department can use it to send out discount coupons on the customer's birthday.

With the owners of the cards established, the user can go about loading the cards. A number of different pass types are available: daily, multi-day, and yearly. In addition, there are now three different ski areas to consider. Passes can be valid for just a single ski area or for multiple ski areas. Each customer can purchase multiple passes, all of which are assigned to the same physical card. In scenarios where the customers already have their ski cards no further work is required. The system remembers the customer list for each login as well as the association from customer to physical card.

Finally, the user is prompted to enter payment information and complete the checkout process. This triggers mailing out physical cards if needed or existing cards are immediately activated, allowing users to complete the purchase in their cars on the way to the ski hill.

Once at the ski hill with their cards, the customers don't need take any additional steps. Their cards are active and they can jump on the first available lift, comfortable in the knowledge that they skipped any irksome lines.

Even though this is a basic prototype, the user experience for the website should still be as enjoyable as possible. Always a hotly debated topic, a decision needs to be made about using a single page application or a multi-page application. Single page applications don't reload the entire page on each page load. Instead they reload a small portion of the page, commonly by combining data retrieved from the server via JSON with a client side template. Many single page application frameworks handle the data model, view, and controller in a similar fashion to ASP.NET MVP. The advantage to single page applications is that the user experience tends to be better. Without having to reload a swath of the webpage each time the user navigates single page applications tend to be snappier to respond and are less jarring for users.

On the other hand, single page applications are heavy in their use of JavaScript, which many developers still have a degree of discomfort with. Developing a single page application in the past has always been complicated and more time consuming than building many pages. The rise of JavaScript and the near endless bounty of a JavaScript framework for building SPAs might have removed the barrier or at least lowered it to the point where the difference between building a SPA and a traditional multi-paged application is minute.

As part of the experimentation culture being fostered at Alpine Ski House, the client side of the application is written using server side view rendering rather than client side. Rendering the HTML on the server side can be more efficient for some devices that have more bandwidth than computation power to crunch through client side JavaScript code. It can also be easier to build server side views than to take on the significant mental tax that is writing different parts of the application in different languages. Even with a server rendered application there is some need for JavaScript so don't feel like you have escaped that particular issue. The need for JavaScript is significantly lower than with single page applications.

The API

RFID scanners are relatively cheap and easy to set up. The fictional scanners in this book are the RT5500s, which work over HTTP. They are hooked up to a simple gate which opens for a period of time when it encounters an RFID signature that validates. In order to validate whether a pass is valid, the scanner relies on sending a message out over the network to a validation service. The validation service needs to be written but the spec is very easy.

The scanner sends out the physical ID of the scanned card encoded in JSON as a GET request and it expects to receive back either a "true" or a "false." That is the extent of the interaction. There is no authentication scheme on the default implementation of the RT5500s, which could lead to some issues down the road. For instance, it is possible that an enterprising individual could send repeated requests to the GET API until they found a valid Id and then spoof it to go skiing for free. Unsecured Internet of Things (IoT) devices are going to be a major problem in coming years. Already, we see that many people are buying Wi-Fi enabled cameras and leaving them unsecured, making it possible to scan the Internet for them and watch what people are doing in their own homes. Scary! Will the decision to not implement any additional security come back to bite the team? We'll have to wait and see.

Almost every web framework out there has some sort of an easy approach to constructing a RESTful service. Thus the API has very little impact on selecting a technology. You could even think of the API as a mostly self-contained microservice. This opens the door to implementing it in any language or technology you choose. The idea being that on such a small project, making a mistake and selecting the wrong technology is not crippling. By using small batch sizes, the rework in the event of a problem can be limited.

Unfortunately, the communication scheme is the easiest thing to implement for the scanners. The rules to determine if a card is allowed are complicated and nuanced. First, the list of passes for a card need to be looked up and the correct pass selected. It is possible that more than one pass is valid at any time, so a consistent way of picking them needs to be decided upon. Next the pass needs to be activated if it is new. Finally, the scan information related to that pass needs to be written. The pass validation logic is certain to be one of the hardest parts of the application to get right.

The Admin View

I'm sure it was Arthur C. Clark who said:

> Any system which is sufficiently complex will require an administrative interface.

As such, the system for the Alpine Ski House needs to have some administrative capabilities. Right away there is a need to see how many people are skiing on that day. This is information that needs to be provided to the insurance company in order to ensure that the coverage is at an appropriate level. In addition, the management team would like to have reports showing how many people are buying new cards to gauge how successful the project is.

This requirement is driven by a desire to know right a way if the experiment is working. Stolen from the concept of a lean start up, Alpine Ski House would like to be able to do minimum cost experiments during the development process. The results of these experiments guide where development resources are spent. The initial version of the administrative view into the application is minimalist in nature, but it's expected to grow quickly when the business starts to get a handle on the sort of insights that can be gleaned from the application.

The admin application is largely a reporting application, which means that it has a lot of snazzy graphs and charts. These are the sorts of things that managers and executives love to see: high level reports from which conclusions can be drawn. In effect, you have an analytics dashboard.

Erring on the side of a better user experience, the admin facing portion of Project Parsley is written using a client side framework interacting with WebAPI. It is believed that this provides for the best user experience without losing too much productivity. It is also a great testing bed for rolling out the less well known approach over the entire application. It is more important to ship the customer facing application than to ship it in a completely finished state. This is also part of the lean start up mentality.

Pulling the Pieces Together

The application we're building is actually three applications: the client side, the admin side, and the API. All of these services need to talk to each other in some way as the data they're using is shared. Many applications of this sort are built around a shared database that does the integration. Using a database as a shared kernel can cause some difficulties as multiple services attempt to write to the same tables. Changing the structure in one part of the application might break other parts of it. The issue is that it is difficult to build an abstraction layer out over a SQL database. Typically, we would like to build out at least an anti-corruption layer to prevent changes to the data model from breaking the application.

We have divided our data model into isolated chunks called bounded contexts. A bounded context is a term taken from the domain driven design world. It is a difficult concept to describe but in effect is a grouping of data and functionality that is distinct and disconnected from the rest of the application. Within a context, names maintain the same meaning. Sound confusing? Consider the concept of a customer. For the shipping department a customer is really just an address, whereas the marketing department's customer is a collection of preferences and attributes that define how a customer is marketed to. The shipping department is a bounded context as is the marketing department. Communication between these bounded contexts should be well defined and explicit.

An anti-corruption layer is an abstraction over the access to bounded contexts, specifically when you must join together several bounded contexts. The pattern is often implemented using an adapter or façade pattern. The adapter translates from the representation in one bounded context to another. For example, both the client side application and the API need to work against a table containing scan information. The client side application needs to read the data to get back a picture of where a rider traveled during the day. The API needs to write records to the scans table. The API is the service writing to the table so it is the canonical source of truth for scan data. This means that any data changes to scan information should be made through the API service.

Should the API team decide that the scan table needs to move from storing dates in local time to storing them in UTC, we'd like to limit the impact on the consumers of this data, namely the client application. To read the scan data, the client application should use an adapter to change the dates back into the representation expected by its code base.

An example mapper might look like the following:

```
public class ScanDataAdaptor{
    public Client.Scan Map(API.Scan scan){
        var mapped = Mapper.Map(scan);
        mapped.ScanDate = ConvertToLocalDate(mapper.ScanDate);
        return mapped;
    }
}
```

Here an automapper is used to map the similar fields from the domain representation in the API to the domain representation in the customer application. Finally, the new UTC style date is converted into the expected local time. A method like this is easy to construct and test You'll be making use of an anti-corruption layer whenever you're communicating between bounded contexts.

Defining our Domain

The domain for Project Parsley is divided into a number of bounded contexts. You can see the Entity Relationship ER diagram, as shown in Figure 4-2, divided into a number of bounded contexts. You'll notice that the applications don't map to a specific bounded context. We're going to allow our applications to talk to more than one bounded context. If we were striving for a pure DDD or microservices approach we might not allow a single application to talk to multiple bounded contexts. For our applications, we're not going to worry too much. We are, of course, keeping the anti-corruption layer in place to prevent breaking data inadvertently.

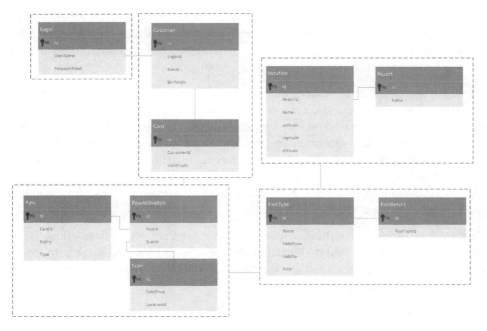

FIGURE 4-2 ER Diagram of the application split into domains

We have five bounded contexts. Starting in the top left of the diagram and moving clockwise, the first is the login context. This context is responsible for authenticating and authorizing users in the customer and admin applications. For this we're using the standard ASP.NET Identity functionality. Next we have a customer bounded context. The customer context holds information related to the people who are skiing or snowboarding. We track some personal details about them and also the cards that they have. Next, we have a location bounded context. The location and the resort name are tracked in this context. We can use this information to calculate things like the number of meters skied in a day. The penultimate bounded context holds information about the pass types. A pass type is typically a set of rules that govern the validity of a pass on a particular day at a particular resort. Types of passes are things like "3-day pass," "yearly pass," and so forth. The final bounded context governs the assignment of passes to cards and their validity.

Summary

We have scoped out three applications and a database. This is a lot of work to get done inside of a few sprints. However, we're confident that we can set out on this journey and build a fantastic solution. Soon people will be using their new reloadable ski cards to bypass ski pass lines and get right onto the hill. In Chapter 5 we'll look at how to get our application building. We're doing it early so that we can start deploying from day 1.

Builds

The team was only a couple of days into the first sprint and things were getting heated already. Danielle was worried the team wasn't gelling properly. They were bickering about broken code when Danielle made an errant push to the repository. She had added a new project to the code base, but had forgotten to check in the solution file. It was a common mistake, and something anyone on the team could have done, but the team was already on edge and every bump hurt a little more than the last.

"Marc," she said, "I've checked in the project file so it should be fixed now."

"It is fixed, but we wasted a good hour on it. We need to get this project out fast. Missing the easy things...that's the sort of thing we don't have time for."

"Calm down, Marc," Adrian comforted. "Nobody is perfect and there are going to be mistakes. What we need to do is find some way to avoid these sorts of problems in the future."

Balázs rolled in just then "Ah good, I was waiting for you folks to come up with a solution instead of bickering and complaining. What can we do to prevent these problems in the future? More pair programming?"

"I think that will help" said Danielle, "but what we really need to do is fail fast. We have to find a way to pave over the differences we have in our environments and avoid people claiming that it works on their machine."

"That sounds hard," Balázs countered. "How do we make it easy?"

"Well, we can set up a build server and have it run builds every time we check in," suggested Danielle.

"Good," said Balázs. "Let's get it done. Now back to work people."

It is no surprise that computers speak a different language than we do. It isn't just that computers speak Esperanto, because they speak in a language that is fundamentally different from our human languages. Human languages tend to be full of ambiguities that cannot be permitted in programming. Computers deal only in hard truths and are perfectly logical beings. So, while humans may be able to understand the intended meaning of the phrase I *love cooking cats and Lego* in spite of some missing commas, a computer unfortunately assumes that cats and Lego are on the menu. It is very difficult for humans to think in a language that computers understand correctly, and because computer language is highly verbose, we introduce higher level languages. Creating human readable programming languages is a difficult task, because there is a need to balance terseness with understandability. The selection of language is a highly personal one that is all too frequently influenced by coding standards inside companies. No matter what language you choose to write your ASP.NET Core application in, you need to translate your high level language into something a computer can natively understand. To do this, you need to pass your code through a compiler. If you're writing VB.NET or C# code, use the Rosslyn compiler and if you're using F#, it has its own compiler.

In this chapter we examine how to build an ASP.NET Core project, the motivation behind build servers, and how to set up a build pipeline.

Command Line Builds

Many people are afraid of the command line. Perhaps afraid isn't the right word; they are uncomfortable with the command line. The truth is, however, that being able to build a solution from the command line is very useful. Build servers frequently lack a UI that is able to express the complex details to run builds. It takes but a single modal dialog box to ruin a build. The command line tooling in .NET Core has received quite a lot of attention, and using it to perform builds is now easier than ever.

Simple command line builds for a single project in .NET Core are as straightforward as running the command from the project level:

```
dotnet build
```

This outputs something like:

```
Project AlpineSkiHouse.Web (.NETCoreApp,Version=v1.0) will be compiled because inputs were
modified

Compiling AlpineSkiHouse.Web for .NETCoreApp,Version=v1.0

Compilation succeeded.
    0 Warning(s)
    0 Error(s)

Time elapsed 00:00:07.3356109
```

It is as simple as that. If your project has external dependencies, you may need to restore them first by running:

```
dotnet restore
```

This command reaches out to any defined Nuget sources and attempts to restore the packages listed in the project.json. The output of this command looks something like the following:

```
dotnet restore
log  : Restoring packages for C:\code\AlpineSkiHouse\src\AlpineSkiHouse.Web\project.
       json...
log  : Installing Serilog.Sinks.File 3.0.0.
log  : Installing Serilog.Sinks.RollingFile 3.0.0.
log  : Installing Serilog.Formatting.Compact 1.0.0.
log  : Installing Serilog 2.2.0.
log  : Installing Serilog.Sinks.PeriodicBatching 2.0.0.
log  : Installing Serilog 2.0.0.
log  : Writing lock file to disk. Path: C:\code\AlpineSkiHouse\src\AlpineSkiHouse.Web\
project.lock.json
log  : C:\code\AlpineSkiHouse\src\AlpineSkiHouse.Web\project.json
log  : Restore completed in 27179ms.
```

Of course, very few projects these days are small enough to be contained in a single project. You can read more about the actual need for multiple projects in Chapter 24, "Feature Organization." If you plan to build more than one project at a time, you need to lean on something else.

> **Note** We mention the project.json file here and in various other places in the book. This file governs what frameworks your projects supports, the output options, what packages it uses, and what additional command line tools are provided to the dotnet command. This file is going to be altered greatly in a soon-to-be-released version of .NET. The final form of the project file is not yet known, but it is likely that it will move back to XML and be, once again, called .csproj. There will be a seamless upgrade path provided, so don't worry about having to upgrade your project.json to a .csproj.

For years the standard approach to having multiple projects has been to have a solution file at the root of your project. Solution files are very simple files that basically define a collection of configurations, such as Debug and Release, as well as the projects that are to be built for each configuration profile. So, perhaps you have a Release build that builds the core project, but does not build some auxiliary tools that are only needed during debugging. These solution files are understood by both Visual Studio and MSBuild. You can build a solution on the command line by running:

```
Msbuild.exe AlpineSki.sln
```

This iterates over all the projects in a solution and executes the build on them. In the case of .NET Core, it is called the dotnet build command.

If your project works in the default MSBuild file, you're set. If your project is slightly different from the default, however, you may want to look at some alternative build tools. One alternative is PSake, a PowerShell-based build tool (*https://github.com/psake/psake*). If functional programming is an area of interest for you, the F#-based FAKE build runner may be just what you're looking for. FAKE defines a domain specific language (DSL) for setting up builds. It can be found at *http://fsharp.github.io/FAKE/*.

No matter what tool you select, it is likely that for a sizable project there is some need to perform additional tasks above and beyond simply compiling the projects, such as assembling packages, running tests and uploading files to a symbol server. The best solution for that is really a discussion for your team, so try some tools out and see which one is the best fit.

Did you find one? Great! Now you can install it on your build server. You do have a build server don't you?

Build Servers

The importance of having a build server cannot be overstressed. Building your software frequently is a great way to catch errors early, hopefully before they've made it to your user base.

You may be familiar with the programmer's catch phrase, "Works on my machine." This mantra is common in programming circles. Developer workstations tend to have a lot of tools and libraries installed that you might not find on computers in the general population. All too frequently, we find that code works locally, but after it is deployed to the production environment, it fails to work. Nobody wants to find themselves uttering "works on my machine," but the differences in environments make it probable.

Avoiding this embarrassment can be as easy as setting up a build server that compiles and tests your software in another environment. Even on a team of one, having rapid feedback is immensely useful when you've checked in something that breaks the build. If the build worked an hour ago and now it is broken, the number of changes that are suspect is limited to those in the last hour.

On larger teams, the importance of continually integrating with your teammates' code is even more important. For example, if Danielle checks in something that conflicts with Mark's latest change, it would be ideal to surface those problems as soon as they happen, rather than weeks later during a production deployment.

In addition to performing continuous integration builds to test that changes don't conflict, it is also important to run nightly builds. There are can be changes in the environment or in a dependent package that break a piece of software nobody has touched in months. Updated node modules are a prime example of this. While it is possible to fix on a version of a node module, it is not possible to fix the versions of dependent libraries. Thus, upstream changes can break your software without you even knowing it.

We call them build servers, but a build server can do a lot more than simply build software. The build server should be responsible for coordinating an entire build pipeline.

The Build Pipeline

Releasing software can be quite difficult to do. Many companies struggle to release their software even once a month, let alone weekly or daily. Companies such as Flickr do multiple software releases a day because they have a high degree of confidence in their build and release processes. Every time a developer checks code into the main branch, a build is kicked off and some minutes later the changes are rolled out to the site. This is known as continuous deployment, where software is deployed all the time.

The advantage to being able to do this is that it reduces the time from idea to profit. When the business has a new idea to change the product and make more money, there doesn't have to be a huge delay just to get the change shipped. Continuous deployment is also helpful for discovering security holes. Instead of having to wait six weeks for the next build to be released, it can be fixed and deployed inside of a day.

If this seems too ambitious for your team, continuous delivery might be more your style. Continuous delivery is just one step removed from continuous deployment, because while you still execute the build pipeline and generate artifacts, perhaps even deploying it to the pre-production environment, the builds are not pushed to production. There is still great comfort in knowing that every build is tested and can be pushed to production if needed. It takes time to get comfortable enough with the build and deployment process to feel that you don't need to have human intervention in the process of deploying to production.

A build pipeline is what we call the process of taking code from Checkin to some final state, whether to production or just deployed to a test environment ready for manual testing. Typically, a build pipeline starts with a trigger such as a Checkin to a source control tool. You can see a sample deployment pipeline in Figure 5-1.

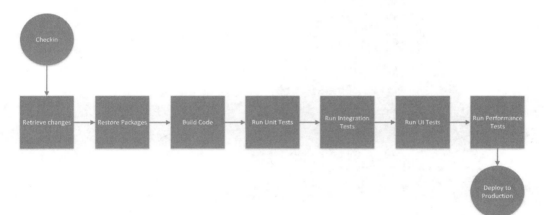

FIGURE 5-1 A deployment pipeline

The build server retrieves the changes from the source control server and starts the process of getting the code to its destination. A typical first step is to restore the packages. For an ASP.NET Core project, the package restore is likely to include both the restoration of nuget packages and node packages. It may even involve restoring JSPM or bower packages. You can read more about JavaScript packages in Chapter 15, "The Role of JavaScript" and about nuget in Chapter 16, "Dependency Management."

The next step is to build the project code. We've already discussed how to do that with the command line. Next, we run our tests. You can read more about different testing approaches in Chapter 20, "Testing." Suffice it to say that there are many different approaches to testing, and several different phases. Here, we're most interested in failing quickly, so we run our fastest-to-complete tests first, which are the unit tests. After that, we move onto the more expensive tests, such as the integration tests and acceptance tests.

Note Several times in this chapter we've mentioned the importance of failing fast. You may be wondering why it is important to fail quickly and the answer is that it is cheaper to fail as soon as possible rather than later in the process. Consider the cost of failure: If you catch the problem on the developer workstation, it is cheaper because it hasn't cost the rest of the team any time at all, and the company only loses the cost of some developer time. If the code makes it all the way out to the customer, the cost can be quite high, including lost sales, incorrect pricing, and all kinds of other problems. The earlier in the process you can move and identify the failure, the lower the cost to the business.

A common rule is that you should have far more unit tests than integration tests, and more integration tests than acceptance tests. The testing pyramid in Figure 5-2 shows this relationship.

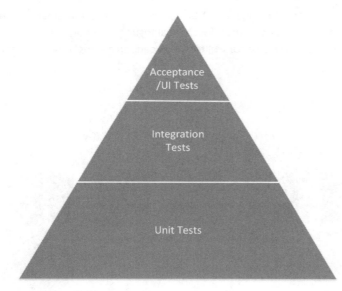

FIGURE 5-2 Testing pyramid

The final piece of testing to complete is performance testing. When deploying a new feature, it is crucial to ensure that there has been no regression in performance that either makes things unpleasant for your users or damages the stability of the system as a whole. One company that is very open about their deployment and testing regimes is GitLabs. During their deployments, they take measurements of hundreds of key metrics and are very careful to improve them strategically.

Taken from one of GitLab's recent blog posts, Figure 5-3 shows how a change to a memory setting can improve HTTP queue timings.

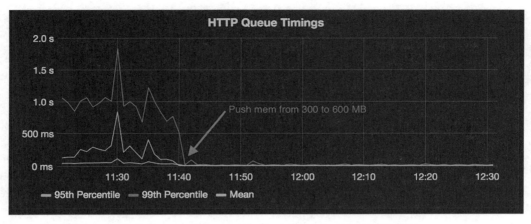

Figure 5-3 HTTP queue timings are vastly improved after a change to memory settings

There are quite a few excellent choices on the market for build servers. TeamCity is a popular choice from JetBrains. Atlassian, who has been expanding its application lifecycle management offerings has an offering in Bamboo. On the open source side, there is Jenkins as well as a handful of Apache projects that show some promise. If you do not want to run your own build server, there are companies, such as CircleCI or Travis CI, that run builds for you on their own infrastructure. Frequently, this infrastructure is hosted on the same cloud you're using to host your software, so you don't even use another data center.

Microsoft's offering in the build runner area is Team Foundation Server (TFS). There are both in-house and hosted versions of TFS. Let's take a closer look at how to set up a build of Alpine Ski House on TFS.

Building Alpine Ski House

As mentioned, TFS offers both a hosted and an on premise install option. Alpine Ski House doesn't have a lot of time to set up a build server on its own hardware, so they have selected the hosted option. In most cases, this is the better approach. Except for a very few situations, if hosting a source control server is not your company's specialty, why not leave infrastructure concerns like these to the experts and focus on your core competencies?

The first thing you need is a Visual Studio Team Services (VSTS) account. VSTS is the hosted version of the venerable Team Foundation Server (TFS). If your company happens to subscribe to Microsoft Developer Network (MSDN), each developer has access to free build minutes on VSTS. Even after these minutes are exhausted, the incremental cost of adding more build minutes is minor. The hosted build agents, the machines that actually run the build, are good for most builds because they have a wide variety of tooling installed on them. If your project requires something special, say an install of Oracle, you can provision your own build agents in the cloud. You can even hook up on premise build agents to talk with the hosted VSTS server. This allows you to keep super-secret proprietary information inside your network, while still getting the advantage of using a hosted solution. Alpine Ski House has no need for this level of security nor does it have anything unusual in its builds, so the hosted agent works fine.

In VSTS, start by creating a new project for Alpine Ski House. To do this from the main dashboard page simply click the Add button under the list of projects. In the dialog box, enter the name of the project and a description as shown in Figure 5-4. You are also prompted for the process template. This can be ignored if you're only using VSTS for builds, because the process template controls the issue tracking and story features in VSTS. If the template controls are something you're interested in exploring, there is plenty of documentation available on the Microsoft website for that topic. For source control, select Git, although again, this doesn't matter. Alpine Ski House is hosted on GitHub rather than in VSTS and the setting is simply for picking the source control tool to use in the project. If you are hosting your source control in VSTS, Git is almost certainly the better option, since it has been highly adopted in the industry.

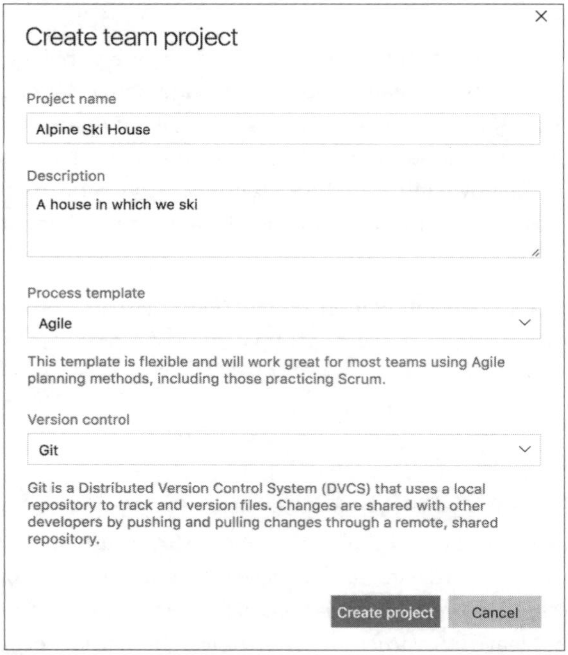

FIGURE 5-4 Creating a new team project in visual studio team systems

With the project created, you can now move on to creating the build. This can be done from the builds tab by selecting New. There are a myriad of build definition templates that you can base your build on as shown in Figure 5-5, but for our purposes, either the Visual Studio build or empty build are good selections.

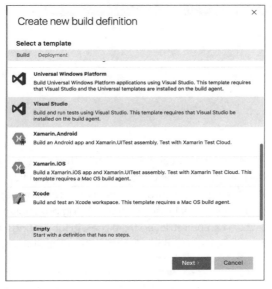

FIGURE 5-5 Selecting a build template

Next, you need to set up the repository where your source code resides, or the source of the source if you like. Figure 5-6 shows the various source control options.

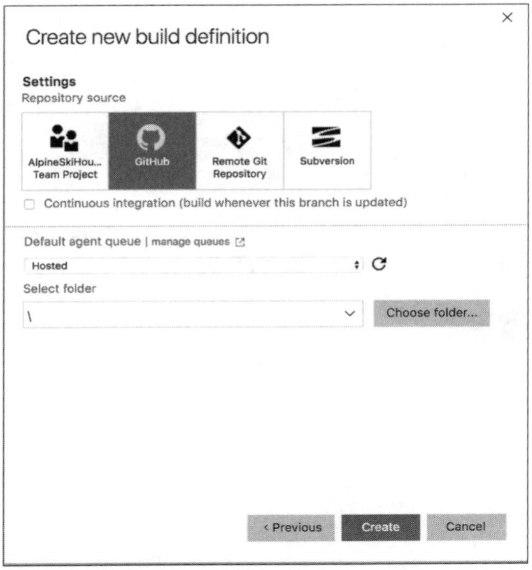

FIGURE 5-6 Selecting the source control tool in use

The dialog box in Figure 5-6 doesn't set up the GitHub credentials, but we'll cover that in a moment. After the build definition has been created, you are directed to an empty build definition page (see Figure 5-7).

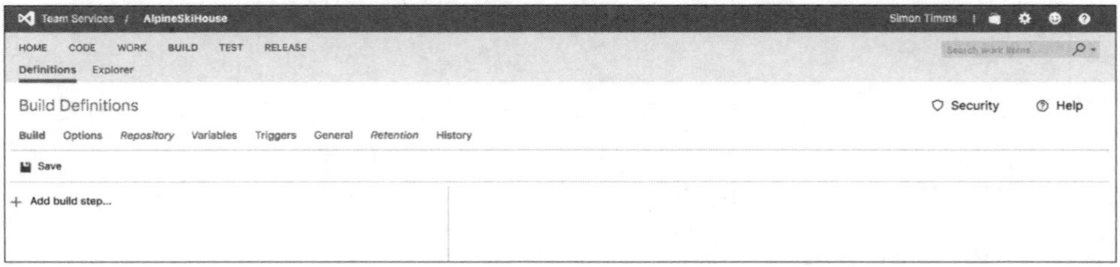

FIGURE 5-7 The build definition page

Let's set up a repository so the build knows where to get your code. Fortunately, there is some great integration between VSTS and GitHub. We can start by going to the Control Panel, which can be accessed by clicking the settings icon (the sprocket) in the top-right corner of the page. From the Control Panel, select services, click New service endpoint, and then select GitHub. In the dialog box shown in Figure 5-8, select either a personal access token, which can be retrieved from the GitHub settings, or Grant Authorization and then proceed through the authorization flow. This uses OAuth to authorize VSTS to act on your behalf at GitHub.

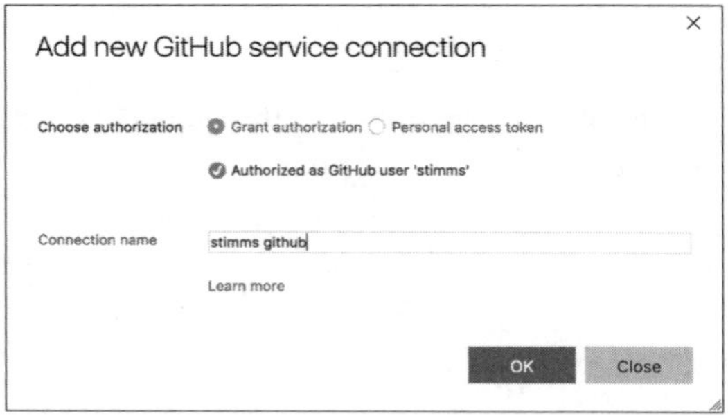

FIGURE 5-8 Granting VSTS access to github

After you've hooked up VSTS and GitHub, you can return to the build definition and select your newly created GitHub account as the source repository, as shown in Figure 5-9.

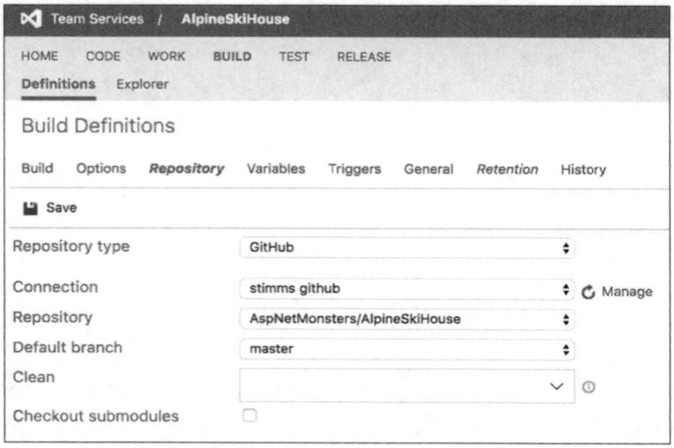

FIGURE 5-9 The repository settings for the build definition

With all of the source control settings in place, you can begin setting up the build process itself. There are many ways to do this. Here, we take a very basic approach and focus on using the command line tools we've already explored instead of relying on MSBuild. You can see an example build process in Figure 5-10.

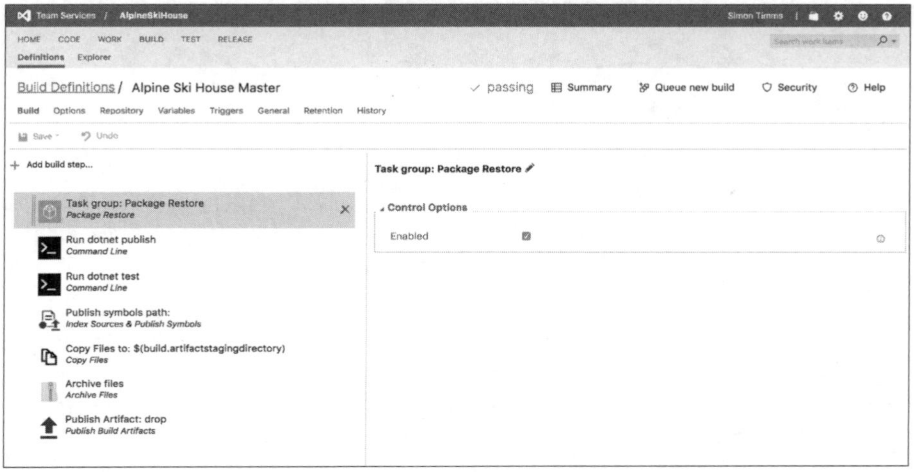

FIGURE 5-10 A simple build definition

The first step in the build process is to restore packages. We have a couple of projects in our solution, so we can either run package restore manually for each one, or write a script to run package restore for each of them. If we had more projects, a script would certainly be the way to go. At the moment, the task group simply runs package restore tasks for each project.

The next step is to call dotnet publish. With a default project file, this simply builds the project and moves files into place in a publish directory. Our project however, has a couple of additional tasks defined by the project.json file:

```
"scripts": {
    "prepublish": [ "npm install", "bower install", "gulp clean", "gulp min" ],
    "postpublish": [ "dotnet publish-iis --publish-folder %publish:OutputPath% --framework
%publish:FullTargetFramework%" ]
  }
```

These tasks run as part of the publish step. These calls go out to npm, bower, and gulp to build up the JavaScript and CSS for the site. The post publish step sets up a web.config file for use with IIS.

We run the tests in Chapter 20 by using the dotnet test command. In the case of Alpine Ski House, at this juncture, unit tests are simple and good to use.

The next step is to move the files we need into a staging directory, pack up the staging directory, and publish the artifacts. These files can then be deployed as part of the release process that we outline in Chapter 6, "Deployment."

Finally, we set up a trigger to run the build whenever somebody checks in the code. This can, rather predictably, be done from the Triggers tab in VSTS. As we discussed earlier in the chapter, we want to run builds both as part of a continual process of checking commits, and on a nightly basis. VSTS supports this scenario as you can see in the configuration shown in Figure 5-11.

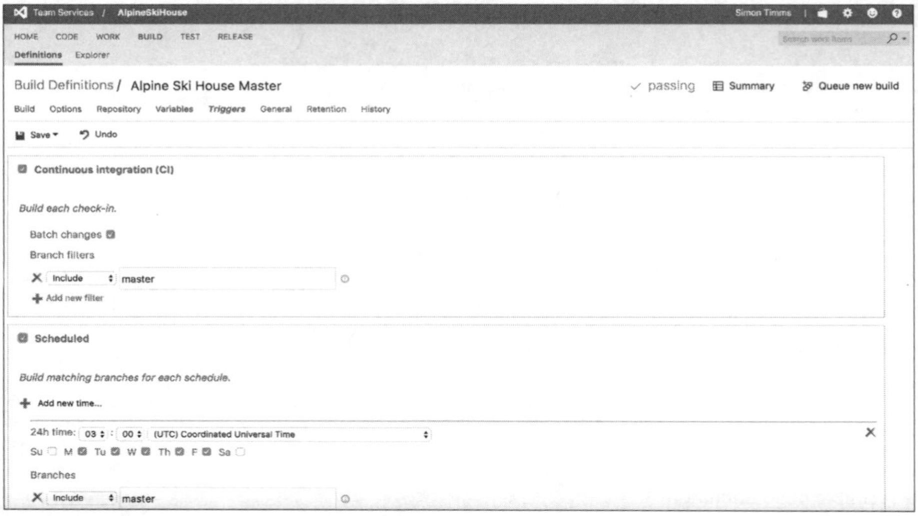

FIGURE 5-11 The alpine ski house triggers

You might also want to build branches located in the main repository. In theory, these branches mostly consist of pull requests, so building them before they are merged into the master further improves your chances of catching code problems before they become an issue that can slow down the entire team.

VSTS has greatly improved with the new build model and is now much closer in feel to something like TeamCity. What's certain is that the simple approach we took to building here, using only command line tools, is portable to just about any build tool. There are more options that you can play with as part of setting up a build, however, the parts we've configured here are sufficient for most projects. After all, simply having a build server, and running builds is a big step up for many teams.

Summary

In this chapter, we took a look at the importance of builds and where they fit inside the entire deployment pipeline, something the Alpine Ski House team was able to use to reduce friction when bringing the code together. Building frequently ensures that you can catch problems as early as possible in your development cycle and be ready to deliver the latest version of your software very quickly. We set up an entire build in VSTS through a series of prompts and dialogs to show just how easy it is to set up a build with modern tooling. All of these pieces helped to set up the team for success in deployment, and in the next chapter, we push our builds out to the cloud.

## CHAPTER 6

Deployment

Balázs wasn't a big fan of emails. He was all about ad hoc meetings. He called them "Jam Sessions," like some sort of band practice. Everybody seemed pretty keen on them and the enthusiasm was so infectious that Danielle was quickly on board. Basically it was mob programming where the whole team would get together and "jam" on a single problem. The idea was that it would make for fewer mistakes and allowed small groups to spin off to tackle parts of the problem asynchronously. If the main team is working on querying the database, another team might spin off to research how to enable encryption on database connections. The splinter would rejoin with its new knowledge and integrate their discoveries into the main product. In this way the team could avoid being blocked on issues which might side track a single developer.

Today's jam session was about getting deployments working. To Danielle it seemed like it was really early in the process to get something deployed. All they really had was a landing page. They hadn't put everything else together yet, but Balázs explained it. "Deployments are always a last minute thing and people rush to get them done in the final minutes before a deadline. That's how mistakes are made. Deployments are hard so let's do it now and do it over and over again until it isn't hard anymore."

"Why would it get easier if we do it a lot?" asked Danielle. Deployments weren't like squats; you weren't going to get strong just because you do them a lot.

"Ah", said Balázs, "do you like having to edit these configuration files manually each time we deploy?"

"Heck no!" replied Danielle.

"So then, why don't you make it easier on yourself and write a script to do it for you? That way the process is repeatable and you don't have to worry about making a mistake," Balázs suggested.

Danielle nodded--things were becoming clearer to her. "If we examine the process each time we do it and make improvements then it will get easier." Not like squats exactly, but they would get stronger at deployment with introspection. "I sure hate having to log into the production servers to update packages."

"Now you're driving the Lada" exclaimed Balázs. He always had the best eastern European sayings. "Let's try jamming on getting deployments working."

In this deployment chapter we look at putting up a Kestrel server, fronting it with a more fully featured web server. We will get the Project Parsley builds from the previous step deployed into the wider world. We'll look at how to do binary deployments to a Linux box, and we'll also look at leveraging Microsoft Azure. We'll create a site that anyone can access to do testing, and we'll make the deployment process so easy and repeatable that it will be possible to put up one-time test environments to play with individual fixes and patches.

Picking a web server

For many years the choices of web servers for hosting ASP.NET applications have been pretty limited. The vast majority of people did their hosting using IIS, the web server that comes with Windows. There were some administrators who ran ASP.NET on Apache on Linux using Mono, which is unlikely to be common. More recently the option of using a web server like NancyHost, which implements the Open Web Interface for .NET (OWIN), became available.

Microsoft IIS is a very efficient and fully featured web server. It supports hosting multiple sites in an isolated fashion, meaning that it can be used to host many different websites on a single instance. Support for SSL, gzip, virtual hosting, and even HTTP2 is all built in out-of-the box. If you're deploying an ASP.NET web application to a Windows environment, there is very little need to look further than IIS.

.NET Core, however, runs on a multitude of platforms, most of which have no support for IIS. In these scenarios the Kestrel web server is the way to go. Kestrel is a lightweight web server that supports .NET Core and runs on all the platforms you love: Linux, macOS, and Windows. At the heart of Kestrel is the asynchronous eventing library called libuv. If this library sounds familiar to you, it's because it is the same library that is at the heart of Node.js.

Kestrel

.NET Core web applications are actually just executable files. In previous versions of ASP.NET, the end result of the compilation was typically a library that could be passed into a web server. The default project contains a Program.cs, the contents of which are:

```
public static void Main(string[] args)
        {
            var config = new ConfigurationBuilder()
                .AddCommandLine(args)
                .AddEnvironmentVariables(prefix: "ASPNETCORE_")
                .Build();

            var host = new WebHostBuilder()
                .UseConfiguration(config)
                .UseKestrel()
                .UseContentRoot(Directory.GetCurrentDirectory())
                .UseIISIntegration()
                .UseStartup<Startup>()
```

```
            .Build();
    host.Run();
}
```

You can see that first we set up a configuration that is read from the command line and the environment. Next, we construct a WebHost and run it. The WebHost it built using a fluent builder pattern and here we start by adding Kestrel hosting and by telling it to use the current directory as its root. Next, IIS integration is added. This is how IIS can communicate with the application. The final configuration step is to specify a startup file that is responsible for performing additional site specific configurations. We'll look at the settings for the application in Chapter 12, "Configuration and Logging." With all the configuration hosting options in place, you can now build the configuration into a host and run it.

There are a handful of other options available to configure at this point. For instance, the CaptureStartupErrors(true) directive catches exceptions in the startup process and throws up an error page instead of simply exiting the application. This might be useful for development, but for production environments, it is better to fail hard and exit the application.

The hosting configuration options are not particularly numerous. All of the configurations for hosting are found inside the application entry point, typically Program.cs. Settings for the application are located in the Startup.cs.

Kestrel is a very important component in any application hosting story with ASP.NET because it is what actually runs the ASP.NET code. Up until this release of ASP.NET Core, ASP.NET has been hosted in the IIS worker process, w3wp.exe. In ASP.NET Core, IIS works as a reverse proxy sending requests onto Kestrel.

> **Note** ASP.NET MVP Rick Strahl has written a great blog post comparing how ASP.NET has been hosted in IIS up until now, and how it differs from the new ASP.NET Core way. It also covers some great tips on avoiding using IIS as part of your development workflow. *https://weblog.west-wind.com/posts/2016/Jun/06/Publishing-and-Running-ASPNET-Core-Applications-with-IIS.*

Reverse Proxy

To understand how IIS communicates with Kestrel, it is important to understand exactly what a reverse proxy does. Proxy servers have long been used to save on ongoing bandwidth or restrict the sites a computer inside a network can see (see Figure 6-1).

FIGURE 6-1 A proxy server

The proxy server takes HTTP requests and decides if they are legal requests. If the request is for a file that it has recently seen and cached, it serves the cached file instead of incurring additional bandwidth and latency costs by sending the request over the public Internet. This technique both saves on bandwidth and reduces latency for the user. Internet service providers might use this technique in their own data centers for files commonly requested by their users. For instance, if a new trailer for a popular movie is released, the proxy prevents the upstream servers from being overloaded. Generally, the experience is better for all involved although it does add to the complexity of invalidating cached resources when the cache is distributed.

A reverse proxy, shown in Figure 6-2, flips the proxy around and places it in front of the web servers. Just as a normal proxy does, the proxy server here caches resources. HTTP GET requests do not modify data on the server, or at least they shouldn't in accordance with the specification, so their content can be saved for a time on the proxy server. This reduces the load on the web servers which tend to have to work much harder to serve a request than the proxy.

FIGURE 6-2 A reverse proxy

Reverse proxies can also be used to act as an abstraction layer around a number of web servers. A proxy (see Figure 6-3) can sit in front of a muddle of microservices so they appear, to outside parties, to be a single service.

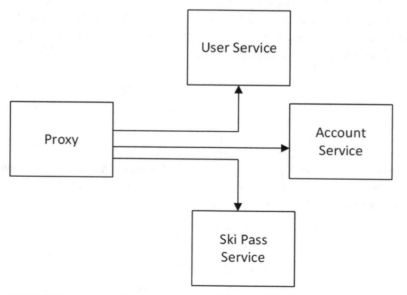

FIGURE 6-3 A proxy can route to numerous different services

For many years IIS has been the "go to" for serving websites on the Windows platform. ASP.NET Core ships with a new IIS module called Asp Net Core Module. This native module passes requests from IIS directly to Kestrel, which is running in a separate process, over HTTP. This is an interesting departure from the approach that has been used previously. The integrated IIS pipeline has been the recommended approach for years, but it couples ASP.NET very tightly to IIS. To allow ASP.NET Core to run on any platform, this coupling had to be broken.

To enable IIS hosting of an ASP.NET Core application, a number of things must be in place. The first is the UseIISIntegration, as was previously suggested. The second is to include a web.config file which loads the ASPNetCoreModule:

```xml
<?xml version="1.0" encoding="utf-8"?>
<configuration>
  <!--
    Configure your application settings in appsettings.json. Learn more at https://
go.microsoft.com/fwlink/?LinkId=786380
  -->
  <system.webServer>
    <handlers>
      <add name="aspNetCore" path="*" verb="*" modules="AspNetCoreModule"
resourceType="Unspecified"/>
    </handlers>
    <aspNetCore processPath="%LAUNCHER_PATH%" arguments="%LAUNCHER_ARGS%"
stdoutLogEnabled="false" stdoutLogFile=".\logs\stdout" forwardWindowsAuthToken="false"/>
  </system.webServer>
</configuration>
```

As you can see in this example, there are some flags that can be passed through to IIS. One of the most interesting of which is the ability to forward windows authentication tokens to Kestrel. This allows your Kestrel applications to continue to use NTLM authentication for single sign-on scenarios. Also specified is the path to launch when requests come in.

The AspNetCoreModule takes all the requests sent to IIS and sends them via HTTP onto Kestrel and then returns whatever Kestrel returns to the client. This can be seen in Figure 6-4.

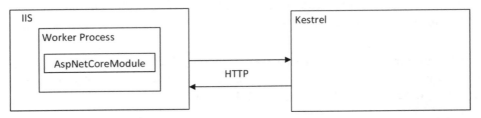

FIGURE 6-4 IIS hosts a worker process, which runs the ASP .NET Core Module to route requests to Kestrel

In the web.config file the handler passes on all requests to the Kestrel process but the requests can be filtered so only a certain class is passed on. For instance, you can change the handler registration to the following:

```
<handlers>
    <add name="aspNetCore" path="/new/*" verb="*" modules="AspNetCoreModule"
resourceType="Unspecified"/>
    </handlers>
```

This passes on just the requests that match the path /new. This allows you to create a hybrid application where some of your requests are handled by ASP.NET Core, and some by another application.

> **Note** The configuration options for the AspNetCoreModule are well documented in the official documentation at *https://docs.asp.net/en/latest/hosting/aspnet-core-module.html*. Pay special attention to the recycleOnFileChange setting, which restarts the Kestrel service if any of the dependent files change. This allows a faster site recycle if you're doing deployments to it.

Because IIS no longer needs to process any managed code, it is possible, even advisable, to disable managed code in IIS for any web applications making use of ASP.NET Core. This should further improve performance.

Nginx

Nginx is a high performance web server that runs on a number of operating systems including Windows, Linux, and OSX. It also provides reverse proxy support for a number of protocols including MTP, POP3, IMAP, and HTTP. Additionally, it can serve static files, provide SSL termination, and even provide HTTP2 support.

Nginx fills the same role as IIS, but on a wider variety of operating systems. Instead of having a web.config file, you can create an nginx.conf file that contains the required configuration settings.

> **Note** A more complete Nginx sample, which includes setting up SSL and HTTP2, can be found on the ASP.NET Monsters website at: *http://aspnetmonsters.com/2016/07/2016-07-17-nginx/* and *http://aspnetmonsters.com/2016/08/2016-08-07-nginx2/*. You can also catch video walkthroughs of the same content on the ASP.NET Monsters Channel 9 at: *https://channel9.msdn.com/Series/aspnetmonsters*.

This configuration file sets up a simple Nginx proxy to Kestrel. It also includes SSL termination. Because Kestrel is super-lightweight, it doesn't actually support SSL and instead relies on an upstream server to do terminations and send unencrypted HTTP requests to it.

```
#number of worker processes to spawn
worker_processes  10;
```

```
#maximum number of connections
events {
    worker_connections  1024;
}

#serving http information
http {
    #set up mime types
    include       mime.types;
    default_type  application/octet-stream;

    #set up logging
    log_format  main  '$remote_addr - $remote_user [$time_local] "$request" '
                      '$status $body_bytes_sent "$http_referer" '
                      '"$http_user_agent" "$http_x_forwarded_for"';
    access_log  /var/log/nginx/access.log  main;

    #set up certificates
    ssl_certificate /etc/letsencrypt/live/ski.alpineskihouse.com/fullchain.pem;
    ssl_certificate_key /etc/letsencrypt/live/ski.alpineskihouse.com/privkey.pem;

    #uses sendfile(2) to send files directly to a socket without buffering
    sendfile        on;

    #the length of time a connection will stay alive on the server
    keepalive_timeout  65;

    gzip on;

    #configure where to listen
    server {
        #listen over http on port 443 on ski.alpineskihouse.com
        listen       443 ssl;
        server_name  ski.alpineskihouse.com;

        #set up SSL certificats
        ssl_certificate       cert.pem;
        ssl_certificate_key   cert.key;

        ssl_session_cache      shared:SSL:1m;
        ssl_session_timeout    5m;

        #disable terrible, broken ciphers
        ssl_ciphers  HIGH:!aNULL:!MD5;
        ssl_prefer_server_ciphers  on;

        #by default pass all requests on / over to localhost on port 5000
        #this is our Kestrel server
        location / {
            #use the proxy to save files
            proxy_cache aspnetcache;
            proxy_cache_valid  200 302  30s;
            proxy_cache_valid  404      10m;
            proxy_pass http://127.0.0.1:5000/;
        }
    }
}
```

Unlike IIS, Nginx does not launch a copy of Kestrel for you, so you need to start them independently in your production environment. For local development, there is usually no need to leverage Nginx unless your local development explicitly requires one of the features provided by the Nginx infrastructure. You can think of Nginx as being similar to a load balancer in your production environment: not something you need to replicate locally for the majority of testing.

> **Note** Although Nginx runs just fine on Windows, there hasn't been a huge amount of work done to optimize how it interacts with Windows. As a result, it is far less efficient on Windows than on IIS. If Windows is your hosting environment, IIS should remain as your go-to web server, at least for the near future.

Publishing

The approach to publishing varies depending on your publishing destination and the maturity of your processes. Visual Studio has always been able to create deployment packages directly from your development machine. This is typically done by right-clicking the website and selecting "Publish" (see Figure 6-5).

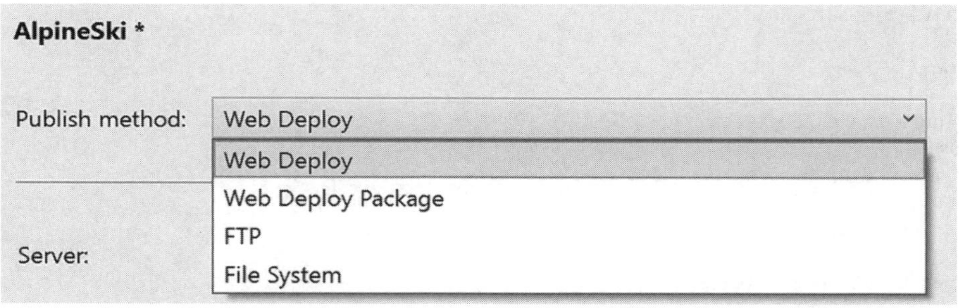

AlpineSki *

Publish method:	Web Deploy ⌄
	Web Deploy
	Web Deploy Package
	FTP
Server:	File System

FIGURE 6-5 The Publish method dialog box

There are a number of options for publishing in this dialog box, including publishing directly to Azure and also publishing using Web Deployment, FTP, or just to a location on the File System. Of these options, Web Deploy is likely the most desirable because it either publishes to a remote location or builds a package for publishing to a remote server using a tool. The direct publishing settings allow you to specify a username and password combination, which is used to authenticate against an IIS instance that supports Web Deploy extensions. If you're running your own instance of IIS, you can install this package (see Figure 6-6) to empower publishing packages easily.

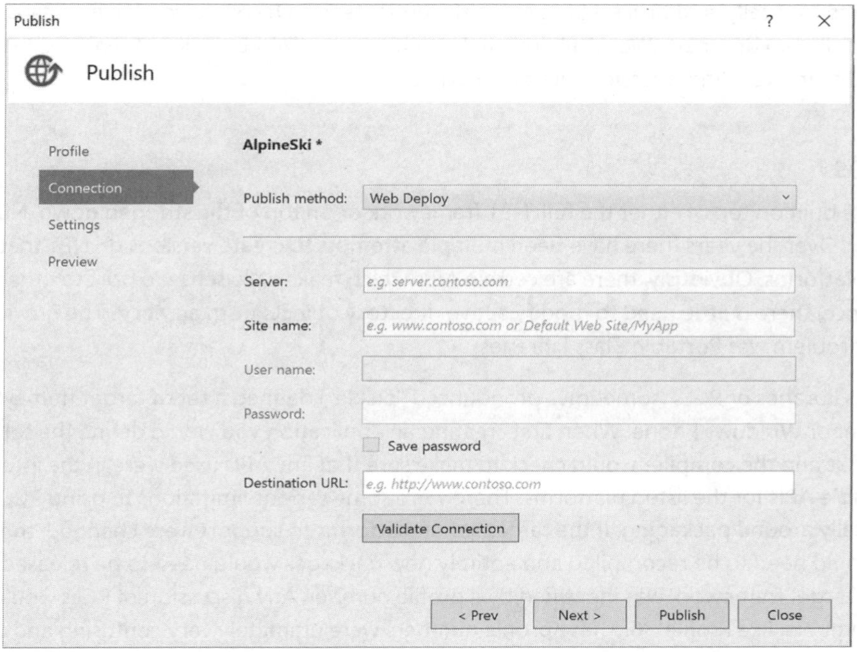

FIGURE 6-6 The full Publish dialog box

Of course if you're publishing your application from Visual Studio, you're doing it wrong. Publishing from Visual Studio is a brittle and difficult to replicate process. If you're on vacation and somebody else needs to publish the application, they are either unable to or they publish it from their computer which is likely to have radically different settings. Right-click deployment in Visual Studio is somewhat anachronistic, referencing a past age when we didn't understand the importance of reproducible builds. It is difficult to set up a build server to continuously build, test, and deploy your application. The Application Lifecycle Management group, whom advises Microsoft on matters related to best practices for DevOps, have long lobbied for deployment from Visual Studio to be removed from the product. Fortunately, there has been a great deal of work put into creating powerful and easy to use tools such as TeamCity, Jenkins, and the TFS Build. These tools automate monitoring a repository for changes, pulling the new code, building it and running tests. If these are too much work to set up, there are hosted solutions such as AppVeyor or Visual Studio Team Services, which are free for small teams. If you have an MSDN license, you've already got licenses for Team Services which aren't being put to good use.

Building on a centralized build server allows everybody on the team to have good visibility into the current state of the builds. It also helps eliminate embarrassing problems where the code works on your local machine, but fails spectacularly after somebody else on the team downloads it. A single build server also allows for performing tests in a single location, which makes them easier to craft and runs them more reliably. Have you ever checked in a seemingly inconsequential change, opted to skip running the unit tests locally, and broken the test for the entire team? Of course you have, because running the tests locally can be a pain. We've all done it. Having a centralized build server ensures that the tests are run and that errors and omissions are caught quickly.

Build Types

.NET Core can be built on top of either the full .NET framework or on top of the stripped down .NET Standard Library. Over the years there have been multiple attempts to create versions of .NET that run on a variety of platforms. Obviously, there are certain APIs which make little sense to port to other platforms. For instance, there is little need to modify active directory objects from an Xbox. The previous solution to the problem was Portable Class Libraries.

Portable class libraries or PCLs (sometimes pronounced "pickle") defined a set of target frameworks such as Silverlight or Windows Phone. When first creating an application you would define the set of target frameworks and the compiler would check to make sure that any APIs used were in the intersection of available APIs for the listed platforms. There were some serious limitations to using PCLs however, especially around packaging. If the target set of platforms to support were changed, the whole library would need to be recompiled and entirely new packages would need to be released. Each combination of target framework was identified by a profile number. Any discussion of PCLs would likely include numbers, like Profile136. These profile numbers were ultimately very confusing and didn't lend much to the discussion.

.NET Standard was developed as a way to solve many of the same problems as PCLs, but in a less convoluted fashion. Instead of having each target framework define a set of APIs it supported, .NET Standard defined a base set of APIs that needed to be defined for any framework claiming to support .NET Standard 1.0. The set of APIs in .NET Standard 1.0 is quite small as it needs to be supported by everything from Xboxes to phones to frameworks running on Linux. .NET Standard defines a number of API sets, each one numbered like a release. Every version number higher than 1.0 supports at least the same set of APIs as the previous layer. So .NET Standard 1.1 supports everything in .NET Standard 1.0 as well as `System.Collections.Concurrent`, `System.Runtime.Numerics`, `System.Runtime.InteropServices`, and a handful of others. Ideally your application would target as low a version of .NET Standard as possible.

A new application in .NET Core comes out of the box configured to run in portable mode. This is the mode that almost all applications have been built in historically. The end result of building the application is a relatively small collection of files: the assembly which is produced and any third party libraries needed to make it run. Any runtime files are expected to already exist on the target computer, typically by virtue of having been installed by a .NET Runtime Installer. Most modern versions of Windows come with a version of .NET already install, although it might not be exactly the version expected by your application. In this mode, the files output from the build are architecture neutral files. During the first run of your application deployed in portable mode, the Just-In-Time compiler produces and caches a local version of the neutral file in native machine code. This allows for subsequent runs to be much faster because they can skip the compilation step.

The alternative to building in portable mode is to build in self-contained mode. In this configuration, the application and all its dependencies are compiled down to machine specific code at build time instead of at run time. The deployment of a self-contained mode application also includes all of the libraries needed to run the application, even the ones from the .NET framework. Specifying the operating system and architecture of the target environment might seem odd after having spent many years working in an environment that supported compile once run anywhere. Doing so is required because the actual .NET runtime is a natively compiled application even if the applications that run on top of it aren't.

One of the best new features in ASP.NET Core is that it is fully bin deployable. In previous versions of ASP.NET, the correct version of the .NET runtime needed to be deployed on the server. This created all manner of conflicts between development teams who wanted the latest and greatest on the server and operations teams who want stability. .NET Core bundles the entire runtime with deployment so the risk of installing potentially conflicting .NET runtimes and breaking an already installed application is eliminated.

Building A Package

Let's start by packaging up a .NET application in portable mode. As this is the out-of-the-box configuration for almost every template, very little additional work is needed. The new dotnet command line tool can be used to assemble a directory from the application. From a command line in the directory of the project file, simply run:

```
dotnet publish
```

This produces a directory structure with all you need to publish your application to a server that already has the .NET framework installed. There are some rudimentary command line options that might be passed into the publishing step such as the mode to build in, usually debug or release mode, and the destination directory.

This directory can be zipped up and dropped in whatever production folder is needed. If you happen to be using a deployment tool, such as Octopus Deploy, the output directory can easily be assembled into a nuget package. Nuget packages are actually the default deployment mechanism for .NET Standard libraries. To ease the burden of creating these packages a mechanism is built in to construct Nuget packages directly from a project. Again, this can be accomplished by using the dotnet command line tool like so:

```
dotnet pack
```

The end result of this build is a pair of .nuget files. This contains the binaries generated from the build and the other contains the symbols for the build for upload to a symbol server for debugging purposes. These packages can be distributed just as you might any other nuget package: uploaded to an Octopus server or distributed via a site such as nuget.org or MyGet.

> **Note** If you're a developer who prefers using visual tools for building and packaging your applications, you might be wondering why we're dwelling so much on command line tooling. The truth is that all the automated build tools, and all the visual build tools, are really just calling command line tooling. It is therefore somewhat important to know what is going on beneath the covers.

If it's possible for your project to make use of self-contained packages, then some updates are needed to the build and packaging steps. First the project.json must be updated. Remove the following line from the frameworks section of netcoreapp 1.0:

```
"type": "platform",
```

Next, a list of runtimes needs to be added to build against. If you want to build against Mac OS X and Windows 10 64-bit, this would be the correct section to add:

```
"runtimes": {
      "win10-x64": {},
      "osx.10.11-x64": {}
   }
```

A full list of package identifiers can be found at: *https://docs.microsoft.com/en-us/dotnet/articles/core/rid-catalog*.

When building or publishing the application the runtime can be specified on the command line by using the –r flag:

```
dotnet publish –r win10-x64
```

With the deployment packages created, you can now concentrate on getting the packages deployed to somewhere people can use them.

The Case for Azure

There are countless ways to host an application so that people can use it. For a long time, people and companies ran their own datacenters. There was nothing wrong with this approach, and indeed many people still do it. The challenge is finding the right people to design and maintain a datacenter for you. There are physical challenges like how to run HVAC properly and how large of a uninterruptable power supply is needed. There are also infrastructure challenges like how to ensure that there is sufficient storage available and how to manage a pool of virtual machines. Managing backups is often the work of several people and who really has time to test restores?

These challenges are neither easy nor cheap to solve. What's more is that these challenges are not part of the company's core business. If the company's primary role is to extract and refine oil, Information Technology (IT) is still going to be seen as an expense rather than a core part of the business no matter how important it is to the success of the business. This frequently leads companies to look outside of an internal IT structure to host applications.

There is a spectrum of options when it comes to external hosting. At the most basic level, a company can simply rent space to collocate their machines. The data center provides physical security and solves some of the infrastructure concerns like cooling and power, but not much more. Frequently these facilities contain cages for each of the companies co-located there in order to isolate the machines from one another.

Further along the spectrum are companies who rent out virtual machines or access to physical machines on a monthly basis. They provide a bit more hardware management, but the clients remain largely responsible for the software and for provisioning enough space and compute power.

Even further along the spectrum are companies who provide a collection of hosted services that provide an abstraction over top of the hardware the services are running on. In this scenario you would tend to rent not a computer for your database server, but instead a database instance complete with certain performance guarantees.

Both the renting of virtual machines and the use of hosted services fall into the category of cloud computing. The term "cloud computing" has become a very hazy one (if you'll excuse the pun) due to a great deal of marketing confusion. In effect, it simply suggests that the computing resources you're using are virtualized and can be easily scaled up or down. You are only charged for the resources you use instead of being charged for a baseline of resources as you would be in a regular data center. This is known as elastic computing.

Elastic computing is ideal for companies who experience "spiky" loads, that is to say, have periods of high usage and low usage. Alpine Ski House is a perfect example of such a company. During the summer months there are very few users on the site because there is no snow to ski on, but come the first cold snap in the winter, demand spikes. With traditional hosting, Alpine Ski House would be forced to pay for beefy hardware all year round when it is only needed for a portion of the year. What's more is that the load on the ticket site is much higher in the morning before people hit the ski slopes than during the day when they're already on the ski slopes. So not only does demand for Project Parsley spike during the year, it is spiky over the course of a single day. Without elastic hosting, Alpine ski house would need to spec its hardware to match peak load.

Microsoft Azure is constantly performing in the leader's quadrant of Gartner's Magic Quadrant Reports. Its infrastructure as a service (IaaS) offerings are approximately in line with other cloud providers, but where it really shines is with its platform as a service (PaaS) offerings. IaaS is the most tunable version of cloud hosting, allowing you to run you own virtual machines and hook them together with custom networking, including dedicated connections between Azure and your on-premises data center. Building on top of this are PaaS offerings that provide an abstraction layer over the IaaS. This layer includes things like a scalable document database, a service bus, services related to audio and video processing, machine learning, and far more.

To borrow an excellent analogy from Scott Hanselman, owning your own data center is like owning your own car: you're responsible for charging it, maintaining it, and driving it. IaaS is like renting a car. You still have the responsibility to drive it and charge it, but a lot of the maintenance concerns are alleviated. Finally, PaaS is like using a taxi. You simply need to tell the driver where you want to go and all the details are taken care of for you. With a service like DocumentDB there is no need to worry about how to scale it or back it up; you simply need to use it.

Azure is an incredibly broad suite of technologies with more than 40 major product offerings. We are going to focus on a single one: App Services.

Azure Deployments

There is no shortage of methods for deploying web applications to Azure App Services. Files can be manually copied to an FTP site in real 1990s site deployment style, copied to a Dropbox or OneDrive account, or Azure can pull directly from a source code repository such as Git (see Figure 6-7).

FIGURE 6-7 The deployment source options on Microsoft Azure app services

Using OneDrive or Dropbox for deployments has always felt somewhat amateurish. There are certainly some scenarios where simply putting a file on Dropbox is all that is required to make a change to the live website, but these tend to be scenarios where the client is a Mom and Pop shop looking for the simplest way possible to update a website. Source control is a crucial part of any deployment strategy so it is tempting to make use of it for deploying.

When hooking up Azure App Services to publish from source control, a simple push to a branch in source control is sufficient to kick off a build and deployment. Thus you can set up your source control to have a test branch and a master branch so that pushing to the test branch kicks off a build and deploys on a test server and pushing to the master branch kicks off a build and deploys on the live site. This does couple your source control tightly to your build and deployment. It becomes very easy to accidentally deploy your site by pushing to the wrong branch and there is no guarantee that what is in the test branch is what gets deployed to master when the time is right. There could be extra commits in master that have not been correctly backported to test, causing unexpected behavior. Ideally the binaries deployed to master are the exact same ones that were deployed to the testing environment. This provides you some assurances that code continues to work in production as it did in test.

What we'd like to do is deploy a package to test, run some regression testing on it, and, when we're comfortable, deploy the exact same binaries to production. There are many tools that can help with this, tools like TeamCity, Jenkins, and Team Foundation Server. For our purposes, we're going to hook up our Azure account to the hosted version of TFS which is now called Visual Studio Team Services (VSTS).

For a long time, the build tools in Team Foundation Services have been very lacking. Builds were defined in painfully difficult to edit WorkFlow files and deviating from the standard build required expert knowledge. With the latest version of TFS however, the builds have been brought more in line with the way builds are constructed in Team City or Jenkins. They are easier to change and the library of pre-written tasks is only growing. For many builds, all that is needed is to couple together a handful of existing build steps.

We already have a build running that produces packages, all that is needed is to hook up a release for the binaries.

> **Note** If you're having trouble automatically hooking up your Azure account to VSTS, then the article at *https://blogs.msdn.microsoft.com/visualstudioalm/2015/10/04/automating-azure-resource-group-deployment-using-a-service-principal-in-visual-studio-online-buildre-lease-management/* might be of some help.

Hooking up VSTS to deploy to Azure is a relatively painless process. For more complex deployment scenarios, you might need to set up a number of tasks. For our simple scenario, however, you can actually get away with a single task in the deployment (see Figure 6-8).

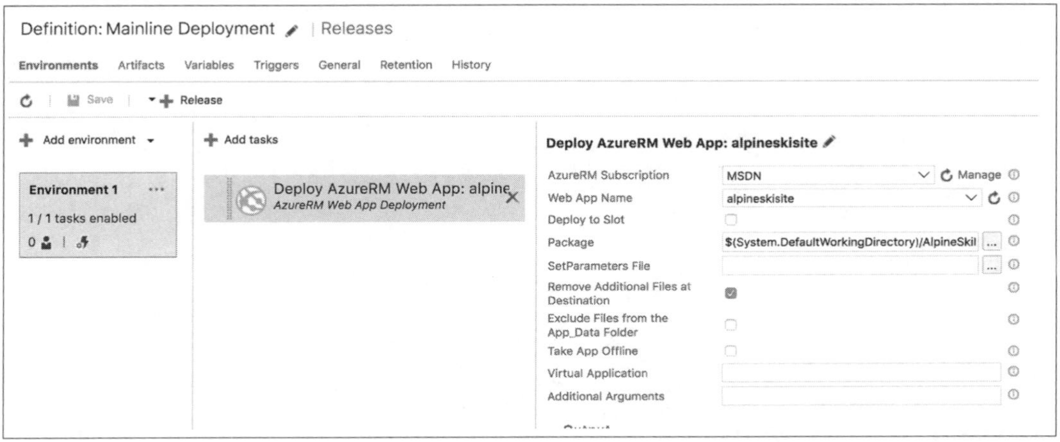

FIGURE 6-8 Deploying a package to Microsoft Azure

Using the newer resource manager, you only need to specify the web application name and select the package you're going to deploy. Selecting Remove Additional Files At Destination is always a good idea to ensure that builds are actually repeatable. Of course this simple configuration is lacking a lot of functionality. The build requires that the web app is already allocated, which means that there is some manual intervention required. Ideally the build creates the resources as part of its processing. This allows you to specify an entire environment: web server, database, firewalls, etc. for testing purposes in a file allowing for a complete, repeatable deployment instead of manually clicking through the portal.

This can easily be achieved with Azure Resource Manager (ARM) templates. These are JSON based files that define entire environments. For instance, this can be a visualization of a simple deployment of Umbraco, an ASP.NET based CMS. This entire collection of virtual machines, network infrastructures, and storage accounts is defined in a 500 line JSON document that can easily be source controlled and versioned. This is an example of infrastructure as code. Azure resources are grouped together into "resource groups". These collections of resources allow you to logically group all the resources for a specific environment. Deploying a resource group from within the release cycle can be done via a PowerShell script or, if using VSTS, via a built in task. An ARM template is shown being deployed as part of a release here in Figure 6-9.

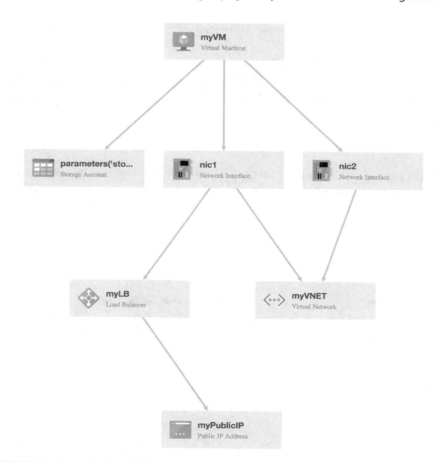

FIGURE 6-9 A visualization of the resources described by an ARM template

ARM templates can also be easily deployed from PowerShell with the appropriate Azure PowerShell tooling installed. In this command, a template is deployed with the administrative login skiadmin.

```
New-AzureRmResourceGroupDeployment -ResourceGroupName alpineski -administratorLogin skiadmin
-TemplateFile alpineski.json
```

Templates can be parameterized so they can handle slightly different scenarios. For instance, they could take in the number of web server instances to create: one for testing or twenty for production.

There are countless other tasks that can be added to the build pipeline. For instance, you might be interested in doing blue/green deployments where your application is deployed to a hot spare before switching users over to it. Perhaps there are web tests that you'd like to run as part of the deployment to ensure things really are working, which are also available in VSTS (see Figure 6-10).

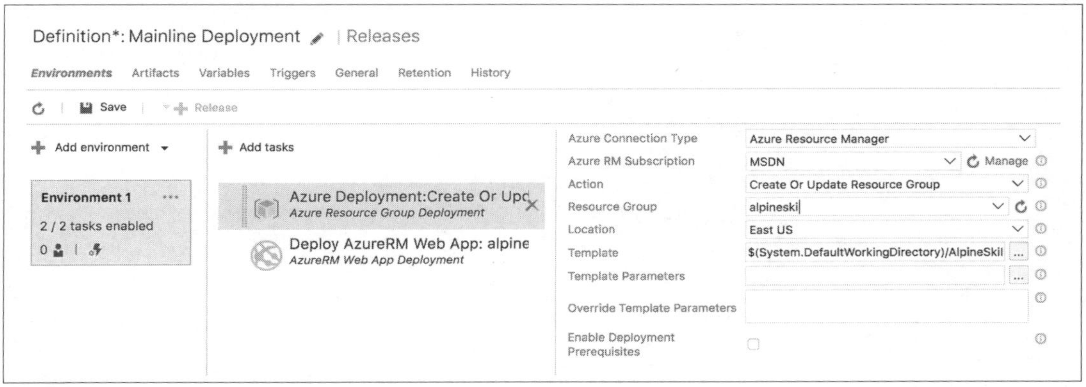

FIGURE 6-10 A resource manager template being deployed from VSTS

Container Deployments

If you or your company aren't quite ready to move to the cloud, there are alternatives that offer some advantages of the cloud locally. Docker and containerization, in general, is perhaps the most impressive change to deployments in the last decade. The entirety of Chapter 9, "Containerization" is dedicated to using containers for deploying ASP.NET Core applications.

Summary

Releasing software is often thought of as being very difficult. Some companies struggle to put out even a single release in a year due to the complexities of their release process. The continuous deployment movement applies the old saying, "If something hurts, do it more," to the release process. By reducing the time between releases, we force ourselves to optimize and improve the process, typically by using automation. The advantages to being able to deploy rapidly are numerous: security flaws can be fixed quickly, time can be spent on improving the product instead of deploying, and releases become repeatable reducing the chances of making manual deployment errors.

Although this chapter has focused a lot on deployments to Azure using VSTS, there is nothing here that cannot be done using the command line or an alternative build tool. The important takeaway is that builds and deployments can and should be automated. ASP.NET Core makes the process even simpler because it can be deployed to a wider variety of platforms and without concerns about clobbering installed applications using other frameworks.

#### PART 2

Sprint Retro: A Journey of 1000 Steps

Danielle was feeling a bit preoccupied. She was in the middle of a boxed set of X-Files she had picked up in a Black Friday deal the previous November. She had just watched an episode where nuclear waste on a Russian ship had created a human-fluke worm hybrid. It had attacked somebody while they used a pit toilet, dragging them down into... well she didn't like to think what was under the pit toilet. It certainly wasn't Narnia. She had never liked pit toilets in the past and this was pretty much the last straw. Only proper running water from now on, and maybe she would buy some fluke worm medicine and keep in on hand, just as a precaution.

A throat clearing sort of sound pulled her back to reality. The first sprint retrospective was starting up. They were a week into the project and what a week it had been. It was hard to believe that only one week ago the news had come down about the new project: Project Parsley. Danielle had rather grown to like the code name they'd come up with. It made her think of a fresh new start, something to remove the taste of the pervious course. A lot of people didn't eat the parsley they got in fancy restaurants but Danielle always did.

Balázs was up and the front of the room in front of the whiteboard. He was waving the marker around seemingly in the midst of a conversation with Tim. Danielle suspected he was actually trying to catch a wiff of the whiteboard markers. The hill had, through a slight ordering mistake almost a decade ago, bought a huge number of the really potent whiteboard markers which used to be the norm. They were excellent.

"Okay, let's get started," called out Balázs. "The point of a retrospective is to figure out what we need to start doing, stop doing, and continue doing." He divided the whiteboard into three columns and wrote "Start," "Stop," and "Continue" at the top of each column.

"Come on, everybody grab a marker and start writing! These are great markers, by the way."

Suspicions confirmed, Danielle picked up a green Expo marker and headed up to the board. Under continue she wrote "Using .NET" and "Continuous deployments." Other members of the team were picking up markers and jostling for space in front of the board. After a few minutes they had come up with:

Start	Stop	Continue
Actually building stuff	Having stand-ups in the morning, can they be at the end of the day?	Using .NET
Kale in the break room	Working only on getting builds going	Continuous deployments
Tutorials on the principles of MVC and other patterns (lunch and learn?)	Messing about with Linux (too difficult)	Using Azure
Using more messaging patterns	Quit using Windows (not powerful enough)	

A lot of the suggestions were jokes, but also the sign of a team that was stating to have fun together.

Balázs seemed pretty happy with the whole thing. "So, reading this, folks, it seems like there aren't any real big things we need to work on. There is a theme that we need to get started on, but I think we're actually doing a lot better than everybody acknowledges. We've managed to put together a solid build pipeline that will remove all of the barriers to getting out code in the future."

He continued, "I've seen a lot of teams fail to get deployments down early in the process and they find themselves scrambling at the last minute to get code, which worked locally, and deployed to the production environment."

Marc didn't seem all that impressed. "We've managed to deploy a site that does nothing. I don't know how we're going to hit any deadlines like this."

"I know it looks that way," said Balázs "but writing code is what our second sprint is all about."

"I suppose," said Marc. "I'm chomping at the bit to get started on some stuff."

"Great!" replied Balázs "We'll need that energy on the next sprint. I also see a need here to do some training to bring the team up on some of the ideas behind MVC. I think we have some really strong developers on the team who've worked in this space before. We can get something figured out. I'm sure we can spring for a lunch, too." Balázs looked over, eyebrow raised at Tim who nodded in agreement. Tim wasn't the sort of fellow to skimp on free lunches.

"I'm glad that Azure is popular," continued Balázs "because the management team is pretty happy about how the pricing for that is working out. I know Tim here is looking at getting rid of everything in the server room and moving to the cloud."

"Yep" said Tim "It is tough to maintain servers out here— it takes forever to get parts and, comparatively, electricity is expensive. Plus, now that we have these new people on staff, we might be in need of some more office space, and so reclaiming the server room will help immensely."

"Okay then," said Balázs, "We've got a path forward on most everything. Let's get back to work and actually ship some code!"

"I don't feel like we've addressed the lack of Kale in the breakroom," complained Danielle, "but I suppose the actual project is going okay. I'd still like to put more super-foods on the backlog for this sprint."

## CHAPTER 7

Building Web Applications with Microsoft Azure

"Nice work, Danielle. This is really coming together." Marc was reviewing the build steps that Danielle had configured to ease the burden of producing builds. "How long does this take to run?"

"From merge to deploy? About 4 minutes." Danielle felt like she had achieved the "make it easy" merit badge for builds, and rightfully so.

"So this is it, eh?" Marc continued with a bit of apprehension. He knew in the next sprint there was going to be some work involved in writing out the card data for their third-party provider to print the cards, and felt compelled to spike something out, especially in these new, cloudy waters. "We're running in the cloud now. And...that's cool, I guess. I mean, we have all kinds of things to sort out, but this should be cool. I hope. Right?" He paused uncomfortably, then resumed with a bit of skepticism. "So where are we going to save the card export data again? We're not going to have a file system, right?"

"No, you're right there. We have a file system in our deployment, but we don't have unlimited disk space. I think we have a bunch of options though. It looks like we can throw the data into queues and process it as we need it, but that doesn't feel quite right," Danielle said. "I wonder if it makes sense to try table storage? Or maybe document storage? I don't want to force it to fit just to use something new."

"Exactly!" said Marc, happy that someone was on the same page as him. "There has been a lot of buzz words floating around here lately." He suddenly spoke in a lower voice, "Would you believe Tim came by and told me to look at the Event service? He talked about how we should think of our skiers as IoT event streams. I'm not sure he gets what we're doing here. But at the heart of it, A. Datum is expecting ski card data to come as CSVs right? So why not just write out CSVs?"

"Yeah, totally Marc, I get what you're saying. We don't need astronaut architecture here, for sure. What do you think about blob storage? Using it is almost as easy as configuring a database from what I've seen."

"Right, I think you're on to something there," he replied. "Our outputs here are files. Let's treat them like files and save them in the file-like place in Azure. It seems to make the most sense."

Confident in the direction they had started moving, Danielle pulled a chair into Marc's cubicle to pair up. They started a branch and were off.

Thinking of Platform as a Service

If this is your first foray into cloud provider service offerings, or if this is your return trip to the cloud after a few years away, it's going to look like there are a lot of shiny new things to try out. Indeed there are, but over-reaching into new tech has been the pitfall of many applications.

Here's a good rule of thumb that you can use to help you evaluate these glorious old-made-new again features—use what you are comfortable building. That's not to say that you should stay inside your comfort zone. In fact, we encourage you to go beyond whatever felt comfortable on your last project. What this rule of thumb does mean is that the services you use should be a fit for your project. We tend to find that the best services to bring into a project are the ones that fill a need and fit like a glove, rather than the one that doesn't fit quite right. Like forcing a certain defendant to wear gloves on national television during a murder trial, and then regretting it.

As your application matures, you often end up with patterns and services that emerge naturally based on the type of work you're doing. For example, if you do batch processing, you make doing batches easy. Even the .NET Framework itself builds up these types of services as part of the base class library, which is why we don't have to write FTP client libraries any more.

It is those types of patterns and services that you should look for in your cloud offerings. Much like Danielle and Marc trying to avoid equating ski hill patrons to water sensors, we shouldn't put the round-shaped things in the square-shaped openings. In Azure, the Platform as a Service (PaaS) offerings tend to allow for problems of many different sizes and shapes to be solved without having to reinvent the wheel.

Platform Services

A lift-and-shift strategy is sometimes employed by an organization, meaning they take what runs locally in their environment and they move it to the cloud. For some companies this means a deployment to a cloud virtual machine, and for others it means doing a "physical to virtual" migration, and pushing a virtual machine to the cloud. But let's be clear, if you do lift-and-shift and claim to have a cloud strategy, you have failed. To say it another way, if all you do is migrate your virtual machines to AWS or Azure, you do not have a cloud-optimized organization or software offering. Lift-and-shift is a small part of the story, and it's only marginally different than in-house virtualization. True, it doesn't require sums of money to purchase new server hardware, so it might seem like a good option from a monetary perspective, but it fails to capitalize on many of the benefits of embracing the cloud.

As harsh as some of that last paragraph might sound, lift-and-shift can actually be a good part in a longer-term plan for moving to the cloud. For instance, after your application is deployed to a virtual machine in Microsoft Azure, you might start using queues to deliver messages to new services you craft, or to start writing your log files to blob storage. Over time, you can move your site into a web app or wrap your API with the API Management services to start sharing it with other organizations. Slowly, your application can lean less on infrastructure, which is the virtualized machines you're deployed to, and move in the direction of running on the platform services that the cloud can offer.

If we're being honest, listing out the entire breadth of services that are available in the cloud is kind of like trying to count ants in a colony. They keep changing in number, they keep moving around, and they sometimes birth an entirely new generation of services you may not know about. Regardless, look at Table 7-1 for some of the more mature and exciting services that you can start to incorporate into your application.

TABLE 7-1 A selection of cloud offerings in Microsoft Azure

Category	Services and Offerings
Compute and Storage	Batch Service Fabric Functions Blob Queue Data Lake Store
Networking, Web and Mobile	CDN, Azure DNS Load Balancer App Service API Management Notification Hubs
Data and Enterprise Integration	SQL Database DocumentDB SQL Data Warehouse Redis Cache Service Bus Logic Apps
Intelligence and Analytics	Machine Learning Cognitive Services (Vision, Emotion and Face APIs)
Internet of Things	Stream Analytics Event Hubs
Security, Identity and Monitoring	Azure AD Azure AD B2C Multi-Factor Authentication Access Control Service Key Vault Backup AutoScale Azure Resource Manager
Developer Tools	Visual Studio Team Services Load Testing Azure DevTest Labs HockeyApp

By taking the building block approach, you can quickly compose an application and you do not have to work through the monotony of rebuilding all the known-commodity pieces that are part of every project. Back in 1999 James was hired as part of a two-man team to build a simple web-based Create/Read/Update/Delete (CRUD) application to help maintain a few tables in a database. The site had to be secured by user credentials and have two roles for users, with one group being able to add to a Category table. He was awarded the contract and barely finished the application within the allotted 120 hours. Today, you can build a CRUD application by using Microsoft Azure AD B2C for authentication, Microsoft Azure SQL Database to back the data, and by putting together three controllers in an ASP.NET Core MVC application. You can do all of this and create your application with this same level of functionality in under 4 hours.

There are, in fact, over 100 aspects of Microsoft Azure that you can exercise to build your application, but putting them together in a repeatable way is critical to the success of your project.

Scaffolding, Destroying, and Recreating Your Services

In Chapter 6, "Deployment," we covered the Microsoft Azure Resource Manager Templates and how they can be employed as part of your deployment process. The templates are JSON-based and contain all of the information you need to create a new instance of the service you've configured. The templates are parameterized in such a way that you can use an external JSON file to tailor the resource to fit each environment that you want to deploy to. But, after identifying the resource that you want to include in your deployment, how do you build the template to use in your script?

Thankfully you don't have to build this by hand. Any service that you create as part of a Resource Group in Microsoft Azure can be viewed using the powerful Azure Resource Explorer, located at *https://resources.azure.com*. This tool allows you to browse any resource that you have created, as shown in Figure 7-1, and extract the template that you need with all of the pre-configured options and settings in place.

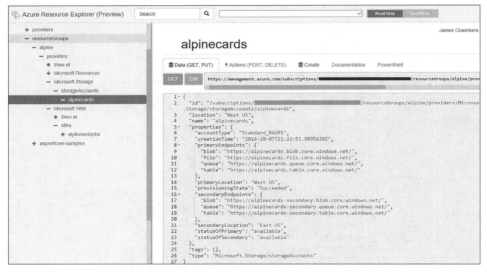

FIGURE 7-1 The Azure Resource Explorer

Alternatively, you don't have to go through the process of building the resource all the way to completion before you can start to work with the template. In Figure 7-2, we show how the Azure Portal itself can be used to generate not only the template, but also all the source code you need in either .NET, Ruby, PowerShell, or from the CLI. You can access this screen by clicking Automation Options before finalizing the creation of a service.

```
Template                                                                              _  □  ×
⬇ Download   🗐 Add to library   ⬆ Deploy

ℹ    Automate deploying resources with Azure Resource Manager templates in a single, coordinated operation. Define resources and configurable input parameters and deploy with script or code. Learn more about template    ⧉
     deployment.

Template    Parameters    CLI    PowerShell    .NET    Ruby

▶ 🔷 Parameters (4)          1  {
  🗋 Variables (0)            2      "$schema": "https://schema.management.azure.com/schemas/2015-01-01/deploymentTemplate.json#",
▼ 🔷 Resources (1)            3      "contentVersion": "1.0.0.0",
  🗋 [parameters('name')] [Microsoft.St...   4      "parameters": {
                            5          "name": {
                            6              "type": "string"
                            7          },
                            8          "accountType": {
                            9              "type": "string"
                           10          },
                           11          "location": {
                           12              "type": "string"
                           13          },
                           14          "encryptionEnabled": {
                           15              "type": "bool",
                           16              "defaultValue": false
                           17          }
                           18      },
                           19      "resources": [
                           20          {
                           21              "apiVersion": "2016-01-01",
                           22              "name": "[parameters('name')]",
                           23              "location": "[parameters('location')]",
                           24              "type": "Microsoft.Storage/storageAccounts",
                           25              "sku": {
                           26                  "name": "[parameters('accountType')]"
                           27              },
                           28              "kind": "Storage",
                           29              "properties": {
```

FIGURE 7-2 A Viewing a template in the Azure Portal

Use the templates and parameter files you download to build out your services and update your build scripts as required. If you are looking for more information on building and customizing the templates and parameters, you can find further reading at: *https://azure.microsoft.com/en-us/documentation/articles/resource-group-authoring-templates/.*

Building Applications Using Platform Services

Let's look at one feature of the application that the Alpine Ski House team needs to solve. When users create ski cards for their accounts, they are prompted to upload a profile picture. The ski cards are later printed by a third-party company that uses a laser printing process to put a black and white picture of the ski card holder on the card. The photo that is uploaded must be resized to specific dimensions and converted to grayscale using a specific conversion standard for the best printing results.

The Alpine Ski House team found a couple of complimentary Microsoft Azure components for their needs, including a simple Storage Account with processing backed by App Services. Storage accounts allow you to store arbitrary data through the use of binary large objects or "blobs." The blob service also provides a backing store for WebJobs, a part of App Services that allows scheduled or triggered jobs to be processed by a number of different mechanisms.

The blob services in storage accounts are just one of the facilities that you can use from the offering. Storage accounts also give you access to unstructured data in the form of the NoSQL table storage, file storage, and finally a simple communication channel through queue storage.

WebJobs are a part of the App Service body of components that also includes mobile services, API development, and the ability to host websites at scale in the Web Apps offering. App Service supports not only .NET languages, but also Java, Node.js, Python, and PHP. You can create one or more components inside of an App Service under the same set of performance and scaling tiers and all services you create in the instance count toward the same bucket of usage, egress, and billing constraints.

Armed with blobs and jobs, the Alpine team married the two with a trigger based off of message in a queue. To make all of this come together, we bring in several components, some of which we expand upon later in the book. After you have gained familiarity with these components, you'll agree that this type of solution, a composition of services offered by the Azure ecosystem, can be quite elegant.

Creating a Storage Account

To get started using these platform features, first you need to create a storage account using the Azure portal, the CLI, PowerShell, or the Visual Studio through the Connected Services dialog.

To use Visual Studio, right-click the project in Solution Explorer and select Add, then click Connected Service. This opens the starting page of the wizard, which is similar to the one you see in Figure 7-3. If you are already signed in to your Microsoft Account, and that account has an Azure Subscription associated with it, you have the option to use an existing Storage Account or one you create as you go.

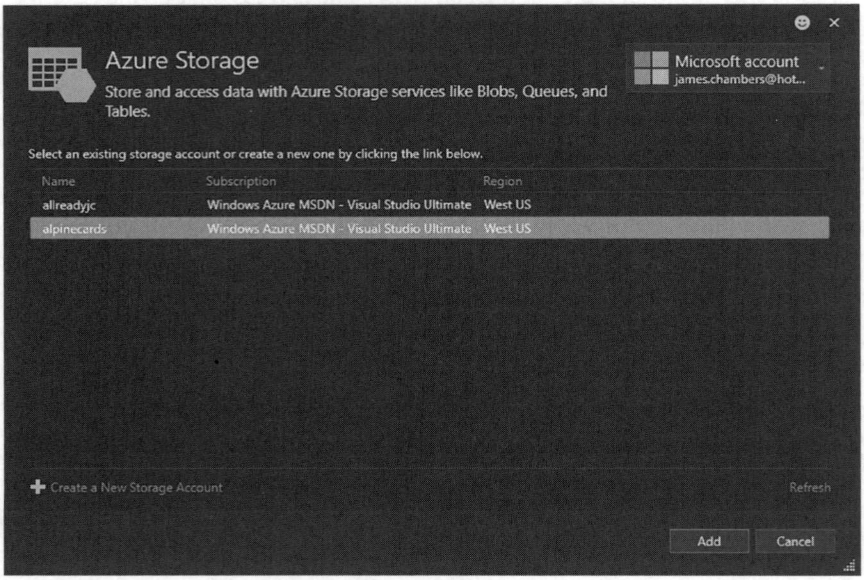

FIGURE 7-3 The Azure Storage Connected Service Wizard

Upon completing the wizard, your project is updated with the requisite packages and a configuration file called `config.json` that contains the connection string your application needs to connect to the storage account in your subscription.

> **Note** You should move the connection string information in your project out of the default location that the Connected Services dialog uses to store it. While it is convenient to have this information added for you automatically, it's not a best practice to leave restricted information in a file that is checked into source control. Learn more about protecting sensitive information in Chapter 12, "Configuration and Logging."

If you elect not to use the Connected Services Wizard, you need to grab the connection string for the storage account from the Azure portal. The connection strings are called key1 and key2, and are located in "Access keys" under the settings group of options as shown in Figure 7-4. The connection strings form part of your project configuration, which is covered in Chapter 12, and they are provided to your services through a pattern called Inversion of Control, which we cover in Chapter 14, "Dependency Injection." For an example of the configuration mechanics in action, you can refer to the AlpineConfigurationBuilder class where the settings are loaded into the configuration collection, as well as the BlobFileUploadService where the actual connection string is parsed and used by the application.

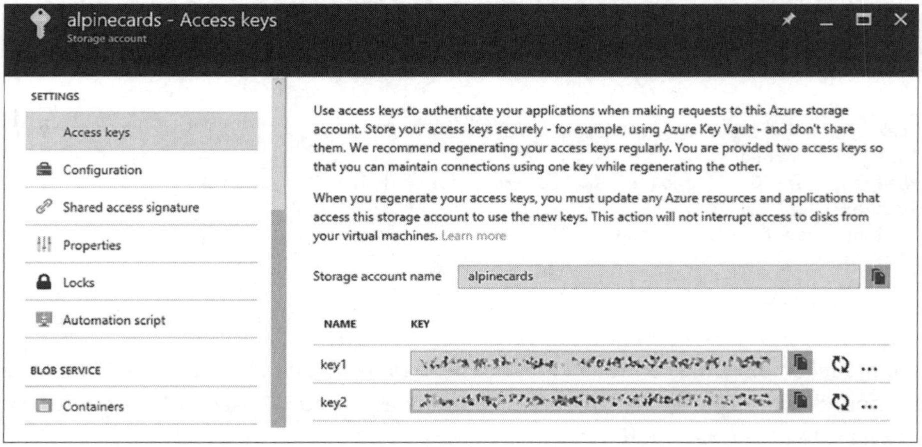

FIGURE 7-4: Accessing the access keys for your storage account

You also need to add a few packages to your project from project.json by selecting Manage NuGet Packages from the right-click context menu of your project in Solution Explorer or from the Package Manager Console in Visual Studio. If NuGet is new to you, you can fast forward to Chapter 14, "Dependency Injection," or come back to this chapter later on. For now, the packages you need include:

- WindowsAzure.Storage

- System.Spatial

- Microsoft.Data.Edm

- Microsoft.Data.OData

- Microsoft.Data.Services.Client

In the companion project to this book, you'll find that the team has also created a console application that is deployed as the web job for the application. That application has taken on the following package dependencies as well:

- Microsoft.Azure.WebJobs

- ImageProcessorCore

The WebJobs package adds helper classes and attributes that can be used to expedite the creation of automation jobs that are deployed to Azure. ImageProcessorCore is the ASP.NET Core-compatible imaging library that is currently in development in the open source community to serve as a replacement for System.Drawing. We look at both of those packages later in this chapter.

Storing Images in Blob Containers

Danielle finished the view for the ski card form and included the form element to allow a file upload as part of the ski card creation process, and the code is shown in Listing 7-1. In the view, we use a feature of Razor and MVC called tag helpers, which we touch on in Chapter 11, "Razor Views," and cover in more detail in Chapter 19, "Reusable Components."

LISTING 7-1 View updates to capture an uploaded image

```
// The new field in the view, Views/SkiCard/Create.cshtml
<div class="form-group">
    <label asp-for="CardImage" class="col-md-2 control-label"></label>
    <div class="col-md-10">
        <input asp-for="CardImage" />
    </div>
</div>
```

Thanks to model binding, the controller does not need to be updated because the HTML file element type is bound to the IFormFile property in our model. Listing 7-2 uses an IFormFile to show the property we extend our view model class.

LISTING 7-2 Updates to the View Model to support automatic model binding

```
// The new field as a property in the view model, CreateSkiCardViewModel.cs
[Display(Name = "Image to be Displayed on Card")]
public IFormFile CardImage { set; get; }
```

We're able to use the BlobFileUploadService in this controller to make a single call that takes care of the upload process for us, calling the UploadFileFromStream method. In the extract from the UploadFileFromStream method in Listing 7-3, we set up the connection to our container and asynchronously upload the file. We have what you could call a "sanity check" in place to ensure that the container exists by calling CreateIfNotExistsAsync, which is a lightweight call with limited overhead.

LISTING 7-3 Uploading an image to blob storage in Azure

```
// prepare the client
var storageAccount = CloudStorageAccount.Parse(_storageSettings.
AzureStorageConnectionString);
var blobClient = storageAccount.CreateCloudBlobClient();
var container = blobClient.GetContainerReference(containerName);
await container.CreateIfNotExistsAsync();

// push image to container
var blob = container.GetBlockBlobReference(targetFilename);
await blob.UploadFromStreamAsync(imageStream);
```

As a point of optimization, code that checks for the existence of cloud resources can be moved to an initialization routine that is executed at application startup. Although it's not terribly burdensome to make the call to CreateIfNotExistsAsync inline, it's also not needed for each time you connect to the service.

Incorporating Storage Queues

At the tail end of the BlobFileUploadService.UploadFileFromStream call, we raise an event that is handled by another block of code in the application. The messaging details here aren't too important, but the handler that responds to the event is worth taking a look at. What the application does at this point is transfer the responsibility of the image processing to something outside of the current request. We want the user's experience to be as quick and as smooth as possible, and to do that, we must defer all resource-bound operations to other processes.

Listing 7-4 contains part of the code from the QueueResizeOnSkiCardImageUploadedHandler class. Much like in the code that we used to connect to the blob services, we have to instantiate a client and ensure that the resource we are trying to access actually exists.

LISTING 7-4 Sending a message to an Azure storage queue

```
        // prepare the queue client
var storageAccount = CloudStorageAccount.Parse(_storageSettings.
AzureStorageConnectionString);
var queueClient = storageAccount.CreateCloudQueueClient();
var imageQueue = queueClient.GetQueueReference("skicard-imageprocessing");
await imageQueue.CreateIfNotExistsAsync();

// prepare and send the message to the queue
var message = new CloudQueueMessage(notification.FileName);
await imageQueue.AddMessageAsync(message);
```

When our connection is set, we create a message containing the name of the file we uploaded to a known location, and then we can return to the primary job of our website, which is to serve up pages. We also send a message off to signal that work needs to be done by some other service, and then we return to rendering views. To continue the chain of processing the image, we have to jump into the web job project the team created to help with processing images outside of the web server's workload.

Automating Processing with Azure WebJobs

Every now and then, a development comes along in your ecosystem that radically changes how you approach problems, and we believe the evolution of Azure WebJobs is one such instance.

> **Note** WebJobs continues to evolve and will be known as Azure Functions going forward. Azure Functions will provide new features, better isolation, and value outside of the boundaries of Web Apps, but they are currently in Preview status and not yet available in all Azure regions around the globe. To find out more about Azure Functions, please visit *https://azure.microsoft.com/en-us/services/functions/*.

WebJobs come from the need to run arbitrary, but often time-consuming code like processing uploaded files, parsing blog contents, or sending email messages on some kind of frequency, either on a set schedule, running continuously in the background, or as something that is triggered from an event in or outside of the application. Web jobs can be any executable or script file that you create. You put the code you need to run in a ZIP file and upload it to Azure.

For Danielle and Marc, this is where Platform-as-a-Service really started to shine. Without having to write the plumbing code for talking to queues or reading blobs from a container, they were able to process their image queue with just three lines of code, as shown in Listing 7-5. After pulling in the WebJobs SDK from the NuGet package they added earlier, they were able to compress what would normally be over 40 lines of configuration, connection and processing code down to this brief snippet.

LISTING 7-5 A queue-triggered Azure web job that processes an image

```
public class ImageAdjustments
{
    public static void ResizeAndGrayscaleImage(
        [QueueTrigger("skicard-imageprocessing")] string message,
        [Blob("cardimages/{queueTrigger}", FileAccess.Read)] Stream imageStream,
        [Blob("processed/{queueTrigger}", FileAccess.Write)] Stream resizedImageStream)
    {
        var image = new Image(imageStream);

        var resizedImage = image
            .Resize(300, 0)
            .Grayscale(GrayscaleMode.Bt709);

        resizedImage.SaveAsJpeg(resizedImageStream);
    }
}
```

Sure, it certainly reads longer than three lines on paper, but to the compiler we only have two variable instantiations and a call to SaveAsJpeg in this block of code. The parameters in the signature of the method are decorated with attributes from the WebJobs SDK as follows:

- **QueueTriggerAttribute:** Indicates what type of storage-based event trips the event alarm and executes this code. The attribute is given the name of the queue to listen to.

- **BlobAttribute:** Used to populate a parameter from the location specified in the template, in this case with read/write permissions on the streams. The SDK takes care of creating and hydrating the streams as well as garbage collection.

It is also worth pointing out that the three lines of code here are made possible by the increasingly popular ImageProcessing library developed by James Jackson-South and a healthy and growing list of open source contributors at *https://github.com/JimBobSquarePants/ImageProcessor*. We initialize an image from the input stream and store it in the image variable. Next, we use the fluent syntax of the library to first resize the image to a width of 300px while maintaining the aspect ratio, thus the 0 as the height parameter, and then convert it to the desired grayscale color space. Finally, we save the image to the output stream.

It takes many more words than lines of code to explain everything that is going on here, but with a little lifting and the use of just a few platform services, we are able to create a speedy web application that is capable of handing the bulk of processing off to external services.

Scaling Out Your Applications

As was discussed in the last chapter, the elastic cloud is what makes it possible for small organizations with periods of bursting traffic to accommodate traffic surges and transient processing demands. For medium-sized organizations like Alpine Ski House, elasticity in the platform allows for growth and enhanced services without having to pay for the infrastructure to support it up front. By easily expanding and contracting to meet the size of the load, it can also save large organizations incredible sums of money by only having to pay for the cycles that are needed, and not having to pay for slow time or outright downtime when business processes are offline and not in use.

Scaling in Multiple Directions

One of the most beneficial aspects of using a PaaS approach to development is the ease with which you can scale your resources. While it is getting easier to maintain virtual machines and change the size of them through Azure Resource Manager, in many cases there are still limitations around deployment clusters and sizing, and even more so if you're on classic virtual machine images. Virtual machine scale sets have given organizations the opportunity to spin up VMs on the fly to help meet demand, but you're still largely responsible for the operating system maintenance and the other aspects of your virtual server inventory. PaaS lets you craft your solution from a different vantage point, giving you a set of turn-key services that can scale vertically or horizontally without worrying about the hardware or operating system underneath.

Scaling vertically, or "scaling up," is akin to buying more powerful hardware in your server farm. From an infrastructure point of view, there are different pricing tiers in the virtual machine sp̄ range from a few dozen dollars per month, up to several thousand dollars per month for ea

Pricing and tier selection also applies in the PaaS space, where you can select from a range of free services through an entry level service called "shared" and then onto the paid tiers with basic, standard, and premium hardware capabilities. In both scenarios, the more money you spend equates to more cores, higher processing speeds, and larger memory sizes. The different tiers also allow access to more ingress and egress, disk space, and additional features such as security, integration services, or custom domains.

Scaling horizontally, or "scaling out," on the other hand is a lot like buying more servers for your farm. Rather than spending the cash on larger capacities in the machine for one large worker, you spend the money on purchasing additional workers to help you divide the work load in hopes that the work can be evenly distributed and processed in parallel. In Azure, the machines and services you scale out with are the same size as the first one you provision, so you can think of horizontal scale as a factor along with the machine size when estimating your total costs.

If you would like to experiment with the different options for pricing tiers and families, you can visit Microsoft's Azure Pricing Calculator located at https://azure.microsoft.com/en-us/pricing/calculator/.

Scaling with Elasticity

After picking your vertical level of scale, or the processing power, you can then combine your selection with your horizontal scale, or the number of workers, to achieve elastic scale. As you would imagine, paying more gets you more features, as shown in Figure 7-5 which provides examples of tier capabilities from the Premium, Standard, and Basic tiers. A paid tier is required for scaling capabilities, and a minimum of the Standard tier is required for auto-scaling capabilities.

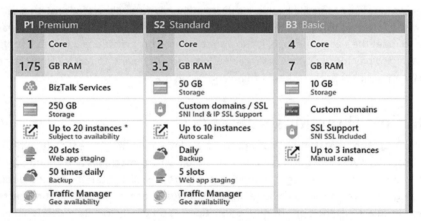

P1 Premium		S2 Standard		B3 Basic	
1	Core	2	Core	4	Core
1.75	GB RAM	3.5	GB RAM	7	GB RAM
	BizTalk Services		50 GB Storage		10 GB Storage
	250 GB Storage		Custom domains / SSL SNI Incl & IP SSL Support		Custom domains
	Up to 20 instances * Subject to availability		Up to 10 instances Auto scale		SSL Support SNI SSL Included
	20 slots Web app staging		Daily Backup		Up to 3 instances Manual scale
	50 times daily Backup		5 slots Web app staging		
	Traffic Manager Geo availability		Traffic Manager Geo availability		

FIGURE 7-5 Samples of feature sets attributed to various levels of service

In the Basic tier the only way to scale your application is to manually slide the instance count control, as illustrated in Figure 7-6. This means that if your application requires more processing power you'll need to log into the portal to make the appropriate change.

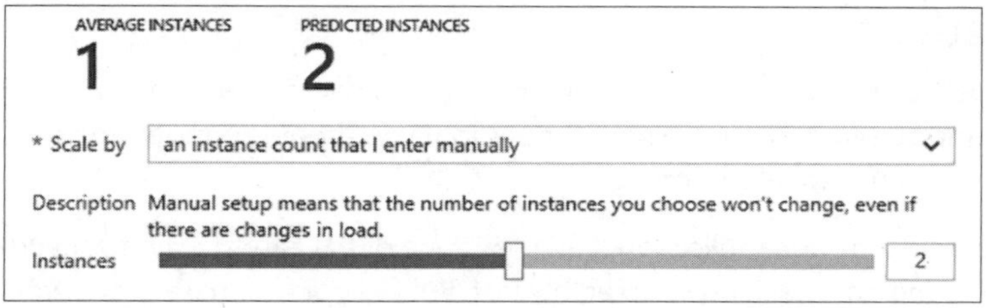

FIGURE 7-6 Manually scaling the instance count of your application

In the Standard and Premium tiers, you have the added option of being able to scale out as required, using cues from your application performance and resource utilization, or in time with events that you know might be around the corner. For instance, you might want to automatically scale up prior to an expected load from a web campaign, just before the start of your work day, or before peak hours on your site. As you can see in Figure 7-7, you have the ability to send out emails based on performance or schedule constraints. You can email out notifications, or you can send data to a webhook end point that you can further use in custom monitoring applications.

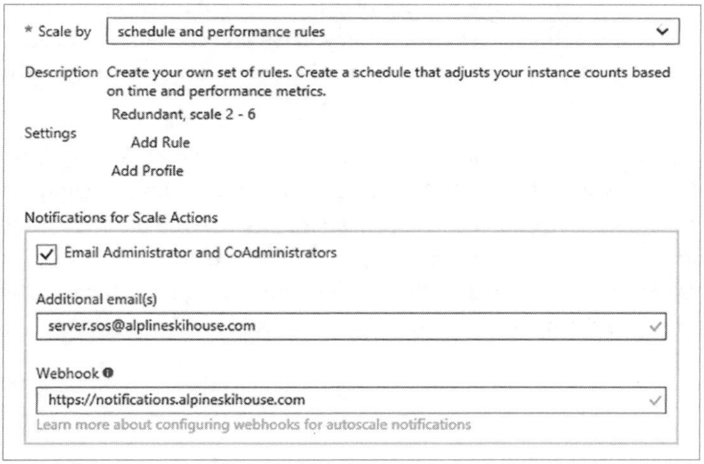

FIGURE 7-7 App service tiers

Obviously, the Standard tier is more expensive than the Basic tier, but it is not nearly as much as what it would cost to purchase a server and maintain it. Taking the smallest Standard tier that is suitable for your business model allows you to keep costs down for your production environment while maintaining your ability to scale up automatically under load and only pay for the processing time you use.

If you're just starting out, you might allow your site to scale between one to two servers at first, which allows you to gauge when load increases. You might be able to find cost savings in higher tiers if you can run fewer instances, or in lower tiers if you don't need all the features at higher price points. Also, don't forget that there are other options to just scaling up and out when you treat your platform as a service, as we're about to discuss.

Scaling Considerations

These scaling benefits are part of a larger picture that can simplify your overall development requirements, but they can also come at a cost. There are implications that you should consider, and possibly rethink your approach on, that can help reduce costs.

Consider, for example, caching in your application. Caching is one of the easiest ways to speed up your application and using in-memory caching is incredibly fast. But as your user base grows, you might find that your cache is eating up your App Service resources, thus requiring scaling and additional instances in order for your website to remain functional. Furthermore, if you have multiple instances configured in your App Service, each one needs to maintain their own in-memory cache. There is an easy alternative though. You could instead move to a distributed cache, which both reduces the memory footprint of your application and allows you to share the cached resources in a centralized location.

Another example of resource utilization is logging. Each tier has an increasing amount of space available to your application that is proportional to the price you pay, but you have to remember that the disk space should be considered volatile and transient. Writing to a local log file on disk has several consequences. First, if you are chasing an error, you are required to hunt down all relevant log files from all then-running servers. Second, and more importantly, the way that scaling and operating system patches occur means that you actually lose data when your site is recycled or moved to an updated instance. For these reasons you should really consider an alternate mechanism for capturing logs, which we look at in greater detail in Chapter 12.

One last example that might trip up your site is the egress, or outbound traffic, of your application. While this limit is relatively high, there is still a threshold that, when crossed, disables your App Service for a period of time. This tends to happen in resource-rich applications where large file sizes are the norm and users consume vast amounts of bandwidth. Again, approaching the problem from a PaaS perspective, you can move those resources to more suitable storage options in Azure, such as using Media Services to stream video and leveraging Azure CDN for static assets.

Summary

Microsoft Azure has evolved into a powerful toolset of services that runs on an infrastructure that we don't have to maintain. This enables developers and folks in operations to focus more on the deliverables and less on how they're going to do it. We can easily duplicate the resources we need into multiple environments and use an elastic scale strategy as we need to or as we can afford. With ready-built options for creating resource templates and a building-block approach to composing our application, we can move past many of the friction points we commonly see in software development while benefitting from the reliable, well-tested services of the cloud.

Even though Azure is a cloud offering from Microsoft it makes no assumptions about what development environment you will use or even the tech stack you work on. In the next chapter, we'll look at a few of the options you have in developing, building and deploying applications with ASP.NET Core MVC.

## CHAPTER 8

Cross-Platform

Just like a snowflake, every developer is a special, unique creature. Danielle didn't have six sides, but she did have a frosty disposition when it came to macOS. She found the whole operating system to be a mess. It was difficult to rename files and there was always this beach ball bouncing around on her screen. No, she liked her Windows development environment. Adrian on the other hand was a proponent of macOS, while the Marks spent at least half an hour a day deep in conversation about their favorite Linux distributions. Mark likes Ubuntu, while Marc was all about Manjaro Linux. Danielle usually went for a walk when that discussion started up because she didn't want to hear another thing about Btrfs vs. Ext4.

It was amazing though. Even with everybody using a different operating system and a different text editor, everybody was working on the same code base without any real issues. Once in a while somebody with a case insensitive file system uses the wrong capitalization or the wrong path separator, but running their builds on both Windows and Linux soon shook those sorts of problems out. Tim was really interested in being able to run their new site on any platform.

Tim had been pricing out Windows and Linux machines as well as various developer workstations, so the idea that everybody can use whatever they want is pretty compelling. There are also some projects coming down the line after Project Parsley is done that have to interact with services running on Linux. It would be helpful if they can standardize on one language or at least one technology. Maybe this .NET Core thing would be exactly what is needed.

Perhaps one of the most surprising aspects of .NET Core and ASP.NET Core is the first class support available for a number of Linux distributions and macOS. This opens .NET up to a much larger audience of developers, including students who are interested in learning programming and who happen to carry MacBooks. We now live in a world where your operating system of choice is no longer a limiting factor when it comes to .NET. This is great from the perspective of new people learning programming and it's also great for development teams because this now eliminates a reason why some teams would not even consider .NET in the past. For Linux and macOS based development teams, .NET is now a very real option.

Many companies use Linux production environments for a variety of reasons. Tooling can still be easier on Linux than on Windows. For instance, Docker support on Windows lags behind Linux, and configuration management tools, such as Chef and Puppet, are still better on Linux than on Windows. When Node.js was first released it only ran on Linux, so there was no choice but to run on something other than Windows. Other tools such as Nginx also run better on Linux than Windows. There are plenty of examples where Linux is a better technical choice, but being able to run .NET tools on the same platform as the rest of your architecture is compelling.

Up and Running on Ubuntu

The AlpineSkiHouse project was initially created on Windows using Visual Studio, but this doesn't mean we are limited to using Windows and Visual Studio forever. Some of the Alpine team members are more comfortable using Linux as their primary operating system. Rather than having a Windows Virtual Machine specifically for working on the AlpineSkiHouse project, let's look at what it takes to setup the .NET Core SDK on the AplineSkiHouse team's favorite Linux desktop, Ubuntu.

Installing .NET Core

The methods of acquiring the .NET Core SDK vary based on your operating system and are well documented at http://dot.net. In Ubuntu's case, .NET Core is installed via the apt-get package manager.

First, we need to add the apt-get feed containing the dotnet package:

```
sudo sh -c 'echo "deb [arch=amd64] https://apt-mo.trafficmanager.net/repos/dotnet/ trusty main"
> /etc/apt/sources.list.d/dotnetdev.list'
sudo apt-key adv --keyserver apt-mo.trafficmanager.net --recv-keys 417A0893
sudo apt-get update
```

Next, install dotnet:

```
sudo apt-get install dotnet
```

The .NET Core SDK is now installed and you can get started building .NET applications on a Linux desktop.

The dotnet CLI

The dotnet command line interface (CLI) is an important part of the .NET Core SDK. It is used to compile and run .NET Core applications. While many developers using Visual Studio with .NET Core projects might not be familiar with the dotnet CLI and its commands, there is a good chance they are using it every day. Visual Studio is actually using the dotnet CLI to perform operations like restoring NuGet packages, compiling your application, and even running unit tests. Even if you plan to use Visual Studio as your IDE, it is helpful to understand the dotnet CLI because it can be useful when setting up automated build scripts. Developers using other operating systems and lightweight code editors need to be more familiar with the dotnet CLI.

The dotnet CLI contains everything necessary to create, compile, and run .NET Core applications. Table 8-1 shows some commonly used dotnet commands.

TABLE 8-1 Common dotnet commands

Command	Description
dotnet new	Creates a basic .NET project
dotnet restore	Restores dependencies specified in the .NET project
dotnet build	Compiles a .NET project
dotnet publish	Prepares a .NET project for deployment
dotnet run	Compiles and immediately executes a .NET project
dotnet test	Runs unit tests
dotnet pack	Creates a NuGet package

Let's take a look at the steps for creating and running a simple Hello World application using the dotnet CLI. First, we execute the `dotnet new` command. This command adds two new files to the current directory, including a project file containing information about the project and a `Program.cs` file containing the code for a simple Hello World application. Figure 8-1 shows the generated `Program.cs` file.

FIGURE 8-1 A very basic .NET Core application on Ubuntu

Note The dotnet command line can create a number of different types of projects. You can choose the project's language by using the -1 flag and either csharp or fsharp. The -t flag defines what type of project to create and can be either console, web, lib, or xunit-test. The project types are far more limited than you might be used to in Visual Studio. If you're creating a new web project on Linux, you might want to investigate yeoman which is a well-known scaffolding tool that can be found at *http://yeoman.io/* or installed via npm using npm install -g yeoman.

The next step is to run the dotnet restore command, as shown in Figure 8-2. This restores any NuGet packages that the application needs.

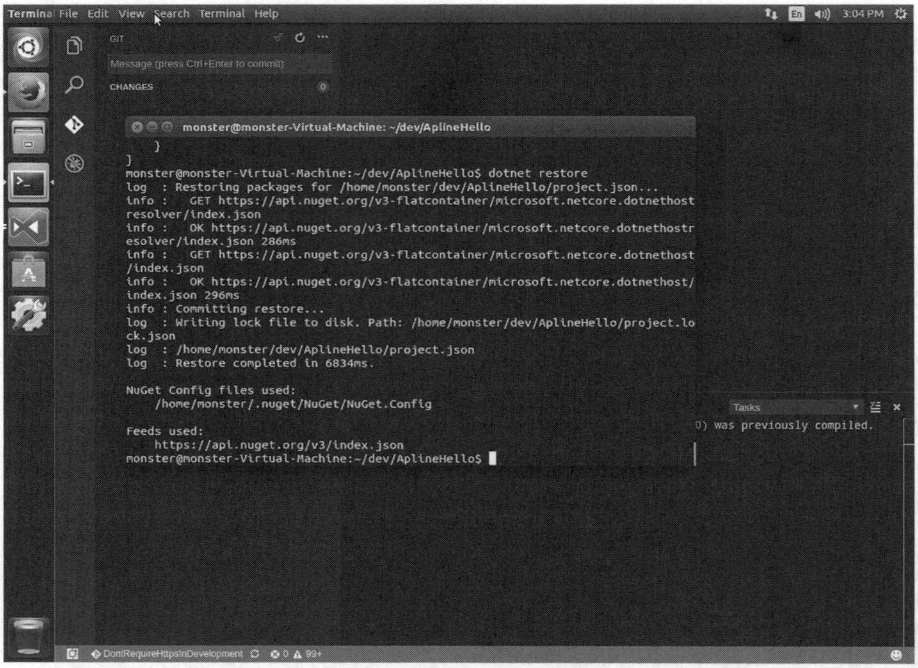

FIGURE 8-2 Restoring the nuget packages in a new project

Now we can compile the application using the dotnet build command, as shown in Figure 8-3.

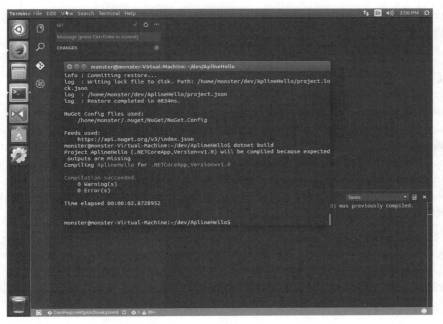

FIGURE 8-3 Running .net build

Finally, we can run the application using the dotnet run command, as shown in Figure 8-4.

FIGURE 8-4 Running our new dotnet on Linux

Restore, build, run, and test are the primary commands that most developers use on a daily basis. We cover the `dotnet test` in more detail in Chapter 20, "Testing."

Choosing a Code Editor

Most developers on Linux and macOS have a favorite code editor. If that's the case, you can certainly use that editor for .NET applications. Many developers who have used Visual Studio feel like they are missing out when using a lightweight code editor because of the lack of IntelliSense. Fortunately, this problem has now been solved by the smart folks at OmniSharp (*http://www.omnisharp.net/*). OmniSharp builds plugins for many popular cross-platform code editors, enabling IntelliSense-style auto-completion for .NET projects. If you have a code editor that you know and love, stick with that but be sure to check if there is an OmniSharp plugin available to enhance your experience.

If you're looking for an editor, Visual Studio Code is worth taking a closer look at. Visual Studio Code is a light-weight, cross platform code editor built by the Visual Studio team at Microsoft. It provides the same excellent syntax highlighting and IntelliSense as Visual Studio without all the bloat of a full IDE. It includes an excellent debugger and also sports a rich plugin ecosystem. We use Visual Studio Code in our examples for the remainder of this chapter.

Alpine Ski House on Linux

With .NET Core installed and our favorite code editor set up for .NET development, let's look at what it takes to run the AlpineSkiHouse.Web project on an Ubuntu developer machine.

```
$ dotnet build
$ dotnet run
```

In Figure 8-5, some errors state that we are missing the user secrets required at startup. So first off, we need to add these user secrets by using the `dotnet user-secrets` command.

```
Terminal File  Edit  View  Search  Terminal  Help

  monster@monster-Virtual-Machine: ~/dev/monster/AlpineSkiHouse/src/AlpineSkiHouse.W
Web$ dotnet run
Project AlpineSkiHouse.Web (.NETCoreApp,Version=v1.0) will be compiled because i
nputs were modified
Compiling AlpineSkiHouse.Web for .NETCoreApp,Version=v1.0

Compilation succeeded.
    0 Warning(s)
    0 Error(s)

Time elapsed 00:00:02.5957823


Unhandled Exception: System.Reflection.TargetInvocationException: Exception has
been thrown by the target of an invocation. ---> System.Collections.Generic.KeyN
otFoundException: A configuration value is missing for authentication against Fa
cebook and Twitter. While you don't need to get tokens for these you do need to
set up your user secrets as described in the readme.
    at AlpineSkiHouse.Startup.Configure(IApplicationBuilder app, IHostingEnvironm
ent env, ILoggerFactory loggerFactory)
    --- End of inner exception stack trace ---
    at System.RuntimeMethodHandle.InvokeMethod(Object target, Object[] arguments,
 Signature sig, Boolean constructor)
    at System.Reflection.RuntimeMethodInfo.UnsafeInvokeInternal(Object obj, Objec
t[] parameters, Object[] arguments)
    at System.Reflection.RuntimeMethodInfo.Invoke(Object obj, BindingFlags invoke
Attr, Binder binder, Object[] parameters, CultureInfo culture)
    at Microsoft.AspNetCore.Hosting.Internal.ConfigureBuilder.Invoke(Object insta
nce, IApplicationBuilder builder)
    at Microsoft.AspNetCore.Hosting.Internal.WebHost.BuildApplication()
    at Microsoft.AspNetCore.Hosting.WebHostBuilder.Build()
    at AlpineSkiHouse.Program.Main(String[] args)
monster@monster-Virtual-Machine:~/dev/monster/AlpineSkiHouse/src/AlpineSkiHouse.
Web$
```

FIGURE 8-5 Running Alpine Ski House on Linux

```
$ dotnet user-secrets set Authentication:Twitter:ConsumerKey "some consumer key"
$ dotnet user-secrets set Authentication:Twitter:ConsumerSecret "some consumer Secret"
$ dotnet user-secrets set Authentication:Facebook:AppId "some app id"
$ dotnet user-secrets set Authentication:Facebook:AppSecret "some app secret"
```

Next, we also need to set the ASPNETCORE_ENVIRONMENT variable to Development because the application is set up to only load user secrets when in Development.

```
$ ASPNETCORE_ENVIRONMENT=Development
$ export ASPNETCORE_ENVIRONMENT
```

Now we can run the application, right?

```
$ dotnet run
```

Okay, so now kestrel fires up as expected, listening on localhost:5000 and the main page loads as expected when we browse to that URL in Firefox. Unfortunately, everything falls apart as soon as we do anything that tries to interact with the SQL Server database, as shown in Figure 8-6.

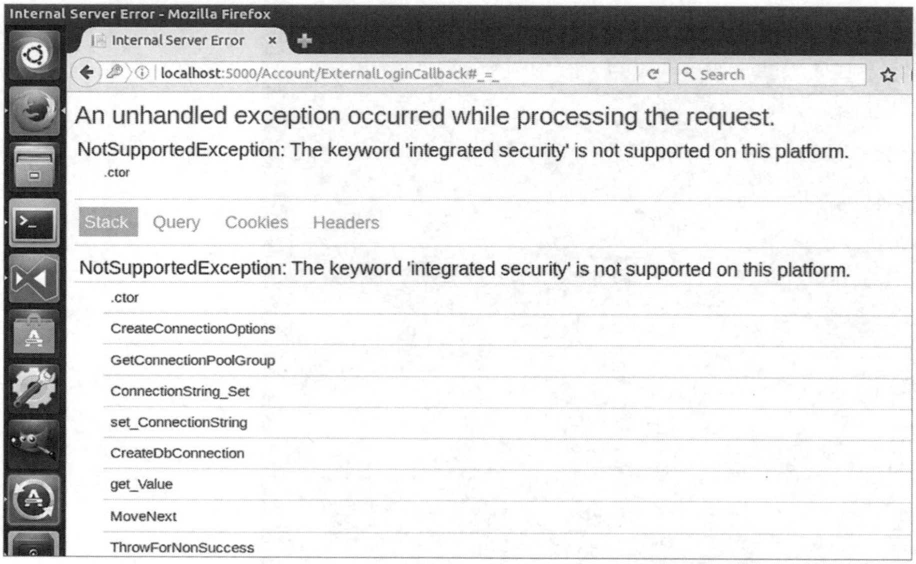

FIGURE 8-6 An error message showing unable to connect to the SQL database

As discussed in Chapter 10, "Entity Framework Core," the application is configured to use SQL Server LocalDB. This works great on Windows, but at the time of writing, SQL Server is not available on Linux. Although the folks at Microsoft are hard at work porting SQL Server to Linux, we need another option to keep our Linux and/or macOS based developers productive.

The best solution currently is to have an instance of SQL Server available on the local office network or in the cloud. On that SQL Server instance, each developer would have rights to create and drop their own databases for development purposes. Don't try to share databases between developers, because you definitely run into versioning issues if you do. Each developer needs to connect to their own unique database for development purposes. Also, make sure this isn't the same SQL Server instance that hosts the production databases.

Now Linux and macOS based developers only need to provide configuration to override the default LocalDB connection string. The configuration can be overwritten by using user-secrets or by adding a new configuration file named *appSettings.Development.json*.

```
$dotnet user-secrets set ConnectionStrings:DefaultConnection "Data Source=tcp:192.168.0.30,3071;
Database=AlpineSkiHouse_Dave;User ID=Dave;Password=Password"
```

appSettings.Development.json

```
{
  "ConnectionStrings": {
    "DefaultConnection": " Data Source=tcp:192.168.0.30,3071;Database=AlpineSkiHouse_Dave;User
ID=Dave;Password=Password"
  }
```

And with that, Alpine Ski House is up and running on Ubuntu! Of course, we should also make sure the unit tests run properly, as shown in Figure 8-7.

```
$ dotnet build
$ dotnet test
```

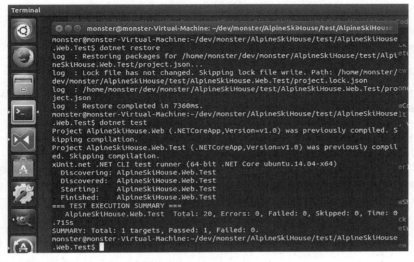

FIGURE 8-7 Running Alpine Ski House tests on Linux

Getting Alpine Ski House up and running on Linux is actually quite simple. This is not an accident, however, and many projects are not simply able to run on Linux or macOS. Alpine Ski House targets .NET Core rather than the full .NET framework. .NET Core deserves its own heading.

.NET Core

There is a tendency to say that an application runs on .NET and then to leave it at that, but there are actually many different versions of .NET and even different flavors of .NET. It is helpful to start by thinking about what makes up the thing we commonly call .NET. First are the languages like C#, F#, and VB.NET. Each language has its own standard, but they are all compiled to a common intermediate language, known as IL by the compiler. The compiler was recently rewritten in C# so it is completely managed and the new compiler is called Roslyn. This language looks like the following:

```
IL_0000: ldarg.0        // this
IL_0001: ldfld          int32 class System.Linq.Enumerable/'<CastIterator>d__94'1'<!0/*TResu
lt*/>::'<>1__state'
IL_0006: ldc.i4.s       -2 // 0xfe
IL_0008: bne.un.s       IL_0022
IL_000a: ldarg.0        // this
IL_000b: ldfld          int32 class System.Linq.Enumerable/'<CastIterator>d__94'1'<!0/*TResult*/>:
```

```
:'<>l__initialThreadId'
IL_0010: call          int32 [mscorlib]System.Environment::get_CurrentManagedThreadId()
IL_0015: bne.un.s      IL_0022
IL_0017: ldarg.0       // this
IL_0018: ldc.i4.0
IL_0019: stfld         int32 class System.Linq.Enumerable/'<CastIterator>d__94'1'<!0/*TResu
lt*/>::'<>l__state'
IL_001e: ldarg.0       // this
IL_001f: stloc.0       // V_0
IL_0020: br.s          IL_0029
IL_0022: ldc.i4.0
```

This code is assembly language that is taken by the Just-In-Time compiler or JITer. Keeping with the trend of rewriting things going the 64-bit, JITer was also rewritten as the RyuJIT project. RyuJIT's goal was to increase the efficiency of compilation and produce more efficient 64-bit code.

All the .NET languages can make use of the base class library or BCL. This library is made up of thousands of classes that can perform tasks as varied as talking to an SMTP server or zipping a file. The breadth of functionality in the base class library is, perhaps, the best part of programming in .NET. There is no need for thousands of small libraries, such as what you might find in a Node.js project, and instead developers can rely on a well-tested and optimized set of functions in the BCL.

The BCL's contents has grown across the versions of .NET. Silverlight, for instance, was a restrictive version of the framework. Many classes in the full framework were missing or had a different surface area in Silverlight. .NET Core is in a similar position where a number of classes were removed or replaced, giving the API a different surface area. Unfortunately, all of the efforts around creating new frameworks were piecemeal and disjointed. It was nearly impossible to tell what classes would be available on any platform and to write code that could run on any of them.

Portable class libraries were used in an attempt to allow developers to write portable code, but they rapidly became overly complex. Microsoft has started on an effort to normalize the interfaces available over a number of platforms, including their recently acquired Xamarin properties.

This standardization effort is known as .NET Standard. .NET Standard defines a number of compatibility levels supported on different platforms. The initial version defines levels 1.0 through to 1.6 and describes the platforms that support each level. Level 1.0, for instance exposes the smallest API surface area and is supported by every platform, including Silverlight. As we move up to 1.1, it is supported on every platform but Silverlight. Below is a chart provided by Microsoft describing the availably of the APIs on their various different platforms.

.NET Platform	.NET Standard							
	1	1.1	1.2	1.3	1.4	1.5	1.6	2
.NET Core	→	→	→	→	→	→	1	vNext
.NET Framework	→	4.5	4.5.1	4.6	4.6.1	4.6.2	vNext	4.6.1
Xamarin.iOS	→	→	→	→	→	→	→	vNext
Xamarin.Android	→	→	→	→	→	→	→	vNext
Universal Windows Platform	→	→	→	→	10	→	→	vNext
Windows	→	8	8.1					
Windows Phone	→	→	8.1					
Windows Phone Silverlight	8							

An arrow indicates that the platform supports the standard features and the additional features found to the right. You might also note that the next version of each platform is listed in the matrix as well. If we look at something like .NET Framework 4.6.1 that supports .NET Standard 1.4, we need to realize that .NET Framework 4.6.1 actually supports far more API surface area than what is described in .NET Standard 1.4, but it supports all of 1.4 as shown in Figure 8-8.

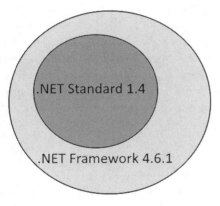

FIGURE 8-8 .NET Standard is a subset of the APIs provided by .NET Framework 4.61

Each higher version of the standard supports more surface area than the previous version, with the exception of 2.0. As you might expect with a large standardization effort like this, there are going to be odd gaps and .NET Standard 2.0 is one of those gaps because it actually supports a smaller surface area than .NET Standard 1.4 or 1.5, as shown in Figure 8-9.

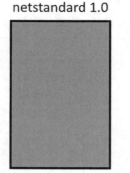
netstandard 1.0

netstandard 1.0 +
System.Collections.Concurrent

FIGURE 8-9 .NET STandard 1.0 and 1.0 with additional packages

Let's assume that your application runs on .NET Standard 1.0, but also needs some functionality from *System.Collections.Concurrent*. There are two possible solutions. First, the application could be moved to support .NET Standard 1.1, which adds support for the concurrent collections namespace. This is a rather awkward approach because it bumps up the version of .NET Standard needed and reduces the number of devices your application can target. Instead, option two is to base the application on .NET Standard 1.0 and simply include the NuGet package for *System.Collections.Concurrent*. As part of the .NET Standardization process, the monolithic framework was broken into a large number of packages. In fact, if you look at the dependencies of a basic application in Visual Studio, you can see in the dependency tree that it takes a whole list of very granular packages, such as *System.Threading. Thread*, to make up the .NET Standard runtime. As long as the package being added is constructed from managed code, there is no need to bump up the version of the supported framework.

Summary

The efforts to bring some level of standardization to .NET APIs have been a long time coming and are certainly welcome. Having cross platform support available for .NET is likely to drive adoption in markets that are not traditionally welcoming to .NET technologies. Even the detractors who object to the closed source nature of Microsoft have to re-examine their objections because so much of the stack, including the BCL and compiler, are open source. The ease of getting up and running on Linux however, might actually drive more traditionally Windows based developers to OSX and Linux. In either case, the operating system that your application runs on is no longer a huge consideration when selecting .NET. In the next chapter we will cover containers, focusing on Docker.

## CHAPTER 9

Containers

"The build is working and all the tests are passing, but I just can't get this thing working right on my machine, Danielle." Adrian was getting frustrated and Danielle could see it. There were a lot of moving parts to the application. Although Danielle hadn't worked with a sizable team like this for years, she remembered how difficult it could be to get an environment set up the same way across different machines. As applications get more complicated, so do their deployments.

"It took me ages too, Adrian. Did you look at the environment set up document?"

"Ugh, that thing? It is 15 pages long and is never up to date. It still references setting up that database thingy we haven't used in a couple of weeks. Nobody has time to update that document."

"You're right!" exclaimed Danielle. "We should go see Balázs about this and get him to put higher priority on keeping our documentation up to date."

Daniel and Adrian steamed over to Balázs' desk like a train pulled by dual ALCO Century 855s. "Balázs, we can't get the environment set up properly on local dev boxes because the documentation hasn't been kept up to date. We need more resources assigned to work on the documentation."

"We don't have time to document everything and keep it up to date. We just need one person who is responsible for setting up environments," suggested Balázs.

"That job would be the worst, and I don't like how you're looking at me."

"You're right, Adrian. We need to find some way to make environments more reproducible and portable." Balázs massaged his temples.

Something about the idea of reproducible environments triggered a memory in Danielle. "I've been hearing about this Docker thing that is supposed to make creating environments and deployments easier."

"That sounds like a really good idea! I'd much rather we have some code or something that creates our environment than have a long and difficult to understand document. Let's do it!"

Repeatable Environments

Deploying applications and setting up build environments have long been thought of as completely different things. You set up a production environment once, perhaps mirror it to a test environment for pre-deployment testing, and then you leave it alone. Development environments are far more fluid because developers come and go, and in order to stay on the cutting edge, it is required that developer's hardware be replaced frequently. As it turns out, however, deploying applications and setting up build environments are actually two sides of the same coin. Ideally, development environments should mirror production environments as closely as possible and production and testing environments should be created easily and quickly, but that hasn't been possible. Fortunately, the realization that creating environments should be easy has driven the development of tooling to make everything easier.

There are many options for building environments in a repeatable fashion. The earliest efforts involved simply mirroring hard drives using Symantec Ghost or PowerQuest Drive Image, and by passing around the image. Reimaging an entire machine is a serious task, but it also makes sure developers use the same tools as other developers because they are encouraged to use whatever tools come preinstalled on the image. In the past, if an older software version needed to be supported, an image needed to be retained to handle that software. Often it was easier to just keep older computers around to do patch releases. Ancient computers would be hidden away around the office with notes attached to them, such as "PSM 1.7 build machine – DO NOT FORMAT." Of course, such notes were lost and machines were formatted anyway, which led to panicked attempts to recreate environments needed to build decade old software.

Virtual machines helped address some of the limitations of using physical machines for isolation. Images are much easier to create and version and also make it possible for developers to run their own tools and simply share files between their local machine and the virtual machine. Multiple virtual machines can be run on one physical machine, which reduces the chance that a critical machine is repurposed. The level of isolation offered is still good compared with simply running multiple versions on the same operating system install because there is very little chance that installing an update on one virtual machine would break a different virtual machine.

Isolating applications and data from interfering with one another has been the goal of operating systems since operating systems were first created. Even without a virtual machine, one application should not be able to interfere with other processes on the machine. Isolation is also frequently desirable within a single process. Threads, lightweight in process isolation, provide a form of isolation, as does variable scoping.

While isolation is a desirable property, it does not come without a cost. There is always some overhead to be paid and, predictably, the more that is isolated the higher the overhead. Virtual machines provide a high degree of isolation, but the cost is that a whole physical machine must be virtualized to provide it. Display drivers, disk drivers, and CPUs must all be virtualized. Threads, which lie at the other end of the spectrum, require very little overhead but also provide little in the way of isolation. This is demonstrated in Figure 9-1.

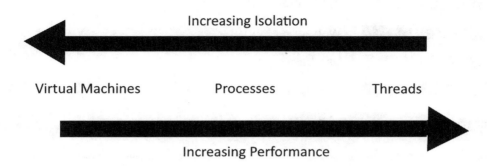

FIGURE 9-1 There is an inverse relationship between isolation and performance

To this mixture we can now add containers. Although containerization is not a new concept, it has really come into its own over the past couple of years. Containers sit in a sweet spot for performance and isolation between virtual machines and processes. Containers do not virtualize the entire machine, but rather provide abstractions over the operating system that make it seem like each container is totally isolated. For instance, if you are working inside of a single container, getting a list of processes only shows the limited set of processes running inside that container and not processes that are running in user-land on the host operating system or in another container on the same host. Equally, a file written to disk inside the container is only visible to that container and is not visible to anything outside the container. The kernel is shared between containers however, so each container must have the same architecture and even the same kernel as the underlying host. Therefore, it is not possible to run a Linux container on Windows or a Windows container on Linux without putting a virtual machine in-between.

While this level of isolation would be compelling on its own, the more interesting characteristics of containers center around packaging and composability. File systems on containers are implemented as a series of layers or slices, each one stacked on top of the previous layer. This is similar to a delectable slice of baklava where phyllo pastry layers stack together to create a sort of tower.

Containers start with a base image that is typically a minimalist image containing only the bare essentials to get the operating system running. The CoreOS Linux distribution is an example for Linux based environments and Windows Nano is an example for Windows based environments. Various additions are stacked on top of this base image. Imagine you're building a container that runs a web server and database. Typically, containers only run a single process, but let's put that aside for now. The base layer would be the operating system and on top of that, install the database server, the web server, and finally the data for your application (see Figure 9-2).

Application files

Web server

Database server

Operating system

FIGURE 9-2 The layers of a system

The layers can easily be composed to build complete images. If there is a need to update the web server, the bottom two layers can be taken and a new web server layered on top of that and then the application files put in place on top of that. These minimalist images can be quickly spun up because they don't require any of the boot time associated with full virtual machines. What's more, these images are small enough that they can be distributed and shared easily. If you're a software vendor whose software is commonly installed on client servers, can you imagine how much work would be saved by knowing that all your clients would have a reproducible, isolated environment for your software? Instead of shipping difficult to maintain installers, you can distribute complete images that your clients can spin up.

We mentioned previously that a container should run only one process. While it might seem like this would serve simply to add unnecessary overhead, as each process would have the overhead of isolation, it actually creates a more stable, scalable environment. The lightweight nature of containers means that far more of them can be spun up on the same hardware were it to be used to run virtual machines. Keeping applications isolated inside a container provides guarantees about shared library and tooling compatibility. Historically, Windows has suffered from DLL Hell, where multiple applications install different global versions of libraries that conflict. Installing the software inside of a container eliminates this problem.

Containers do not need to be limited to a single machine. A large application deployment might require dozens of different services, all deployed at a different scale. For instance, a dozen web servers, half a dozen search servers, and two database servers might be required. Creating environments like this on physical hardware has always been difficult while containers allow the resourcing of servers to become more of a software problem than a hardware one. Rather than dedicating a machine as a web server, it can simply be dedicated as a container host. A container orchestration system knows about the pool of servers available to it. By reading a configuration file, it can deploy containers to the servers in any configuration. This diagram shows multiple containers deployed across a collection of physical machines, as shown in Figure 9-3.

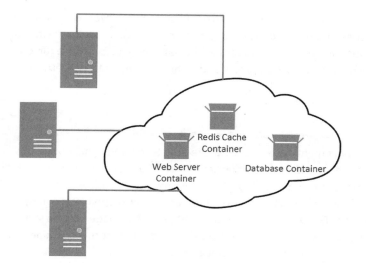

FIGURE 9-3 Containers deployed to a container orchestration system sitting on multiple physical servers

Because containers can be spun up and down quickly, the orchestration system can choose to move containers between physical machines while maintaining the health of the application. The containers do not know where they are running, and any communication between the containers can be orchestrated by the container orchestration system.

Networks within container environments can be constructed using software -based definitions. For instance, you might want the web server container to be able to communicate with the database container and the Redis cache container, but the database container should not be able to talk to the Redis container. What's more, the only externally facing ports would be the web server and, perhaps, some service management ports, as seen in Figure 9-4.

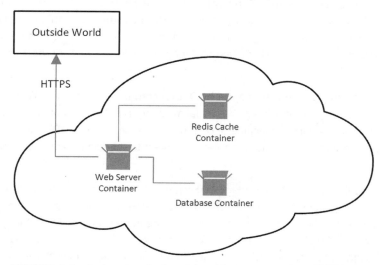

FIGURE 9-4 A private network of containers that expose only an HTTPS connection to the outside world

The ability to build environments in code so that they can easily be scaled, moved, or reproduced is invaluable. Containers and orchestration provide advantages of a reproducible cloud infrastructure, but with portability between clouds and onsite infrastructure. The full environment can be run on a local developer's machine, allowing accurate development and testing with minimal concern.

Docker

You may have noticed how we haven't mentioned a specific container technology until now in this chapter. As with all good technical ideas, there are multiple implementations of container technology. Docker is the best known of all the container technologies. Docker provides a consistent set of tools over the virtualization features that already exist inside the Linux kernel. It also provides a common image format to ship images around. The Docker Registry is a location where images can be stored and retrieved, making image construction easier. Docker can also be used to run Windows containers in Windows Server 2016, and in the Anniversary Update to Windows 10.

In addition to Docker, rkt (pronounced rocket) is a similar container technology direct from the CoreOS team. Rkt provides a standard, open container format that does not require a daemon to run. Rkt's security model prevents image hijacking and has less of a monolithic architecture than Docker, because rkt allows for components to be swapped out as technologies change. Both rkt and Docker are built on the same cgroups functionality embedded in the Linux kernel. Arguably, rkt is a better implementation but, as with Betamax, the superior technology doesn't always win.

In this section we'll take a look at how to run an ASP.NET Core application inside a Linux container. First, you need to install Docker. If you're using Windows, you probably want to install Docker for Windows, which can be found at *http://www.docker.com/products/docker#/windows*.

Docker leverages the HyperV hypervisor within Windows to run a Linux virtual machine. It is on this machine that the Docker daemon runs. The containers here are native Linux containers that can be installed into a Linux server in the cloud or in your data center. You can certainly run Windows containers natively, and we'll cover that in the next section. The concepts remain the same, so if you're anxious to run Windows containers, keep reading this section before moving on.

With Docker installed, you can create your first image. The Docker command installed on Windows connects to the Docker daemon that resides on the virtual machine. The tool can connect to any Docker daemon, whether it is on a local virtual machine or one that resides in the cloud. Docker for Windows automatically sets up your environmental variables to connect to the daemon on the virtual machine.

Microsoft has been kind enough to build a Docker image that comes with the latest version of .NET Core preinstalled. Use this as the base image for your Dockerfile. Microsoft actually produces a whole bunch of Docker images with various different combinations of the SDK and base operating systems. For instance, the image microsoft/dotnet:1.0.0-preview2-sdk contains the latest (at the time of writing) SDK on top of a Linux operating system, while the image microsoft/dotnet:1.0.0-preview2-nanoserver-sdk contains the latest SDK on top of Windows Nano. A complete list of Microsoft supplied containers is available at *https://hub.docker. com/r/microsoft/dotnet/.*

Let's start with a blank text file in the root of your project and enter the following information:

```
FROM microsoft/dotnet:1.0.0-preview2-sdk

COPY . /app

WORKDIR /app

RUN ["dotnet", "restore"]

RUN ["dotnet", "build"]

RUN ["dotnet", "ef", "database", "update"]

EXPOSE 5000/tcp

ENTRYPOINT ["dotnet", "run", "--server.urls", "http://0.0.0.0:5000"]
```

This file contains instructions for Docker to build an image for deployment. The first line is the base image that you're building the final image from. A specific version has been specified here, but you might want to use microsoft/dotnet:latest if you are working on the cutting edge. The next line copies the contents of the current directory over to the /apps folder on the image. There is, of course, a standard on Linux for where files should be placed, but because these images are transient, we're ignoring it and shoving files straight on the root like a high school student who has just been handed a copy of Red Hat 5.2 on a burnt CD. Ah, memories.

Set the working directory to your newly copied /app folder. In that folder, run a package restore, by running dotnet restore, and then a build to get the application ready to run. Next, allow connections over TCP to the container on port 5000. Finally, run the dotnet command to spin up a copy of Kestrel on port 5000. The entry point is the command that is run when the container is launched. The rest of the command is run during the build.

The command output is quite lengthy, because it contains the verbose package restore. However, the build ends with:

```
Step 8 : ENTRYPOINT dotnet run --server.urls http://0.0.0.0:5000
 ---> Running in 78e0464bc9fe
 ---> 3a83db83863d
Removing intermediate container 78e0464bc9fe
Successfully built 3a83db83863d
```

The final alphanumeric string produced is the id of the container.

With the Dockerfile in place, run the following:

```
docker build -t aplineski
```

This creates your first Docker image, creating a new image tagged with alpineski. You might want to be more specific with your naming, however, if you're going to distribute these images. The created image is placed into the inventory on the machine. This inventory can be managed using a number of commands. To list the images, use:

```
docker images
```

To remove an image, use:

```
docker rmi <image id>
```

After you have a container running, you can make changes to it and commit the changed container as an image that can be used as a future base image. This is done using:

```
Docker commit <container id> <image name>
```

In most cases, you want to use a Dockerfile to create the image rather than committing a modified running container because it is more reproducible this way.

To launch the container you created, run:

```
docker run -d -t -p 5000:5000 3a83db83863d
```

This starts up a background container that forwards port 5000 from the Docker host to the container. Starting the container prints out another very long hash, like the one in the following example:

```
731f082dc00cce58df6ee047de881e399054be2022b51552c0c24559b406d078
```

You can find a shorter version of this and a list of all the running containers by using docker ps.

```
docker ps
CONTAINER ID        IMAGE               COMMAND               CREATED          STATUS
     PORTS                        NAMES
731f082dc00c        3a83db83863d        "dotnet run --server."  19 seconds ago   Up 20
seconds
        0.0.0.0:5000->5000/tcp    angry_shirley
```

The first field container id is a short form of the Id. To see what the container has actually output, you can use the following Docker logs command:

```
docker logs 731f082dc00c
Project app (.NETCoreApp,Version=v1.0) was previously compiled. Skipping compilation.
info: Microsoft.Extensions.DependencyInjection.DataProtectionServices[0]
      User profile is available. Using '/root/.aspnet/DataProtection-Keys' as key repository;
keys will not be encrypted at rest.
Hosting environment: Development
Content root path: /app
Now listening on: http://*:5000
Application started. Press Ctrl+C to shut down.
```

The contents here are probably familiar because they are the tail end of the output from a dotnet run. After you're done with your container, you can shut it down by using:

```
docker stop
```

If you just want to pause your running container, you can issue:

```
docker pause
```

To resume the container, you can issue:

```
docker unpause
```

Data storage is another important aspect of Docker containers. Containers might seem to make a lot of sense for transient data and functionality. A web server, for instance, is stateless so shutting down and destroying one container and starting up another shouldn't have much effect on serving webpages. A database server, however, needs to maintain the state of information all the time. For this purpose, you can mount a directory from the machine that is running Docker into the running image. This allows you to shut down the container and start up another with the same volume attached seamlessly. When running a container the -v flag mounts a volume. For instance, run:

```
docker run -d -t -v /var/db:/var/postgres/db -p 5000:5000 3a83db83863d
```

This mounts the /var/db into the container as /var/postgres/db. The mounted directories can even reside on iSCSI, so you can mount volumes directly from a SAN providing good redundancy.

The Docker file for Alpine Ski is going to be more complicated than the default file you created. There are a number of variations that need to be handled. There are a number of different data contexts, each of which must be updated independently. You also need to deal with the Twitter and Facebook variables, which can be set using an environmental variable. Finally, you need to set the hosting environment to development to ensure that you're not redirected to a non-existent SSL version of the site.

```
FROM microsoft/dotnet:1.0.0-preview2-sdk

COPY . /app

WORKDIR /app

RUN ["dotnet", "restore"]

RUN ["dotnet", "build"]

RUN ["dotnet", "ef", "database","update", "--context=ApplicationUserContext"]
RUN ["dotnet", "ef", "database","update", "--context=PassContext"]
RUN ["dotnet", "ef", "database","update", "--context=PassTypeUserContext"]
RUN ["dotnet", "ef", "database","update", "--context=ResortContext"]
RUN ["dotnet", "ef", "database","update", "--context=SkiCardContext"]

EXPOSE 5000/tcp

ENV Authentication:Facebook:AppSecret FacebookAppSecret
ENV Authentication:Facebook:AppId FacebookAppId
ENV Authentication:Twitter:ConsumerSecret TwitterSecret
ENV Authentication:Twitter:ConsumerKey TwitterKey
```

```
ENV ASPNETCORE_ENVIRONMENT Development

ENTRYPOINT ["dotnet", "run", "--server.urls", "http://0.0.0.0:5000"]
```

Sharing containers with Docker is a little bit complicated, and in fact it's one of the places where rkt really shines. With rkt, it is possible to export images and then load them directly to a webserver where they can be pulled by others. Docker still allows exporting containers using the Docker save command, but these files must be imported manually into other Docker instances. To share Docker images, you really need to run a Docker registry, which can be deployed using a Docker image. Alternatively, you can upload the image to the public Docker registry called Hub. Of course, this means that your image is public for all to see. Private versions of the registry are available from various vendors for a fee.

Windows Containers

The rampant success of containers on Linux has led to the inclusion of container technology in Windows Server 2016 and Windows 10 Anniversary edition. It is not installed by default, however, and must be enabled. What's more, if you happen to run Windows within a virtual machine your success can vary.

To start you need to enable the container service and the HyperV hypervisor. This step is where failure can occur if you don't have a version of Windows that is compatible with containers. Unfortunately, a restart is required in this step. One day, someone will invent an operating system that can be reconfigured without a required restart, but apparently today is not that day.

```
Enable-WindowsOptionalFeature -Online -FeatureName containers -All
Enable-WindowsOptionalFeature -Online -FeatureName Microsoft-Hyper-V -All
Restart-Computer -Force
```

> **Tip** If you're using Windows 10, you can install the container support from the Programs and Features dialog in the control panel. But don't you feel better using the command line?

After the reboot is complete, you need to download and set up Docker. It is distributed as simply a zip file that can be expended and added to your path.

```
Invoke-WebRequest "https://master.dockerproject.org/windows/amd64/docker-1.13.0-dev.zip"
-OutFile "$env:TEMP\docker-1.13.0-dev.zip" -UseBasicParsing
Expand-Archive -Path "$env:TEMP\docker-1.13.0-dev.zip" -DestinationPath $env:ProgramFiles
# For quick use, does not require shell to be restarted. $env:path += ";c:\program files\docker"
# For persistent use, will apply even after a reboot. [Environment]::SetEnvironmentVariable("Pa
th", $env:Path + ";C:\Program Files\Docker", [EnvironmentVariableTarget]::Machine)
```

With Docker installed, it can be registered as a service and started.

```
dockerd --register-service
Start-Service Docker
```

If you have more than one Docker installed on your machine, be sure to specify the correct one to use with Windows containers. The install will have added Docker tools to the path, but because the new tools are at the end, they might not be executed.

Now you can test your new Windows container-based solution by creating a new Dockerfile to target it. Most of the existing Dockerfile can be reused because the commands are very similar between operating systems.

```
FROM microsoft/dotnet:1.0.0-preview2-windowsservercore-sdk

COPY . /app

WORKDIR /app

RUN ["dotnet", "restore"]

RUN ["dotnet", "build"]

RUN ["dotnet", "ef", "database","update", "--context=ApplicationUserContext"]
RUN ["dotnet", "ef", "database","update", "--context=PassContext"]
RUN ["dotnet", "ef", "database","update", "--context=PassTypeUserContext"]
RUN ["dotnet", "ef", "database","update", "--context=ResortContext"]
RUN ["dotnet", "ef", "database","update", "--context=SkiCardContext"]

EXPOSE 5000/tcp

ENV Authentication:Facebook:AppSecret FacebookAppSecret
ENV Authentication:Facebook:AppId FacebookAppId
ENV Authentication:Twitter:ConsumerSecret TwitterSecret
ENV Authentication:Twitter:ConsumerKey TwitterKey
ENV ASPNETCORE_ENVIRONMENT Development

ENTRYPOINT ["dotnet", "run", "--server.urls", "http://0.0.0.0:5000"]
```

Notice that this container is based on Windows Server Core. Building Windows Nano containers seems to only work from within Nano containers currently, unless you make use of the less efficient Hyper-V containerization. The Dockerfile should work on most instances of Windows. Windows containers come in two flavors: Hyper-V and Windows Server Containers. Windows Server Containers are lighter weight and closer to the cgroups based containers on Linux and the kernel is shared between all the containers on the system. Hyper-V containers are containers that exist inside a virtual machine. They are more isolated, but also suffer from lower performance than the native containers.

> **Note** If you're having problems with Docker containers on your local Windows install, you might want to try them out on Azure where there is a Windows container that comes with Docker pre-installed. The only caveat is that you are unable to run Hyper-V containers on it because it is already a Hyper-V container.

Windows containers are still very young. At the time of writing, Windows Server 2016 is not yet released and the container support on Windows 10, although not in beta, probably should be. As we move forward, and containers become more important, the effort put into making them better and more robust only increases. Although predicting the future is a fool's game, it feels safe predicting that in five years' time containers will be the default deployment mechanism not just for web applications, but for desktop applications as well. Before that time we'll have to solve some of the problems associated with running containers in production.

Docker in Production

At the time of writing, running Docker in production with Docker Swarm, the official Docker orchestration tool, is unstable. There are many reports of networking failures and nodes in the swarm being unable to properly communicate with one another; however, Docker Swarm is still in its early days. There are also some alternatives that support Docker in a distributed fashion, but are without the official Swarm components.

Apache Mesos is a cluster management tool that aims to abstract the data center away and treat is as if the entire data center is a single computer. First released in 2009, it has grown to be a well-accepted tool and is even the backing technology for Azure's container distribution technology (*https://azure.microsoft.com/en-us/documentation/videos/azurecon-2015-deep-dive-on-the-azure-container-service-with-mesos/*). It is backed by a commercial entity known as Mesosphere. At its core, Mesos is a distributed scheduling tool, but by building on top of it, you can easily use it to distribute containers. Marathon is likely the best known tool for doing container management on Mesos.

Never one to be left behind, Google created and has open sourced a similar tool known as Kubernetes. While Mesos had container management grafted onto it long after it was first created, Kubernetes was created from the beginning to manage and orchestrate containers. Kubernetes has a number of fundamental building blocks: pods, labels, controllers, services, and nodes. A pod is a collection of containers that run together on one machine. If you have containers that should run in close proximity, you might want to organize them into a pod. Labels are just that, key value pairs that can be assigned to any node or pod. You might label a pod with a front-end role and production level to denote a production front-end server. Controllers are responsible for reconciling the actual state of the system with the desired state of the system. For instance, imagine that you want to have two web server containers, a database container, and a Redis container, but your actual state only has a single web server, as shown in Figure 9-5.

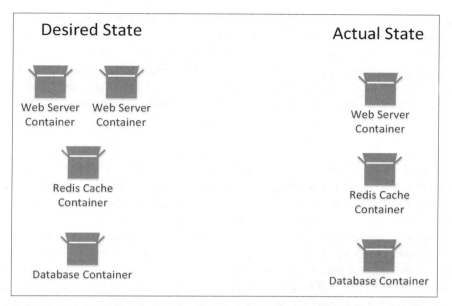

Desired State

Web Server Container   Web Server Container

Redis Cache Container

Database Container

Actual State

Web Server Container

Redis Cache Container

Database Container

FIGURE 9-5 The desired state and the actual state—Kubernetes performs the required operations to bring the actual state in line with the desired state

Upon receiving the new desired state, the Kubernetes system performs a reconciliation loop until the actual state of the system matches the desired state. This way, you can avoid having to do difficult, manual comparisons between the actual and desired states. Kubernetes calculates what operations need to be run to bring the systems into convergence.

Finally, a service in Kubernetes is a collection of pods that work together to provide a piece of functionality. Keep in mind that Kubernetes is designed around the idea of microservices, so a service might be quite small. The number of services deployed is a scalability point, allowing you to scale up a microservice as demand requires. Services can provide routable end points that can be exposed to other services or outside of the cluster.

On the Cloud

There are numerous options available to host containers in the cloud. All of the major cloud providers have some sort of a solution related to cloud computing. Google's compute engine offers container based cloud computing using their own Kubernetes orchestration engine. Google has more experience with containerization than any of the other vendors and their offering seems to be the most mature.

The Google container implementation is closer to what we have come to expect from Platform as a Service (PaaS) offerings in the cloud. There is no need to allocate your own cluster of virtual machines. Instead, your containers run as part of the general computer cloud. Both the AWS and Azure offerings currently require that the end user allocate their own collection of virtual machines to build the container cluster on.

Cloud computing is an incredibly competitive area at the moment. Every major cloud player is falling over themselves to attract as many of the companies who have yet to move to the cloud as possible. Despite the theory that moving between clouds should be simple, there is not really a huge value proposition for most companies to make the move, making it important to attract the final few companies and lock them into a vendor specific cloud. Despite containerization preventing vendor lock in, there will no doubt be significant effort made to improve the ease of use of containers.

Summary

Containerization of services might seem like a technology that is still in its infancy, but it is growing up very rapidly, especially if you believe all of the hype. Microsoft has heavily invested in containerization on their server and desktop operating systems, as well as in Azure. It is indeed a fundamental change in how services are built and deployed. It encourages applications to be split into smaller fit-to-purpose pieces. Of course containers aren't a panacea, and there are certainly still places where the older, monolithic approach to building applications is perfectly suitable. Even if your architecture doesn't demand being broken up into smaller parts, containers might still be useful for providing a consistent build and testing structure for your application. Having developers run their own container instances can speed up testing and ensure a consistency between their environment and all the others on the team.

Containers are certainly worth investing a week of your team's time to see just how containers can help out with your current bottle necks. In the next chapter we'll take a look at how we can leverage an entity framework to make database access easy and efficient.

## CHAPTER 10

Entity Framework Core

Work was progressing well on Project Parsley, the new lift ticketing system for Alpine Ski House. Danielle felt like things on the team were starting to click and that they had a shared goal. It was about then that Marc, in his booming voice, started singing,

> *"It's not about the data, data, data.*
> *We don't need your data, data, data,*
> *We just wanna make the world ski*
> *Forget about the index"*

Danielle squinted. "Are you singing Jessie J?" she asked.

"Of course" replied Marc. "She is the Bach of the 21st Century. But actually I have data on my mind. We've got to put a bunch of data in the database and take it out again. You'd think that problem would be a solved by now, but I'm still writing raw SQL in my code."

Danielle knew there wasn't necessarily a perfect solution for every data access problem and that raw SQL might well be the best solution for some data access stories. "We've talked a bit about NOSQL stores and decided that none of us have enough experience to use them for this project. That leaves us with a SQL store, or probably SQL server since we're hosted on Azure – path of least resistance, you know. I've been using Entity Framework for most of my data access."

"Oh" pondered Marc, "I've never used Entity Framework, but it sounds super enterprizy. Is this Enterprise Java Beans again? Am I going to need to create a SkiPassEntityFactoryBeanFactoryStrategy? I don't think we have time for that, Danielle."

Danielle laughed, the big man's sense of humor was starting to grow on her. "Don't worry, even though they reset the version number on Entity Framework Core, it is based on many years of experience with full Entity Framework (EF). EF can get your data efficiently and easily. Grab a chair and I'll see what I can show you before you start singing again."

It could be argued that data is the most valuable aspect of a business application. Not surprisingly, it can be common to see a large percentage of an application's codebase dedicated to data storage and retrieval. This includes retrieving data from a data store, tracking changes, and saving changes back to that same data store. Over the years, several .NET technologies have emerged to help make this easier and aside from Tabs vs. Spaces, few decisions have been more polarizing than choosing a technology and approach to storing and retrieving data in your application.

Entity Framework (EF) Core is the latest data access technology built by the ASP.NET team and is the recommended framework when building ASP.NET Core applications. EF Core is an Object Relational Mapper (ORM), meaning that it can handle the complexities of mapping from between a relational store and an object oriented domain model in your application. EF Core is not the only ORM available for .NET Core applications. Dapper is a popular micro-ORM while nHibernate is a fully featured ORM. Both frameworks are fully open-sourced and community driven, but at the time of writing this, only Dapper has support for .NET Core. The main difference between micro-ORMs and a fully featured ORM like Entity Framework is that micro-ORMs typically require you to manually specify the SQL statements that are executed, whereas full ORMs generate most SQL statements for you based on the information it knows about your entities and your database. The choice of ORM vs micro-ORM ultimately depends on the team and the problems you are trying to solve.

The Alpine Ski House team decided to use EF Core because the team members are familiar with previous versions of Entity Framework and they like the direction the ASP.NET team has taken with EF Core, making it relatively lightweight and more extensible than previous versions of EF. Another advantage is EF Core's LINQ support, which is used to efficiently query the model by expressing rich queries in C# code. EF Core also provides an easy way to use raw SQL when needed, whether for performance reasons or simply for convenience.

It's all System.Data

It's worth noting that regardless of which ORM you choose to use in your application, they are all built on top of System.Data. The System.Data APIs that have been a part of .NET since version 1, provide an abstraction for interacting with databases in the form of IDbConnection, IDbCommand, IDataReader, and IDbTransaction. Virtually every ORM ever written in the history of .NET is written on top of these four interfaces. That's actually pretty amazing when you think about how long .NET has been around, and is a testament to the excellent design work that went into the creation of .NET.

Different database providers can provide their own implementations of the common System.Data interfaces. Microsoft provides an implementation for SQL Server out of the box in System.Data.SqlClient and many other providers are also available, including common providers such as MySQL, Oracle, PostgreSQL, and SqlLite. The Alpine Ski House team uses SQL Server because it has excellent cross platform support in .NET Core along with solid production support.

Entity Framework Basics

When using Entity Framework as a data access layer, the domain model is expressed using Plain Old CLR Objects (POCOs). For example, a Ski Card domain entity would be expressed simply as a SkiCard class. Entity Framework takes care of mapping the properties of that class to the columns of a particular table in a database. Entity Framework manages this mapping and any interaction with the database via an instance of a class that inherits from DbContext.

Before diving deep into the Alpine Ski House domain, let's examine a simplified example. Consider a very simple SQL Server database that stores a list of all the resorts managed by Alpine Ski House in a Resorts table (see Table 10-1).

TABLE 10-1 The Resorts database table

Resorts	
Id	int
Name	nvarchar(255)
OperatingSince	date

The application models the Resort record with a POCO named Resort. We refer to these as entity classes.

```
public class Resort
{
  public int Id { get; set; }
  public string Name { get; set; }
  public DateTime OperatingSince {get; set;}
}
```

Now you need to add a reference to the Microsoft.EntityFrameworkCore.SqlServer package, which pulls in all of the EF Core pieces that you need. At this point, EF doesn't know anything about the Resort entity. You can tell EF about the Resort entity by creating a DbContext class that contains a DbSet for the Resorts.

```
    public class ResortContext : DbContext
    {
        public DbSet<Resort> Resorts {get; set;}

        protected override void OnConfiguring(DbContextOptionsBuilder optionsBuilder)
        {
            //Do not specify connection strings here in real-world applications
            //In an ASP.NET application this is configured using dependency injection.
            //See Chapter 11 & Chapter 13
optionsBuilder.UseSqlServer("Server=(localdb)\\MSSQLLocalDB;Database=ResortDBs;Integrated
Security=true");
        }
    }
```

That's all you need to start using Entity Framework. The mapping conventions in EF take care of mapping the Resort class to the Resorts table in the database. These conventions can all be overridden as needed, but first let's explore the basic DbContext API, which provides a useful abstraction of the database. To access the data in the database, start by creating an instance of the ResortContext.

```
var context = new ResortContext();
//Use the context
context.Dispose();
```

It's important that the Dispose method is called after you are done working with an instance of a DbContext. Calling the Dispose method ensures that any associated database connections are released back to the connection pool. Without returning the connection to the connection pool, you risk starving the connection pool and eventually causing connection timeouts. When creating a context manually, it is a good idea to make use of the using pattern to ensure that the Dispose method is called when the code block is completed.

```
using(var context = new ResortContext())
{
//Use the context
}
```

In an ASP.NET application, use the built in dependency injection framework to handle creation of and disposal of the context. We cover that in more detail in Chapter 14, "Dependency Injection."

Querying for a single record

When querying for a single record based on a primary key, use the DbSet.Find method as follows:

```
var resort = context.Resorts.Find(12);
```

When querying for a single record based on criteria other than the primary key, use the First method and specify a lambda expression, which returns true for the matching record:

```
var resort = context.Resorts.First(f => f.Name == "Alpine Ski House");
Resulting Query:
SELECT TOP(1) [f].[Id], [f].[Name], [f].[OperatingSince]
FROM [Resorts] AS [f]
WHERE [f].[Name] = N'Alpine Ski House'
```

The First method throws an exception if no matches are found. Alternatively, you can use the FirstOrDefault method, which returns Null if no matches are found.

Another option is to use the Single and SingleOrDefault methods. These methods work almost exactly like the First and FirstOrDefault methods, but they throw an exception if multiple matching records are found.

```
var resort = context.Resorts.Single(f => f.Name == "Alpine Ski House");

Resulting Query:
SELECT TOP(2) [f].[Id], [f].[Name], [f].[OperatingSince]
FROM [Resorts] AS [f]
WHERE [f].[Name] = N'Alpine Ski House'
```

Notice how EF generated a SELECT TOP(2) for the Single instead of SELECT TOP(1) like it did for the First query. The SELECT TOP(2) is needed so EF can throw an exception in the case when multiple records are found. Use Single when you expect only one matching record as this more clearly states the intent of the query and provides a clear error if that expectation does not hold true.

Querying for multiple records

In many cases, you will want to query the database for multiple records that match some specific criteria. This is accomplished by calling the `Where` method on the `DbSet`, which returns all of the records matching the specified lambda expression.

```
var skiResorts = context.Resorts.Where(f => f.Name.Contains("Ski")).ToList();

Resulting Query:
SELECT [f].[Id], [f].[Name], [f].[OperatingSince]
FROM [Resorts] AS [f]
WHERE [f].[Name] LIKE (N'%' + N'Ski') + N'%'
```

EF does not immediately call the database when you call the Where method. Instead, it returns an `IQueryable<T>` where T is the type of the entity being queried. The actual execution of that query is deferred until a method on `IQueryable<T>` is called that would require the query to be executed. In this case, we forced the execution immediately by calling the `ToList` method. The deferred query execution is an important feature of EF that allows you to chain multiple methods together and build complex queries. This is an example of the lazy instantiation pattern where the creation of an object or calculation of a value is delayed until the first time it is needed.

Saving Data

DbContext also provides a mechanism for tracking changes to entities and saving those changes back to the database. Let's take a look at the basics of saving changes.

Inserting data is accomplished by adding a new entity to a DbSet, and then calling the DbContext's SaveChanges method.

```
var resort = new Resort
{
    Name = "Alpine Ski House 2",
    OperatingSince = new DateTime(2001, 12, 31)
};
context.Resorts.Add(resort);
context.SaveChanges();

Resulting Query:
INSERT INTO [Resorts] ([Name], [OperatingSince])
VALUES (@p0, @p1);
```

You can also add multiple entities to the DbSet before calling SaveChanges. Entity Framework keeps track of all the new entities. EF sends insert commands to the database when SaveChanges is called. At that point, a transaction is created and all the insert commands are executed within that transaction. If any one of the insert commands fail, they are all rolled back.

Change Tracking

The DbContext's change tracker also tracks changes to existing entities and issues Update commands when SaveChanges is called.

```
var resort= context.Resorts.Find(12);
resort.Name = "New Name";
context.SaveChanges();

Resulting Query:
UPDATE [Resorts] SET [Name] = @p1
WHERE [Id] = @p0;
```

Only the [Name] column is updated. The other columns are not updated because the change tracker knows those columns have not been changed. A certain amount of overhead is associated with change tracking. When loading entities for a read-only purpose, it can be advantageous to turn off change tracking. This can be done on a case-by-case basis using the AsNoTracking() extension method.

```
var lastYear = new DateTime(2015,1,1);
var newResorts = context.Resorts.AsNoTracking().Where(f => f.OperatingSince > lastYear);
```

The DbSet.Remove method is used to delete an entity.

```
var resort= context.Resorts.Find(12);
context.Resorts.Remove(resort);
contex.SaveChanges();

Resulting Query:
DELETE FROM [Resorts]
WHERE [Id] = @p0;
```

Using Migrations to Create and Update Databases

So far, our simple example assumed that a database already existed that matches our entities. In many cases, including the Alpine Ski House application, you might be working with an entirely new database. Developers need an easy way to create a local test database and also to define and execute migration scripts when changes are made to the database. EF provides command line tooling to automate these tasks. The command line tooling is referenced via NuGet by adding a tooling dependency to the Microsoft.EntityFrameworkCore.Tools package and is executed using the dotnet ef command. We cover dependency management in more detail in Chapter 16, "Dependency Management."

Creating a new database

Use the dotnet ef database update command to create a new database.

```
> dotnet ef database update
```

The command compiles your application and connects to the database using the connection string configured for your local development environment. We cover configuration in more detail in Chapter 12, "Configuration and Logging."

If the specified database does not exist, a new database is created. If the database does exist, any required migration scripts are applied to update the database to match the domain classes in the application.

You can also explicitly specify the name of the DbContext class you would like the command to use.

```
> dotnet ef database update -c AlpineSkiHouse.Data.ResortContext
```

The -c (or --context) option can be specified for any of the dotnet ef commands and is required when your application has more than one DbContext class. As you can see in the Alpine Ski House application, this option is used extensively.

Running the dotnet ef database update command on the ResortContext results in a new database that contains only the __EFMigrationHistory table, as shown in Figure 10-1.

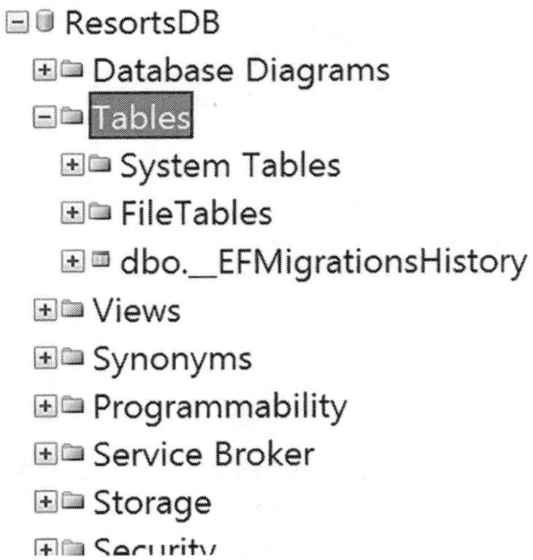

FIGURE 10-1 A new database created by the dotnet ef database update command

The database doesn't contain the expected Resorts table because you have not yet defined any migrations for the ResortContext.

Adding Migrations

Entity Framework Migrations are used to upgrade, or downgrade, the database from one version to another. A migration is defined as a C# class that inherits from the Migration class. The class contains two methods: Up(), which is used to migrate up to the version specified by this migration and Down(), which is used to migrate the database back to the previous version.

Defining these migrations manually would be very tedious, which is why Entity Framework provides the `dotnet ef migrations` add command to do most of the heavy lifting for you. In the case of a new DbContext, an initial migration is needed in order to create the tables for your model.

```
dotnet ef migrations add CreateInitialSchema
```

This creates a new class called `CreateInitialSchema` in a Migrations folder next to the specified DbContext.

```
public partial class CreateInitialSchema : Migration
{
    protected override void Up(MigrationBuilder migrationBuilder)
    {
        migrationBuilder.CreateTable(
            name: "Resorts",
            columns: table => new
            {
                Id = table.Column<int>(nullable: false)
                    .Annotation("SqlServer:ValueGenerationStrategy",
SqlServerValueGenerationStrategy.IdentityColumn),
                Name = table.Column<string>(nullable: true),
                OperatingSince = table.Column<DateTime>(nullable: false)
            },
            constraints: table =>
            {
                table.PrimaryKey("PK_Resorts", x => x.Id);
            });
    }

    protected override void Down(MigrationBuilder migrationBuilder)
    {
        migrationBuilder.DropTable(
            name: "Resorts");
    }
}
```

In this case, the Up method adds the Resorts table with a column for each property in the Resort class. The Down method drops the Resorts table. In your local developer environment, this Cre-ateInitialSchema migration is considered a pending migration because it has not yet been applied to your local database. Running the `dotnet ef database update` command applies the pending update and creates the Resorts table, as shown in Figure 10-2.

```
dotnet ef database update
```

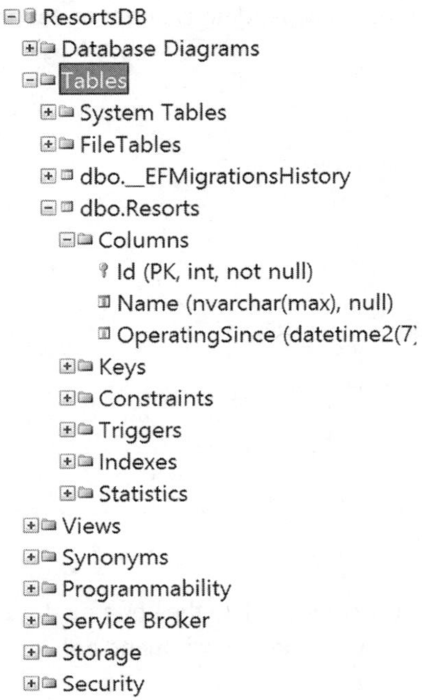

```
⊟ ▣ ResortsDB
  ⊞▢ Database Diagrams
  ⊟▢ Tables
    ⊞▢ System Tables
    ⊞▢ FileTables
    ⊞▢ dbo.__EFMigrationsHistory
    ⊟▢ dbo.Resorts
      ⊟▢ Columns
          ⸙ Id (PK, int, not null)
          ▯ Name (nvarchar(max), null)
          ▯ OperatingSince (datetime2(7)
      ⊞▢ Keys
      ⊞▢ Constraints
      ⊞▢ Triggers
      ⊞▢ Indexes
      ⊞▢ Statistics
    ⊞▢ Views
    ⊞▢ Synonyms
    ⊞▢ Programmability
    ⊞▢ Service Broker
    ⊞▢ Storage
    ⊞▢ Security
```

FIGURE 10-2 The ResortsDB database with pending changes applied

> **Note** You might be surprised by the nvarchar(max) datatype used for the Name column. If no additional options are specified, Entity Framework maps .NET string types to nvarchar(max). We cover the use of data annotations and model configuration later in this chapter.

If a change is made to a domain class or if new classes are added, a new migration must be defined in the migrations folder. A common example is adding a new property to a domain class.

```
public class Resort
{
    public int Id { get; set; }
    public string Name { get; set; }
    public string MailingAddress { get; set; } //this was added
    public DateTime OperatingSince { get; set; }
}
```

After adding the property, the domain model and database are out of sync and a migration is needed in order to bring the database up-to-date with the model. Start by calling the dotnet ef migrations add command, and specifying a descriptive name for this migration.

```
> dotnet ef migrations add AddedMailingAddress
```

Entity Framework now compiles your application and detects any pending changes to your entity classes. A new class is added to the Migrations folder.

```
public partial class AddedMailingAddress : Migration
{
    protected override void Up(MigrationBuilder migrationBuilder)
    {
        migrationBuilder.AddColumn<string>(
            name: "MailingAddress",
            table: "Resorts",
            nullable: true);
    }

    protected override void Down(MigrationBuilder migrationBuilder)
    {
        migrationBuilder.DropColumn(
            name: "MailingAddress",
            table: "Resorts");
    }
}
```

In this case, the Up method adds the new MailingAddress column while the Down method drops the MailingAddress column. Calling the dotnet ef database update command applies the pending migration.

The EF migrations tool does a good job of generating code to change the structure of a database but sometimes you also need to make changes to the data using UPDATE, INSERT, or DELETE statements. Data changes can be achieved by passing any valid Sql statement to the migrationBuilder. Sql method in the Up or Down method as needed. It is even possible to add a migration when no model changes have occurred. Calling the dotnet ef migrations add command when there are no model changes results in an empty migration. Here is an example of a migration that simply adds rows to the Resorts table.

```
public partial class AddResortsAndLocations : Migration
{
    protected override void Up(MigrationBuilder migrationBuilder)
    {
        migrationBuilder.Sql(
            @"INSERT INTO Resorts(Name)
                VALUES('Alpine Ski House'),
                      ('Nearby Resort'),
                      ('Competing Resort')");
    }

    protected override void Down(MigrationBuilder migrationBuilder)
    {
        migrationBuilder.Sql(
            @"DELETE Resorts WHERE Name IN
                ('Alpine Ski House',
                 'Nearby Resort',
                 'Competing Resort')");
    }
}
```

> **Note** In general, entity classes and DbContext classes don't contain any database provider specific logic. Migrations however, are specific to the provider that was configured at the time the migration was created. As such, you cannot expect to create a migration for SQL Server and then have a developer on another computer run that migration against SQL Lite. If you choose to support multiple database providers, you might want to manage your migration scripts manually outside of Entity Framework.

Creating Update Scripts for Production Servers

The dotnet ef database update command line tool works great for developer workstations, but might not always work when trying to deploy to a production database server. In cases when your build server is not able to apply migrations directly, you can use the dotnet ef migrations script command to generate a database script that can be used to apply pending migrations to a database.

```
C:\EFBasics>dotnet ef migrations script
Project EFBasics (.NETCoreApp,Version=v1.0) was previously compiled. Skipping compilation.
IF OBJECT_ID(N'__EFMigrationsHistory') IS NULL
BEGIN
    CREATE TABLE [__EFMigrationsHistory] (
        [MigrationId] nvarchar(150) NOT NULL,
        [ProductVersion] nvarchar(32) NOT NULL,
        CONSTRAINT [PK___EFMigrationsHistory] PRIMARY KEY ([MigrationId])
    );
END;
GO
CREATE TABLE [Resorts] (
    [Id] int NOT NULL IDENTITY,
    [Name] nvarchar(max),
    [OperatingSince] datetime2 NOT NULL,
    CONSTRAINT [PK_Resorts] PRIMARY KEY ([Id])
);
GO
INSERT INTO [__EFMigrationsHistory] ([MigrationId], [ProductVersion])
VALUES (N'20160627025825_CreateInitialSchema', N'1.0.0-rc2-20901');
GO
ALTER TABLE [Resorts] ADD [MailingAddress] nvarchar(max);
GO
INSERT INTO [__EFMigrationsHistory] ([MigrationId], [ProductVersion])
VALUES (N'20160627030609_AddedMailingAddress', N'1.0.0-rc2-20901');
GO
```

Using the default options, this command outputs all the migrations for the specified DbContext. The From and To options can be used to generate a script to migrate from a specific version to a specific version.

```
>dotnet ef migrations script 0 InitialResortContext
Project AlpineSkiHouse.Web (.NETCoreApp,Version=v1.0) was previously compiled. Skipping
compilation.
IF OBJECT_ID(N'__EFMigrationsHistory') IS NULL
BEGIN
```

```
    CREATE TABLE [__EFMigrationsHistory] (
        [MigrationId] nvarchar(150) NOT NULL,
        [ProductVersion] nvarchar(32) NOT NULL,
        CONSTRAINT [PK___EFMigrationsHistory] PRIMARY KEY ([MigrationId])
    );
END;
GO
CREATE TABLE [Resorts] (
    [Id] int NOT NULL IDENTITY,
    [Name] nvarchar(max),
    CONSTRAINT [PK_Resorts] PRIMARY KEY ([Id])
);
GO
CREATE TABLE [Locations] (
    [Id] int NOT NULL IDENTITY,
    [Altitude] decimal(18, 2),
    [Latitude] decimal(18, 2),
    [Longitude] decimal(18, 2),
    [Name] nvarchar(max),
    [ResortId] int NOT NULL,
    CONSTRAINT [PK_Locations] PRIMARY KEY ([Id]),
    CONSTRAINT [FK_Locations_Resorts_ResortId] FOREIGN KEY ([ResortId]) REFERENCES [Resorts]
([Id]) ON DELETE CASCADE
);
GO
CREATE INDEX [IX_Locations_ResortId] ON [Locations] ([ResortId]);
GO
INSERT INTO [__EFMigrationsHistory] ([MigrationId], [ProductVersion])
VALUES (N'20160625231005_InitialResortContext', N'1.0.0-rtm-21431');
GO
```

Now that we have covered the basics pieces of Entity Framework, let's take a look at how we can use it to deliver features in the Alpine Ski House web application.

The ApplicationDbContext

When we created the AlpineSkiHouse.Web project using Visual Studio, we selected the Web Application template using Individual User Accounts. Selecting this option created a context in the application named ApplicationDbContext, a DbContext for the ApplicationUser entity. Let's take a look at the entity and context that were added to the project:

Models\ApplicationUser.cs
```
namespace AlpineSkiHouse.Models
{
    // Add profile data for application users by adding properties to the ApplicationUser class
    public class ApplicationUser : IdentityUser
    {
    }
}
```

The ApplicationUser class inherits common user properties from the IdentityUser class such as an EmailAddress and unique Id. As the comment states, this class can be extended by adding your own properties. This is exactly what is needed for the current sprint, but first let's take a look at the ApplicationDbContext.

Data\ApplicationDbContext.cs

```
namespace AlpineSkiHouse.Data
{
    public class ApplicationDbContext : IdentityDbContext<ApplicationUser>
    {
        public ApplicationDbContext(DbContextOptions<ApplicationDbContext> options)
            : base(options)
        {
        }

        protected override void OnModelCreating(ModelBuilder builder)
        {
            base.OnModelCreating(builder);
        }
    }
}
```

Much like the ApplicationUser class, the ApplicationDbContext class inherits properties from a base class: IdentityDbContext. In the case of the ApplicationDbContext, these properties are DbSets for ASP.NET Identity related entities including Users, Roles, Claims, and Tokens. We explore the ASP.NET Identity entities in more detail in Chapter 13, "Identity, Security & Rights."

Rather than hard coding configuration in the OnConfiguration method, configuration options are passed into the constructor. This allows you to specify the configuration as part of your application startup and use the built in dependency injection framework to inject this option into the DbContext for you. Use this constructor signature for all the DbContext classes you define in your application. Using this method of configuration simplifies the testing of your DbContext classes, which we explore in more detail in Chapter 19, "Testing."

When you start adding features to the Alpine Ski House application, it might be tempting and even initially convenient to place all your entities in the ApplicationDbContext class. Instead, it is much easier to maintain the application if you create separate DbContext classes for each of the bounded contexts outlined in Chapter 4, "Scoping the Project." The ApplicationDbContext maps to the login bounded context, but the name is misleading as it implies it is the single DbContext for the entire application, so rename the ApplicationDbContext to ApplicationUserContext.

```
public class ApplicationUserContext : IdentityDbContext<ApplicationUser>
{
    public ApplicationUserContext(DbContextOptions<ApplicationUserContext> options)
        : base(options)
    {
    }

    protected override void OnModelCreating(ModelBuilder builder)
    {
        base.OnModelCreating(builder);
    }
}
```

Extending ApplicationUserContext

Now that a clear boundary exists in your domain, you can add additional user account details to the `ApplicationUser` class. Mildred, the sales and marketing expert at Alpine Ski House, would like to capture names in order to personalize messages. Mildred would also like to capture users' contact information, such as email address and phone number, so she can notify users of activity related to their accounts or send them summaries of their activities after a day of skiing at one of our resorts.

`EmailAddress` and `PhoneNumber` properties are already part of the base `IdentityUser` class, but you do need to add the `FirstName` and `LastName` properties:

```
public class ApplicationUser : IdentityUser
{
    [MaxLength(70)]
    [Required]
    public string FirstName { get; set; }

    [MaxLength(70)]
    public string LastName { get; set; }
}
```

Data Annotations are used here to specify which properties are required and also the maximum length for string properties. These attributes are used for validating the state of an entity before saving it, and are also used by Entity Framework when generating column data types for the database. By specifying the `MaxLength` as 70 for `FirstName` and `LastName`, the column type is `nvarchar(70)` instead of `nvarchar(max)`. We chose to leave `LastName` optional since some people have only a single name. While this situation is generally pretty rare in North American cultures, you don't want to exclude anyone from skiing at the resort because of an arbitrary restriction around last names. We also want Cher and Madonna to keep coming back to Alpine Ski House for their annual ski trip.

Now that you have made changes to the entity class, you need to create a migration in order to add these columns to the database.

```
dotnet ef migrations add AddNamePropertiesToApplicationUser

public partial class AddNamePropertiesToApplicationUser : Migration
{
    protected override void Up(MigrationBuilder migrationBuilder)
    {
        migrationBuilder.AddColumn<string>(
            name: "FirstName",
            table: "AspNetUsers",
            nullable: false,
            defaultValue: "");

        migrationBuilder.AddColumn<string>(
            name: "LastName",
            table: "AspNetUsers",
            nullable: true);
    }

    protected override void Down(MigrationBuilder migrationBuilder)
```

```
    {
        migrationBuilder.DropColumn(
            name: "FirstName",
            table: "AspNetUsers");

        migrationBuilder.DropColumn(
            name: "LastName",
            table: "AspNetUsers");
    }
}
```

To apply this migration, run the `dotnet ef database update` command.

Ski Card Context

Ski cards represent an important concept for Project Parsley. A ski card is the physical card that a customer wears on the hill and is recognized by the scanners at lifts and other locations on the ski hill. A ski card is the representation of a customer within the system. The original model had the customer and card modelled as two entities. Since a ski card has one-to-one mapping with a customer, and one can never exist without the other, we decided to merge these into a single `SkiCard` entity. After logging in, users have the ability to create one or more ski cards for themselves and members of their family.

First, create a new `DbContext` called `SkiCardContext`.

```
public class SkiCardContext : DbContext
{
    public SkiCardContext(DbContextOptions<SkiCardContext> options) : base(options)
    {
    }

    public DbSet<SkiCard> SkiCards { get; set; }
}
```

It might seem strange to have a context with only one or two entity types, but there is nothing wrong with keeping things small. The overhead of having multiple contexts in the system is very minimal and you can always refactor this at a later date.

For now, configure the `SkiCardContext` to store data in the same database as the `Application-UserContext`. The connection string configuration is done in the `ConfigureServices` method of the `Startup` class.

```
services.AddDbContext<SkiCardContext>(options =>
    options.UseSqlServer(Configuration.GetConnectionString("DefaultConnection")));
```

The `SkiCard` class contains a unique identifier, the date and time the card was created, and some basic information about the customer whom we refer to as the card holder.

```
public class SkiCard
{
```

```
    public int Id { get; set; }

    /// <summary>
    /// The Id of the ApplicationUser who owns this ski card
    /// </summary>
    public string ApplicationUserId { get; set; }

    /// <summary>
    /// The date when the card was created
    /// </summary>
    public DateTime CreatedOn { get; set; }

    [MaxLength(70)]
    [Required]
    public string CardHolderFirstName { get; set; }

    [MaxLength(70)]
    public string CardHolderLastName { get; set; }

    public DateTime CardHolderBirthDate { get; set; }

    [Phone]
    public string CardHolderPhoneNumber { get; set; }
}
```

The Alpine Ski House team agreed that they need to extend the SkiCard entity in the future, but this gives them a good starting point to support the goal in Sprint 2, which is to allow customers to login and create ski cards for their family members. Now that the initial version of our ski card bounded context has been created, let's create the initial migration using the dotnet ef migrations command and update the local development database using the dotnet ef database update command.

```
dotnet ef migrations add InitialSkiCardContext -c AlpineSkiHouse.Data.SkiCardContext
dotnet ef database update -c AlpineSkiHouse.Data.SkiCardContext
```

Relationships crossing Context Boundaries

Anyone with experience in relational database design is probably horrified with what we've done here. By defining boundaries around the DbContext classes in the application, we have disconnected tables that would normally be connected by a foreign key. How can you ensure referential integrity without foreign keys? Take ski cards for example. The SkiCard table has a column named ApplicationUserId that refers to the primary key of the ApplicationUser who created that SkiCard. If these entities had been in the same bounded context, we would have explicitly modelled the relationship between ApplicationUser and SkiCard using navigation properties. With the navigation properties in place, EF would have defined a foreign key between the two tables and the referential integrity of the data would have been enforced by the database.

As it stands, the relationship is not explicitly defined. The Alpine Ski House team debated the pros and cons of this. One of the main concerns is what happens if a user decides to delete her account. Without the explicit relationship between ApplicationUser and SkiCard, you can end up with orphaned `SkiCard` records. The team considered a couple of options. The first option is to manually define the foreign key using a migration.

```
dotnet ef migrations add AddSkiCardApplicationUserForeignKey -c AlpineSkiHouse.Data.
SkiCardContext
```

Since there are no model changes, this creates an empty migration where you can manually add the foreign key.

```
public partial class AddSkiCardApplicationUserForeignKey : Migration
{
    protected override void Up(MigrationBuilder migrationBuilder)
    {
        migrationBuilder.AddForeignKey("FK_SkiCards_ApplicationUser_ApplicationUserID",
            "SkiCards", "ApplicationUserId",
            "AspNetUsers", principalColumn: "Id",
            onDelete: ReferentialAction.Cascade);
    }

    protected override void Down(MigrationBuilder migrationBuilder)
    {
        migrationBuilder.DropForeignKey("FK_SkiCards_ApplicationUser_ApplicationUserID",
"SkiCards");
    }
}
```

This ensures that you never have any orphaned `SkiCard` records at the relational database level, however, this method might cause other problems. If a user decides to delete his user record, the business users don't necessarily want the `SkiCard` record to be deleted. The business users still want to know that a ski card exists and to know what passes have been used for that card. Deleting the ski card records causes historical reports to be inaccurate. You can change the `onDelete` value to `ReferentialAction.SetDefault`, but the team can quickly realize they are discussing functionality that is out of scope for the current sprint. Users have no way to delete their accounts anyway, so we shouldn't be wasting our time guessing at future requirements. For now, the decision was made to remove the foreign key migration, deferring the decisions on this functionality to a future date.

Deleting a user account is a non-trivial operation that has implications across several bounded contexts. Instead of trying to handle all of this logic via foreign keys, it might be easier to understand and more extensible to handle this using events. When an `ApplicationUser` is deleted, the application user bounded context raises an `ApplicationUserDeleted` event. Any actions that need to happen as a result of the `ApplicationUserDeleted` event are implemented as event handlers in other bounded contexts. This is a better approach and should be considered if this feature is required.

Wiring up the Controller

Now that the context is available, you need to implement a controller for the `SkiCard` entity. The controller exposes endpoints for viewing a list of ski cards, creating a new ski card, and editing details for an existing ski card.

This controller needs access to the SkiCardContext and the UserManager<ApplicationUser>, which is passed into the constructor. These dependencies are resolved by the built in dependency injection framework as discussed in Chapter 14.

```
[Authorize]
public class SkiCardController : Controller
{
    private readonly SkiCardContext _skiCardContext;
    private readonly UserManager<ApplicationUser> _userManager;

    public SkiCardController(SkiCardContext skiCardContext, UserManager<ApplicationUser>
userManager)
    {
        _skiCardContext = skiCardContext;
        _userManager = userManager;
    }

}
```

Adding the [Authorize] attribute to the SkiCardController ensures that only users who have logged in have access to the action methods on the SkiCardController. We discuss authentication and authorization in more detail in Chapter 13.

Index Action Method

Start by implementing the Index action method. The index action method does not take in any arguments and is responsible for getting all the ski cards for the current user, converting each ski card to an instance of a SkiCardListViewModel, and passing the list of view models to the View to be rendered as HTML. Based on the standard MVC routing configuration, the URL for this endpoint is /SkiCard.

To retrieve the list of ski cards for the current user, first get the current user's userId from the UserManager instance.

```
var userId = _userManager.GetUserId(User);
```

You can then query for all the ski cards with ApplicationUserId, matching the userId via the DbSet _skiCardContext.SkiCards.

```
_skiCardContext.SkiCards.Where(s => s.ApplicationUserId == userId)
```

Rather than executing this query and iterating over the results to create an instance of the SkiCardListViewModel for each SkiCard, you can define a LINQ projection using the Select method projection to query the database directly for only the properties needed to create SkiCardListViewModels.

```
_skiCardContext.SkiCards
        .Where(s => s.ApplicationUserId == userId)
        .Select(s => new SkiCardListViewModel
        {
            Id = s.Id,
            CardHolderName = s.CardHolderFirstName + " " + s.CardHolderLastName
        });
```

The Select projection, which takes advantages of the deferred query execution feature discussed earlier, specifies that instead of returning instances of the SkiCard class, instead return instances of the SkiCardListViewModel class using property values of the SkiCard class.

The Entity Framework is smart enough to generate a query here that returns only the data needed to populate the SkiCardListViewModel properties.

```
SELECT [s].[Id], ([s].[CardHolderFirstName] + N' ') + [s].[CardHolderLastName]
FROM [SkiCards] AS [s]
WHERE [s].[ApplicationUserId] = @__userId_0
```

Here is the completed Index action method that passes the list of view models to the view. We take a closer look at defining the views using Razor in Chapter 11, "Razor Views."

```
// GET: SkiCard
public async Task<ActionResult> Index()
{
    var userId = _userManager.GetUserId(User);
    var skiCardsViewModels = await _skiCardContext.SkiCards
        .Where(s => s.ApplicationUserId == userId)
        .Select(s => new SkiCardListViewModel
        {
            Id = s.Id,
            CardHolderName = s.CardHolderFirstName + " " + s.CardHolderLastName
        })
        .ToListAsync();

    return View(skiCardsViewModels);
}
```

Async/Await

We use async/await in most of our action methods that involve querying the database or dealing with some external resource. For more details on async and await in ASP.NET applications, check out this excellent video on Channel 9: *https://channel9.msdn.com/Events/aspConf/aspConf/Async-in-ASP-NET.*

Create Action Methods

Next, we implement the Create action methods that are used to create a new ski card. The SkiCard controller contains two Create action methods that both map to the URL SkiCard/Create. The first action method does not take in any arguments and is accessed via the GET method and returns a view containing a form that the user fills in. The second action method takes in a CreateSkiCardViewModel argument and is accessed via the POST http method. The POST action method is responsible for validating the view model values and creating a new SkiCard entity. Upon successfully creating the SkiCard entity, it redirects the user to the Index action method. This pattern is commonly referred to as the Post/Redirect/Get pattern.

A typical GET action method for the create action doesn't contain much logic. In this case, you want to pre-populate the CreateSkiCardViewModel with some default values. In particular, you can assume the PhoneNumber for the card holder is the same as the PhoneNumber for the current user.

You can also assume that if the user doesn't have any existing ski cards, the ski card he is creating is probably for himself. You can prepopulate the FirstName and LastName properties using the current user's first name and last name. Of course, the user is given the opportunity to change these values in the form in case the prepopulated data is incorrect.

```
// GET: SkiCard/Create
public async Task<ActionResult> Create()
{
    var userId = _userManager.GetUserId(User);
    var currentUser = await _userManager.FindByIdAsync(userId);
    var viewModel = new CreateSkiCardViewModel
    {
        CardHolderPhoneNumber = currentUser.PhoneNumber
    };

    //If this is the user's first card, auto-populate the name properties since this card is
    //most likely for that user. Otherwise assume the card is for a family member and leave
    //the name properties blank.
    var hasExistingSkiCards = _skiCardContext.SkiCards.Any(s => s.ApplicationUserId == userId);
    if (!hasExistingSkiCards)
    {
        viewModel.CardHolderFirstName = currentUser.FirstName;
        viewModel.CardHolderLastName = currentUser.LastName;
    }

    return View(viewModel);
}
```

Based on the information provided using the Any method, EF generates a very efficient query for checking whether there are any existing ski cards for the specified user.

```
SELECT CASE
    WHEN EXISTS (
        SELECT 1
        FROM [SkiCards] AS [s]
        WHERE [s].[ApplicationUserId] = @__userId_0)
    THEN CAST(1 AS BIT) ELSE CAST(0 AS BIT)
END
```

The POST method validates the state of the view model by checking ModelState.IsValid. We cover model state validation in more detail in Chapter 11. If the model is valid, a new SkiCard is created with the ApplicationUserId set to the current userId, and the CreatedOn DateTime is set. The remaining properties are set based on the values passed in via the view model instance. Finally, the ski card is added to the SkiCards DbSet and call SaveChangesAsync to save the changes to the database. After the save is complete, redirect the user to the Index action method where he would see the new ski card appear in the list.

```
// POST: SkiCard/Create
[HttpPost]
[ValidateAntiForgeryToken]
public async Task<ActionResult> Create(CreateSkiCardViewModel viewModel)
{
    if (ModelState.IsValid)
```

```
    {
        var userId = _userManager.GetUserId(User);

        SkiCard skiCard = new SkiCard
        {
            ApplicationUserId = userId,
            CreatedOn = DateTime.UtcNow,
            CardHolderFirstName = viewModel.CardHolderFirstName,
            CardHolderLastName = viewModel.CardHolderLastName,
            CardHolderBirthDate = viewModel.CardHolderBirthDate.Value.Date,
            CardHolderPhoneNumber = viewModel.CardHolderPhoneNumber
        };

        _skiCardContext.SkiCards.Add(skiCard);
        await _skiCardContext.SaveChangesAsync();

        return RedirectToAction(nameof(Index));
    }

    return View(viewModel);
}
```

Edit Action Methods

The Edit action methods follow the same post/redirect/get patterns as the Create action methods. The main difference is that the Edit method takes in a single Id parameter that indicates the Id of the ski card that is being edited.

Special care must be taken to ensure that users are not able to edit other user's ski cards. You can do this by adding a filter for the current ApplicationUserId when retrieving ski cards to edit. If no results are found, return NotFound() returns a 404 result to the browser.

```
// GET: SkiCard/Edit/5
public async Task<ActionResult> Edit(int id)
{
    var userId = _userManager.GetUserId(User);

    var skiCardViewModel = await _skiCardContext.SkiCards
        .Where(s => s.ApplicationUserId == userId && s.Id == id)
        .Select(s => new EditSkiCardViewModel
        {
            Id = s.Id,
            CardHolderFirstName = s.CardHolderFirstName,
            CardHolderLastName = s.CardHolderLastName,
            CardHolderBirthDate = s.CardHolderBirthDate,
            CardHolderPhoneNumber = s.CardHolderPhoneNumber
        }).SingleOrDefaultAsync();

    if (skiCardViewModel == null)
    {
        return NotFound();
    }

    return View(skiCardViewModel);
}
```

A projection is used to create an EditSkiCardViewModel for the SkiCard. The EditSkiCard-ViewModel does not contain all of the properties of the SkiCard entity because the ApplicationU-serId and CreatedOn properties are read only and do not appear in the edit form.

The POST action method starts by checking if the model state is valid. If the view model is valid, start by retrieving the specified SkiCard. Again, add a filter to only return ski cards for the current user. If the ski card is not found, return a 404 response using the NotFound() method.

If the specified ski card was found and does belong to the current user, modify the SkiCard properties based on the values passed in to the Edit method via the view model and call SaveChange-sAsync in the ski card context. At this point, the EF change tracker detects any changes that were made and generates an update statement to update the specified record in the database. After the save is complete, redirect the user to the Index action method.

```
// POST: SkiCard/Edit/5
[HttpPost]
[ValidateAntiForgeryToken]
public async Task<ActionResult> Edit(EditSkiCardViewModel viewModel)
{
    if (ModelState.IsValid)
    {
        var userId = _userManager.GetUserId(User);

        var skiCard = await _skiCardContext.SkiCards
                    .SingleOrDefaultAsync(s => s.ApplicationUserId == userId && s.Id ==
viewModel.Id);

        if (skiCard == null)
        {
            return NotFound();
        }

        skiCard.CardHolderFirstName = viewModel.CardHolderFirstName;
        skiCard.CardHolderLastName = viewModel.CardHolderLastName;
        skiCard.CardHolderPhoneNumber = viewModel.CardHolderPhoneNumber;
        skiCard.CardHolderBirthDate = viewModel.CardHolderBirthDate.Value.Date;

        await _skiCardContext.SaveChangesAsync();

        return RedirectToAction(nameof(Index));
    }
    return View(viewModel);
}
```

With the database context and controller in place, the application is ready to process requests related to creating and editing ski cards. Creating the views related to the ski card controller is covered in Chapter 11.

Pass Types

The pass types bounded context contains information about the different types of passes. It consists of three entities: PassType, PassTypeResort, and PassTypePrice. The PassType entity consists of a name and description, as well as other properties describing when and at which resorts the passes can be used. The PassTypePrice entity defines a price for a particular PassType for customers of different ages. For example, a standard day pass has a higher price for an adult, and a lower price for young children.

```csharp
public class PassType
{
    public PassType()
    {
        PassTypeResorts = new List<PassTypeResort>();
        Prices = new List<PassTypePrice>();
    }

    public int Id { get; set; }

    [MaxLength(255)]
    [Required]
    public string Name { get; set; }

    public string Description { get; set; }

    public DateTime ValidFrom { get; set; }

    public DateTime ValidTo { get; set; }

    /// <summary>
    /// Maximum number of times a pass of this type can be activated.
    /// For example a standard day pass would have max activations of 1.
    /// an annual pass might have max activations of 265 (number of days the ski hill is open)
    /// </summary>
    public int MaxActivations { get; set; }

    public List<PassTypeResort> PassTypeResorts { get; set; }

    public List<PassTypePrice> Prices { get; set; }
}

public class PassTypeResort
{
    public int ResortId { get; set; }

    public int PassTypeId { get; set; }
}

public class PassTypePrice

{
    public int Id { get; set; }

    [Range(0, 120)]
```

```
    public int MinAge { get; set; }

    [Range(0, 120)]
    public int MaxAge { get; set; }

    public decimal Price { get; set; }

    public int PassTypeId { get; set; }
}
```

The PassTypeContext contains a single DbSet for the PassTypes. You don't need to define a DbSet for PassTypeResort or PassTypePrice, because all operations on these two entities are done via instances of a PassType entity. EF still recognizes the PassTypeResort and PassTypePrice entity as part of this context because of the relationships defined on the PassType entity.

The primary key for PassTypeResort entity is a composite key that you specify using the ModelBuilder in the context's OnModelCreating method. The model builder can be used to specify additional information about primary keys, foreign keys, property types, and other constraints. In general, the conventions built in EF are sufficient for your entities, but from time to time you do need to override these conventions in the OnModelCreating method.

```
public class PassTypeContext : DbContext
{
    public PassTypeContext(DbContextOptions<PassTypeContext> options)
        :base(options)
    {
    }

    public DbSet<PassType> PassTypes { get; set; }

    protected override void OnModelCreating(ModelBuilder modelBuilder)
    {
        modelBuilder.Entity<PassTypeResort>()
            .HasKey(p => new { p.PassTypeId, p.ResortId });

        base.OnModelCreating(modelBuilder);
    }
}
```

The Alpine Ski House admin application will eventually provide a mechanism for creating pass types. For this sprint the Alpine Ski House team decided to use a migration to insert the basic pass types.

Passes and Validation

The final bounded context implemented in this sprint is the Ski Pass context. Ski passes are related to a ski card in that a pass gives a card holder access to the lifts on a particular resort for a period of time. The period of time and the particular resort depends on the properties of the associated pass type.

The first version of the ski pass bounded context contains three entities: Pass, PassActivation, and Scan. The Pass entity represents a particular pass type (TypeId) that was purchased for a particular ski card (CardId). The Scan entity represents each individual occurrence of a Card being scanned at any of the various locations at a resort. The PassActivation entity represents the usage of a ski pass at a resort on a particular day. A pass activation is created by the pass validation service the first time a ski card is scanned at a lift on a particular day. Each SkiPass is allowed only a certain number of pass activations as defined by the MaxActivations property on the associated PassType entity. Customers are denied access to the ski lift if there are no more pass activations remaining on their ski card.

The patterns for defining these entities classes and their DbContext class should look very familiar at this point.

```
public class Pass
{
    public Pass()
    {
        this.Activations = new List<PassActivation>();
    }

    public int Id { get; set; }

    public int CardId { get; set; }

    public int PassTypeId { get; set; }

    public DateTime CreatedOn { get; set; }

    public List<PassActivation> Activations { get; set; }
}

public class PassActivation
{
    public int Id { get; set; }

    public int PassId { get; set; }

    public int ScanId { get; set; }

    public Scan Scan { get; set; }
}

public class Scan
{
    public int Id { get; set; }

    public int CardId { get; set; }

    public int LocationId { get; set; }

    public DateTime DateTime { get; set; }
}

public class PassContext : DbContext
{
    public PassContext(DbContextOptions<PassContext> options)
        :base(options)
    {
```

```
    }

    public DbSet<Pass> Passes { get; set; }

    public DbSet<PassActivation> PassActivations { get; set; }

    public DbSet<Scan> Scans { get; set; }
}
```

Events and Event Handlers

Customers can purchase passes online via the website, but payment processing and its associated bounded context are out of scope for this sprint. By modeling the interaction between bounded contexts as events, you can implement the logic for creating ski passes without requiring a fully functional payment processing system.

When a purchase is completed, an event is raised by the purchases bounded context. This event will provide information about the types of passes that were purchased for different types of cards. We want the passes bounded context to create new SkiPass entities when this event is raised.

To accomplish this, use a publish-subscribe messaging pattern in which a publisher creates event notifications and publishes them on a message bus. The message bus then notifies any subscribers who are interested in that particular type of event notification. An advantage of using this pattern is that the publisher does not need to know any details about the subscriber or subscribers. The pattern promotes an application structure that it is easy to test, easy to extend, and easy to understand. In this case, it also allows you to implement logic in the pass bounded context without requiring a fully functioning purchase and checkout subsystem.

In this example, we are using the MediatR[1] library to implement this pattern for Project Parsley. MediatR allows for simple, in-process messaging in .NET applications. Events are represented as POCO classes that implement the INotification interface. PurchaseCompleted is the event raised by the purchases bounded context after the checkout process is completed. It contains relevant information about a purchase.

```
public class PurchaseCompleted : INotification
{
    public string UserId { get; set; }
    public DateTime Date { get; set; }
    public string TransactionId { get; set; }
    public decimal TotalCost { get; set; }
    public List<PassPurchased> Passes { get; set; }
}
public class PassPurchased
{
    public int PassTypeId { get; set; }
    public int CardId { get; set; }
    public decimal PricePaid { get; set; }
    public string DiscountCode { get; set; }
}
```

---

[1] https://github.com/jbogard/MediatR

When the purchases bounded context is implemented, it publishes an instance of the PurchaseCompleted class using the MediatR bus.

```
_bus.Publish(purchaseCompletedEvent);
```

In the case of the passes bounded context, we are interested mostly in the PassTypeId and CardId for each of the PassPurchased instances. You can subscribe to the PurchaseCompleted event by creating a class that implements the INotificationHandler<PurchaseCompleted> interface, and by adding your logic to the Handle method.

```
public class AddSkiPassOnPurchaseCompleted : INotificationHandler<PurchaseCompleted>
{
    private readonly PassContext _passContext;
    private readonly IMediator _bus;

    public AddSkiPassOnPurchaseCompleted(PassContext passContext, IMediator bus)
    {
        _passContext = passContext;
        _bus = bus;
    }

    public void Handle(PurchaseCompleted notification)
    {
        var newPasses = new List<Pass>();
        foreach (var passPurchase in notification.Passes)
        {
            Pass pass = new Pass
            {
                CardId = passPurchase.CardId,
                CreatedOn = DateTime.UtcNow,
                PassTypeId = passPurchase.PassTypeId
            };
            newPasses.Add(pass);
        }

        _passContext.Passes.AddRange(newPasses);
        _passContext.SaveChanges();

        foreach (var newPass in newPasses)
        {
            var passAddedEvent = new PassAdded
            {
                PassId = newPass.Id,
                PassTypeId = newPass.PassTypeId,
                CardId = newPass.CardId,
                CreatedOn = newPass.CreatedOn
            };
            _bus.Publish(passAddedEvent);
        }
    }
}
```

The handler starts by creating new instances of the Pass class based on the information passed in the event notification. The new passes are then added to the pass context and the changes are saved to the database. Finally, the handler publishes a `PassAdded` event for each new created pass. We don't currently have any handlers for the `PassAdded` event, but this provides for a simple extension point in the application. Any logic triggered when a pass is added is implemented as a class that implements `IN otificationHandler<PassAdded>`.

An instance of the `PassContext` and `IMediator` are passed into the handler's constructor. This is handled at runtime by ASP.NET Core's built in dependency injection, which we explore in Chapter 14.

Summary

With Entity Framework Core, Microsoft has provided an easy to use API for retrieving data from and saving data to a database. Many of the common pitfalls associated with ORMs can be avoided by splitting larger data models into smaller and more manageable bounded contexts. While EF Core is not the only data access library available for ASP.NET Core, it should be considered as the default option in many applications.

In the next chapter, we will explore the Razor view engine.

## CHAPTER 11

Razor Views

Candice was busy tapping away on her keyboard and humming along to the music playing in her ears. She was in the zone, dialed right in, and working at refactoring her views to take advantage of the bits she was learning in Razor. She didn't hear Chester approach and ask why she was working late, and when he peeked over her shoulder to get her attention, she certainly didn't mean to throw a right jab to Chester's chin, sending him directly to the carpet.

"Oh my goodness!" she yelled. "For the love of Moose Jaw, what are you doing?!"

"It hurts, Candice," Chester replied from the floor. He was looking up at the ceiling tiles. "What was that for?"

"You scared me, you jerk. And I'm a black belt in Taekwondo, you know that. You don't come up on me like that." As she stood up from her desk to help Chester off the floor, she realized the sky outside had darkened and no one else appeared to be in the office. "Geez, what time is it?"

"Owww," he moaned. "It hurts, Candice."

"Yeah, I know. Sorry. Here, get up you oaf." She helped Chester off the floor and sat back down. "End of day I guess, eh? Are you locking up?"

"No, Tim's still here. And, I'm telling Tim on you," he chuckled. "If that leaves a bruise you owe me lunch. What are you still doing around? You'd usually be gone at least an hour ago."

"I know, right? But I'm just geeking out here over these views. I finished up my cards on this sprint a little early, ya know? Danielle and I were hacking through some of this Razor stuff earlier this week, and it's actually pretty cool. It's just, really smart. So I checked with Balázs and he cleared me to take a couple days to clean up the views a little."

"Huh, so our Ruby programmer is coming around? Jumping on the Microsoft boat?"

"Well I wouldn't go that far," Candice laughed. "But yeah, I have to give a little credit here. This is saving a ton of time. Do you remember how we were frustrated with all that markup? You should check this out." She was pulling up the view code for creating ski cards as she asked, "Have you seen these Tag Helpers?"

"No. I mean, yes I remember complaining, but no, I haven't seen the Tag Helpers."

"Okay, well, grab a seat and I'll show you some Razor, then you'll owe me lunch. And then we'll sit around and reminisce about that time you tried to sneak up on me."

Creating Web Sites as a Developer Today

One of the most interesting things about web development today is that we don't write HTML any-more, despite the fact that it's a critical part of the user's in-browser experience. It might sound unbelievable, but it's true. Sure, there are fragments scattered all over the place, but in reality, what are we doing? We write applications that generate HTML, so actually HTML is the byproduct of our work, but not the direct fruits of our labor.

Today, we use a mixture of tools designed to use the context of the user's request and translate that into something the browser can interpret. But because HTML isn't a programming language itself, we certainly can't say that we write our applications in HTML. Even in single-page applications, front-end developers are more likely to be writing templates and binding code than writing pure HTML. We find ourselves using tooling, templating, and languages that are more suited to interoperate with code on the server and the output of all of that, as far as the browser is concerned, is where we find the HTML.

There are many ways to produce HTML output from C# because, after all, HTML is really just a string. You can append strings together to create the HTML.

```
var html = "<html>";
html += "<body>";
html += "<div class=\"exciting\">Hello" + name + "!</div>";
html += "</body>";
html += "</html>";
```

This method however, is ugly and super difficult to maintain. Perhaps we can make use of C# 6's new string interpolation to make things prettier.

```
var html = @$"<html>
                <body>
                    <div class='exciting'>Hello {name}!</div>
                </body>
              </html>";
```

While better than the previous version, it would still be nice to have some way to build HTML that provides IntelliSense and avoids the common pitfalls, like forgetting to HTML encode strings. There is just such a tool: Razor.

Building on Previous Successes and Learnings

It is worth pointing out that there is a rich history of informed development behind the Razor view engine, but it's also a departure from the file-per-page approach of previous efforts. It moves away from the required, explicit notation of "bumblebee syntax" of angle brackets and percentage symbols used in web forms and simplifies reuse of your work when it is used as designed. It was a deliberate choice to build a template markup syntax that allowed C# to be interwoven with HTML and to feel familiar to anyone who was comfortable working in a .NET language. Razor also enables IntelliSense, HTML encoding, and all sorts of other syntactic niceties and provides a base set of helpers to make the view development workflow more fluid than its predecessors.

Razor is maturing and has continued to improve with each release. It was introduced during the era of the MVC 3 Framework and was first released in June of 2010.

Understanding Razor's Role

Razor is the default and only mature view engine in ASP.NET Core MVC, but Razor's definition has become somewhat blurred in meaning due to the variety of amenities it offers projects. When we refer to Razor, we're likely talking about the syntax contained in our view or perhaps the file itself. But Razor also includes a parser and tokenizer to bring the syntax alive, edit-time features to support IntelliSense in Visual Studio, and a C# generator complete with a plethora of so-called chunk generators to build out a C# class file to represent our view.

Some of these things happen at edit time and others happen at runtime, and while all of the pieces are critical to make our edit time experience enjoyable and our runtime experience functional, the syntax side of Razor and a few of its conventions are really what we need to know as developers.

Razor lets you flip back and forth, seamlessly and almost magically, between HTML and C# as you create a view. It implicitly understands the context of HTML elements and the rules of the typed C# language, but it also lets you set explicit boundaries to denote which parts are markup and which parts are code. You can template out your pages, include optional parts set upon conditions that you create, or surface to the view.

Ultimately the intended purpose of Razor is to provide you with a method of controlling the way the view is rendered, an important fact that should not be lost on you. Views are not the place to store business rules and validation. You should not be initiating connections, handling events, or going multiple levels deep into conditional logic to decide if part of your view should be rendered or if you should make a call out to a service. Such code becomes brittle, hard to maintain, and isolates part of your business logic into something that is difficult to test. Here's some advice from a key contributor on the Razor project:

> Razor is just a language. Try not to put too much logic into the view itself. Abstract that out into components and modules if you can. -Taylor Mullen, SDE on the Razor Team at Microsoft

So, there it is: keep it simple. While Razor allows you to do some incredible and complex things, the idea with Razor is actually to help you develop views that are simple, easy to read, and functional when given the correct inputs.

Mastering Razor Essentials

You'll remember from Chapter 3, "Models, Views, and Controllers" that the responsibility of a view is to play a part in generating the user experience that is delivered to the client. A view often contains HTML that, in turn, can hold references to CSS and JavaScript, but you can't directly look at a view in your browser. Remembering that your view is being turned into a C# class is perhaps a good way to think about it, knowing that if you're not writing in C# code, what you are writing is being turned into C# code.

Peeking Behind the Curtain

Arguably, the internals of the Razor view engine are not visible in your project. Indeed, it's the kind of thing that many developers do not require a deep understanding of, however, if we have a look at what's going on back stage, we can remove some of the "magic" that appears to be happening. If you would rather leave the magician alone and not force him to reveal his trick, this section is not for you!

You've already seen throughout this book, and likely in the companion sample project, a number of views and the code they contain. If you've experimented a little and broken a view, and that remember experimentation is highly recommended, perhaps you've also seen an error message with a line number. If you stop and think about that, it's a little weird, right? You actually see something similar to Figure 11-1, which appears to be a compiler error in your view.

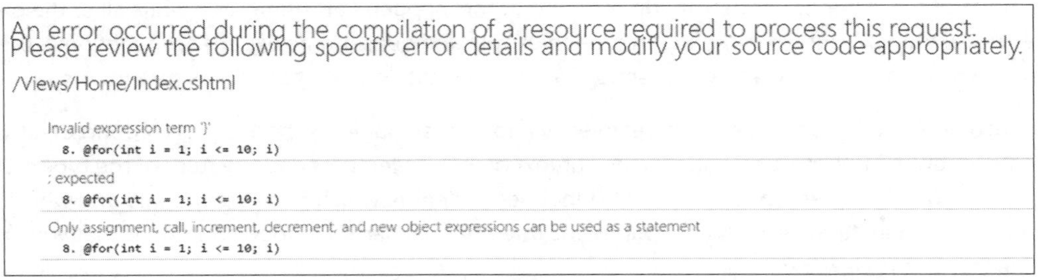

An error occurred during the compilation of a resource required to process this request. Please review the following specific error details and modify your source code appropriately.

/Views/Home/Index.cshtml

    Invalid expression term ')'
       8. @for(int i = 1; i <= 10; i)

    ; expected
       8. @for(int i = 1; i <= 10; i)

    Only assignment, call, increment, decrement, and new object expressions can be used as a statement
       8. @for(int i = 1; i <= 10; i)

FIGURE 11-1 An example of an error in a Razor view compilation

The example compilation error shows a number of suspected reasons for the error, with the guilty party here being a missing increment operator on the i variable of the for statement. The compiler reveals the correct line number as the source of the error from our view, not from the generated C# class view, because that would carry a lot less meaning for developers.

Here's how that works. When your view is parsed, it is evaluated and broken down into parts. Some of those parts are already in C#, while others are chopped up into bits of text and inserted into a structure that becomes a C# class. Take for example the code in Listing 11-1, where we have a simple block of code in a Razor view file that alternates between C# and HTML and outputs a message.

LISTING 11-1 Example Razor syntax with C# code from the fictional SampleView.cshtml view

```
@for(int i = 1; i <= 5; i++ ) {
    <p>This is index #@(i)</p>
    i += 1;
}
```

In order for us to get meaningful information from the debugger at runtime, there has to be a lot going on behind the scenes. Listing 11-2 shows what part of that block of Razor view code from Listing

11-1 turns into after being parsed. Of course, this is not a complete listing. We have not included the using statements, namespaces, class declarations, or function names because these are quite verbose, but this is the core representation of the Razor code from Listing 11-1.

LISTING 11-2 Part of the generated C# class from a Razor view

```
        #line 1 "SampleView.cshtml"
  for(int i = 1; i <= 5; i++ ) {

#line default
#line hidden

        Instrumentation.BeginContext(19, 4, true);
        WriteLiteral("    <p>This is index #");
        Instrumentation.EndContext();
        Instrumentation.BeginContext(29, 1, false);
#line 2 "SampleView.cshtml"
            Write(i);

#line default
#line hidden
        Instrumentation.EndContext();
        Instrumentation.BeginContext(31, 6, true);
        WriteLiteral("</p>\r\n");
        Instrumentation.EndContext();
#line 3 "SampleView.cshtml"
  }
```

You can see evidence of the native C# code directly in the output, as well as where the class generator makes calls to `WriteLiteral` to add the HTML to the document. There are also calls to begin and end instrumentation contexts, but perhaps the most interesting thing here is the use of the `#line` compiler directives to hint at the file of origin and the line number that the code is mapped to. This is what allows the compilation error to surface at runtime with information appropriate to our view.

That's right, it happens at runtime, and in another departure from previous versions of the MVC Framework, Razor views are compiled to C# classes in memory as a string. The string is passed to the MVC compilation service that compiles the view out into another in-memory artifact, the view's own assembly, and the runtime then loads the result into memory.

> **Note** At the time of this writing, there aren't many facilities to support build-time compilation of Razor views in ASP.NET Core MVC without a few workarounds and heavy lifting. This means that views can't be rendered down to classes and put in separate assemblies that can be loaded from outside the project, but the ASP.NET team has said that they are working on a solution for folks who need this capability.

As part of an assembly the view can be used like any other class. When requested implicitly by using `View()` on a controller or explicitly by name, a view locator service resolves the underlying type and invokes the generated method asynchronously.

We understand what happens behind the scenes a little better when we've finished our view and we attempt to run it. Now let's rewind a little bit and review the things we need to know to build our views out and, in particular, the constructs we can use to control the view engine and fully expose our view for the .NET class it is.

Writing Expressions with Razor Syntax

By default, Razor assumes you're working in HTML which is great if all you're doing is writing markup. Even if most folks don't understand that there is an application running behind the scenes, they still have the expectation that something relevant is in front of them. If we want to start interleaving the static parts with more meaningful, contextual information that makes the page relevant to our users, we're going to need to let Razor know it's time to write some C#. Consider the following statement:

```
<p>Today is @DateTime.Today.ToString("D"). What a wonderful day.</p>
```

The previous statement generates the following resultant HTML:

```
<p>Today is October 13, 2016. What is a wonderful day.</p>
```

We open by using straight HTML, but then we inject a formatted date using the @ character to let Razor know we've starting writing code. What's interesting is that we follow the call to `ToString` with a period, but the parser is able to determine that we're not trying to invoke a method or access a property. We call this type of code an implicit expression.

When an implicit call doesn't work, for instance when we're trying to perform a calculation or lead our code with a non-obvious C# element, we can instead use an explicit expression like so:

```
<p>Half of 10 is @(10 / 2).</p>
```

The output from that is expectedly:

```
<p>Half of 10 is 5.</p>
```

To create an explicit expression, you have to wrap the code you're writing with parentheses, and the closing parenthesis is the signal that you intend to switch back to HTML. For both the implicit and explicit methods, you can only use one expression. If you want more code in place, you'll likely prefer to use a code block.

Switching to Code

Previously in Listing 11-1, we had a look at some code that contained a `for` statement, in which we flipped into HTML. The block of code as a whole was wrapped in a @{ . . } character sequence, which is referred to as a code block. Let's now consider a bit of an expanded example in Listing 11-3 where we introduce more code.

LISTING 11-3 An extended code block with additional C# statements in it

```
@for (int i = 1; i <= 5; i++)
{
    <p>This is index #@(i)</p>
    for (int j = 0; j < 10; j++)
    {
        if (j >= 5)
        {
            <p>Multiplied by the inner index, the product is @(j * i).</p>
        }
    }
    i += 1;
}
```

What is great here is that our code is very fluid and we are still able to move back and forth between HTML markup and C# statements. What is different inside a code block, however, is that the parser expects C# rather than HTML because C# is outside of the code block. The parser is stricter here because it has to be. Entering an HTML tag is obvious to the parser because <p> is not valid C# code, but to get out of the HTML block we need to explicitly end the tag. HTML does not require that we have a closing tag, and outside of a code block in a Razor file that is still true, but if we're going to open a tag inside a code block, we must also remember to help Razor out and close it.

Again, moving back into HTML is fairly easy because we just have to wrap our content in a tag, like the <p> tag in the code previously discussed. Because the Razor view engine's expectation is that C# is the default inside a code block however, it's important to note that it would no longer be valid to have plain text standing alone without markup, as shown in Listing 11-4.

LISTING 11-4 Invalid character content inside a code block

```
@if(true)
{
    Hello.
}
```

That code is not valid inside a code block because `Hello.` is not a valid C# statement. But...it almost could be! If by chance `Hello` or any other set of characters also appeared as a class in our application, there is no way for the parser to know if we're talking about the string literal "Hello." or if we're trying to access a property on the `Hello` class. This might seem like a bit of a predicament if you're trying to add content inside of a code block, but there's a solution to that as well by switching to explicit markup mode.

Explicitly Using Markup

We can fix the code from Listing 11-4 by wrapping our friendly greeting in a `<text>` tag. Here in Listing 11-5, we demonstrate two ways to get the parser to interpret the message the way we intend for it to.

LISTING 11-5 Examples of correctly denoting text in a code block

```
@if(true)
{
    <text>Hello.</text>
}

@if(true)
{
    @:Hello.
}
```

The `<text>` tag is part of the Razor syntax and is not some newly devised HTML markup. `<text>` tags are handled server-side and are removed from the response that is sent to the client. Everything that you put inside the tag is rendered as though you were outside of the code block. `<text>` tags can span multiple lines.

In a way, you can think of the `@:` character sequence as shorthand for `<text>` tags, the single difference being that it only instructs the parser to treat the remaining text on the line as text. If you spill over to a second line, the parser again assumes C# as the default for anything you write.

Razor Parser Control Cheat Sheet

In addition to the basics that we've covered so far, there are a few other gems that you should know about so that you can put them to use. We've included them altogether here in Table 11-1 in a handy cheat sheet.

TABLE 11-1 Razor Parser Control Cheat Sheet

Syntax	Meaning
@	Implicit expression causing an inline switch to C# code, continued until the first non-C# characters are encountered
@@	Escape sequence for the @ character, not needed when working with email addresses as Razor understands the structure of an email address and implicitly treats it as text
@()	Explicit expression, the code in the parentheses is interpreted as C#
@{ ... }	Explicit code block, everything in the braces is assumed to be C# unless you use another control sequence to switch the parser back to text

`<text>...</text>`	A server-side tag that is not output to the client, in which anything found by the parser is rendered as text in the response
`@:`	Explicit text mode from this character sequence forward, terminated at the end of the current line
`//` `/* ... */`	C# style comments, valid only when the parser is in C# mode and treated as literal output when in text mode
`@* ... *@`	Razor style comments, any contents of which are ignored by the parser and it is not rendered in the final output in the client response

One thing to remember about most of these flow control statements is that you're only instructing Razor to prefer one mode or the other. You're still free to switch between modes by nesting these sequences together. The recommendation here, however, is similar to what we'd suggest for when you're writing code: as your view complexity increases, so too does the effort required to maintain it. If you find you're not able to do something easily within a view, it might be best to explore moving some of the logic to your view model, a view component or even JavaScript where, in any of those cases, it can be properly tested.

> **Note** The ASP.NET Monsters got to sit down for a chat with Taylor Mullen, one of the Software Developer Engineers who has contributed a good portion of the code in the Razor view engine in ASP.NET Core MVC. Check out the episode on Microsoft Channel 9 where the Monsters mash with Taylor about the Razor view engine, located at *https://channel9.msdn.com/Series/aspnetmonsters/ASPNET-Monsters-59-Razor-with-Taylor-Mullen.*

Bringing in More C# Features

There's more to Razor than just the basic syntax features. We'll explore a few of those here and later in the book, particularly in Chapter 19, "Reusable Components," and Chapter 21, "Extensibility."

Using C# Types in Your Views

As with every other block of C# code, you need to bring into context the namespaces and types that you want to work with by means of a `using` statement. This can include types that you have defined in your assembly or types that are brought in through dependencies on external libraries.

```
@using AlpineSkiHouse.Models
```

To help keep your code organized, you should place your `using` statements at the top of the file, but this is not required because all using statements are hoisted up into the start of the generated class anyway. In a bit of a departure from C#, you are able to litter your `using` statements throughout your code, but due to readability and maintainability concerns it's not wise to do so.

Defining a Model

Razor has the concept of "strongly-typed views," meaning that your view is aware of the type of object it represents. This allows you to easily interweave your own model's properties into the view. First, you have to signal to Razor the type you want to use.

```
@model SkiCard
```

You can then access properties of your model throughout the page.

```
Welcome to your Ski Card summary, @Model.CardHolderFirstName.
```

This is where understanding the flow control of the Razor parser comes in handy. The observant reader sees the implicit expression in the middle of a block of text and knows that the view engine handles it accordingly.

While you can define the model type that you want to use in the view itself, it is the controller that ultimately instantiates your model, or has it instantiated, and passes it to the view. It's also the controller's responsibility to ensure that the type passed in to the view matches what is expected by the view, otherwise you get an exception at runtime.

Using View Data

If we are to maintain a level of pragmatism in our development workflow, we have to accept that the academically "right" way to do things might not be right for our particular scenario. While it is easy to preach that "everything should be strongly-typed" and that "view models are the correct way to pass data from your controller to your view," in practice there are other realities that set it. Take, for example, the title that is rendered out in the header of a webpage. What is the correct way to set it? Surely it's not some kind of template, as the title could change from page to page. Setting it in the view seems right, but what if the view is dynamic and needs to render different titles for each type of item being viewed? This starts to sound like, "well, yeah, we need to have a view model where the properties can be set on the controller and passed to the view." To solve that, you might then require a view model for every page. But, what about if the view model is like the SkiCardViewModel type? The page title has nothing to do with the view model of a SkiCardViewModel, so why would we put it in there? And in other scenarios, such as in the use of a model like an IEnumerable<SkiCardViewModel>, where is the best place to store the title then?

The point is that there might be no right place after all, at least not for every situation. You can likely work with another developer to find a good solution that works for you both, but then the next developer walks into the room and it's wrong again. Everyone's opinions differ, and that's okay. The beauty of the language and the framework is that we're allowed to have different points of view. In the same unassuming way, ASP.NET Core MVC maintains the idea of View Data that can be accessed through a couple of properties without the use of a strongly-typed object. This facilitates an alternate way to store data in the controller and retrieve it in the view without having to hardwire things into place. Especially in the case when you legitimately only have one thing to forward, such as with the title of a page, you can't really go wrong with using Razor's view data mechanisms.

In its simplest form, you're going to do something like the following in your controller action:

```
ViewData["Message"] = "Thanks for reaching out.";
```

And you're going to retrieve the data like so in your view:

```
<h3>@ViewData["Message"]</h3>
```

The view data is backed by an IDictionary<string, object>, so you can store whatever you want in it. It works for simple types like int and string, as well as for more complex objects like SkiCardViewModel. Overlaid onto that dictionary is another mechanism for accessing the view data in a dynamic property of the view called the ViewBag. By using the ViewBag you can access any of the keys of the dictionary as though they were properties:

```
<h3>@ViewBag.Message</h3>
```

For both usages, if there is no entry present in the dictionary for the key you provide, you do not receive an error message when you attempt to display view data in this way.

If you try to access the value, say to put the object in the text of the page, you find that Razor treats it much like a Console.WriteLine would in that it invokes the object's ToString() method. To access the properties of an object, you are better served by creating a view-scoped variable in a code block at the top of the view that can be used throughout, like so:

```
@{
    var skiCard = (SkiCardViewModel)ViewData["SkiCard"];
}
```

Remember, Razor is just going to end up being C#, so you are still subjected to things like null reference exceptions and casting conversions if you're not careful. And while view data can be an easy way to shuttle data around, it's time to talk about a few best practices regarding the use of view data.

First of all, the previous example that stores a complex object in view data was to illustrate how casting can work in a view, just like anywhere else you would use a cast. You might find a reasonable use case for this, but the preferred way to pass a full view model from the controller to the view is obviously through the use of the @model syntax. If your page is composed of many parts with different view models to support each part, you might want to look at View Components, which we cover in Chapter 19.

Secondly, a good way to infer if you should be using view data is to think about if the data you are storing is about the subject of the model or if it's a concern of the view. Just as storing the view model in the view data isn't a good approach, neither is breaking down properties from an object and storing them independently. The following is another example of what you should avoid:

```
ViewData["SlopeName"] = "Knee Bender";
ViewData["Altitude"] = "3317m";
ViewData["SnowDepth"] = "12dm";
```

While we hate to keep showing code that is outside the bounds of what you should be doing, we also think it's important to know what it looks like so that you can identify what can become problematic in your code. In the example code block, it's not reasonable to assume that the depth of snow on a particular slope is a concern of the view in terms of controlling flow or setting the title in the <head> of the HTML. Therefore, it would be wise to compose a view model that exposes those properties and again moves them to the view via the @model.

Finally, the best advice is just to make reserved use of the view data. View data was kept in to help keep a balance between functionality, maintainability, and the friction of getting simple data out and into a webpage.

Working with Layouts

Since the very early days of the web, we've been dealing with the problem of repeated page elements, things like headers and footers that are relevant to a particular page, but are also branding elements that were designed to appear on all pages of a site. These elements are easy enough to code once, but if they are copied-and-pasted around from page to page, they become difficult to keep in sync. Early frameworks allowed us to include these components as static elements in our pages.

As the web evolved, so too did the needs of web-based applications. Include files to cover aspects like headers and footers were no longer enough to handle more complicated designs, such as those that might be similar to what Figure 11-2 shows. Shopping carts, recommended product lists, and user account management all need to render dynamic content based on the state of the user's current experience and so the template had to mature.

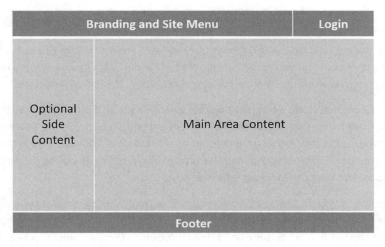

FIGURE 11-2 A template with interactive, replacable components

In ASP.NET 2.0, WebForms gave us page templating via a concept called Master Pages that allowed us to compose a page using an outer template and then fill it in through nested pages. Those pages had special indicators and custom server-side tags that wrapped content and made sure that it was injected in the correct place.

In Razor, things operate a little differently because the view is rendered before the layout. This means that you have the ability to set values, like the title of the page, through view data properties and then use those values in the layout. Let's now dive into what kind of code you would need to represent the design surface that we see in Figure 11-2.

Foundations of Layouts

Let's quickly look at how layouts and views fit together. Remember from Chapter 3 that a controller is able to return a view by convention using the name of the action method, or it can explicitly request a particular view by name. The view itself doesn't have to contain much layout nor does it have to specify a layout, though you might choose to do both. If these things are missing, however, we have to figure out where to get them from.

Putting together a templating engine is non-trivial, so to manage most considerations around how to set up defaults and where things are located, a set of conventions was created to make layouts work in Razor. The first order of business was solving the starting point to pull templates together. Thus, the Views folder has a file called _ViewStart.cshtml in the root that allows you to set a template to be used in code. In the default project template, the layout selection is going to be fairly trivial, something like the following:

```
@{
    Layout = "_Layout";
}
```

This simple assignment lets Razor know that we are using the file called _Layout.cshtml as our template. The next convention is that the use of the _ViewStart.cshtml is tied to the location of the views. Any folder that has a _ViewStart.cshtml uses that as the starting point. Any folder that does not have a _ViewStart.cshtml uses the one from its closest ancestor in the tree, working back to the root of the Views folder if required.

As we're all now painfully aware, Razor is just C# code and the _ViewStart.cshtml is not exempt. In this file you can write code, manipulate view data, or determine which layout to use as the default based on a configuration setting or piece of business logic. The layout set here is used for any view that is rendered, but you have the option to override that view either on your controller or in the view itself.

In Listing 11-6 we see the contents of a nearly-barebones layout, just enough to sketch out the essentials to meet our goals from Figure 11-2. Working from the outside in, we have the DOCTYPE definition, and then the outer <html> tag that contains both the <head> and the <body> tag.

LISTING 11-6 A sample of a layout file using multiple Razor features

```
<!DOCTYPE html>
<html>
<head>
    <title>@ViewData["Title"] - My Site</title>
    <link href="~/css/site.css" rel="stylesheet" />
</head>
<body>
    @await Html.PartialAsync("_Toolbar")
    <div class="container body-content">
        @RenderSection("sidebar", required: false)
        @RenderBody()
        <hr />
    </div>
    @Html.Partial ("_Footer")
    @RenderSection("scripts", required: false)
</body>
</html>
```

The `<title>` element includes the only Razor feature in the `<head>`, which is an implicit expression that we've seen a few times now. There's nothing preventing you from putting more in to the `<head>`. In fact, we'll circle back here later in the chapter for a great example on ways to build from this starting point when we talk about Tag Helpers.

The most important of the remaining features in use here is the call to RenderBody, but don't worry, we'll talk about `PartialAsync` and `RenderSection` as well. RenderBody is the location in the document where Razor renders the requested view.

If you don't call RenderBody, you receive an error at runtime unless you make an explicit call to IgnoreBody, in which case the view requested by the controller is not rendered.

> **Note** Even when you call IgnoreBody it's important to note that the execution still passes through your view. While the result of the view is not returned in the response to the client, any resources that would normally be created, services that would be invoked, View Components that would be executed, or any operation that would otherwise cause a side effect still run. If IgnoreBody turns out to be the right path for your solution, be mindful of any unwanted side effects, which might include server resource utilization, logging, and connections to databases.

Including Sections from Views

If we can think of a view as a class, we can think of a section as a function that is invoked from the calling parent. The parent defines where the sections are, and the children choose what goes inside. In the case of Listing 11-6, the parent would be the layout and it would be up to the views to implement the sections. Any section that is defined is required by default and Razor ensures that it is present in any view based on the layout where the section is defined.

It's relatively easy to include a section in your view. After defining the section in your layout, as we have done in Listing 11-6, you need to add the following code to your view:

```
@section sidebar {
    <p>There are currently @cart.Count items in your cart.</p>
    <nav>
        <a asp-action="index" asp-controller="cart">View My Cart</a>
        <a asp-action="index" asp-controller="checkout">Check Out and Pay</a>
    </nav>
}
```

Regardless of where this section appears in the view, it is rendered in the location where the section is defined in the layout. A section is just like any other part of the page and you can flow seamlessly from Razor's text mode to code mode as you need.

The sections we've defined so far live in our layout. You can define sections at various levels, but they do not work "up" the chain. For instance, a parent in the view hierarchy does not know about the sections that children define. You can define a section in a layout and implement it in a view, but if you define a section in, say a partial view, you won't be able to access it in the layout.

Sections that appear in views must be defined in the layout that the view is rendered to, unless you explicitly ignore the section in the layout with a call to IgnoreSection("sectionName"). The code located in any ignored section is not invoked. This might be useful if you want to build a layout that has a required section for every page, but is conditionally excluded based on some criteria you define, perhaps predicated on the absence or presence of a signed in user.

Defining and Consuming Partial Views

Partial views are a good way to share a small part of a template or user experience between different views in your application. You can think of partials as a child to the view that they are rendered from. They are akin to the WebForms User Control feature and are similar in ways to the include files that we had in the early days of web applications. They are a good way to break down an otherwise complex layout or feature and isolate the complexity away from the parent document. You can include a partial in your view with the syntax we saw before:

```
@Html.Partial("_Footer")
```

A partial view is just a view fragment. It shares the same cshtml file extension that normal views have and is located using the same strategies that you would use to locate views. While it is not required, most folks tend to prefix the names of their partial views with an underscore so that they are a little easier to spot in the view folders.

As with a full view, a partial view can be strongly-typed with a model definition, the mechanics of which are identical to views as we saw previously. There is no controller in play when we're working with a partial however, so the model is passed into the partial from the view.

```
@Html.Partial("_VolumeBarChart", Model.DailyRiderVolumeData)
```

This method of using of partials and view models can be extremely useful in situations where you can leverage a composite view model to craft something like a dashboard of reports.

> **Note** Partial views should be kept simple. If what you are trying to display through a partial needs access to services or the backing of any amount of business logic, you should consider using View Components, which will be visited in Chapter 19, "Reusable Components."

Partial views operate in a bit of a different way from the other view features in Razor. One difference is that partials don't get to participate in things like sections that are defined in the layout, so you can't define a scripts section to include JavaScript particular to the partial in the rendered page. Another difference is that when a partial is rendered, it is given a copy of the view data, but not a reference to the view data, so there is no way to change or set values in the view's main view data dictionary. This means you aren't able to set a page title through the wiring you defined in your template from a partial view. Finally, partials aren't rendered inside of a layout because they expect to be part of a view that does so already. These choices are actually deliberate to keep partials simple, straightforward, and speedy to render.

Enhancing Views with Advanced Razor Functionality

It's likely already obvious that Razor isn't a single purpose or feature limited view engine. There are some great new features in ASP.NET Core MVC that give developers even greater flexibility over how views are constructed and that add capabilities to our tool chest.

Injecting Services into a View

When many developers heard that there was going to be a form of dependency injection built into the view engine for ASP.NET Core MVC there were protests, petitions, and several class action lawsuits filed in the state of Washington.

Okay, that didn't happen, but folks were legitimately concerned that developers were bleeding into territory where business logic and service access were dripping into views, allowing views to start doing things that controllers and models should be doing. After all, what is the point of a framework that separates the models from the controllers from the views if they can all act in the same way?

But if you stop to consider what is at play, you realize that services are injected for you behind the scenes all the time already. Things like HTML helpers and the URL helper are there behind the scenes and are available for you to use to perform actions like resolving controller and action routes. Again, this is about achieving balance and finding the tool that's fit for the right purpose. This isn't an "instead of view models" or "instead of controllers" scenario, this is a "both, and" scenario that provides a way to limit the amount of work you need to do on each controller. It also helps to ensure that a service is created in one place, that it can be properly tested, and that it can be used reliably throughout our views.

You can use any service registered in the services container in a view by using either a combination of a using statement and an inject statement, or an inject statement with a fully qualified service name.

```
@using AlpineSkiHouse.Services
@inject ICsrInformationService customerServiceInfo
```

Here, we're injecting an instance of an `ICsrInformationService` and naming it `customerServiceInfo`. We can then use the `customerServiceInfo` variable anywhere in our view.

```
Call us at @customerServiceInfo.CallCenterPhoneNumber today!
```

> **Note** You can find more information about putting services in the container in Chapter 14, "Dependency Injection."

Service injection can, however, be used incorrectly. The point here is that something like a partial view might require information about some other aspect of the user's session, such as their profile or what is in their shopping cart. We wouldn't want to pollute the view model with information about our upcoming events with that kind of information, and it would be frustrating to have to put that logic in every controller. On the flip side of the service injection coin, it would be a terrible misuse of the feature to inject a database context into a view to fetch records on the fly. But, by injecting a service that can retrieve the data we still maintain a good separation of responsibility, you are still able to isolate and individually test services, and you don't have to expose our controllers or view models to concerns that are unrelated to the task at hand.

Working with Tag Helpers

The latest version of Razor brings us the powerful Tag Helper feature, which is a way to introduce server-side processing without muddying up our HTML. The ability to express server-side processing through elements that appear similar to HTML is not new to Razor, as you can see in Listing 11-7 with a sample of code from a WebForms project. In this example, Web Controls are used as placeholders for HTML `<input>`, `<label>`, and `<span>` tags.

LISTING 11-7 Using Web Controls in WebForms to render a required field

```
<div class="form-group">
    <asp:Label runat="server" AssociatedControlID="Email" CssClass="col-md-2 control-
label">Email</asp:Label>
    <div class="col-md-10">
        <asp:TextBox runat="server" ID="Email" CssClass="form-control" TextMode="Email" />
        <asp:RequiredFieldValidator runat="server" ControlToValidate="Email"
            CssClass="text-danger" ErrorMessage="The email field is required." />
    </div>
</div>
```

In WebForms, we had to mark every control with the appropriate prefix. Most controls that Microsoft provides use `asp:` by default, but third party vendors can create their own. We can create our own, or we can modify the prefix and point it at whichever namespace we want to. We also had to include the `runat="server"` attribute on each control to ensure proper processing.

But the thing that trips up designers, adding a learning curve for newcomers to ASP.NET, and providing a source of frustration for many is the fact that these placeholders are just placeholders and not actual HTML. There are very few options that allow a designer to tweak the page, and every draft of a webpage that comes from a designer needs massive restructuring to enable server-side capabilities. Even the attribute used to set CSS classes on the element differ from the corresponding valid HTML. You must set aside your knowledge of a broadly known syntax and pick up something that won't work with the rest of the industry.

Contrast that experience with the code in Listing 11-8, where Tag Helpers come into play with Razor. The syntax is much more fluid, the code is valid HTML even with the custom attributes, and we clearly see what elements are in use. We don't have to learn what components become a `<label>` or a `<span>`, and we can again use the element attributes, such as for the CSS class assignment.

LISTING 11-8 Using Tag Helpers in Razor to render a required field

```
<div class="form-group">
    <label asp-for="Email" class="col-md-2 control-label"></label>
    <div class="col-md-10">
        <input asp-for="Email" class="form-control" />
        <span asp-validation-for="Email" class="text-danger"></span>
    </div>
</div>
```

This is Razor flexing its smarts, and there are a couple of powerful things going on here. First, none of the Tag Helper attributes will be rendered as-are to the client. Things like `asp-for` are helping to both give context to the Tag Helper and assistance to you as a developer. That custom attribute is able to interact with Visual Studio to provide IntelliSense behind the scenes, as you can see in Figure 11-3. In this case, the `label` Tag Helper is aware of the view's model and is coded to accept a property of the model. This allows suggestions based on the model's type, and the public properties are available to this sort of "binding" syntax. IntelliSense is integrated well enough to recognize enum properties and provide appropriate auto-completion options.

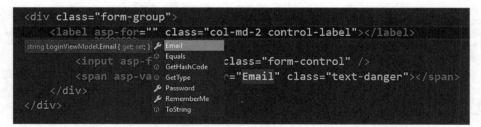

FIGURE 11-3 Visual Studio IntelliSense for Razor Tag Helpers

After the server-side execution is complete, the final result of the code in Listing 11-8 results in what is shown in Listing 11-9. All of the Tag Helper attributes have been stripped, and the HTML elements are now decorated with the attributes they need to provide the desired user experience. The `<input>`

element is decorated with the client-side validation messages and the `<label>` and `<span>` are set up in their relationship with the `<input>`.

LISTING 11-9 The HTML output from a form created with Tag Helpers

```html
<div class="form-group">
    <label class="col-md-2 control-label" for="Email">Email</label>
    <div class="col-md-10">
        <input class="form-control" type="email" data-val="true" data-val-email="The Email
field is not a valid e-mail address." data-val-required="The Email field is required."
id="Email" name="Email" value="">
        <span class="text-danger field-validation-valid" data-valmsg-for="Email" data-
valmsg-replace="true"></span>
    </div>
</div>
```

If you don't care for the implicit use of Tag Helpers, you can also opt to use a more explicit syntax. One of the concerns that arose from the development community is the complete inverse of the designer and newcomer argument: "How does my development team know which code is part of the HTML and which is part of the Tag Helper?" In fact, it was a thread that spanned over half a year and generated nearly 200 comments from the community.

> **Tip** The way that the ASP.NET team exposed the design of Tag Helpers and interacted with the community to bring Tag Helpers to a point of balance is a great example of how they are taking open source seriously. Developers are encouraged to take part in the discussion, fork the repo, and make contributions to the codebase at *https://github.com/aspnet/mvc*.

To enable the explicit prefix, you need to add the following line of code to your view.

```
@tagHelperPrefix "th:"
```

You can also enable this syntax at the _ViewImports level, which requires that all views use the same notation. Any HTML element that you want to use a Tag Helper in now has to be prefixed. The same code from Listing 11-8 is revisited in Listing 11-10 with the prefix in place.

LISTING 11-10 Form elements rendered with Tag Helpers using a prefix

```html
<div class="form-group">
    <th:label asp-for="Email" class="col-md-2 control-label"></label>
    <div class="col-md-10">
        <th:input asp-for="Email" class="form-control" />
        <th:span asp-validation-for="Email" class="text-danger"></span>
    </div>
</div>
```

Tag Helpers, as illustrated so far, demonstrate some of the benefits over the Web Controls in that they are lightweight, unobtrusive, and interact easily with the tags they influence. If you prefer the verbosity of the explicit prefix syntax, you can add that back. Tag Helpers are limited in scope and reach and can be combined on a single element to compose a more dynamic result without running the risk of interfering with other parts of your page.

There is also another case for using Tag Helpers where HTML elements are not the target, but the artifact of the Tag Helper used. Take for example the environment Tag Helper in Listing 11-11, which is used to generate the appropriate <link> element based on the current execution environment. In this instance, the Tag Helper's primary function is to remove the complexity of arriving at the result from the view. We don't need to know how to access configuration or write logic in the view to determine which stylesheet should be used.

LISTING 11-11 Using the environment tag helper to choose a stylesheet

```
<environment names="Development">
    <link rel="stylesheet" href="~/css/site.css" />
</environment>
<environment names="Staging,Production">
    <link rel="stylesheet" href="~/css/site.min.css" asp-append-version="true" />
</environment>
```

When used correctly, Tag Helpers add value by abstracting away the complexities of the view from the developer. They are aware of their context and have access to the view's model, which gives them rich capabilities. You can build your own Tag Helpers as well. If you want to find out more about how to do so, be sure to check out the Custom Tag Helpers topic in Chapter 19.

Help from Visual Studio

Visual Studio does a very good job of helping you identify which parts of your view are using Tag Helpers. Figure 11-4 shows a distinction between the tags that were not activated as Tag Helpers and those that were.

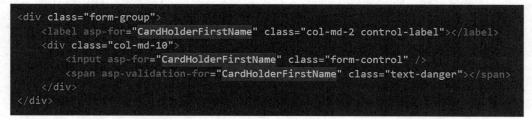

FIGURE 11-4 Tag Helper Syntax highlighting in Visual Studio

In the Visual Studio dark theme, the outer `<div>` in Figure 11-4 is not modified by a tag helper, but the `<label>` immediately inside of it is. While the `<div>` takes on a blue coloring, the `<label>` is a delightful teal. Likewise, HTML attributes like the `class` of the `<div>` are a lighter shade of blue, whereas `asp-for` on the `<label>` is recognized as a server-side attribute of the tag helper. The `asp-for` attribute is called a bound attribute and is not rendered in the final output to the client, whereas the unbound attributes like `class` just flow through as HTML.

Avoiding Duplication in Your Views

There are going to be namespaces from your project that have a high level of reuse. Rather than adding using statements to the top of every view, you can leverage _ViewImports to bring those namespaces into every view in your application. The same is true for services that you inject into views as well as Tag Helpers. Here's an example of a few statements that appear in the Alpine Ski House _ViewImports in the root of the Views folder to allow the models and Tag Helpers the team has created to be used throughout the views:

```
@using AlpineSkiHouse
@using AlpineSkiHouse.Models
@addTagHelper *, AlpineSkiHouse.Web
```

_ViewImports follows the same inheritance model as other view engine components. All views in the folder share the statements contained within. If you want to override the settings from a parent folder you can do so by adding another _ViewImports in the child folder. You also have the option to override service definitions.

Using Alternate View Engines

Before we close the door on the conversation about Razor, we should probably mention that you don't have to use Razor if you don't want to. You can write your own view engine by implementing IViewEngine should you fancy such a venture, or perhaps you could blend in a view engine from another framework and use that instead.

```
services.AddMvc().AddViewOptions(options =>
    {
        options.ViewEngines.Clear();
        options.ViewEngines.Add(MyIViewEngine);
    });
```

In the early days of ASP.NET MVC there were a number of alternative view engines that gained some traction. Most of them have fallen by the wayside since the adoption of Razor however.

Of course, writing a view engine is a non-trivial task. Perhaps you don't need the full nuclear option, and instead you want to just inherit from the existing RazorViewEngine class and make a few small tweaks. If that is your path, you can add your version of Razor to the mix at startup in the ConfigureServices method of your Startup class:

```
services.AddSingleton<IRazorViewEngine, YourCustomRazorEngine>();
```

And finally, if Razor's not doing all the things you like, for instance if perhaps you need to expand the list of file providers or change the locations included by default when locating views, you can go an even simpler route and just modify some of Razor's default settings:

```
services.Configure<RazorViewEngineOptions>(options =>
{
    // modify options
});
```

Summary

As far as view engines go, Razor has already proven itself as a competent and mature tool to handle the server side aspects of rendering a user experience. There is a low level of friction as you shift from writing HTML and C# code, and syntax allows you to easily incorporate framework and language features. Having a syntax that closely mirrors vanilla HTML is far easier on designers than frameworks that radically depart from the well-known syntax are. The use of layouts and partials make composing a web application that looks consistent from page to page something that is achievable in short order, while strongly-typed models, service injection, and Tag Helpers bring the power of the platform to your views.

Throughout the book we've glanced over alternate configuration a few times, including here with the Razor view engine, and now it's time to look at that more closely. In the next chapter we're going to have a deep dive into Configuration and Logging, two areas of ASP.NET that have seen significant changes and improvements.

## CHAPTER 12

Configuration and Logging

"Right, got it. Thanks for the heads up, Chapman. It's not going to help us, but it probably won't kill us either." Tim waited until he was sure Greg had hung up, then he slammed the phone down. "Aw, Man!"

Greg Chapman was the Partner Integration Manager at The Phone Company and the current product owner of the telephony and customer service system Alpine was using. Unfortunately, the version of the software that was installed at Alpine did not have a direct upgrade path without the purchase of additional hardware, meaning the dev team at Alpine wasn't going to get the service they were expecting to code against for service center information to be displayed on the site.

The Marks were in the hallway outside of Tim's office when they heard the call end. "So, yeah," started Marc peeking around the door, "when you end a call with 'Aw, Man!' and then slam down your end of the phone, should we assume that's going to affect us?"

"Humph," grumbled Tim, "come on in." He made the invitation, but the Marks were already through the doorway. "Greg is an old friend of mine from when we worked at A. Datum, so I reached out to him to make sure I could keep the upgrade of the CSR software moving forward. He looked into our licensed version for me to see if he could expedite our request, but it's off-the-charts old. We can't even upgrade the system until we get new servers in place, meaning basically..."

"...that we aren't getting our shiny new API," Marc finished for him. "Great."

"Yeah. I know you guys were wanting that for the website," continued Tim, "but I don't think we're going to get it before we have to ship. We're stuck with what we got."

"Well that may not be entirely a dead end, right?" asked Mark. "I mean, it writes that info file out whenever anyone signs in on their VOIP phone. I know it was meant for that old usage report, but we could just tell it to overwrite the file every time. Remember, Marc? Danielle was telling us about those custom configuration providers."

"Right...let's mash on that!" Mark was enthused to flex some new know-how and show it to Danielle. "Tim, hold on. We're going to pair on this for a bit and figure out if this is actually a problem. Give us three hours to spike it and see where we land?"

In production, logging and configuration are extremely important. This chapter covers the new configuration system in ASP.NET Core as well as the powerful new logging tools to help you improve how you create, store, and share information about your application and how it executes.

Moving Away from web.config

Traditionally, we have had the luxury and the burden of being able to store our application configuration in web.config. Although over time, web.config has both evolved in capability and devolved in focus. You can explicitly set library bindings, grant access to a specific user, modify settings of a view engine, specify connection strings, and set the default color of your site's background if you choose to do so. There is just too much going on in that file.

This complexity was one of the primary motivators for moving away from web.config. The name itself implies that there is configuration about something to do with "web," but web what? A web application? A web server? A web of lies?

The .NET community is accustomed to a few rules that most applications operate under. Here are a few examples of these rules. First, we should develop the application in Visual Studio. Next, the hardware that we deploy on in production should run Windows Server and that server should have the .NET Framework installed on it. There should also be a copy of IIS to host the website and related host configuration. We should likely write code to talk to an installation of SQL Server to store our application data. Because these assumptions fall by the wayside in ASP.NET Core, web.config, also has to fall by the wayside.

That last statement is true, at least from an application point of view. If you're going to host your application in IIS, you still need web.config, but it won't be what powers your application configuration in ASP.NET Core. Breaking free from web.config means the tooling that you use doesn't have to understand web.config. If you want to host your application outside of IIS, you probably won't natively use web.config, because the host won't understand it. And, if we're honest about what ends up in most web.config files, there is enough unrelated information and configuration in there to scare off a pack of three horned monsters.

But, by far, one of the biggest and most frustrating things about web.config is that it is the bullied kid. The system-wide inherited configuration from higher folders in IIS (applicationhost.config or machine.config) can seep unknowingly into your application, making troubleshooting an application difficult to figure out. Settings at parent levels can introduce and lock in behaviors or providers that you are unaware of and that didn't exist in other environments, causing unintended side effects at runtime.

In ASP.NET Core you'll observe that you are free to choose the type of configuration you can read in, that the host and server configurations can be clean and separate from application settings, and that you can leverage a more powerful configuration system in your project.

Configuring Your Application

Each environment you create has different settings that are appropriate to its own context. When running on a local development machine, you might want to use the developer emulator for Azure Storage Tools, but in higher environments you want to use the real deal.

There's a clear signal through the use of the `ConfigurationBuilder` that you can instruct your application to read these values in from the appropriate, environment-driven source in the constructor of the `Startup` class:

```
var builder = new ConfigurationBuilder()
    .SetBasePath(env.ContentRootPath)
    .AddJsonFile("appsettings.json", optional: true, reloadOnChange: true)
    .AddJsonFile($"appsettings.{env.EnvironmentName}.json", optional: true);

if (env.IsDevelopment())
    builder.AddUserSecrets();

builder.AddEnvironmentVariables();
Configuration = builder.Build();
```

From this code, you can likely come to the conclusion that the environment you are running in has some effect on the configuration you use. You can see the env.EnvironmentName token used to apply a configuration file based on the environment you're running in. This token is picked up as an environment variable natively through the operating system or, in the event that you're using Visual Studio, through the process-bound environment variables that are set in the project's debug settings. The technique of conditionally adding configuration sources allows you to easily substitute values without any additional build or deployment steps. The call to .AddJsonFile based on the environment name also has the optional parameter set to true, meaning that you only need to create those files as required to suit your needs. Likewise, due to the way the configuration values are stored, you needn't worry about creating all of the values for all of the environments. It is okay to define a connection string in your development environment file that doesn't exist elsewhere.

> **Note** Certain types of data are not appropriate to store in your application configuration files, particularly if you work on public repositories. Even within a team, there are configuration aspects that should not be shared among developers. We cover how to store these types of values in Chapter 13, "Identity, Security, and Rights Management" when we discuss User Secrets.

The code also highlights the idea that there might be values that are stored in multiple files, or even sourced from different configuration providers. There are calls in there for JSON files and environment variables. If the code is executing the development environment, it also loads configurations from the User Secrets store.

The order that you load configurations in is important because each configuration provider is called in the order that they were added. Values that exist in multiple configuration sources overwrite previous entries without warning, and only appear after they are in the application's configuration store. If appsettings.json and appsettings.development.json both contain a value for StorageKey, and that same key also exists in an environment variable, the value from your environment variables is what your application uses at runtime.

All values from configuration are stored as key-value pairs, even though you might want to express some measure of hierarchy when you store them. Typically you see a set of values like what we have in our appsettings.json file:

```
"Logging": {
  "IncludeScopes": false,
  "LogLevel": {
    "Default": "Debug",
    "System": "Information",
    "Microsoft": "Information"
  }
}
```

Again, you only have the ability to store the configuration information in key-value pairs, so the above configuration is deserialized into something that can work in such a structure. If you set a breakpoint at the end of the Startup constructor and examine the Configuration property, you'd see that the values have been transformed into the corresponding values in Table 12-1.

TABLE 12-1 Hierarchical keys from configuration and their mapping to logging level values

Key	Value
Logging:IncludeScopes	False
Logging:LogLevel:Default	Debug
Logging:LogLevel:System	Information
Logging:LogLevel:Microsoft	Information

The configuration provider walks the tree of values in the JSON document to the end node where it extracts the value. For all other property names along the way, it uses the names of those nodes to build up a corresponding key.

Using Stock Configuration Providers

There is a growing number of framework-provided components for reading configurations, as well as a push from the community to add support for additional types of storage. You will find that any of the mature providers are equipped with extension methods off of ConfigurationBuilder to facilitate chaining in the fluent syntax and to make it easier to wire up your sources.

Here, from the ASP.NET configuration repository on GitHub, are the available providers at the time of writing with sample invocations:

- Configuration.Azure.KeyVault – Reads data from the specified key vault, given the client ID and secret you provide. This is a good way to allow developers to use cloud resources while maintaining granular control over which assets they have access to.

  ```
  builder.AddAzureKeyVault(vaultUri, clientId, clientSecret);
  ```

- Configuration.CommandLine – Allows you to provide arguments from the command line. This is less likely to be used in ASP.NET Core MVC applications, but can be wired up if you perform a few extra steps.

  ```
  builder.AddCommandLine(args);
  ```

- Configuration.EnvironmentVariables – Reads configuration information from the process that the application is running in. Keep in mind that when you start a process, the environment variables for the user and the system are loaded and not refreshed, so Visual Studio processes and sub processes do not pick up on changes you make in your settings. If you want to work with changing values, consider setting the environment variables on the Debug tab of your project's Property pages. You can optionally filter your environment variables with a prefix that is removed from the key name.

```
builder.AddEnvironmentVariables("AlpineApi-");
```

- Configuration.Ini – While not commonly thought of in the context of web applications, INI files are actually a reasonably good container for storing configuration. They support named sections, are largely free of extra "cruft," and are human readable.

```
builder.AddIniFile("loadbalancerinfo.ini", optional: false, reloadOnChange: true);
```

- Configuration.Json – The de facto provider used in the ASP.NET Core MVC project template. While it is not the least verbose format by far, JSON files provide nested structure capabilities and can be validated for document correctness. There are many "pretty print" utilities that make it easy to visually assess a document and understand its contents.

```
builder.AddJsonFile("appsettings.json", optional: true, reloadOnChange: true);
```

- Configuration.Xml – A traditional ASP.NET storage format that most developers on the .NET stack are familiar with. As an added benefit, if you previously used custom configuration sections and want to migrate them, you might be able to port those settings with minimal effort to your ASP.NET Core MVC project. The XML configuration provider allows you to inspect both attributes and node values from XML.

```
builder.AddJsonFile("webserviceendpoints.{envEnvironmentName}.json", optional: true);
```

The file-based providers for XML, INI, and JSON files all support making configuration files optional and also support automatic reloading on change at runtime without requiring you to restart your application. Setting the reloadOnChange parameter to true when adding these types of configuration files enables this feature and changes are immediately surfaced to your application.

Building a Custom Configuration Provider

When the Marks decided to tackle the issue of Customer Service Representative (CSR) availability on the site, they set their sights on a file that contained the information they needed and decided to treat it as a configuration source. The file contained a header row with the call center's phone number, an additional line for each call center representative that was online, the extension they could be reached at, and the time that they logged in. They grabbed a sample file to examine the details:

```
ACTIVE_PHONE_NUMBER|555-SKI-HARD
STAMMLER, JEFF|4540|2016-09-12T08:05:17+00:00
ILYINA, JULIA|4542|2016-09-12T13:01:22+00:00
SCHUSTIN, SUSANNE|4548|2016-09-12T12:58:49+00:00
CARO, FERNANDO|4549|2016-09-12T10:00:36+00:00
```

Let's examine how you would build support for such a file in your application. Begin by writing a class that can parse out the information from the file and build the configuration values. This is important because you can then build and test this logic and functionality separate from your other concerns. We're actually interested in two specific points: the phone number of the call center and the number of CSRs that are online. Extract and compute those values, then store them in a dictionary with a key that is prefixed with `CsrInformationOptions`. Here is the `Parse` method that reads a stream and performs the bulk of the work:

```
public IDictionary<string, string> Parse(Stream stream)
{
    _data.Clear();

    using (var reader = new StreamReader(stream))
    {
        // first line contains the phone number
        var line = reader.ReadLine();
        var phoneNumber = ExtractPhoneNumber(line);

        // all subsequent lines contain contact information
        var onlineCount = 0;
        while ((line = reader.ReadLine()) != null)
        {
            onlineCount++;
        }

        // assign to the config store
        _data.Add("CsrInformationOptions:PhoneNumber", phoneNumber);
        _data.Add("CsrInformationOptions:OnlineRepresentatives", onlineCount.ToString());
    }

    return _data;
}
```

Implementing a custom configuration provider requires that you write an implementation of `IConfigurationSource`, which is responsible for configuring and returning an instance of `IConfigurationProvider`. In the case of a file-based configuration source, you can leverage the pre-built `FileConfigurationSource` from the framework that has the properties you need to describe a file and that gives you the ability to support automatic reloads when files change on disk.

```
public class CsrInformationConfigurationSource : FileConfigurationSource
{
    public override IConfigurationProvider Build(IConfigurationBuilder builder)
    {
```

```
        FileProvider = FileProvider ?? builder.GetFileProvider();
        return new CsrInformationConfigurationProvider(this);
    }
}
```

The provider exposes a set of methods to access your internal list of values. The configuration system uses these methods to access values that you read from your configuration source. Here, you implement `CsrInformationConfigurationProvider`, which inherits from `FileConfigurationProvider` and relies on the parser previously built to read the values from the stream provided.

```
public class CsrInformationConfigurationProvider : FileConfigurationProvider
{
    public CsrInformationConfigurationProvider(FileConfigurationSource source) : base(source) {
}

    public override void Load(Stream stream)
    {
        var parser = new CsrInformationParser();
        Data = parser.Parse(stream);
    }
}
```

While not explicitly required, you might also want to surface the use of your configuration source through an extension method that you hang off of `IConfigurationBuilder`. This makes it easy to chain your configuration source into the other configuration sources at startup. The `CsrInformationExtensions` class contains these extensions methods in the Alpine project and, in the end, allows for a single line of code to add the configuration file to the project in `Startup.cs`:

```
var builder = new ConfigurationBuilder()
    .SetBasePath(env.ContentRootPath)
    .AddCsrInformationFile("config\\TPC_ONLINE_AGENTS.INFO", reloadOnChange: true)
    .AddJsonFile("appsettings.json", optional: true, reloadOnChange: true)
    .AddJsonFile($"appsettings.{env.EnvironmentName}.json", optional: true);
```

Arguably, this approach is one of many hammers and it might not be right for your nail. You should always examine which aspects of your application's inputs should be considered data sources rather than configuration sources.

> **Note** At the time of this writing, `FileConfigurationSource` providers do not reload as designed when you change them on disk. This is a known issue in version 1.0.1, and the ASP. NET team has set a milestone on GitHub to resolve the issue in the 1.1.0 release.

One final reminder here. Even though we created a custom configuration provider to extract a very specific set of values from a unique file format, we rendered the properties down to key-value pairs and stored them in a common bucket. This means that any configuration source added to the application after ours might contain a value for the keys that we configured.

Employing the Options Pattern

The goal of configuration in ASP.NET Core is to simplify how we provide and consume configuration. JSON, XML, and custom data sources all speak to the "provide" side of that equation, and it is the option services that simplify consumption. The options services allow us to use dependency injection to provide configuration information to our services, controllers, and other objects in our application.

To take advantage of these services in full, we need an object that can be injected, so we'll start there. Remember that our customer service configuration information essentially boils down to two properties: the call center phone number and the number of CSRs that are currently logged in. From that, we can also derive if the call center is open. Option objects are plain old CLR objects, which means that building an options class is a fairly straightforward chore to implement.

```
public class CsrInformationOptions
{
    public string PhoneNumber { get; set; }
    public int OnlineRepresentatives { get; set; }
}
```

We want to expose this data to the options services that are available for the lifetime of the application, so we return to the `Startup` class in the `ConfigureServices` method to wire things up. A call to `Configuration.GetSection` allows us to retrieve a group of data with a shared name prefix. This can be a section of a configuration file or, in this case, the values that we added to the configuration store with a prefix of `CsrInformationOptions`. We pass the result of this call to the `Configure<T>` method and type it to the options class that we previously created.

```
services.Configure<CsrInformationOptions>(Configuration.GetSection("CsrInformationOptions"));
```

When our application runs, we now have the ability to ask for our configuration object, pre-loaded with all its properties loaded from various configuration sources. You can see a sample of this in the *CsrInformationService* constructor.

```
public CsrInformationService(IOptions<CsrInformationOptions> options)
{
    _options = options.Value;
}
```

In the constructor, notice that we accept a parameter of type `IOptions<CsrInformationOptions>` rather than just a `CsrInformationOptions` proper. This is due to how the options services work, registering a single service in the application that is capable of resolving any configured options object.

Options services are typically enabled by default through various code paths that the default project template uses. If you receive an error that the `IOptions<TOptions>` is not configured in your application, you can resolve this by adding a call to `services.AddOptions()` in the `ConfigureServices` method in `Startup`.

Logging as a First-Class Citizen

Thank goodness we weren't actively logging anything; it would have made diagnosing this production issue much more difficult.

– No one, ever.

In a world of mixed conventions, formats, and participation in the practice of logging, there is one truth: You cannot start logging retrospectively to diagnose an error that has already happened. If you aren't logging when something happens, you've missed a critical opportunity to simplify the task of finding the root cause of an issue. Logging is more honest than a user, more timely than an escalating help desk ticket, and more even-keeled than an upset DevOps manager. Without it, we would be nearly blind to the inner workings of our application at runtime and we would miss out on an important tool in preventative maintenance.

Taking those cues, ASP.NET Core has moved logging up a notch in visibility and accessibility for developers. Rather than reaching out to third-party libraries and fetching config files from samples online, the project template now ships with everything you need to easily use logging throughout your application. Consider the following fields and the `CsrInformationService` constructor:

```
private ILogger<CsrInformationService> _logger;
private CsrInformationOptions _options;

public CsrInformationService(
  IOptions<CsrInformationOptions> options,
  ILogger<CsrInformationService> logger)
{
    _options = options.Value;
    _logger = logger;
    logger.LogInformation("Entered the CsrInformationService constructor.");
}
```

You don't even have to create an instance of a logger to start logging in your application, it is provided to you by the services made available through dependency injection, which we look at more closely in Chapter 14, "Dependency Injection." At runtime, a logger factory creates an instance of an `ILogger` typed to our service class, which sets the category of the logger, and we can use the logger as soon as we're in scope. All we need to get logging in our service is a backing field, a parameter in our constructor, and one line of code.

More importantly, everything to do with logging is an abstraction over the logging concepts. We see more of this toward the end of this chapter when we swap out the built-in logging for an alternate logging library, which allows us to easily use our library of choice.

Creating Logs That Provide Clarity

If you log clearly, you have the opportunity to detect a failing service, to monitor performance impacts of changes in a release, and of course, to better understand what transpired when things go completely off the rails. The best log file is one you never have to look at, but in the event that you must, it is better to be equipped with the information that positions you for early success.

Here are a few suggestions on how you can write more helpful logs from your applications:

- **Be clear:** You likely learned the "5 W's" in a writing class at some point in school: who, what, where, when, and why. In many circumstances these are good details to include in the messages you generate for your log files. Including information about the user (more specific), the request ID (more anonymous), the executing operation, the service in question, the timing, and any effort you made to recover from an ill-fated circumstance are all helpful.

- **Don't overdo it:** Try to anticipate when information might be helpful and include it routinely throughout your request, but also limit yourself to relevant information for your scenario. When a user is trying to update their profile, you likely don't need to record the number of processors on the server.

- **You probably can't overdo it:** Disk space is cheap and time is precious during investigations. Provided you are *Doing It Right*, the verbosity of the information that is in-context can be quite helpful in your application's darkest hours. Any transient information that is not available outside of the scope of the request could be intensively valuable down the road. Likewise, any information that can help you group and extract information about a wider context is also valuable. The one caveat here is to make sure that you're not logging to the point where you affect performance.

- **Understand what is in place:** You don't have to do what is already done. Turn up the verbosity of your dependencies' logging, which is discussed in the next section, and see what those libraries are offering through the default logging services. If the library you are leaning on is already capable of providing you with the information you need, dial back the filters on a per-namespace basis and let them do their best to annotate themselves.

- **Understand what's at stake:** The information you provide can play a key role in being able to provide a speedy reaction to misbehaving applications, but be mindful of the data you select for logging purposes. Susanne Schustin, for example, is a great person and doesn't need anyone to know that she lives at 1744 North Cypress Blvd, Winnipeg, MB, R0M 2J4 with a Canadian Social Insurance Number of 636 192 352. So, please, dear reader, mind your manners when logging. It is unfair to put someone in DevOps at risk of violating a Personal Identity Information policy that your organization is bound to just by simply opening a log file.

Setting Expectations for Exceptions

The advice you would receive about what you should do when it comes to logging around exceptions is about as varied as you might find. If you're going to just throw again, why bother logging? If you don't have every single detail, how can you know what went wrong? Perhaps we should look at exceptions from a different point of view, and consider the state of the application that lead us to generating an exception in the first place.

Exception handling is something that we do in *exceptional* circumstances, when we have a critical execution path in our application and the power to do something about an error, should that error occur. We shouldn't be handling exceptions that we're not going to try to recover from, unless it provides us with some valuable insight into the state of the application.

When you do land in scenarios where a high-risk operation might reveal mission-critical information, follow the suggestions for clarity previously mentioned. We'll talk about the logging levels in just a moment, but consider the following logging strategy pattern as a proactive approach that you might take to troubleshooting a problem at runtime:

```
try
{
    _logger.LogDebug($"Entering critical path for {resource.Id}...");
    _service.InvokeRiskyManeuvre();
    _logger.LogInformation("Successfully completed barrel roll for {resource.Id}.");
}
catch (UnexpectedStateException ex)
{
    _logger.LogError($"Unable to complete operation, resource {resource.Id} in {resource.Status}
state. Error: {ex.Message}");
    throw;
}
```

Under different logging configurations you would see different log results, but in all scenarios you would know which resource you're working with. In the debug configuration, you could track your progress line by line. In higher-level environments, your application might be configured to reveal success messages. Further, in the case of an exception, you're explicitly trapping an exception you know about, doing your part to isolate errors you anticipate and then providing information about the resource that would help you understand what went wrong.

Logging as a Development Strategy

Now that you've caught the bug for logging, you might be inclined to start Logging All The Things. Sure, why not? When you are working on your local machine, logs can provide a quick insight into how services are running at times when your application isn't under load and the order of events is easy enough to discern. Here are some scenarios where logging can really augment the debugging experience:

- Discerning what transpires when events happen asynchronously in your application.

- Building a service that responds to commands from an IoT source rather than your application.

- Developing a microservice that communicates with many other services; locally, you could be debugging one service and allow logging to capture peripheral information for others.

- When locally reproducing a difficult defect that pertains to sensitive information, you can capture that data and reveal it through a local log stream.

While that last point might cause some of you to cringe, chances are you might be missing out on a powerful aspect of logging. Locally, you're likely the one to be entering the data, and you already know the secrets. Using trace-level logging in conjunction with higher-level logging is a great way to capture details that paint the full picture of what has transpired in your application.

```
_logger.LogDebug($"Created new resource {resource.Id}...");
_logger.LogTrace($"Resource private token {resource.Token}");
```

This type of information getting dropped into a production environment would surely be frowned upon, so you'll be happy to know that trace-level logging is off by default. ASP.NET Core allows you to specify the verbosity level of your logging, which can help to reduce the peripheral noise in your application log files.

Logging Levels in ASP.NET Core

By now you've realized the position-switching we've taken on putting sensitive information into your logs, but we've also been hinting at the logger's ability to read your cues of discernment to avoid any significant problems. You've also likely noticed a few of the methods that we can use to log, so now let's take a look at how the Alpine Ski Team put those to work by first starting to define the logging levels themselves. These levels are stated in order below, ranging from most useful in development to most meaningful in production.

- **Trace:** This level is disabled by default. Use this level of logging locally to help triage problems with sensitive data. Because it's considered "safe" by other developers, you should never enable it in environments in of production.

- **Debug:** At this level you can help distinguish between motivations for strategy selection, states of toggles or flags, and the types of things that are more interesting to a developer, such as GUIDs or process IDs.

- **Information:** Brings value to the logs for individuals working in operations or data that can be used in log analysis tools to help build alerts, notifications, and enabling other kinds of monitoring.

- **Warning:** This level is where things are not yet completely dark, but are not exactly bright either. The ideal scenario for using the Warning level is when you are able to recover from an error via some sort of second level retry, where things failed, giving you hope.

- **Error:** If you have to abort an operation that is critical to the business and need to log out information that is vital to an investigation, this is the vehicle to do so. These errors might be particular to a request, signaling a failure in a particular circumstance.

- **Critical:** This level is for wider spread failings in an application, like when critical infrastructure cannot be reached or when some other calamitous situation arises. You're not pumping the brakes here, because you're already in the ditch.

Now, let's look at how to put these levels in play for our application, namely how we configure the application to log at the expected level. Jump back into your appsettings.config and you'll see the same configuration that we were looking at earlier in the chapter, which was set up by the Alpine team.

```
"Logging": {
  "IncludeScopes": false,
  "LogLevel": {
    "Default": "Debug",
    "System": "Information",
    "Microsoft": "Information"
  }
}
```

The default for all logging is "Debug," but there are entries for the System and Microsoft namespaces that set logging levels as well. The team decided that these are useful settings for most developers when they pull the code down locally and run the application. You can see the fruits of these in Figure 12-1 by running the application from the console using the dotnet run command; however, you see that there can be a lot of noise when you're performing typical actions, like navigating from view to view.

FIGURE 12-1 Lots of information in the default logging configuration

> **Note** This noise is the exact kind of thing that we were hoping to avoid, so the team has decided to use User Secrets to mute some of the details on their own machines. We talk more about User Secrets in Chapter 13.

To filter these informational messages out of production, the team has also added an environmental configuration file, appsettings.production.json, which has the desired level of logging that you might expect in production:

```
{
  "Logging": {
    "IncludeScopes": false,
    "LogLevel": {
      "Default": "Information",
      "System": "Error",
```

```
        "Microsoft": "Error"
    }
  }
}
```

This is the same structure as the one that exists in the main configuration file. Remember from earlier in the chapter, we said that the same values can appear in multiple configuration sources, but the last one in wins. In this case, the overrides help to clear away the informational messages that are part of the System and Microsoft namespaces, allowing us to see the evidence that we need to see more clearly, as in Figure 12-2.

FIGURE 12-2 Modified logging configuration to produce cleaner logs

To get these settings into our application, we actually need to configure the logging middleware appropriately by passing the Logging section into the AddConsole extension method:

```
var loggingConfig = Configuration.GetSection("Logging");
loggerFactory.AddConsole(loggingConfig);
loggerFactory.AddDebug();
```

Note that there are actually two calls here, and it might not be apparent at first glance what is going on. First of all, it's worth pointing out that some extension methods are more capable than others. There are two here that we use to wire up logging. The first adds logging to the console and the second adds logging to the Debug output window in Visual Studio. The call to AddConsole allows us to pass in an instance of an IConfiguration, which we do in the previous block of code. The AddDebug method on the other hand does not. This means that AddConsole has the ability to use the settings we've stored to filter log messages based on namespaces. AddDebug does not contain an overload that allows us to pass settings in for a filter, so the Alpine team has instead elected to write their own.

```
loggerFactory.AddDebug((className, logLevel) => {
    if (className.StartsWith("AlpineSkiHouse."))
        return true;
    return false;
});
```

The filter requires a Func that accepts a string containing the logger category, which is typically the fully qualified class name, and the LogLevel of the message being logged. You don't get to inspect the message itself, nor do you need to as this is just an opportunity for you to determine if logging is appropriate for messages from this category at that point in time. In this trivial implementation of a logging filter, the team has decided to only print messages to the Debug output window if the messages are coming from a namespace that they have crafted themselves.

Using Logging Scopes to Augment Logging

Scopes are a way to better understand where a log comes from by allowing you to reveal part of your call chain. A scope is created automatically for each request and along the way, different parts of the execution pipeline might elect to create a nested scope of their own. As you navigate through a request, new scopes are entered and exited like little Russian dolls. You can add your own as well and wrap a scope around a process that spans multiple classes. You might open a scope before entering a critical aspect of a business process, like performing all the work required to complete a purchase and collect payment from a third-party service, closing the scope when the operations are complete. In ASP.NET Core, scopes live for the lifetime of the HTTP request.

The Alpine team wanted to be explicit about understanding the steps that were being executed from the perspective of each incoming request, particularly when it related to adding new ski card data. To enable this, they first modified the logging setting to include scope information in appsettings.json by changing the setting to "IncludeScopes": true. This exposes the scope information in the logs as follows:

```
info: Microsoft.AspNetCore.Hosting.Internal.WebHost[1]
    => RequestId:0HKV5MFUPFPVU RequestPath:/
    Request starting HTTP/1.1 GET http://localhost:5000/
```

The scope information is preceded by a chain of one or more => symbols, so the only scope active at this point is the root of the request itself. You can see nesting form as additional log entry segments are appended to the output. This becomes more evident when the log entry comes from an action on a controller:

```
info: Microsoft.AspNetCore.Authorization.DefaultAuthorizationService[1]
  => RequestId:0HKV5MFUPFPVV RequestPath:/skicard
  => AlpineSkiHouse.Web.Controllers.SkiCardController.Index (AlpineSkiHouse.Web)
  Authorization was successful for user: james@jameschambers.com.
```

The team further enhanced the scoping information they were receiving by instructing the logger to include custom scopes around the key business scenarios. Here's an example in the SkiCardController where a custom scope is used to wrap the code employed to add a ski card to a user's account. Note the calls to _logger and where they sit in relationship to beginning the CreateSkiCard scope:

```
if (ModelState.IsValid)
{
    var userId = _userManager.GetUserId(User);
    _logger.LogDebug($"Creating ski card for {userId}");
    using (_logger.BeginScope($"CreateSkiCard:{userId}"))
    {
        SkiCard skiCard = new SkiCard
        {
            ApplicationUserId = userId,
            CreatedOn = DateTime.UtcNow,
            CardHolderFirstName = viewModel.CardHolderFirstName,
            CardHolderLastName = viewModel.CardHolderLastName,
            CardHolderBirthDate = viewModel.CardHolderBirthDate.Value.Date,
            CardHolderPhoneNumber = viewModel.CardHolderPhoneNumber
        };

        _skiCardContext.SkiCards.Add(skiCard);
        await _skiCardContext.SaveChangesAsync();
        _logger.LogInformation($"Ski card created for {userId}");
    }
    _logger.LogDebug($"Ski card for {userId} created successfully, redirecting to Index...");
    return RedirectToAction(nameof(Index));
}
```

The log output for creating a user's ski card now looks like so, with explicit information about where in the call chain the logs are coming from:

```
dbug: AlpineSkiHouse.Web.Controllers.SkiCardController[0]
   => RequestId:0HKV5MFUPFQ01 RequestPath:/SkiCard/Create
   => AlpineSkiHouse.Web.Controllers.SkiCardController.Create (AlpineSkiHouse.Web)
   Creating ski card for f81d8803-304a-481b-ad4f-13ef7bcec240
info: Microsoft.EntityFrameworkCore.Storage.Internal.RelationalCommandBuilderFactory[1]
   => RequestId:0HKV5MFUPFQ01 RequestPath:/SkiCard/Create
   => AlpineSkiHouse.Web.Controllers.SkiCardController.Create (AlpineSkiHouse.Web)
   => CreateSkiCard:f81d8803-304a-481b-ad4f-13ef7bcec240
   Executed DbCommand (1ms)...
   ...WHERE @@ROWCOUNT = 1 AND [Id] = scope_identity();
info: AlpineSkiHouse.Web.Controllers.SkiCardController[0]
   => RequestId:0HKV5MFUPFQ01 RequestPath:/SkiCard/Create
   => AlpineSkiHouse.Web.Controllers.SkiCardController.Create (AlpineSkiHouse.Web)
   => CreateSkiCard:f81d8803-304a-481b-ad4f-13ef7bcec240
   Ski card created for f81d8803-304a-481b-ad4f-13ef7bcec240
dbug: AlpineSkiHouse.Web.Controllers.SkiCardController[0]
   => RequestId:0HKV5MFUPFQ01 RequestPath:/SkiCard/Create
   => AlpineSkiHouse.Web.Controllers.SkiCardController.Create (AlpineSkiHouse.Web)
   Ski card for f81d8803-304a-481b-ad4f-13ef7bcec240 created successfully, redirecting to
Index...
```

Scopes give us information about SQL calls through Entity Framework, the controller and action that are being executed as part of the request, and the request ID itself. This is all powerful information in helping to understand what transpired over the course of a request, and is further enhanced by the fact that calls to the database done in the context of the `SkiCardController.Create` action are easy to identify. This can offer a lot of insight when used wisely.

A final word on scopes would be to use them sparingly and only when they can add significant value that you can't add in other ways. If the request ID is all you need to isolate a series of related logging events, the recommendation is to be mindful of the scope stack and don't add overhead to the logs when it isn't required.

Using a Structured Logging Framework

Structured logging is a concept that allows you to store the data part of your log entry separate from the log message itself. It introduces the concept of a log template and parameters while still supporting the traditional text-only log entries by means of rendering the data into the template. Adding structure to your logging introduces a machine-readable format to your log entries that starts to enable really interesting scenarios.

> Structured logging uses "a consistent, predetermined message format containing semantic information [...]" to enable deeper insights from our logs. (ThoughtWorks Technology Radar, January 2014).

The Alpine team selected the Serilog library and added the appropriate packages, namely the `Serilog.Extensions.Logging` and the `Serilog.Sinks.Literate` packages. You can find these in the `project.json` of the project, which also contains the other logging dependencies. The extensions package is what allows Serilog to flex its structured muscles within ASP.NET Core's logging abstractions, while the Literate library provides a much cleaner, easier to read console output.

The next step is to update the `Startup` class to use the new package, first by removing the configuration of the `LoggerFactor`, including the call to AddDebug, and then replacing it with the following:

```
Log.Logger = new LoggerConfiguration()
    .MinimumLevel.Information()
    .MinimumLevel.Override("AlpineSkiHouse", Serilog.Events.LogEventLevel.Debug)
    .Enrich.FromLogContext()
    .WriteTo.LiterateConsole()
    .CreateLogger();
```

This configuration gives the same levels of error messages that were added previously for console logging and exposes Serilog to the application at runtime.

Using Serilog with Configuration

We would be amiss if we didn't point out that if you wanted your configuration for Serilog to be different from environment to environment, that you should instead use the `Serilog.Settings.Configuration` package, which allows you to read in your settings from a known structure native to Serilog. The same configuration as previously stated would be represented as follows in your appsettings.json:

```
"Serilog": {
  "Using": ["Serilog.Sinks.Literate"],
  "MinimumLevel": {
      "Default": "Information",
      "Override": {
          "AlpineSkiHouse": "Debug"
      }
  },
  "WriteTo": [
    { "Name": "LiterateConsole" }
  ],
  "Enrich": ["FromLogContext"],
  "Properties": {
      "Application": "Sample"
  }
}
```

With your `IConfigurationRoot` previously configured, you would only need the following in your `Startup` class' `Configure` method to load the log settings:

```
var logger = new LoggerConfiguration()
    .ReadFrom.Configuration(Configuration)
    .CreateLogger();
```

You then have the ability to use what you've learned in per-environment configuration and apply it to your logger, overriding settings in User Secrets, environment variables, or in `appsettings.EnvironmentName.json` files as required.

As a simple example of how the team can now approach logging, let's examine a logging statement in the Home controller's `Contact` method, which includes the log template and the data to be rendered into the template:

```
_logger.LogDebug("User visited contact page at {VisitTime}", DateTime.Now);
```

You can think of the thing that you're logging to as a bucket or a "sink." You can have as many sinks as you like and either write to all of them or write to them selectively if you so choose. When non-structured sinks are logging information, such as when writing to a console window or a text file, the previous call to LogDebug is simply rendered as text. But when you log to a sink that understands the parameterized version of our log entry, that's when structured logging really starts to shine. Let's look at one such sink as we think of logging in a different light.

Logging as a Service

Stepping up the value of treating your logs like they are data, requires a logging sink that understands the information you are trying to persist. More importantly, it helps you get that information out. When you start to factor in the idea of using many, many services as part of your application footprint, getting that information out becomes more important. Further, when those services span multiple application servers it becomes increasingly complex. To combat that complexity and mitigate latency risks, the prevailing solution is to use a service to collect your logs.

The Alpine team chose to work with Seq, which is free for developers to use locally, but does require a commercial license for production. While we won't go too deeply into any specific product or service, we do highlight here the Seq engine because it is written by the same folks as Serilog and is easy to stand up and operate with Serilog.

For the latest information on downloading and installing Seq, please visit https://getseq.net/.

Because Serilog is already configured, all the Alpine team had to do was to add an additional package, named `Serilog.Sinks.Seq`, and then add an additional sink to the configuration of the logger in Startup as follows:

```
Log.Logger = new LoggerConfiguration()
    .MinimumLevel.Information()
    .MinimumLevel.Override("AlpineSkiHouse", Serilog.Events.LogEventLevel.Debug)
    .Enrich.FromLogContext()
    .WriteTo.LiterateConsole()
    .WriteTo.Seq("http://localhost:5341")
    .CreateLogger();
```

One significant point in this configuration is the call to *WriteTo.Seq()*, where the location of the Seq server you want to write to is passed as a parameter, *localhost:5341* is the default setting for a local Seq install. The next time you run the application, you start to see information appearing in the Seq interface, as shown in Figure 12-3.

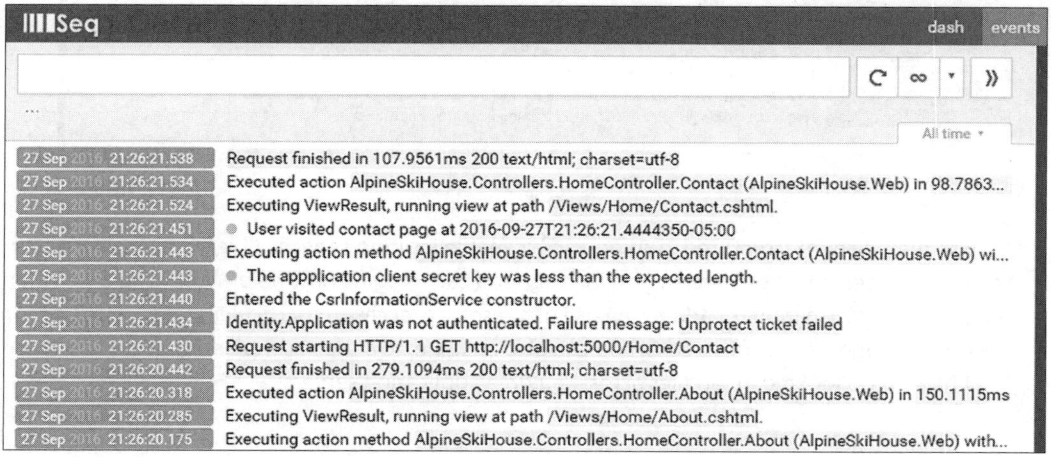

FIGURE 12-3 The Seq Web Interface

It is great to see the clarity that starts to emerge from your logs. Important information is highlighted and different log levels receive different color indicators. The UI is able to give you visual cues about the logs, but what is really compelling here is the ability to drill into a particular log statement. Figure 12-4 shows what is revealed in the same LogDebug message that appeared in the team's Contact action.

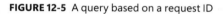

27 Sep 2016 21:26:21.451	● User visited contact page at 2016-09-27T21:26:21.4444350-05:00
	Id ▾ Level (Debug) ▾ Type ($70B15473) ▾ Pin ▾ Raw JSON
	✓✗ ActionId e158733e-2add-4ea5-ab93-cab45e370af2
	✓✗ ActionName AlpineSkiHouse.Controllers.HomeController.Contact
	(AlpineSkiHouse.Web)
	✓✗ RequestId 0HKV78R5K572G
	✓✗ RequestPath /Home/Contact
	✓✗ SourceContext AlpineSkiHouse.Controllers.HomeController
	✓✗ VisitTime 2016-09-27T21:26:21.4444350-05:00

FIGURE 12-4 Drilling into a log entry

Notice the parameter VisitTime that was passed as part of the log entry? We have fulfilled the premise of being able to treat our logs as data, and the proof is in the tooling's inherent ability to provide search capabilities over that data. Figure 12-5 shows an example of a search with a query that was built by using the *RequestId* as search criteria for related requests.

IIISeq	dash events
RequestId == "0HKV78R5K572G"	✕ ▾ C ∞ ▾ »
...	
	All time ▾
27 Sep 2016 21:26:21.538	Request finished in 107.9561ms 200 text/html; charset=utf-8
27 Sep 2016 21:26:21.534	Executed action AlpineSkiHouse.Controllers.HomeController.Contact (AlpineSkiHouse.Web) in 98.7863...
27 Sep 2016 21:26:21.524	Executing ViewResult, running view at path /Views/Home/Contact.cshtml.
27 Sep 2016 21:26:21.451	● User visited contact page at 2016-09-27T21:26:21.4444350-05:00
27 Sep 2016 21:26:21.443	Executing action method AlpineSkiHouse.Controllers.HomeController.Contact (AlpineSkiHouse.Web) wi...
27 Sep 2016 21:26:21.443	● The appplication client secret key was less than the expected length.
27 Sep 2016 21:26:21.440	Entered the CsrInformationService constructor.
27 Sep 2016 21:26:21.434	Identity.Application was not authenticated. Failure message: Unprotect ticket failed
27 Sep 2016 21:26:21.430	Request starting HTTP/1.1 GET http://localhost:5000/Home/Contact
62 events scanned... complete.	

FIGURE 12-5 A query based on a request ID

With the power of structured logging and a capable logging service, all related log entries for a given set of search criteria are easy to identify. You can imagine how helpful this would be when searching for information related to the use of a resource, access to particular assets, or the progression of a user through a series of screens. You can also imagine how much simpler that would be when you don't have to go looking in log files across multiple application servers!

Summary

As development teams work more and more closely with operations, in a world where environments are created and destroyed on the fly, traditional topics that we once relied on, such as configuration and logging, have really had to adapt. In ASP.NET Core we are equipped better than ever to provide configuration and logging structures to our applications. These structures can be shaped by various inputs and bound to particular contexts. Putting it all together and using a logging service can help us extract the information we need more readily to help diagnose troubled times and modern libraries and services can really start to empower our teams. In the next chapter we will cover more about identity, security, and rights management in ASP.NET.

#### PART 3

Sprint Retro:
The Belly of the Beast

Season 3 of the X-Files was letting Danielle sleep a bit better than the previous season. There hadn't been any more human fluke worm hybrids, so that was promising. Alien-human hybrids—there were plenty of those, but Danielle wasn't as worried about them. They mostly seemed interested in putting tiny monitoring devices in peoples' noses. If aliens wanted to know when she blew her nose, that was fine by her. This last sprint had been very productive; they had figured out data access security, logging, dependency injection, and they had an actual site to deploy.

"Welcome, welcome everybody" said Balázs "We're back for retro number two. Before we get started let's take a look back and see if we managed to address some of the problems with sprint 1." He pulled out a notebook and flipped through. "Okay, there was a feeling that we hadn't really shipped a product yet. How are we doing on that?"

"I'm feeling good" said Candice "we got a bunch of pages out there. They might not look pretty but we've got some structure down."

"The database stuff is looking great" said Mark "This Entity Framework stuff makes retrieving and adding data a breeze. I even feel like I understand the async methods."

"I like the support for writing LINQ queries" added Danielle "I've had that before in NHibernate, but it has always been a little weird. EF seems like it was written with LINQ in mind whereas NHibernate kind of slaps it on top."

"I'm really happy" chimed in Tim, who really wasn't supposed to be a participant in the team's meetings. "What is out in production isn't done but we're seeing builds go out a dozen times a day and each one in an incremental improvement. Well mostly."

"Look" said Adrian "I thought that the pink and red color scheme was slick. It reminded me of a SweetTart."

The team laughed. Poor Adrian had been getting flack for that style sheet change all week. "Good," continued Balázs "so that pain point is solved. We also had some lunch and learns on the agenda. We did two of those this week, so thanks Danielle and Mark for putting those on."

"Thanks, indeed" said Tim patting is stomach, "I didn't really understand them, but I thought it was, urrm, important for moral that I attend."

"Let's throw up the retro board and see what suggestions people have this week." Balázs looked disappointedly at the new odor-free pens which had replaced the really good ones. There had been a bit of a safety concern after the last meeting and all the really good pens had been carted away. Rumor had it they were buried next to the lost ET cartridges.

The team again grabbed pens and started writing on the board.

Start	Stop	Continue
Getting our JavaScript figured out	Making such ugly pages	Using .NET
Putting more automated tests in place	Having logins in place on our local machine, it really slows us down	Using dependency injection
Reusing some of the code we have in multiple places		Lunch and learns
Using a more powerful dependency injection container		
Make the site look prettier		

"Not much this week," said Balázs. "It seems like as a team we're working quite well together. I'm interested in this automated tests one; who put that down?"

"That was me," said Adrian "I've seen a couple of issues show up again after we've fixed them. It would be nice to be able to put some tests in there to protect against that."

"Great idea, makes up for that red and pink stylesheet in my mind. I'll second that!" said Mark "I like doing testing as I'm writing my code, but we're in such a panicked rush that I'm having trouble justifying the time spent on writing good tests."

"You're thinking test driven development?" asked Balázs?

"Exactly!" replied Mark "We should be writing tests before we're writing the code. It makes code more adaptable to change as well as giving us a safety net."

"We write tests first?" asked Danielle "I don't understand that."

"Okay" interrupted Balázs "I think maybe that could be the topic of a lunch and learn this week. Is there also some pain around dependency injection?"

"I think so" said Chester, "I mean the built in container is pretty good, but there are some things it doesn't quite do as nicely as things like Autofac."

"Humm, I think we can add that to this sprint. Would you like to head that up, Chester?" Asked Balázs.

"Sounds good," replied Chester.

"Alright," continued Balázs "let's see if we can also do something about the look of the site. I know it is a weird thing to worry about when we don't have all the functionality hammered out yet, but people are more forgiving of a site that looks pretty good. That goes double for upper management. They are all visual people, so let's try to give them something really good to look at."

"Finally it seems like we need to come up with approach to JavaScript. I happen to have seen a couple of checkins related to JavaScript, and they look a bit rough. Perhaps there is an approach that isn't so hacky." suggested Balázs.

"I like that idea" said Chester, "I don't feel like the code we have now will be maintainable once the site becomes bigger. We've been treating JavaScript like it was 2002 again—all single functions embedded in script tags on the page."

"Great" said Balázs, "You can take charge of that Chester. I'm going to go work on some cards for the next sprint. Why don't you all head home, it's getting a bit late."

Danielle didn't have to be told twice, and she had the Quagmire episode of X-Files all queued up and a quinoa salad that had been marinating all day in a mix of olive oil and cilantro. Over the weekend she had some plans to head out on the lake, probably the last time for the season, since the weather was turning. She made a mental note to go to the bathroom before she left to go to the lake, since there were only pit toilets out there.

## CHAPTER 13

Identity, Security, and Rights Management

It wasn't like her to interject, but Danielle was sensing a trend forming and had been for almost a month. Throughout the summer, one by one, the developers were taking a week's vacation to rest up and prepare for the official launch and the onboarding of the new software system. For two weeks in a row she'd overheard other team members talk about some of the security bits as they handed the work off prior to their departures, but she hadn't thought about it until now.

"Okay, so that makes sense," Marc said in response to Mark, "because I can just assign the claims I need as part of the middleware check-in at sign in. But how do I get Facebook authentication working locally?"

"Oh, that's easy," Mark said. "I got our credentials from Tim for the resort's Facebook page and I have them committed in my branch. If you pull it down locally, it'll just work."

"Wait a minute," said Danielle, interrupting. "You mean you're checking in our production credentials to GitHub?"

"Well, yes, but it doesn't matter. The repo is private," replied Mark.

"Sure, I understand," countered Danielle. "But I have at least two problems with this, the first being accountability. The fact that the production credentials are in our repo means that anyone on our team, whether we trust them or not, has access to them. If they pull down the repo on a machine that is compromised, our credentials could get out. Besides, I don't want to be in a position where I know the production access keys for any part of the system at all!" Both Mark and Marc nodded, since they knew where this was headed.

"I get that...I've been in a place where that's gone down bad before," added Marc. "So then, how am I supposed to get this going on my machine?"

"Might be time for us to check out user secrets?" asked Mark.

"Yeah, and we should probably get together as a group to talk a little bit about how we're going to handle this going forward, too. So, who's going to ask Tim to reset the Facebook keys?"

Defense in Depth

Rather than diving right into the technical aspects of security in this chapter, we're going to consider the big picture in this section. While this might seem counter-intuitive in a text that claims to be targeted toward technical folks, not all important aspects are about the technology.

The technology portion is of course very important. It has never been good enough to just put your site behind an SSL certificate and call it secure. There are several elements at play on many levels, and it is your responsibility as a professional to put into play a series of systems, protocols, and mechanisms that not only prevent technical breaches, but also prevent system compromises due to human actions as well. We need to defend our applications and the data our company is amassing in the way that our management, administrators, employees, and other developers use and interact with it. It's just as important to think about how data is used as it is to think about how their use of data might expose the company to additional risk.

> Companies spend millions of dollars on firewalls, encryption and secure access devices, and it's money wasted, because none of these measures address the weakest link in the security chain. – Kevin Mitnick, in testimony at the Senate Governmental Affairs Committee, March 2000.

The scope of this book is not wide enough to help protect your applications against well-engineered social exploits or infrastructure implementation; however, we can discuss ways to build out an application that takes a serious approach to protecting the data it serves. By understanding some of the contexts under which an application might become susceptible to attackers, we can better deal with low-hanging fruit that would be the target of potential perpetrators.

Internal Threats

In the case of the development team at Alpine Ski Resort, they had a strong sense of security with their code base because they trusted each other with sensitive data and believed their source code to be secure in a private GitHub repository.

What we tend to forget, especially on smaller teams, is that the basic nature of our trust is often inherently transient. The team dynamic you have one day can change quickly with the addition of an intern, the resignation of a long-time employee, or a change in department structure. When these variations surface or any other adjustment comes into play, you have no idea how data you have access to today might be used. Therefore, you must ensure that things like production keys, or even access keys from lower-level environments, do not permeate the source code control system. By adhering to principles of least privilege, you can enable employees to do their work without requiring them to be in control of the keys to the kingdom. Failure to adhere to such tenets increases the chance of secrets being exposed, which could happen via an employee with ill-intent, a disgruntled employee or through a security breach where a developer's machine is infected with malware. If that same employee is never given the keys, the breach is much more likely to be isolated.

Most third party services provide developer-level API keys and access tokens that allow you to keep your production codes safely out of the development environment. Generally speaking, it's in the best interest of such parties to do so because it also helps them protect the data and services they provide. If obtaining developer keys is not immediately a visible option, it is worth asking the provider directly to help you out! You can protect your developers from being exploited simply by not giving them the information that would be the target of an attack. If the production access tokens are not in the repository, they can't find their way into malicious hands. We cover access tokens a little later in this chapter in the "User Secrets" section.

Other attack vectors for the exploit or misuse of application services are largely tied to excessive access rights provided by APIs. This might include vulnerabilities created unintentionally, such as when an API is used internally and is assumed safe, so it does not require authentication. Authentication is a good step, but an app or service that grants an authenticated user unrestricted access to the system is also a risk. With the right tools, an attacker can use the application services in an unexpected way, such as skirting around the web UI and using their username and password to access the API directly. As we discuss identity, claims, and policies throughout this chapter, you'll learn how to better segregate authorization from authentication to protect your APIs.

There is one more type of risk: technical debt. All too often we see occurrences of misuse, that otherwise have not been possible, due simply to rushing a feature out the door without proper consideration for security and data integrity. We spoke about the concept of over-binding in Chapter 3, "Models, Views and Controllers," and how by simply running with the same model for read and write scenarios, we open up a vulnerability. A holistic and honest review of your software often reveals susceptibilities that your development team already knows about, and that's without diving into the code.

External Threats

Even when services are meant for internal applications, it is likely that at some point you're going to be consuming data coming from outside sources or interacting with other API services to benefit your users or enable business scenarios. It is an unfortunate reality that we live in a world where we need to think about how those interactions take place and to what extent we trust the data we process, the callers of our application, or the services that we interact with.

Are you importing data? It is important to know where it comes from. Do you validate the entire file as a batch of records, or do you just perform per-line validation? Some exploits are possible because while every row is valid, as a whole, the file or operation orchestrated by the file can constitute fraud. Are users able to create or modify documents in your application? Most of these scenarios are a form of resource manipulation, and can therefore be treated with the appropriate policy application.

Do you expose your data to partner sites? This is a legitimate and often worthwhile scenario that can distinguish your organization from the competition. When you do so, do you include checks to ensure that the site reusing your APIs is one you trust? All major browsers now support the ability to block scripts from loading data if the server does not know the originating caller.

User Secrets

Let's get back to the development team at Alpine Ski Resort. We should all be at least somewhat offended if someone in management is handing out access keys to the development team. In some ways, this is akin to giving all tellers, and perhaps the night security patrol officer, the codes to the bank vault in the basement. If the management team understands the business, production access keys are held in much higher regard.

This is largely where user secrets come in: there is a need for developers to reliably develop and use an application locally that has access to secured resources and services. Rather than assuming rights to sensitive keys, data, and services, developers can register for their own instance of an application service, such as with Facebook, and then locally use their own keys. To do this, developers need a mechanism to store the credentials, to load them into the application when it's executed, and to prevent these keys from being shared with others. This is especially true when those keys can incur costs or cause other side-effects if unintended parties use them, which is why developers should guard their own tokens and keys with a good measure of care.

The other benefit of encouraging developers to use private keys specific to their accounts is related to resource utilization, auditability, and cost. While using vendor provided sandbox services is typically encouraged in higher-level environments, you should investigate to see if the service has limitations or restrictions on how developers interact with the API. If such restrictions exist, those services are likely good candidates for being called with unique keys by each developer.

You can think of user secrets as per-user, per-project environment variables. These are configuration values that are isolated from the project, but made available at runtime through the ASP.NET Core configuration system. User secrets are stored under the user's profile as a JSON file, and most typically consist of key-value pairs, though more complicated structures are achievable as we learned in Chapter 12, "Configuration and Logging."

The basic operation of adding secrets is fairly straightforward:

```
dotnet user-secret set YourKey "The value you wish to set it to"
```

At the time of this writing, there are only a limited set of commands to interact with user secrets from the Command Line Interface (CLI):

- **set:** Assigns the provided value to the specified key

- **list:** Lists all known user secrets for the user given the project

- **remove:** Removes the specified key value pair from the store

- **clear:** Removes all keys from the store without confirmation

The user-secret command can only be run in a directory where a project.json file exists, and the file must contain a value for userSecretsId, doing otherwise would give you an execution failure. The command uses the value for the userSecretsId to access a very specific folder on disk, located under your user profile.

User secrets are stored as a JSON file, and therefore allow for multiple levels of structure and property assignment. From the CLI, the basic commands don't allow you to easily set up more complicated secrets using sections. There are no commands to create complex objects with nested properties, and tasks, like deleting many keys, which can become tedious. You don't need to use the CLI, however, because you can access the file in plain-text form directly. You can find this file at appdata\Roaming\Microsoft\UserSecrets in a directory with the same name as your `userSecretsId`. You can also access this file directly in Visual Studio by right-clicking the project node in Solution Explorer and choosing Manage User Secrets.

Azure-Backed Authentication

In corporate settings, where users are provisioned by administrators and accounts and tied to internal roles and policies, you often find Active Directory (AD) behind the scenes. Active Directory has found its way to the cloud, and is available as an Microsoft Azure offering as a service. There are facilities to link your internal Active Directory to a cloud-hosted instance, and you can import or migrate your internal directory to a permanent, managed solution out in Microsoft Azure, and even tie in users from your organization's Office 365 account. This gives you the benefit of multi-region reliability and failover support, a high SLA for uptime, and the peace of mind knowing you'll be upgraded on-the-fly and hosted by a well-secured infrastructure. It also lets you add features like mobile support, multi-factor authentication, and remote policy enforcement to a myriad of devices.

Options in Azure Active Directory

When choosing Microsoft Azure Active Directory as the authentication mechanism for your application, you have the choice of two configurations:

- **Single-tenant:** Your application is connected to your corporate directory. Users in your domain are able to sign on according to policies that are set by administrators.

- **Multi-tenant:** The application is configured so that multiple directories from your Microsoft Azure account, or those external to your account, can be enabled to support authentication to your application. Each organization has to perform the requisite provisioning for your application, but this allows each of those organizations to access your app.

Microsoft Azure provides you with information about the authenticating organization, so in multi-tenant scenarios, you have the ability to conform the user's experience to one that is appropriate in your context.

While these features might lend well to the success of an internal application, the goal of most consumer-facing applications is to allow self-sign up and administration. Microsoft Azure Active Directory sets its sights on inward-facing users, users that can benefit from centralized administration, and users that otherwise might already have an organizational account. These features do not typically align with the type of application we're building with Alpine, where the external user is our focus.

Users Outside Your Organization

When you want to provide your customers with a personalized experience, you need them to authenticate, but you also don't want the barrier of requiring administrators to create user accounts.There's another set of concerns that don't fit single-tenant or multi-tenant authentication options, either from a workload or a cost perspective:

- We want users to self-provision and manage their accounts, without requiring administrative intervention to sign up or make account changes.

- Users might be transient, generating little or no revenue for our organization before leaving the site and not using its features.

- Users might want to bring their own identity, using an account from a third-party site such as Google or Facebook.

- Users often use the same set of credentials from site-to-site. If those credentials are compromised in another less-secure location, their experience and data in our app could be compromised as well.

For these reasons, Microsoft Azure also has an offering called Azure Active Directory B2C, which boasts the same high availability of Azure Active Directory, because it's built on Azure Active Directory, but with the added benefit of providing authentication sources from social account sites. There is a free tier to help you get started, allowing 50,000 unique users and 50,000 total authentications per month. After authenticating, Azure AD B2C redirects back to your application with a JWT token that contains the information collected about the user through the local data store or the social login service via claims.

To get started with Azure AD B2C, first you need to create a B2C directory in your Microsoft Azure subscription. Be sure to check the B2C box, as shown in Figure 13-1, when creating your directory, because it can't be changed after you've created it. It can take a few minutes for the directory to be fully enabled.

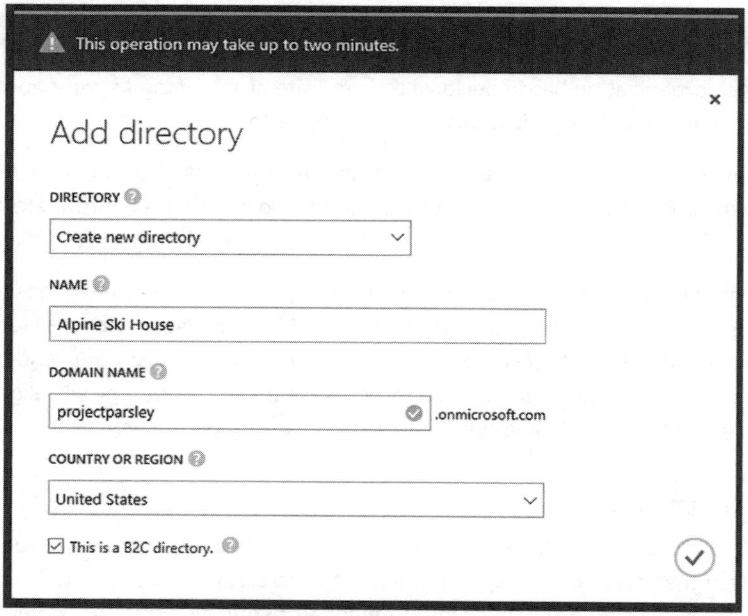

FIGURE 13-1 Creating a B2C Directory

After creating the directory, you need to complete a number of configuration options to get it fully working inside your application, namely adding social identity providers, selecting user attributes, and adding the required settings to your application.

Social identity providers, such as Microsoft Account or Facebook, require that you first register an application within those services. For a list of registration locations for each supported provider, please visit *http://aspnetmonsters.com/2016/09/heres-a-handy-list-of-social-login-providers/*. As you configure the identity providers in Azure AD B2C, you are prompted to complete the form you see in Figure 13-2, which allows the services to communicate and establish the user identity.

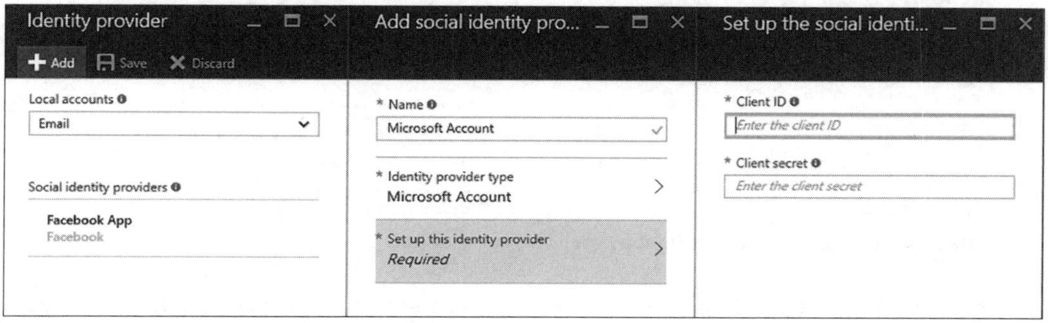

FIGURE 13-2 Adding a Social Identity Provider to Azure AD B2C

When you register with those services, you receive a client ID and secret to use when configuring the B2C service. The interface for each provider is different and we'll leave it as an exercise for you to locate the settings we need, but Figure 13-3 presents such an interface in the developer tools for Facebook applications. In this case, the Client ID is called the App ID and the Client Secret is simply referred to as the App Secret, but these names might vary from service to service.

FIGURE 13-3 Locating Your Client ID and secret in a Facebook application

After the social providers have been added, you can then optionally add user-specific attributes, if it's something that is appropriate for your application's signup process. For instance, the ski size a person typically rents might be a user preference that can be associated with the user, but it's not something that should be required as part of the signup process. Things like a display name and an email address, however, are things that can be provided by many social login services, and, are reasonable to ask users for when they first create an account. To require these fields at the time of signup, you need to create a policy, such as in Figure 13-4, where the attributes you want included are bound to the directory's sign-up policy.

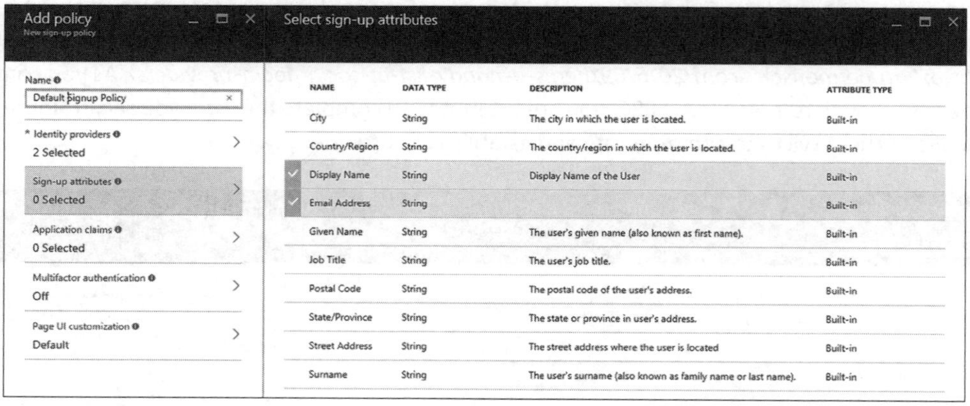

FIGURE 13-4 Configuring a Default Signup Policy for your directory

If you want to use the Display Name and Email Address attributes in your application, you also need to configure the Application Claims section that allows these values to be passed through to your application in the JWT token. Beyond the sign up process, you can also create sign in policies to control multi-factor authentication or configure policies around profile editing or password resets. Policies provide a powerful mechanism for you to describe the identity management experience you would like to offer your users.

Finally, you need to generate the values required for an application to leverage Azure AD B2C. To do this, you must add an application to the tenant, which is shown in Figure 13-5. Note that you also need to ensure that you've selected the options for web app/web API as well as enabling implicit flow. These options are required for you to get Open ID Connect working for your application.

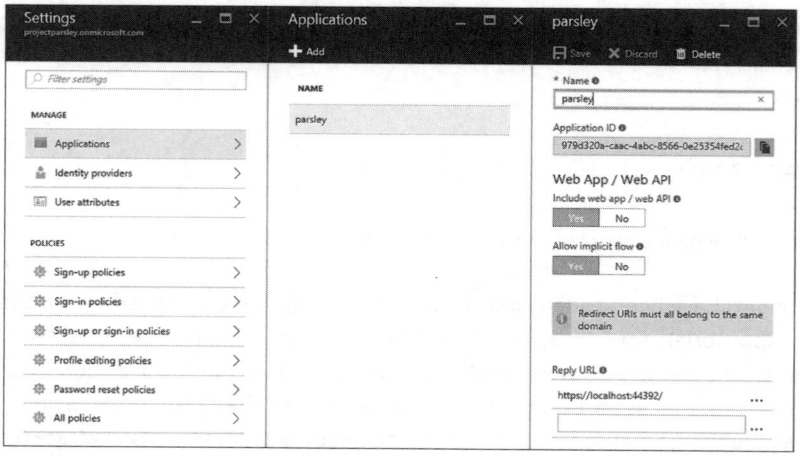

FIGURE 13-5 Registering your application in Azure AD B2C

Next, you need to add those settings to your application. In your appsettings.json file, you can add the following values at the root of your configuration as shown here in Listing 13-1.

LISTING 13-1 The expected configuration elements needed to configure the Azure AD B2C middleware

```
"AzureAd": {
  "ClientId": "CLIENT_ID_FROM_PORTAL",
  "Tenant": "YOUR_TENANT.onmicrosoft.com",
  "AadInstance": "https://login.microsoftonline.com/{0}/v2.0/.well-known/openid-
configuration?p={1}",
  "PostLogoutRedirectUri": "https://localhost:44392/",
  "SignUpPolicyId": "B2C_1_YOUR_SIGN_UP_POLICY_NAME",
  "SignInPolicyId": "B2C_1_YOUR_SIGN_IN_POLICY_NAME"
}
```

Change the tokenized values to your own values, and be sure to set the appropriate endpoint for the redirect URI. As we discussed earlier in the chapter, if these are sensitive values, making use of the User Secrets tooling is worth considering. With these settings in place, the next step is to add the packages to support OpenID Connect to your project.json file. The packages you need to include are:

```
Microsoft.AspNetCore.Authentication.Cookies
Microsoft.AspNetCore.Authentication.OpenIdConnect
```

You now have the pieces you need to configure the requisite authentication middleware for your site, namely the user secrets loaded at startup and the authentication packages to access an OpenID Connect gateway. You need to do this for each policy that you create in Azure AD B2C. To support the two policies added in the configuration in Listing 13-1, you need to create make two calls to `UseOpenIdConnectAuthentication` using the data you added to the configuration, and configure the middleware for each policy, which can look similar to the following:

```
app.UseOpenIdConnectAuthentication(signUpPolicy));
app.UseOpenIdConnectAuthentication(signInPolicy));
```

Finally, you need to create or modify an `AccountController` so that it supports the necessary identity functions. This includes signing up, logging in, and logging out. For instance, to handle sign ups, you can implement the following code in a `SignUp` method:

```
var policyId = Startup.SignUpPolicyId.ToLower();
var authProperties = new AuthenticationProperties { RedirectUri = "/" };
await HttpContext.Authentication.ChallengeAsync(policyId, authProperties);
```

This code captures the `policyId` from the `Startup` class, creates an instance of the `AuthenticationProperties` object, and then responds to the request with an HTTP Challenge. You can implement actions for other policies in a similar fashion.

> **Note** The experience for configuration and implementation at the time of writing this text is still evolving, and while the mechanics remain similar, the code itself is subject to change. It is likely that as B2C matures, middleware and simplified configuration might be available for the offering as a whole. Be sure to visit *https://azure.microsoft.com/en-us/documentation/services/active-directory-b2c/* for the most up-to-date information on integrating Azure AD B2C into your application, including a complete code sample to work with ASP.NET Core MVC.

Each organization, and perhaps each project within an organization, has to make choices about how to establish user identity. Azure Active Directory and Azure AD B2C give you a number of options to consider without burdening you with the need to create and manage an identity store within your application. For Alpine Ski House, we are only expecting approximately a few hundred logins per day. Our policies, roles, and access restrictions are fairly static, and we don't believe that adding the external dependency is going to add value to the project. Instead, we opted to use the components that were built-in to the project template for identity, along with those available via NuGet.

Identity in ASP.NET Core MVC

ASP.NET Core provides authentication, authorization, and user management via the built in ASP.NET Core Identity. While Identity offers an overwhelming number of configuration options, most applications are served well with only minor changes to the default configuration options.

The entities in the ASP.NET Core Identity model are `IdentityUser`, `IdentityRole`, `IdentityUser-Claim`, `IdentityRoleClaim`, `IdentityUserLogin,` and `IdentityUserToken`. When configured to use Entity Framework, as is the Alpine Ski House Web application, these entities are stored in tables, as shown in Figure 13-6. Note that the tables for ASP.NET Core Identity are all prefixed with `AspNet` instead of `Identity`, such as the table for `IdentityRole` is `AspNetRoles`.

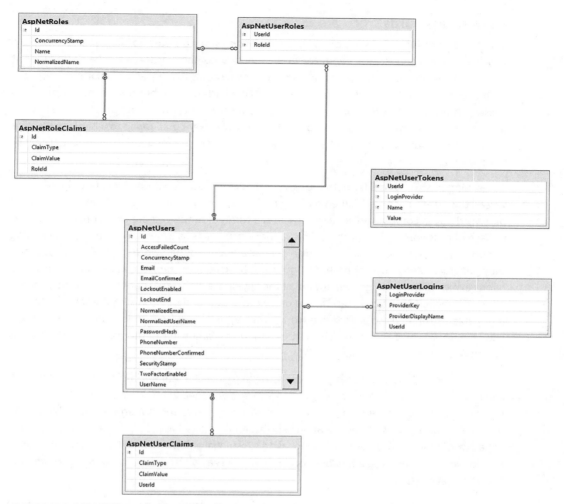

FIGURE 13.6 ASP.NET Core Identity tables

IdentityUser contains information about the users in the application. It is represented by the ApplicationUser class, which can be extended as we discussed in Chapter 10, "Entity Framework Core." The base IdentityUser class contains a unique id and some other optional properties that might or might not be used depending on the needs of the application. For example, if the user creates a password within the application, the PasswordHash property contains a cryptographically strong hash of the user's password. There are also properties to store a user's Email and PhoneNumber, and Boolean values indicating whether or not the Email and PhoneNumber have been confirmed. There is also an option here to keep track of the number of failed login attempts and whether the account has been locked.

Storing Passwords

Storing passwords is always a tricky proposition. When storing a password, there are a couple of ways to do it and almost all of them are wrong. Encrypting passwords seems like a good idea at first, but if the encrypted passwords are leaked, which seems to happen with alarming regularity, an attacker could decrypt the passwords. This is a bad situation because many people reuse passwords from site to site. Not only do you put your own site at risk, but also other sites. With a password and an email address it is possible that the attacker could log in to a banking website or some other high impact site. This is the reason that it is recommended for people to use distinct passwords for each website.

Hashing passwords is a far better idea. A hash is a one-way function that cannot be reversed to reveal a password. When hashing passwords, it is important to hash not just the user's password but to combine it with a salt. A salt is a string of random characters appended to the unhashed password before hashing. This random string acts as protection from an attack using rainbow tables. A rainbow table is a large database that maps passwords with the hashes that they generate. Many popular hashing algorithms have rainbow tables that permit near instantaneous exploration of a large percentage of the key-space. Salts invalidate this approach because the key in the rainbow table maps to the password + salt. Without knowing the salt, an attacker is not able to enter any password that works. The key in the rainbow table is unlikely to be the actual user password and more likely to be a string that simply hashes to the same value, so it is not obvious what the user's password is.

Even when hashing passwords, you need to remain vigilant about the implementation. Many common hashing functions, such as MD5 and SHA, are designed to be as fast as possible. Their purpose is to give a checksum of a file so you know if the file is correct. When you are hashing large quantities of data you want the operation to be as simple and fast as possible. The opposite is true of password hashing. You want hashing to take a substantial amount of time to avoid brute force attacks, preferably by using a tunable algorithm that can easily be made to take longer as computer resources get cheaper.

How easy is it to break a password hashed with a low grade hashing function? Well famed hacker Kevin Mitnick provides a hint:

> I love my new 4 GPU password cracker. Over 60 BILLION NTLM hashes a second.

> :-) Unfortunately, Md5crypt is much slower. I need to add cards. -Kevin Mitnick (@ kevinmitnick)

Attacks on MD5 Hashed Passwords[1], published in 2005 by Robertiello and Bandla, suggested that they could brute force an MD5 password in 96 hours using a simple CPU based approach. Modern GPU approaches coupled with cheap hardware and even elastic computing makes cracking MD5 not only possible, but easy.

---

[1] http://pamsusc.googlecode.com/svn-history/r38/CSCI555/thesis/papers/RAINBOW_report.pdf

> Fortunately, all of this is handled for you by ASP.NET Identity. When configured to use local accounts, ASP.NET Identity hashes passwords using the `PasswordHasher`.
> By default, the `PasswordHasher` in ASP.NET Identity uses a PBKDF2 hash (HMAC-SHA256), a 128-bit salt, a 256-bit subkey, and 10,000 iterations. This is by all measure a very strong hash that would take a substantial amount of time to crack. This hash is stored in the `PasswordHash` column of the `AspNetUsers` table and is used by the `SigninManager` to confirm a user's password when he attempts to log in.

An `IdentityRole` represents a role, and `IdentityUsers` can belong to any number of `IdentityRoles`. Membership to an `IdentityRole` can be used to authorize users to areas or resources within the application, which we discuss in the "Enabling Security Through Attributes" section of this chapter.

ASP.NET Identity makes heavy use of claims. A claim is simply a name-value pair that contains some information about the user. A claim can be issued by a trusted party, such as Facebook, or they can be added by your application. Some examples of claims are a user's email address and a user's birth date. In ASP.NET Core Identity, claims for a specific user are represented by the `IdentityUserClaim` entity. Claims can also be added to a group of users in the `IdentityRoleUserClaims` entity, although this is less common. Claims are an important aspect of Authorization, as we discuss in the "Custom Authorization Policies" section of this chapter.

The `IdentityUserLogin` entity represents a login from a trusted third party. We discuss Third-Party authentication providers, such as Facebook and Twitter, in the "Other Third-Party Authentication Providers" section of this chapter.

`IdentityUserTokens` represent an access token related to a particular user. These tokens are typically used to grant access to an application's public API. An example of this approach is how GitHub allows users to generate a personal access token that can be used to access the GitHub API. We don't plan to use `IdentityUserTokens` in the `AlpineSkiHouse` application.

Referencing ASP.NET Identity

ASP.NET Core Identity is automatically added to applications that are created using the default ASP.NET Core project templates. It is important to understand however, what packages are referenced and how they are configured.

When we created the `AlpineSkiHouse.Web` project, we selected the Authentication: Individual User Accounts option. Selecting this option adds a reference to `Microsoft.AspNetCore.Identity.EntityFrameworkCore,` which in turn references the `Microsoft.AspNetCore.Identity` package. The project template also generates some boilerplate code for managing users in the application. We previously reviewed the `ApplicationUser` class and its associated `DbContext` in Chapter 10.

In the Startup class, we see the following configuration that tells ASP.NET Identity to use the `ApplicationUser` class and that you are using Entity Framework to store the Identity model:

Configuration for ASP.NET Identity in Startup.ConfigureServices

```
services.AddIdentity<ApplicationUser, IdentityRole>()
```

```
    .AddEntityFrameworkStores<ApplicationUserContext>()
    .AddDefaultTokenProviders();
```

Here, you also have the option to specify additional options. For example, you can change how many invalid login attempts it would take to trigger an account lockout.

```
services.AddIdentity<ApplicationUser, IdentityRole>(
    options =>
    {
        options.Lockout.MaxFailedAccessAttempts = 3;
    })
    .AddEntityFrameworkStores<ApplicationUserContext>()
    .AddDefaultTokenProviders();
```

Other options are available to configure password strength requirements, username requirements, paths for user login and logout, the length of time an authentication cookie is valid, and much more.

See Also *For a complete list of options see https://docs.asp.net/en/latest/security/authentication/identity.html or visit the identity repository at https://github.com/aspnet/Identity/blob/dev/src/Microsoft.AspNetCore.Identity/ IdentityOptions.cs.*

The final step in configuring ASP.NET Identity is calling app.UseIdentity(); in the Configure method of your Startup class. This call should occur just before app.UseMvc();.

Local User Accounts

ASP.NET Identity provides mechanisms for managing users and authenticating users via the User-Manager and SignInManager classes respectively. A significant amount of the code for managing local accounts is already created by the default project templates. Let's take some time to explore this code in a little more detail.

Managing Users

The UserManager class is used to manage users in ASP.NET Identity Core. For example, during registration a new user is created by calling the CreateAsync method.

```
var user = new ApplicationUser
{
    UserName = model.Email,
    Email = model.Email,
    FirstName = model.FirstName,
    LastName = model.LastName,
    PhoneNumber = model.PhoneNumber
};
var result = await _userManager.CreateAsync(user, model.Password);
```

The UserManager class provides a ton of functionality that is otherwise very tedious to implement. Examples include mechanisms for confirming email addresses and phone numbers, resetting passwords, and locking and unlocking users account. These mechanisms are well documented on the official ASP.NET docs site, located at *https://docs.asp.net/en/latest/security/authentication/accconfirm.html*.

Authenticating Users

When a user chooses to sign in using their local account, you need to verify the user's identity based on the username and password supplied via the login form. Verifying the username and password is done using the SignInManager that is injected into the AccountController.

```
//
// POST: /Account/Login
[HttpPost]
[AllowAnonymous]
[ValidateAntiForgeryToken]
public async Task<IActionResult> Login(LoginViewModel model, string returnUrl = null)
{
    ViewData["ReturnUrl"] = returnUrl;
    if (ModelState.IsValid)
    {
        var result = await _signInManager.PasswordSignInAsync(model.Email, model.
        Password, model.RememberMe, lockoutOnFailure: false);
        if (result.Succeeded)
        {
            _logger.LogInformation(1, "User logged in.");
            return RedirectToLocal(returnUrl);
        }
        if (result.RequiresTwoFactor)
        {
            return RedirectToAction(nameof(SendCode), new { ReturnUrl = returnUrl,
            RememberMe = model.RememberMe });
        }
        if (result.IsLockedOut)
        {
            _logger.LogWarning(2, "User account locked out.");
            return View("Lockout");
        }
        else
        {
            ModelState.AddModelError(string.Empty, "Invalid login attempt.");
            return View(model);
        }
    }

    // If we got this far, something failed, redisplay form
    return View(model);
}
```

If the specified username and password match, the sign in is successful and the SignInManager adds a special authentication cookie to the HttpResponse. The value of the cookie is an encrypted string that is actually a serialized instance of a ClaimsPrincipal. The ClaimsPrincipal uniquely identifies the user and his or her claims. In subsequent requests, ASP.NET Identity validates the authentication cookie, decrypts the ClaimsPrincipal, and assigns it to the User property of the HttpContext. This way, each request is associated with a particular user without having to pass the username and password with every request. The decrypted and deserialized ClaimsPrincipal can be accessed from any controller action via the User property.

Note The cookie based approach to authentication in ASP.NET Core Identity is implemented using middleware. Cookie middleware can be used independently of ASP.NET Identity via the `Microsoft.AspNetCore.Authentication.Cookies` package. For more details, see *https://docs.asp.net/en/latest/security/authentication/cookie.html*.

The `SignInManager` provides some optional features. One option is whether failed login attempts should count toward account lockout. Locking accounts after a number of failed attempts is an important security measure. The default template disables this behavior because the template does not include a mechanism for system administrators to unlock locked accounts. We are making note of this and adding the lockout functionality in a future sprint. For now, support issues related to lockouts are escalated to the development team where accounts are unlocked manually via the database. Another option is to enable two factor authentication. When two factor authentication, or 2FA, is enabled, the system sends a random code via email or text message after the user has entered a valid username and password. The user is redirected to a page where he can enter the code. The user cannot be signed in until the code has be validated. A complete tutorial on enabling two factor authentication using SMS can found on the official ASP.NET docs site, located at *https://docs.asp.net/en/latest/security/authentication/2fa.html*.

Other Third-Party Authentication Providers

ASP.NET Identity provides easy integration with third-party authentication providers, which are referred to as external login providers. The Alpine team has elected to allow users to log in with Twitter or Facebook as an external source, as illustrated in Figure 13-7.

One of the goals with Project Parsley is to increase customer engagement via social networks, so Facebook and Twitter are a natural choice of authentication providers for the application.

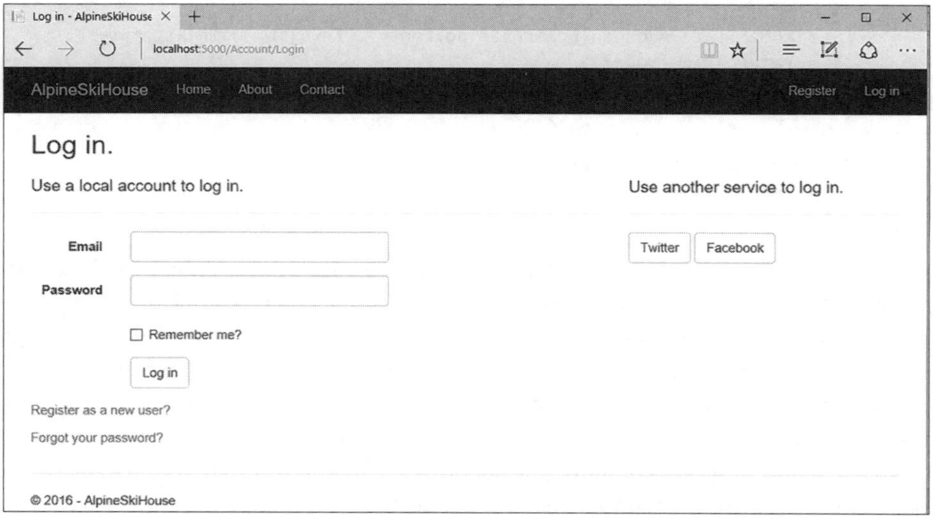

FIGURE 13-7 Logging In with an External Provider

To enable login using Facebook and Twitter, add references to the appropriate NuGet packages.

```
"Microsoft.AspNetCore.Authentication.Facebook": "1.0.0",
"Microsoft.AspNetCore.Authentication.Twitter": "1.0.0"
```

Next, configure the providers in the Configure method of the Startup class.

```
app.UseIdentity();


if (Configuration["Authentication:Facebook:AppId"] == null ||
    Configuration["Authentication:Facebook:AppSecret"] == null ||
    Configuration["Authentication:Twitter:ConsumerKey"] == null ||
    Configuration["Authentication:Twitter:ConsumerSecret"] == null)
    throw new KeyNotFoundException("A configuration value is missing for authentication against
Facebook and Twitter. While you don't need to get tokens for these you do need to set up your
user secrets as described in the readme.");
app.UseFacebookAuthentication(new FacebookOptions
{
    AppId = Configuration["Authentication:Facebook:AppId"],
    AppSecret = Configuration["Authentication:Facebook:AppSecret"]
});

app.UseTwitterAuthentication(new TwitterOptions
{
    ConsumerKey = Configuration["Authentication:Twitter:ConsumerKey"],
    ConsumerSecret = Configuration["Authentication:Twitter:ConsumerSecret"]
});
```

Each external login provider requires a set of public and private tokens. The method for obtaining these tokens differs for each provider, so refer to the provider's developer documentation for specific instructions. As we discussed earlier in the "Internal Threats" section of this chapter, these tokens need to be kept private, which is why we are retrieving them from configuration instead of embedding them directly in the code.

On the Login page, you are able to display buttons to log in via any configured external providers. When users select one of these providers, for example the Facebook provider, they are redirected to the Facebook login page where they are prompted to enter their Facebook usernames and passwords. Assuming the Facebook login is successful, the user is redirected to the Account/ExternalLoginCallback endpoint in the Alpine Ski House web application. In this action method, we are able to obtain login information about the user from the SignInManager and then attempt to sign the user in to our application using the external login information.

```
ExternalLoginInfo info = await _signInManager.GetExternalLoginInfoAsync();
if (info == null)
{
    return RedirectToAction(nameof(Login));
}

// Sign in the user with this external login provider if the user already has a login.
var result = await _signInManager.ExternalLoginSignInAsync(info.LoginProvider,
                        info.ProviderKey, isPersistent: false);
```

```
if (result.Succeeded)
{
    _logger.LogInformation(5, "User logged in with {Name} provider.", info.LoginProvider);
    return RedirectToLocal(returnUrl);
}
if (result.RequiresTwoFactor)
{
    return RedirectToAction(nameof(SendCode), new { ReturnUrl = returnUrl });
}
if (result.IsLockedOut)
{
    return View("Lockout");
}
```

If the login does not succeed, we need to give the user an opportunity to create a new account with Alpine Ski House. When creating a new account, we want to capture some additional account details, such as email address, first name, last name, phone number, and age. Some of the external login providers provide some of this information as claims values that can be found on the ExternalLoginInfo's Principal property. For example, the Facebook provider makes the user's email, first name, and last name available, which we are then able to pre-populate for the user. The Twitter provider does not populate any of these claims.

```
// If the user does not have an account, then ask the user to create an account.
ViewData["ReturnUrl"] = returnUrl;
ViewData["LoginProvider"] = info.LoginProvider;
var email = info.Principal.FindFirstValue(ClaimTypes.Email);
var lastName = info.Principal.FindFirstValue(ClaimTypes.Surname);
var firstName = info.Principal.FindFirstValue(ClaimTypes.GivenName);

return View("ExternalLoginConfirmation",
    new ExternalLoginConfirmationViewModel
    {
        Email = email,
        FirstName = firstName,
        LastName = lastName
    });
```

> **Note** Microsoft provides packages that integrate with the built in identity constructs to support authentication via Facebook, Twitter, Google, and Microsoft accounts, all of which can be found on NuGet. It is also possible to support logins from other providers via custom implementations that you or third-parties would write. See *http://aspnetmonsters.com/2016/04/github-authentication-asp-net-core/* for a tutorial on enabling GitHub authentication.

Enabling Security Through Attributes

One of the benefits of having a comprehensive framework in place underneath your application is that many of the opt-in pieces complement each other nicely. After authentication is enabled in your application via middleware, you are now able to leverage it through the use of global filters or through the attributes you decorate your classes and methods with. We look at filters in the next section, but they are something a developer in the MVC realm might already be familiar with. In ASP.NET Core however, they are implemented based on the concept of application policies.

In the simplest form of use, you can require that a user be authenticated simply by decorating the class with the Authorize attribute. You can see this in the definition of the SkiCardController:

```
[Authorize]
public class SkiCardController : Controller
{
  // ...
}
```

Alternately, if you do not want every action to require authentication, you can also use the attribute at the method level:

```
[Authorize]
public async Task<ActionResult> Create()
{
  // ...
}
```

If you have decorated your controller with the Authorize attribute, you might still want to allow an unauthenticated user to access an action that resides within it. This is typically seen in the AccountController and in similar classes where, generally speaking, you want users to be authenticated, but when they are in the process of registering, they do not yet have an account to sign in with. This is enabled by decorating the action with the following attribute:

```
[AllowAnonymous]
public IActionResult Register(string returnUrl = null)
{
    ViewData["ReturnUrl"] = returnUrl;
    return View();
}
```

You can add another level of specificity to the attribute and specify the roles of the authenticated user by passing the values to the attribute constructor like so: [Authorize(Roles = "customer,csr")]. If you use a single attribute, the user must be in at least one of the roles you provide in the comma-separated list. If you use multiple Authorize attributes, they must be in every role that you specify.

When you add an Authorize attribute and specify a role, the framework is working behind the scenes to resolve that role with a RolesAuthorizationRequirement. It makes use of the ClaimsPrinciple.IsInRole() method to iterate over all of the roles that the user belongs to, as presented in their claims. Essentially, if your login process decorates the user with a claim in some way, it is added to the user's identity and the user is allowed into the corresponding parts of your application. You are limited, however, because the roles you specify are fixed at compile time and cannot change at runtime.

The good news is that there is no magic in these parts and the `Authorize` attribute isn't your only option. You have the ability to craft the same types of constructs to define security in the way that suits your organization. Instead of using constants in your code, you can build up rich requirements and policies to protect your application, as we'll discuss next.

Using Policies for Authorization

A policy is a set of requirements used to control access based on the properties of the request, the client that made the request, the claims of the user's identity who initiated the request, and any other factor you might want to build in. Out of the box, you can set up policies that include requirements based on operations, roles, or other claims.

Applying Policies Globally

Globally requiring an authenticated user is a common practice, where anyone who wants to access the site is required to present some kind of identity token. In most scenarios this is handled by the browser from the client side and middleware on the server side, by using cookies and being negotiated through a challenge/login model. Enabling a global rule that requires authentication for all application access includes creating a policy and adding that policy to the `FilterCollection` of the application. While we are not implementing this in the Alpine Ski House application, if we were going to, we'd be doing it during application startup. In the `ConfigureServices` method of Startup.cs, there is a line of code that adds the MVC services to the dependency injection container:

```
services.AddMvc();
```

AddMvc() also contains an overload that accepts an action that then receives an `MvcOptions` parameter. `MvcOptions` gives us access to a number of properties, one of which is the collection of filters we use in our Alpine Ski House application. We can create our filter and add it to this collection as follows:

```
services.AddMvc(options =>
{
    var policy = new AuthorizationPolicyBuilder()
        .RequireAuthenticatedUser()
        .Build();
    options.Filters.Add(new AuthorizeFilter(policy));
}
);
```

Behind the scenes, this is doing the same thing that the attribute is doing by adding a requirement to the pipeline of type DenyAnonymousAuthorizationRequirement. When a request is being executed, this requirement fails for any user who is not logged in. You can still opt out of this filter by using the AllowAnonymous attribute at the controller or action level throughout your application.

Defining Policies for Selected Use

The `AuthorizationPolicyBuilder` isn't a one-trick pony either. You can use it to build policies that:

- Require particular claims

- Require explicit values of claims

- Require specific roles

- Use specific authentication schemes

- Combine any of the stated options into a single rule

Let's take a quick look at what is required to be able to define and use an administrative policy in our application. The requirements for this policy could be fairly trivial. For instance, we need to ensure that we have authenticated users who are in the Human Resources or Accounting departments and have an administrative role in our application. Assuming that we are attributing roles and department claims properly, our policy definition would be as follows:

```
var policy = new AuthorizationPolicyBuilder()
    .RequireAuthenticatedUser()
    .RequireRole("admin")
    .RequireClaim("department", new List<string> { "hr", "accounting" })
    .Build();
```

This resides in the `Startup` class in our `ConfigureServices` method. After defining the policy, we can then add it to the services available throughout our application.

```
services.AddAuthorization(options =>
{
    options.AddPolicy("RefundAccess", policy);
});
```

While it is convenient to use the `AuthorizationPolicyBuilder` with its fluent syntax, it's also possible to define the policies in-line with the lambda overload:

```
services.AddAuthorization(options =>
{
    options.AddPolicy("RefundAccess", policy =>
    {
        policy.RequireAuthenticatedUser();
        policy.RequireRole("admin");
        policy.RequireClaim("department", new List<string> { "hr", "accounting" });
    });
});
```

With a named `RefundAccess` policy in place, we can now decorate any of our controllers or actions with the Authorize attribute as before, but now we are also able to specify the policy name:

```
[Authorize("RefundAccess")]
public class HomeController : Controller
{
    // ...
}
```

These facilities cover many authorization scenarios in an application, but they do have limitations. For example, policies created with the builder or lambda methods mentioned previously, are essentially static throughout the life of the application because they are configured during startup. Further, these approaches do not allow factors at runtime to affect a user's ability to be approved or rejected by a policy. When the requirements and policies that are available through the framework still do not provide you with the level of control you require, you are free to create and integrate your own.

Custom Authorization Policies

Authorization attributes and claims policies provide most of the functionality you need for authorization in our Alpine Ski House application, but there are times when we might need to implement more custom logic to decide whether a user is authorized to do something in the application. In ASP.NET Core Identity, that logic is defined in custom authorization policies. An authorization policy is made up of one or more requirements and a handler that evaluates those requirements against the current authorization context.

A requirement is simply a class containing properties that define the requirement. The requirement class must inherit from IAuthorizationRequirement. A hypothetical requirement, used in the following example, is that an employee has been with the company for more than a specified period of time.

```
public class EmploymentDurationRequirement : IAuthorizationHandler
{
    public EmploymentDurationRequirement(int minimumMonths)
    {
        MinimumMonths = minimumMonths;
    }

    public int MinimumMonths { get; set; }
}
```

The logic for evaluating policy requirements is implemented in an authorization handler. Authorization handlers inherit from the base Authorization<T> class where T is the type of requirement being evaluated. For example, a handler for the EmploymentDurationRequirement can evaluate the minimum number of months of employment based on an employment date claim.

```
public class MinimumEmploymentDurationHandler :
                    AuthorizationHandler<EmploymentDurationRequirement>
{
    protected override Task HandleRequirementAsync(AuthorizationContext context,
EmploymentDurationRequirement requirement)
    {
        if (!context.User.HasClaim(c => c.Type == ClaimTypes.EmploymentDate &&
                            c.Issuer == "http://alpineskihouse.com"))
        {
            return Task.FromResult(0);
        }

        var employmentDate = Convert.ToDateTime(context.User.FindFirst(
            c => c.Type == ClaimTypes.EmploymentDate &&
```

```
                    c.Issuer == "http://alpineskihouse.com")Value);

        int numberOfMonths = (DateTime.Today - employmentDate).TotalMonths;
        if (numberOfMonths > requirement.MinimumMonths)
        {
            context.Succeed(requirement);
        }
        return Task.FromResult(0);
    }
}
```

After the requirements and handlers are defined, a custom policy can be defined in the Config-ureServices method of Startup.cs. cooki that the handler must also be registered with the services collection.

```
services.AddAuthorization(options =>
{
    options.AddPolicy("CompletedProbation",
            policy => policy.Requirements.Add(new MinimumEmploymentDurationHandler(3)));
});
services.AddSingleton<IAuthorizationHandler, MinimumEmploymentDurationHandler>();
```

Custom policies can be referenced just like any other authorization policies.

```
[Authorize(Policy = "CompletedProbation")]
public IActionResult GetSomeFreeSwag()
{
    return View();
}
```

Protecting Resources

It is often necessary to protect access to a particular resource based on authorization logic. An example of this is how a SkiCard can only be edited by the customer who created that SkiCard. In our initial imple-mentation, this was handled with logic in the Edit action method of the SkiCardController. By adding s.ApplicationUserId == userId to the SkiCard query, we are able to ensure that customers are only able to edit their own SkiCards.

```
var skiCard = await _skiCardContext.SkiCards
                    .SingleOrDefaultAsync(s => s.ApplicationUserId == userId
                                            && s.Id == viewModel.Id);

if (skiCard == null)
{
    return NotFound();
}
//Otherwise continue with Edit action
```

This approach works for simple scenarios, but it is potentially error prone and limiting. The restriction that only the owner of the SkiCard can edit the SkiCard is not clearly stated. The application also has a requirement to allow authorized system administrators to edit ski cards on behalf of a customer. Adding that level of complexity to the query makes for some obscure logic.

You can simplify this authorization process by creating a custom AuthorizationHandler for the SkiCard entity. First, you need to define an IAuthorizationRequirement that defines the type of requirement authorized by this handler. In this case, you are editing SkiCard entities, so create a class called EditSkiCardAuthorizationRequirement.

```
public class EditSkiCardAuthorizationRequirement : IAuthorizationRequirement
{
}
```

Next, create a class called EditSkiCardAuthorizationHandler that inherits from the base AuthorizationHandler class, specifying the requirement type and resource type as generic parameters. In the HandleRequirementAsync method, add the logic to check whether the current user can edit the specified SkiCard.

```
public class EditSkiCardAuthorizationHandler :
    AuthorizationHandler<EditSkiCardAuthorizationRequirement, SkiCard>
{
    private readonly UserManager<ApplicationUser> _userManager;

    public EditSkiCardAuthorizationHandler(UserManager<ApplicationUser> userManager)
    {
        _userManager = userManager;
    }

    protected override Task HandleRequirementAsync(AuthorizationHandlerContext context,
                            EditSkiCardAuthorizationRequirement requirement,
                            SkiCard skiCard)
    {
        var userId = _userManager.GetUserId(context.User);
        if (skiCard.ApplicationUserId == userId)
        {
            context.Succeed(requirement);
        }
        return Task.CompletedTask;
    }
}
```

Now the authorization requirements for editing a SkiCard are clearly stated and testable, as discussed in Chapter 20, "Testing." Next, register the AuthorizationHandler in the ConfigureServices method of Startup.cs.

```
services.AddSingleton<IAuthorizationHandler, EditSkiCardAuthorizationHandler>();
```

Finally, modify the SkiCardController to properly authorize users in the Edit action method. Unlike the previous custom authorization policy, you cannot use the declarative approach with the Authorize attribute because the SkiCard resource would not be known at the time the Authorize attribute is executed. Instead, use the IAuthorizationService to authorize users imperatively.

```
private readonly SkiCardContext _skiCardContext;
private readonly UserManager<ApplicationUser> _userManager;
private readonly IAuthorizationService _authorizationService;

public SkiCardController(SkiCardContext skiCardContext,
                         UserManager<ApplicationUser> userManager,
                         IAuthorizationService authorizationService)
{
    _skiCardContext = skiCardContext;
    _userManager = userManager;
    _authorizationService = authorizationService;
}
```

In the Edit action method, call the AuthorizeAsync method of the authorization service, passing in the current user, the ski card, and an instance of the EditSkiCardAuthorizationRequirement. If the AuthorizeAsync method returns true, you can continue. If not, return a ChallengeResult that redirects the user to the Account/AccessDenied.

```
[HttpPost]
[ValidateAntiForgeryToken]
public async Task<ActionResult> Edit(EditSkiCardViewModel viewModel)
{
    if (ModelState.IsValid)
    {
        var skiCard = await _skiCardContext.SkiCards
                    .SingleOrDefaultAsync(s => s.Id == viewModel.Id);

        if (skiCard == null)
        {
            return NotFound();
        }
        else if (await _authorizationService.AuthorizeAsync(User, skiCard, new
EditSkiCardAuthorizationRequirement()))
        {
            skiCard.CardHolderFirstName = viewModel.CardHolderFirstName;
            skiCard.CardHolderLastName = viewModel.CardHolderLastName;
            skiCard.CardHolderPhoneNumber = viewModel.CardHolderPhoneNumber;
            skiCard.CardHolderBirthDate = viewModel.CardHolderBirthDate.Value.Date;

            await _skiCardContext.SaveChangesAsync();
            return RedirectToAction(nameof(Index));
        }
        else
        {
            return new  ChallengeResult();
        }
    }
    return View(viewModel);
}
```

Cross-Origin Resource Sharing (CORS)

Many types of content and behaviors are required to render a rich webpage, from images and stylesheets, to scripts. Some of that content might be data or AJAX requests that have the ability to pull down additional payload to the browser. To prevent such requests from getting maliciously hijacked along the way, the CORS recommendation was incorporated into the recommended standards by the W3C (World Wide Web Consortium) to help establish trust between the client and the server.

For this to work, a browser making a request via AJAX to any domain other than the origin of the webpage itself, must present an Origin header. The server, in kind, needs to respond with an Access-Control-Allow-Origin header to signal that it expects requests from that domain. If it fails to respond with the expected values or header, the browser prevents the script that is requesting the resource from accessing the response returned by the server. While it doesn't protect the client in the event of a security breach on the server side, it does help eliminate much of the risk of cross-site scripting vulnerabilities.

When you intend to open an API to a website that does not originate from the same origin, you need to enable CORS in your application. You can say that two requests share the same origin if they both operate on the same domain, the same port, and the same scheme, HTTP or HTTPs. When enabling CORS, it is wise to enable it where you can modify or invalidate particular origins on the fly. An example of this is where you have an API that is consumed by third-parties who pay to access your API.

To enable CORS support in your application, you must first add the Microsoft.AspNetCore.Cors package to your project.json. Next, you need to add a CORS policy to the service container in your application in Startup.cs via the CorsPolicyBuilder:

```
public void ConfigureServices(IServiceCollection services)
{
  // other service config
  services.AddCors(options =>
  {
    options.AddPolicy("AlpineSkiHouseApiPolicy",
            builder => builder.WithOrigins("https://alpineskihouse.com"));
  }
  );
  // ...
}
```

The call to AddPolicy() allows you to both name and build the policy you want. You can then wire the CORS middleware into the application ahead of the call to UseMvc() in the Configure method of Startup.cs:

```
app.UseCors("AlpineSkiHouseApiPolicy");
```

The breadth of this policy might be too wide for your entire API, so you can actually omit the call to UseCors() altogether, and instead opt to use an attribute-based approach at the controller level.

```
[EnableCors("AlpineSkiHouseApiPolicy ")]

public class SkiPassValidationApiController : Controller
{
  // …
}
```

This approach gives you a more granular approach to enabling CORS for specific aspects of your API. You can also use EnableCors at the action level, or if you want to disable CORS for an action that would otherwise be included in the policy, globally or at the controller level, you can apply the DisableCors attribute.

Summary

There are many facets of security for an application and many volumes of text have already been written on the subject. Given today's atmosphere in the media, customers growing concern for privacy, and the increasing threat of applications being compromised, we must do what we can to ensure that only those we deem permissible have access to the appropriate parts of our application.

Certainly, the internal concerns we have are real and as software developers, we need to think about security as we write every piece of code. Beyond what we do internally, including how we write our code and to whom we allow access, it is also important to consider those attempting to access the system without our consent. For further reading on security as it relates to outward-facing systems, we recommend the Open Web Application Security Project (OWASP) community's body of work, located at *https://www.owasp.org/*.

It's clear that security is a sweeping subject and even though we discussed over a dozen concerns in this chapter, we didn't even touch on more traditional concepts, such as certificates or SQL injection attacks, but not because these topics are less important. Security is clearly something that needs to be at the front of every developer's mind, a topic that should be prevalent in conversations across the organization, and a theme in your project.

Security is just one category of services that will be used in your application. In the next chapter we'll look at how you can make those services available to every component in your project without any of the components needing to know the specifics of service instantiation.

CHAPTER 14

Dependency Injection

"This code is a tangled mess" complained Mark. "I have no idea how I'm going to get it under test. I really want to test this one private method in here, but it is difficult to get at. Maybe I can just make it public."

"Well," replied Danielle, "what's the method called?"

"`CalculatePassStartDate`."

"Okay, what's the class?"

"`PassValidationChecker`."

"Huh," said Danielle, "it sounds to me like that class is doing too many things. Is it a pass checker or a start date calculator?"

"It's both. We need the start date to check if the pass is valid, so it makes sense that they both live in the same class."

"Okay, well which class would have to change if we added a new type of pass?"

"Probably the `PassValidationChecker`."

"And which class would change if we added a new ski hill?"

"Again the `PassValidationChecker`. It has a list of rules for each hill. You'd have to make changes in there too if you wanted to change rules like the age at which youth passes expire."

"Well, then it seems like the class has at least two reasons to change, likely more. That is a sign that it should be several classes. Think about those SOLID principles – the S is for the single responsibility principle. It means that a class should have a focus so narrow that it does one and only one thing, so it has only a single reason to change."

"Gotcha," said Mark. "So, I should extract `CalculatePassStartDate`, maybe `PassStart-DateCalculator`, and then just new one up from inside `PassValidationChecker`."

"Hold on, what do you mean 'new it up'?"

"Well the usual new `PassStartDateCalculator()`."

"That doesn't really fix the coupling problem that you have. It is still hard to isolate the class to test it because you're relying on a concrete implementation."

"Danielle, I have to new it up. It isn't just going to magically show up in the `PassValidation-Checker`."

"It could if you add it to our dependency injection container and resolve it with an interface."

"Oh, good idea, Danielle. Hey, this sounds a lot like inversion of control, or the I in SOLID."

"Yep, dependency injection is one method of easily implementing inversion of control. It couldn't be easier in .NET Core. There is already a built-in container, so you can just register your implementation there."

"Thanks, Danielle. You're a 'SOLID' programmer," Mark said as he started chuckling.

Danielle's eyes rolled back. Twice. "Get out of here Mark."

It's no coincidence that we have referenced this chapter numerous times throughout this book. Dependency injection (DI) is a critical architectural consideration in the design of ASP.NET Core. Some readers might already be experts on the topic, but for many, the concepts here are new. In this chapter, we start with an overview of dependency injection and dive in to the implementation provided out of the box in ASP.NET Core.

What is Dependency Injection?

Before jumping in to the fundamentals of dependency injection, let's take a look at what problem dependency injection is trying to solve. Note that for the purposes of this topic, we refer to all controllers, components, and other classes that make up our application as services.

Resolving Dependencies Manually

Let's take a look at a relatively simple `SkiCardController` from Chapter 10, "Entity Framework Core." To process requests for viewing, creating, and editing ski cards, the `SkiCardController` requires some other services from our application. Specifically, it requires a `SkiCardContext` to access the data, a `UserManager<ApplicationUser>` to access information about the current user, and an `IAuthorizationService` to check if the current user is authorized to edit or view the requested ski card.

Without the use of DI or other patterns, the `SkiCardController` is responsible for creating new instances of these services.

The SkiCardController without DI

```
public class SkiCardController : Controller
{
    private readonly SkiCardContext _skiCardContext;
    private readonly UserManager<ApplicationUser> _userManager;
    private readonly IAuthorizationService _authorizationService;

    public SkiCardController()
    {
```

```
        _skiCardContext = new SkiCardContext(new DbContextOptions<SkiCardContext>());
        _userManager = new UserManager<ApplicationUser>();
        _authorizationService = new DefaultAuthorizationService();
    }

    //Action methods
}
```

This looks relatively simple, but in reality, that code doesn't compile. First of all, we have not speci-fied a connection string or database type for the SkiCardContext, so the DbContext is not actually being created properly. The UserManager<ApplicationUser> doesn't have a default constructor. The only public constructor on the UserManager class has seven parameters:

Public constructor for UserManager<TUser> class

```
public UserManager(IUserStore<TUser> store, IOptions<IdentityOptions> optionsAccessor,
IPasswordHasher<TUser> passwordHasher, IEnumerable<IUserValidator<TUser>> userValidators, IE
numerable<IPasswordValidator<TUser>> passwordValidators, ILookupNormalizer keyNormalizer,
IdentityErrorDescriber errors, IServiceProvider services, ILogger<UserManager<TUser>> logger)
{ //...
}
```

So now, our SkiCardController needs to know how to create all of these other services. The con-structor for the DefaultAuthorizationService also has three parameters. Clearly, it is not feasible for our controllers, or any other service in our application, to create every service that it interacts with.

Aside from the significant amount of code duplication that this implementation would cause, the code is also tightly coupled. For example, the SkiCardController now has specific knowledge about the concrete DefaultAuthorizationService class instead of only having a basic understanding of the methods exposed by the IAuthorizationService interface. If we ever wanted to change the constructor for the DefaultAuthorizationService, we would also need to change the SkiCard-Controller and any other class that uses the DefaultAuthorizationService.

Tight coupling also makes it more difficult to swap out implementations. While it is unlikely that we can implement an entirely new authorization service, the ability to swap out implementations is important because it enables easy mocking. Mocking is an important technique that makes it much easier to test the expected interaction between services in our application, as you will see in Chapter 20, "Testing."

Using a Service Container to Resolve Dependencies

Dependency injection is a common pattern that is used to solve dependencies. With dependency injection, the responsibility for creating and managing class instances is offloaded to a container. Addi-tionally, each class declares what other classes it depends on. The container is then able to resolve those dependencies at runtime and pass them in as needed. The dependency injection pattern is a form of inversion of control (IoC), meaning the components themselves are no longer responsible for directly instantiating its dependencies. You might also hear DI implementations referred to as IoC containers.

The most common approach for injecting dependencies is to use a technique called constructor injection. Using constructor injection, a class declares a public constructor that accepts arguments for all the services it requires. For example, the SkiCardController has a constructor that accepts the SkiCardContext, UserManager<ApplicationUser>, and IAuthorizationService. The container takes care of passing in instances of each of those types at runtime.

SkiCardController using Constructor Injection

```
public class SkiCardController : Controller
{
    private readonly SkiCardContext _skiCardContext;
    private readonly UserManager<ApplicationUser> _userManager;
    private readonly IAuthorizationService _authorizationService;

    public SkiCardController(SkiCardContext skiCardContext,
                            UserManager<ApplicationUser> userManager,
                            IAuthorizationService authorizationService)
    {
        _skiCardContext = skiCardContext;
        _userManager = userManager;
        _authorizationService = authorizationService;
    }
    //Action methods
}
```

Constructor injection provides a clear indication of what dependencies are needed for a particular class. We even get help from the compiler because we can't create a new SkiCardController without passing in the required services. As we mentioned earlier, a key benefit of this approach is that it also makes unit testing much easier.

Another option for injecting depdencies is property injection, where a public property is decorated with an attribute indicating that the property should be set at runtime by the container. Property injection is a little less common than construction injection and is not supported by all IoC containers.

Services are registered with the container when the application starts. The method of registering services varies depending on the container being used. You will see a couple examples later in this chapter.

> **Note** Dependency injection is currently the most popular pattern for solving the problem of resolving dependencies, but it is not the only pattern available. For a period of time, the Service Locator pattern was popular in the .NET community and with this pattern, services are registered with a central service locator. Whenever a service needs an instance of another service, it requests an instance of that service type from the service locator. The main drawback with the Service Locator pattern is that every service now has an explicit dependency on the service locator. For a detailed examination of the two patterns, take a look at Martin Fowler's excellent article on the topic[1].

---

[1] http://www.martinfowler.com/articles/injection.html

Dependency Injection in ASP.NET Core

ASP.NET Core provides a basic implementation of a container with built-in support for constructor injection. Services are registered during application startup in the `ConfigureServices` method of the `Startup` class.

ConfigureServices method in Startup.cs

```
// This method gets called by the runtime. Use this method to add services to the container.
public void ConfigureServices(IServiceCollection services)
{
    //add services here
}
```

Even in the simplest version of an ASP.NET Core MVC project, you're going to need at least a few services in the container to make your application run as intended. The MVC framework itself depends on services that need to exist at runtime to properly support activating controllers, rendering views, and other core concepts.

Using The Built-In Container

The first thing you want to do is add services provided by the ASP.NET Core framework. The `ConfigureServices` method quickly gets out of control if you have to manually register every service from ASP.NET Core. Fortunately, each feature of the framework provides a convenient Add* extension method to easily add the services required to enable that feature. For example, the `AddDbContext` method is used to register an Entity Framework `DbContext`. Some of these methods also provide an options delegate that allows for additional setup of the service being registered. For example, when registering the `DbContext` classes, use the options delegate to specify that the context should connect to the SQL Server database specified in the `DefaultConnection` connection string.

Registering the DbContexts in AlpineSkiHouse.Web

```
services.AddDbContext<ApplicationUserContext>(options =>
    options.UseSqlServer(Configuration.GetConnectionString("DefaultConnection")));
services.AddDbContext<SkiCardContext>(options =>
    options.UseSqlServer(Configuration.GetConnectionString("DefaultConnection")));
services.AddDbContext<PassContext>(options =>
    options.UseSqlServer(Configuration.GetConnectionString("DefaultConnection")));
services.AddDbContext<PassTypeContext>(options =>
    options.UseSqlServer(Configuration.GetConnectionString("DefaultConnection")));
services.AddDbContext<ResortContext>(options =>
    options.UseSqlServer(Configuration.GetConnectionString("DefaultConnection")));
```

Other framework features to add here include Identity for authentication and authorization, Options to enable strongly typed configuration, and finally MVC to enable routing, controllers, and everything else that comes with MVC.

```
services.AddIdentity<ApplicationUser, IdentityRole>()
    .AddEntityFrameworkStores<ApplicationUserContext>()
```

```
    .AddDefaultTokenProviders();
services.AddOptions();
services.AddMvc();
```

The next step is to register any application services that you wrote, or any services from other third-party libraries. The Alpine Ski team has done this as well, ensuring that any services required by any of the controllers, along with anything those services require, are properly registered. When registering application services, it is important to consider the lifetime of the service being added.

> **Note** One of the responsibilities of a container is to manage the lifetime of a service. The lifetime of a service is defined as the time the service exists, from first being created by the dependency injection container, to the time the container releases all instances of it. The ASP.NET container supports the lifetime options shown in Table 14-1.

TABLE 14-1 ASP.NET service container lifetime options

Transient	A new instance is created whenever the service is requested. Use this lifetime for lightweight services.
Scoped	A single instance is created per HTTP request.
Singleton	A single instance is created the first time the service is requested.
Instance	Like singleton but the instance is registered with the container at startup.

When adding a DbContext using the AddDbContext method, the context is registered with the Scoped lifetime. When a request enters the pipeline and follows a route where required services are provided an instance of that DbContext, a single instance is created and is used for all services that might require use of that connection to the database. In effect, the service created by the container is "scoped" to the HTTP request and is used to satisfy all dependencies during the request. When the request is complete, the container releases any usage of the services and allows them to be cleaned up by the runtime.

Here are some examples of application services that you can find in the AlpineSkiHouse.Web project. The service lifetime is specified using the appropriately named Add* methods.

```
services.AddSingleton<IAuthorizationHandler, EditSkiCardAuthorizationHandler>();
services.AddTransient<IEmailSender, AuthMessageSender>();
services.AddTransient<ISmsSender, AuthMessageSender>();
services.AddScoped<ICsrInformationService, CsrInformationService>();
```

As the list of application services grows, it might be helpful to create extension methods to simplify the ConfigureServices method. For example, if your application had dozens of IAuthorization-Handler classes to register, you might want to create an AddAuthorizationHandlers extension method.

Example of an extension method for adding a set of services

```
public static void AddAuthorizationHandlers(this IServiceCollection services)
{
    services.AddSingleton<IAuthorizationHandler, EditSkiCardAuthorizationHandler>();
    //Add other Authorization Handlers
}
```

After services are added to the `IServiceCollection`, the framework takes care of wiring up dependencies at runtime by using constructor injection. For example, when a request is routed to the `SkiCardController`, the framework creates a new instance of the `SkiCardController` passing in the required services via the public constructor. The controller no longer has knowledge of how to create these services or how to manage their lifetime.

> **Note** When developing new features, you might occasionally receive an error that reads something like: *InvalidOperationException: Unable to resolve service for type 'ServiceType' while attempting to activate 'SomeController'*, as shown in Figure 14-1.

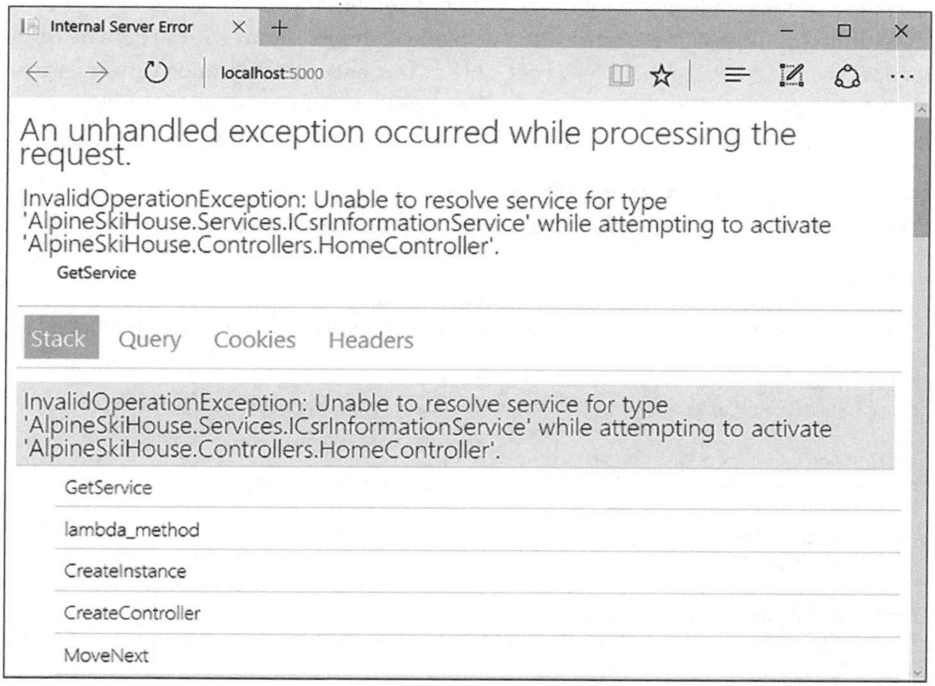

FIGURE 14-1 Example of a developer error page displayed when a required service has not been added to the service collection

The most likely cause here is that you forgot to add the service type in the `ConfigureServices` method. In this case, adding the `CsrInforamtionService` resolves the error.

```
services.AddScoped<ICsrInformationService, CsrInformationService>();
```

Using a third-party container

The built-in container that the ASP.NET Core framework provides only contains the basic features required to support most applications. There are a number of more feature rich and well-established dependency injection frameworks available for .NET however. Fortunately, ASP.NET Core is built in such a way that the default container can be replaced by third-party containers. Let's take a look at how to do that.

Some popular IoC containers for .NET include Ninject, StructureMap, and Autofac. At the time of writing, Autofac is the most advanced in its support for ASP.NET Core, so we are using it in our example. The first step is to reference the `Autofac.Extensions.DependencyInjection` NuGet package. Next, we need to make some modifications to the `ConfigureServices` method in `Startup.cs`. Instead of returning `void`, the `ConfigureService` method should return `IServiceProvider`. Framework services are still added to the `IServiceCollection`, and our application services are registered with the Autofac container. Finally, the `AutofacServiceProvider` is returned, which provides ASP.NET Core with the Autofac container instead of using the built-in container.

Abbreviated version of ConfigureServices using AutoFac

```
public IServiceProvider ConfigureServices(IServiceCollection services)
{
    // Add framework services.
    services.AddDbContext<ApplicationUserContext>(options =>
        options.UseSqlServer(Configuration.GetConnectionString("DefaultConnection")));

    services.AddDbContext<SkiCardContext>(options =>
        options.UseSqlServer(Configuration.GetConnectionString("DefaultConnection")));

    services.AddDbContext<PassContext>(options =>
        options.UseSqlServer(Configuration.GetConnectionString("DefaultConnection")));

    services.AddDbContext<PassTypeContext>(options =>
        options.UseSqlServer(Configuration.GetConnectionString("DefaultConnection")));

    services.AddDbContext<ResortContext>(options =>
        options.UseSqlServer(Configuration.GetConnectionString("DefaultConnection")));

    services.AddIdentity<ApplicationUser, IdentityRole>()
        .AddEntityFrameworkStores<ApplicationUserContext>()
        .AddDefaultTokenProviders();


    services.AddOptions();

    services.AddMvc();

    //Now register our services with Autofac container
    var builder = new ContainerBuilder();
    builder.RegisterType<CsrInformationService>().As<ICsrInformationService>();
    builder.Populate(services);
    var container = builder.Build();
```

```
      // Create the IServiceProvider based on the container.
      return new AutofacServiceProvider(container);

}
```

While the example here is fairly simplistic, Autofac also provides additional advanced features, such as assembly scanning to find classes that match the criteria of your choosing. For example, we can automatically register all of the IAuthenticationHandler implementations in our project by using assembly scanning.

Using assembly scanning to register types automatically

```
var currentAssembly = Assembly.GetEntryAssembly();

builder.RegisterAssemblyTypes(currentAssembly)
       .Where(t => t.IsAssignableTo<IAuthorizationHandler>())
       .As<IAuthorizationHandler>();
```

Another great feature of Autofac is the ability to split configurations into modules. A module is simply a class that bundles the configuration of a related set of services. In their simplest forms, Autofac modules are similar to creating extension methods for the IServiceCollection. Modules however, can be used to implement some more advanced features. Because they are classes, they can also be discovered at runtime and loaded dynamically to implement a plugin framework.

Simple example of an Autofac module

```
public class AuthorizationHandlersModule : Module
{
  protected override void Load(ContainerBuilder builder)
  {
      var currentAssembly = Assembly.GetEntryAssembly();

      builder.RegisterAssemblyTypes(currentAssembly)
             .Where(t => t.IsAssignableTo<IAuthorizationHandler>())
             .As<IAuthorizationHandler>();
  }
}
```

Loading a module within Startup.ConfigureServices

```
builder.RegisterModule(new AuthorizationHandlerModule());
```

Autofac is a mature and feature rich dependency injection tool that we have only briefly discussed here. You can learn more by reading through Autofac's excellent documentation at *http://docs.autofac. org/*.

Summary

The built-in and flexible support for dependency injection in ASP.NET Core is a welcome addition to the framework. Using dependency injection greatly simplifies the instantiation and management of services by shifting those responsibilities to the container. Our application's controllers and services become easier to implement because they only need to declare the services that they depend on. As we discuss in Chapter 20, "Testing," unit testing can be easy when services use constructor injection.

We recommend starting with the built-in container, because the features it provides are sufficient for most applications. The switch to a third-party container can be done at any time if more advanced features are needed. In the next chapter, we cover the role of JavaScript in a modern web application.

## CHAPTER 15

Role of JavaScript

It was only Tuesday and Danielle had a headache already. Last week she lasted until late Thursday before the headache arrived. She called it her JavaScript headache. She really didn't like JavaScript. She thought it was a silly toy language and she just didn't like the way it let her make mistakes, or the way it had functions calling functions generating functions. Massaging her temples, she decided it was time for some coffee.

On her way to the kitchen, she passed by Chester's cubicle. His laptop was always interesting and Danielle paused to check out what new stickers had shown up in the last week. The sticker in the top left of his cubicle looked familiar: jQuery. Danielle knew that one; she knew it all too well. It had been the source of her Friday headache at 11:45 last week.

"That jQuery sticker new, Chester?"

"Sure is," replied Chester. "I'm really getting into the whole JavaScript thing. Look, I just installed this bower package manager using npm, which runs on Node."

"Woah, woah" Danielle held up her hands. "Slow down. I haven't had my coffee yet and I don't know that I can handle JavaScript without it."

"Okay" said Chester, "How about we pair on some of this stuff? There is an awful lot of cool technology that we can make use of. But it can wait until you've had your coffee."

"I don't know about that" said Danielle. "I'm going to have a coffee the size of my headache and I'm not sure how long it's going to take me to drink a swimming pool."

Programming a site on the modern Internet is a mixture of server side and client side programming. On the server, you have an embarrassing richness of languages to choose from. Even if you've settled on using a .NET language there are choices: F#, C#, and even VB.NET are all possibilities. On the client side, however, you're limited to writing JavaScript.

In this chapter we'll look at the penetration of JavaScript in modern web development, discuss how much JavaScript is the right amount, and talk about how to set up a build pipeline for JavaScript. Then we'll look at compiling to JavaScript and examine some of the frameworks that are available to make building pages easier. Finally, we'll examine how to organize your JavaScript code so it doesn't become a mess.

Writing Good JavaScript

JavaScript *was* a language that encouraged poor programming practices. This is perhaps a controversial statement, but consider how the language lacked many fundamental programming constructs, such as classes and namespaces. Of course you can simulate having both classes and namespaces, but the level of knowledge required to do so was quite high. If you look at entry level JavaScript tutorials, none of them start with how to construct classes, but the equivalent tutorials on C# have no option but to introduce classes immediately because they are fundamental to the language. Fortunately, modern JavaScript has fixed some of these shortcomings by introducing new syntax around classes and modules. We use these constructs throughout this chapter and the Alpine Ski House application in general.

The method of including JavaScript on a page is also an opportunity to introduce poor practices. There is nothing stopping you from writing JavaScript inline with your HTML. For instance, this code sets the background of the body of the page to pink after it has finished loading:

```html
<html>
<body onload="document.querySelector('body').style.backgroundColor = 'pink'">
```

Mixing code and markup in this fashion is difficult to maintain and hard to debug. Allowing JavaScript to be executed in the page is also a great way to make your site vulnerable to cross-site scripting attacks (XSS). In this class of attack, an attacker puts JavaScript into an input meant for something else and the modified script is displayed and executed by subsequent visitors to the site. Consider a site like Wikipedia where anybody can edit the site. If Wikipedia was not sanitizing its inputs, an attacker could put the following alert into a page and all the subsequent visitors to the site would receive the following message:

```
alert("You are quite smelly");
```

This is obviously rude, although in some cases probably factual, but it is still just an irritation. A much more nefarious approach could be to inject JavaScript that would steal the contents of a password box and send the information to an attacker.

Sanitizing your input to prevent scripts from being added is an approach to prevent this class of attack. An even better approach however, is to make use of the Content-Security Policy headers. Supported by most modern browsers, these headers instruct the browser not to execute any JavaScript that is inline, which effectively neutralizing the thread of XSS attacks. Instead, only JavaScript that is found in external script files is supported.

> **Note** If you're curious about what browsers support new features, the site Can I Use, located at *http://caniuse.com*, is a fantastic tool. For instance, the support matrix for the Content-Security Policy headers can be found at *http://caniuse.com/#feat=contentsecuritypolicy.*

External script files included on the page via a script tag are certainly the way to go. The other nicety of keeping JavaScript in separate files is that the scripts can be passed directly into a JavaScript engine such as those hosted by Node.js to do unit testing without having to invoke a full browser. You can read more about JavaScript testing and testing in general in Chapter 20, "Testing."

Do We Even Need it?

Back in your father's day, a short 22 years ago, JavaScript didn't even exist. Do you really need to use JavaScript on your website? To be honest, yes. JavaScript provides for all manners of functionality that aren't possible otherwise. Rich user controls, single page applications, and even website metrics are all driven by JavaScript. Without it, all interactions must be driven by communicating back to the server, which adds latency and requires a beefier server that, of course, costs more money. Building a site without JavaScript is crippling your user experience.

You might hear concerns about building your site to degrade gracefully so that users without JavaScript enabled can still have a good experience. The statistics for recent years on how many users browse the web without JavaScript enabled are difficult to find. The numbers have been on the decline for many years however, and it is no longer worth the effort to develop a custom website with all its functionality shifted to the server. Of course, there might be niches where a high percentage of users legitimately do have JavaScript disabled, but these are few and far between, and you're likely to know if you're in that situation.

Organization

ASP.NET Core MVC introduces the idea of a wwwroot directory, which contains all of the content files that are shipped to the web server. These files include CSS, images, and JavaScript files. In the default template, this folder contains a number of resources that exist only in that location. This means that were you to delete the wwwroot folder, you would lose these resources. Thus, if you use the default template, it is advisable to check in the wwwroot folder to your source control.

We suggest however, that this is not the right approach to the wwwroot folder. All the files in the wwwroot folder should be stored outside of that tree and it should be possible to recreate the wwwroot folder by using just our build tools. Let's look at each file type and where they should be coming from.

CSS files control the look and feel of the website. Writing pure CSS for a large website, however, is a complicated process. Historically, CSS has not had support for variables, so it is not a very DRY language. To address this problem, a number of languages have been created that compile down to CSS. Less and SASS are a couple of the more popular tools. Instead of keeping our CSS files in wwwroot, they should be kept outside of the root in a folder such as Style. During the build process, these files should be converted from SASS into CSS and placed in the wwwroot directory.

Image files can also be processed as part of the build process. Images on the Internet are a major source of page bloat. The larger the image, the longer it takes to download, and the less snappy your website feels. Frequently used images can be optimized and can retain their fidelity all while you remove some of the cruft. There are some great JavaScript based tools for performing this optimization, after which the images can be copied into wwwroot.

Finally, JavaScript files almost always require some post processing. They should be minified and possibly concatenated together to create a single JavaScript file. Again, the files should be copied from somewhere else in the tree. We recommend starting with a Scripts folder outside of the wwwroot and putting additional folders within it for the various types of scripts. The exact structure under the Scripts folder can vary from site to site. Folders for Pages, Controls, and Services are good candidates, as you can see in Figure 15-1.

FIGURE 15-1 The layout of the Scripts directory

In short, the wwwroot folder should be treated in much the same way as we treat the bin folder, as a temporary location for build artifacts.

To SPA or not to SPA?

A sure sign of a senior level developer is that they answer "It depends" to technical questions before launching into a long discussion. There are very few simple answers to technology choice questions. Deep diving into the problem space is always required and nothing is black and white.

The same concept applies to the question, "How much JavaScript should I use on my site?" There are as many factors to consider as there are calories in a well-crafted Philly cheesesteak. The spectrum takes us from using JavaScript only to do simple interactions, like validating inputs all the way to a Single Page Application (SPA), to instances where all user interactions require interaction with JavaScript.

Server side applications are a more traditional approach to building web applications. The logic for the application is held on the server that renders pages to HTML and passes them on to the browser. This is the model that comes out of the box in the default MVC template. Every navigation takes the user to a completely new page and communication with the server tends to take the form of either getting a new page or posting back a form. Overall the amount of traffic between the client and server is greater in a server side application than in a SPA, which makes the experience slower for the user. The traffic is spread out over the whole lifetime of the session however.

Single page applications might initially take a larger bandwidth hit to transfer the content to the client, but over the lifetime of a user session, they are likely to be more efficient. You can use a combination of templates and data from the server transferred as JSON to build HTML on the client side by manipulating the document object model (DOM).

The claim that single page applications are harder to create than server side applications is perhaps a bit more tenuous now that it has been in the past. Client side JavaScript frameworks have been improving constantly for the better part of a decade. Developer productivity using these frameworks is likely on par with server side applications. We take a look at some of these frameworks later in this chapter.

Developer productivity has also improved as a result of better tooling. Although JavaScript is the only real client side programming option, it is possible to build languages that compile to JavaScript. Languages such as CoffeeScript and TypeScript have been doing just that for years and have prompted the analogy that JavaScript is the assembly language of the web. In fact, there is a quite interesting project called asm.js, which is a subset of JavaScript that is designed to be more efficient to compile and execute. It is also possible to compile languages such as C++ into asm.js.

There are also some great linting tools for finding JavaScript errors that compile, but still aren't quite right. Unit test runners can also be a part of your build pipeline. The build pipeline itself can be constructed by using any one of a number of powerful tools.

Building JavaScript

Selecting a tool to assemble JavaScript from whatever format you have in your source control tool to whatever form is used on the client is a problem of exploring the embarrassment of riches. There are tools built into Visual Studio and tools that are used by the masses of web developers. The ecosystem moves so quickly that it is a near impossibility to keep up with what the "best" tool is for the job. The thing is that build tools are not a new invention. We've had Make for decades and the problem of building has not changed greatly. Source files still need to pass through a process of being converted from one format to another. In C programming, we convert .c files to .o files and then link them together into a single binary, perhaps a.out. In TypeScript development we take .ts files, convert them to .js files and then bundle them together into a minified single file. The parallels are striking and even the most modern tools don't stray too far from their roots.

> **Note** We are already seeing a move away from the venerable HTTP 1.1 protocol to a brand new HTTP protocol, HTTP 2.0. This protocol, which is inspired by Google's SPDY protocol, adds support for pipelining multiple files over a single connection. This means that you might not need to concatenate your files together into a single file to avoid TCP/IP connection overhead anymore. This is the first major revision to HTTP since 1999 and it brings with it a whole raft of improvements. You can read more about HTTP 2.0 at *https://tools.ietf.org/html/rfc7540*, but it is also worth reading Poul-Henning Kamp's take on it at *http://queue.acm.org/detail.cfm?id=2716278*.

Bundler & Minifier

The simplest tool to use for processing JavaScript is the Bundler & Minifier tool that comes as an extension to Visual Studio and is the recommended tool from Microsoft for new ASP.NET Core projects. Bundler & Minifier sacrifices some power and flexibility for ease of use. For the most part it is as simple as right-clicking a file, selecting Bundler & Minifier, and then selecting Minify File. This can be seen in Figure 15-2

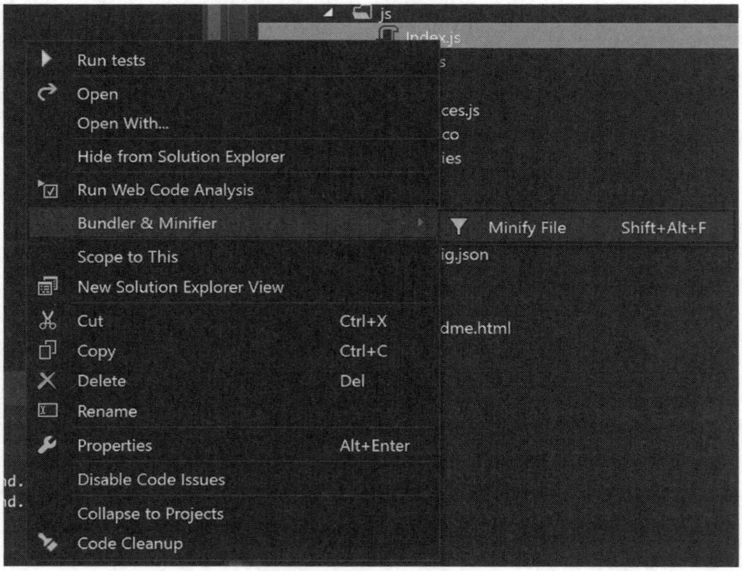

FIGURE 15-2 The Bundler & Minifier menu item

When selecting multiple files there is also an option to bundle the files together. Bundler & Minifier takes its configuration from the bundleconfig.json file, which basically lists a mapping between sources and outputs. The default bundleconfig.json file looks like this:

```
[
  {
    "outputFileName": "wwwroot/css/site.min.css",
```

```
    "inputFiles": [
      "wwwroot/css/site.css"
    ]
  },
  {
    "outputFileName": "wwwroot/js/site.min.js",
    "inputFiles": [
      "wwwroot/js/site.js"
    ],
    "minify": {
      "enabled": true,
      "renameLocals": true
    }
  }
]
```

One of the niceties of Bundler & Minifier is that it can be hooked into the .NET Core command line tools easily. This allows you to run commands like:

```
dotnet bundle
```

This reads the bundleconfig.json and processes the specified concatenation and minification tasks to create the output file. Bundler & Minifier also has the ability to watch files so that it regenerates the output file automatically on save.

We recommend against using this tool for anything but the simplest application because the tool is limited and is not a standard JavaScript tool. Nobody from the node, Go, or Elixr communities is moving to the Bundler & Minifier tool because there are more advanced, if not more complex, tools available. There are all sorts of things that can be done with a fully-fledged JavaScript build tool that cannot be done with Bundler & Minifier.

Grunt

Grunt was the first JavaScript build tool to gain a significant mind share. It was built in JavaScript and could leverage other JavaScript libraries to perform a myriad of actions. It is also branded as a "JavaScript Task Runner," meaning that it does more than simply process JavaScript. There are plugins for manipulating CSS, linting, unit testing, and minifying images. In fact, there are almost 6,000 plugins so the ecosystem is quite mature.

To get started with Grunt, you need to install it by using npm. It can be installed globally by issuing:

```
npm install -g grunt-cli
```

This actually only installs tooling to find and run your Gruntfile, so you still need to install Grunt into your local project, again by using npm.

```
npm install -save-dev grunt
```

This adds a dependency on Grunt to your package.json file. For this example, let's also install the package grunt-ts. This package is a Grunt task that can be used to build TypeScript files. We'll talk about TypeScript later in this chapter, but trust us, it's fabulous.

```
npm install –save-dev grunt-ts
```

With the grunt task installed and in place, we can construct a very simple file called `Gruntfile.js` that governs how Grunt runs.

```
module.exports = function(grunt) {
  grunt.initConfig({
    ts: {
      default : {
        src: ["**/*.ts", "!node_modules/**"]
      }
    }
  });
  grunt.loadNpmTasks("grunt-ts");
  grunt.registerTask("default", ["ts"]);
};
```

Here, we export a function that takes in the grunt object for manipulation. This module is imported into the Grunt, processed, and is used directly. Because this is pure JavaScript, you can write any valid JavaScript in there. In this case, we start by setting up some configuration for the TypeScript or `ts` task. We've used the `src` property to define a glob of files to use in the compilation. Anything inside the `node_modules` directory is ignored and any files ending `.ts` are included.

Next, we load the grunt-ts library, which provides the actual functionality to compile TypeScript into JavaScript by adding the `ts` task. Finally, we register the default task so that it has a dependency on the `ts` task. We can now run this command from the command line.

```
grunt
Running "ts:default" (ts) task
Compiling...
Cleared fast compile cache for target: default
### Fast Compile >>Scripts/chart.d.ts
### Fast Compile >>Scripts/Controls/MetersSkied.ts
### Fast Compile >>Scripts/Controls/MetersSkiedLoader.ts
### Fast Compile >>Scripts/init.ts
### Fast Compile >>Scripts/Pages/Home/Blah.ts
### Fast Compile >>Scripts/Pages/Home/Index.ts
Using tsc v1.8.10


TypeScript compilation complete: 1.86s for 6 TypeScript files.

Done.
```

We can see a number of files are compiled from TypeScript into JavaScript. A subsequent build step might assemble these files into a single file and move it into the wwwroot.

gulp

One of the complaints about Grunt is that it leaves behind a lot of intermediate files. Processing JavaScript can require many steps, and after each step, Grunt leaves the files behind to be cleaned up later. gulp is the answer to this. gulp is based around the idea of streams. Each step in the build process is a stream and we can direct this stream through a number of pipes, as shown in Figure 15-3.

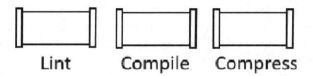

Lint   Compile   Compress

FIGURE 15-3 A build pipeline

The output from each step in the pipe is used as input into the next step in the pipe, so there are no temporary files written to disk.

Streams are a fantastic model for builds in general and the *stream* metaphor is quite commonly used in the problem space. gulp is a very rich ecosystem, just like Grunt. There are many thousands of plugins for it, over 2,500 at this time. Again, the file used to control gulp is a simple JavaScript file, so it can contain anything that is valid JavaScript and can lean on the larger community of modules contained within npm.

Let's take a look at a basic gulp file and then expand upon it to perform all of our build steps.

```
var gulp = require("gulp"),
    rename = require("gulp-rename2"),
    typescript = require("gulp-typescript");

var webroot = "./wwwroot/";
var sourceroot = "./Scripts/"

var paths = {
    ts: sourceroot + "**/*.ts",
    tsDefintionFiles: "npm_modules/@types/**/*.d.ts",
    jsDest: webroot + "js/"
};

gulp.task("typescript", function(){
    return gulp.src([paths.tsDefintionFiles, paths.ts, "!" + paths.minJs], { base: "." })
        .pipe(typescript({
            module: "system"
        }))
        .pipe(rename((pathObj, file) => {
            return pathObj.join(
                pathObj.dirname(file).replace(/^Scripts\/?\\?/, ''),
                pathObj.basename(file));
        }))
        .pipe(gulp.dest(paths.jsDest));
});
gulp.task("default", ["typescript"]);
```

The first three lines of the file pull in a number of modules: gulp itself, a rename library, and the typescript task. These are simple npm modules and are added by using the standard *require* syntax. Next, we set up a number of variables to avoid using magic strings in the rest of the file. You might notice the ** globbing syntax. This matches all directories at any depth so we can keep our TypeScript files in a good folder structure.

The remainder of the file defines a couple of tasks. The first task is the beefiest one. First, we use the gulp.src directive to gather all the source files. Next, we pipe these files through the typescript compiler task. We've set up some options here to emit system style modules, which we'll cover in a later section. Next, we pipe the files through the rename task where we strip off the Scripts prefix. This could have been done by changing the base directory for the TypeScript compilation, but then we wouldn't have had a very good demonstration of pipes. Finally, we pipe the files into the destination directory.

We can pull in some additional libraries to perform actions like optimizing images. There is a great gulp plugin called image gulp-image-optimization that you can use for this purpose. Simply include the following library to use it:

```
var imageop = require('gulp-image-optimization');
```

Next, write a task to perform the optimization:

```
gulp.task("images", function()
{
    return gulp.src(paths.images)
        .pipe(imageop({
            optimizationLevel: 5,
            progressive: true,
            interlaced: true
        })).pipe(gulp.dest(paths.imagesDest));
});
```

Note that this has the same basic structure as the TypeScript compilation, with establishing a stream using src and then piping the output through a number of steps. You can find a complete example of the gulp file used for Alpine Ski house in the GitHub repo. There is almost no limit to the things that can be done with gulp, because it is a fantastic build tool.

gulp is arguably the most popular JavaScript build tool at the moment. Although there is a lot of attention and work going into WebPack.

WebPack

WebPack sells itself as a solution for large projects that need to dynamically load chunks of JavaScript. The issue with large projects is that you either need to pay the price up front and load a huge glob of JavaScript on first load, or juggle loading modules from the server as you need them, which slows down the app.

Note If you're interested in learning more about the different ways to get JavaScript files from the server to the client, the ASP.NET Monsters have recorded a video about just that topic. The video can be found at *https://channel9.msdn.com/Series/aspnetmonsters/ ASPNET-Monsters-Ep-67-Gettting-JavaScript-to-the-Client.*

Let's try applying WebPack to the same TypeScript compilation that we've been using so far. Before we get there however, we're going to need to make a slight detour into the world of JavaScript module types. There are at least five major standards for defining modules in JavaScript, including CommonJS, AMD, System, ES2015, and UMD, and there are likely another two dozen lesser known module formats as well. The problem is that JavaScript didn't define a module format as part of the language until very recently. Nature abhors a vacuum, so naturally, a bunch of module formats up sprang that differ only slightly. The TypeScript compiler can emit any of the five major module formats based on the value of the *module* flag passed into it. WebPack understands CommonJS and AMD modules, but none of the others.

Therefore, we need to ensure that the TypeScript compiler is emitting CommonJS modules. You can do this by using a tsconfig.json file in the root of your project. This file contains settings for the TypeScript in the project. A minimal one might look like:

```
{
    "compilerOptions": {
        "module": "commonjs",
        "noImplicitAny": true,
        "removeComments": true,
        "preserveConstEnums": true
    }
}
```

The most important line in here is the one that defines the module type to create. There are, of course, many other options that can be added to this file, but we won't go into them here. With this file in place, you can go about adding WebPack.

First, you need to install the WebPack tooling globally.

```
npm install -g webpack
```

Unlike Grunt, this actually installs full WebPack, so you don't need to install additional tooling locally just to get WebPack running. You do, however, need to install a plugin for doing typescript compilation:

```
npm install ts-loader –save
```

Now you can create a build file for WebPack called webpack.config.js:

```
module.exports = {
  entry: './Scripts/Init.ts',
  output: {
    filename: 'wwwroot/js/site.js'
  },
  resolve: {
```

```
      extensions: ['', '.webpack.js', '.web.js', '.ts', '.js']
    },
    module: {
      loaders: [
        { test: /\.ts$/, loader: 'ts-loader' }
      ]
    }
  }
}
```

This file is quite interesting not for what it contains, but for what it doesn't contain. There is much less in here than in the equivalent gulp file. The WebPack file defines a few rules based on file extensions. For example, the module section defines which tool to use for a file matching the regex `\.ts$`: any file ending with .ts. These files are all directed to the TypeScript plugin. The next thing to notice is that we define an entry point into the application. From this base location WebPack explores the modules included so it is able to determine which files to include in the output. As an example, we fed it an entry point `init.ts` that included home/`index.ts`, which in turn, included home/`blah.ts`. WebPack was able to determine the files to include in the package and included `init.ts`, home/`index.ts` and home/`blah.ts`, ignoring a number of other .ts files that we had scattered around the project. This means that as long as you're consistent in including your modules using an import statement, WebPack is able to prune dead code from your production JavaScript file.

Let's say that in addition to building the TypeScript and concatenating it to a single file, we also want to minify the JavaScript. This can be done by simply including the `UglifyJsPlugin`. To do this, we need to install WebPack to the local `node_modules` directory.

```
Npm install webpack
```

Next, we need to require it into the webpack.config.js file and add it to the plugins section:

```
var webpack = require('webpack');
module.exports = {
  entry: './Scripts/Init.ts',
  output: {
    filename: 'wwwroot/js/site.js'
  },
  resolve: {
    extensions: ['', '.webpack.js', '.web.js', '.ts', '.js']
  },
  plugins: [
    new webpack.optimize.UglifyJsPlugin()
  ],
  module: {
    loaders: [
      { test: /\.ts$/, loader: 'ts-loader' }
    ]
  }
}
```

That is all that is needed to include minification in our project.

WebPack is a powerful tool, but its inner workings are somewhat obscure. Tools of this nature tend to be good if you follow the canonical way of doing things, but as soon as you stray from the straight path, they become like chains around your ankles as you start to fight them. WebPack is nice because it allows pulling in gulp, or really any pure JavaScript, into the build process. Another very interesting feature of WebPack is that it supports hot reloading of JavaScript into a running webpage. This makes developing complex single page applications a lot easier because you no longer need to do a full page reload every time you make a change to the JavaScript.

Which Tool is Right for me?

It is impossible to say which tool is right for your team because each tool has its advantages and disadvantages. The Alpine Ski House team uses gulp for their work. WebPack, while nice, was just a bit too much magic for them and the stream based approach seemed more natural than Grunt's approach. Chances are, by the time this book is published, all of these tools have fallen off the JavaScript leaders' radar and have been replaced with something new. JavaScript development is the fastest moving technology around, which might not be a good thing. Don't be distracted too much by the new, hot technologies. There is a lot to be said for battle tested tools, such as Grunt and gulp.

TypeScript

We've mentioned TypeScript a few times in this chapter already without delving into exactly what it is. Time for all of that to change. TypeScript is a language that compiles to JavaScript. It is much like the more well-known language CoffeeScript in that regard, but unlike CoffeeScript, TypeScript is a superset of JavaScript. This means that any valid JavaScript is automatically syntactically valid TypeScript. But TypeScript is so much more than a simple superset of JavaScript, because it adds some very useful functionality. We like to think of TypeScript as being two tools in one: a very complete ES2015 to ES5 compiler and a static type checker with the ability to do type inference.

ES2015 to ES5 Compiler

ECMAScript, or ES, is the standard for the language commonly known as JavaScript. JavaScript is a very fast moving community which has, for many years, been been held back by by the very slow pace of evolution for JavaScript itself. In the past few years, this development has accelerated. ES2015 was released in 2015 and defined a huge number of improvements to JavaScript. The plan is that every year a new version of JavaScript is released and is named after the year it was ratified in. There is, indeed, an ES2016 and there are plans in place for ES2017. ES2016 is a fairly minor release so we typically continue to refer to it as ES2015 or ES6, although the latter is frowned upon.

Unfortunately, not all browsers are capable of running the new ES2015. If you've been a web developer for some time, you are likely shaking your head and blaming Internet Explorer for holding the web back once again. This time however, Microsoft is not fully to blame. They have been making great strides in encouraging users to upgrade to the latest and greatest version of Internet Explorer or even to move to Edge, which is a more modern browser implementation. The major culprits these days are actually mobile devices where the vendor locks a user into a version of the browser. These are very slow to upgrade, so allowances must be made. This is where JavaScript compilers or, as they have become known, *transpilers* come in.

There are a number of really excellent transpilers for converting ES2015 JavaScript into the more common ES5 variant. They all have varying levels of support for ES2015+ features, but TypeScript ranks as one of the very best. It is able to take a class that looks like:

```
import {MembershipGraph} from "./MembershipGraph";

export class Index {
    constructor() {
        var graph = new MembershipGraph();
        console.log("Graph loaded.");
        window.setTimeout(()=> console.log("load complete"), 2000);
    }
}
```

And convert it into the ES5 equivalent, which looks like:

```
System.register(["./MembershipGraph"], function(exports_1, context_1) {
    "use strict";
    var __moduleName = context_1 && context_1.id;
    var MembershipGraph_1;
    var Index;
    return {
        setters:[
            function (MembershipGraph_1_1) {
                MembershipGraph_1 = MembershipGraph_1_1;
            }],
        execute: function() {
            Index = (function () {
                function Index() {
                    var graph = new MembershipGraph_1.MembershipGraph();
                    console.log("Graph loaded.");
                    window.setTimeout(function () { return console.log("load complete"); },
            2000);
                }
                return Index;
            }());
            exports_1("Index", Index);
        }
    }
});
```

As you can see, the compiled version is fantastically larger than the original version. Which one of those would you rather maintain? Pay special attention to the lambda syntax that was expanded into the equivalent function. In addition to expanding the lambda syntax, notice that there is an awful lot of code generated related to registering the module with System.register. This is because we asked TypeScript to generate SystemJS style modules. The import of MembershipGraph is expanded into a requirement for loading the Index module. We learn a bit more about module loaders coming up, but this sort of boiler plate code generation is just the sort of thing that TypeScript excels at.

There are far too many marvelous ES2015 features to enumerate and explain in a single chapter of this book. Indeed, there are entire books dedicated to just that. One thing that we would feel amiss not mentioning is the let variable scoping operator. Variable scoping in JavaScript has always been a bit unusual. Most programming languages use block level scoping, but JavaScript uses function level scoping when using the var key word. While this is a powerful feature, especially for lambdas, it can be confusing. Any variable declared with the let key word takes on block level scoping, which is far more understandable coming from almost any other language.

If ES2015+ to ES5 compilation was the only feature of TypeScript, it would still be a strong competitor for other compilers like Babel; however, compilation is only half of what TypeScript can do.

Typing System

One of the many dimensions you can use to classify a language is the typing system. Strongly typed languages perform compile time type checking of types, meaning that if you attempt to perform a string operation like replace on an integer, the compiler stops you. Examples of such languages are F#, Java, and C#. Dynamically typed languages are at the other end of the spectrum, where checks are performed only at run time. Dynamic languages couldn't care less about what the whole object looks like and focuses on whether it has the one specific method you are calling. JavaScript is a dynamically typed language, as are Ruby, Python, and PHP.

It is very much possible to build large and complex applications in dynamically typed languages. It is sometimes nice, however, to have compile or edit time suggestions about problems. Typically, it is cheaper and easier to solve problems before runtime than at runtime, so the earlier in the process we can move error detection, the better. TypeScript adds a typing system on top of vanilla JavaScript and it does it in such a way that there is next to no added friction.

Let's consider a function that multiplies two numbers together:

```
function multiply(one, two){
return one * two;
}
```

There would be no problem with writing multiply(2,"elephant") until you reached runtime, at which point you would get NaN. By adding an annotation that one and two are numbers however, TypeScript is able to throw an error:

```
function multiply(one: number, two: number){
return one * two;
}
```

The error thrown during compilation is "Argument of type 'string' is not assignable to parameter of type 'number.'" This might seem to be a rather small and trivial example, but as you build more and more complex applications, the usefulness of the typing system quickly becomes apparent. Not every variable requires a type to be assigned to it. For some of them, the compiler can infer their types and, for those it can, TypeScript assumes they are of the type any, which means that it won't perform any checking against it.

If you happen to be using a library, such as d3.js, that wasn't originally written in JavaScript, you might find that a definition file is useful. A definition file is similar to a header file in C in that it defines what functions a library has and what all the ingoing and outgoing types are. Almost every popular JavaScript library has definition files available that make sure you're interacting with the library correctly. For instance, the Alpine Ski House team has taken a dependency on chart.js and has built a definition file to check that they are correctly calling the graphing functions. An excerpt of the definition file looks like:

```
interface Chart {
    Line(data: LinearChartData, options?: LineChartOptions): LinearInstance;
    Bar(data: LinearChartData, options?: BarChartOptions): LinearInstance;
    Radar(data: LinearChartData, options?: RadarChartOptions): LinearInstance;

    PolarArea(data: CircularChartData[], options?: PolarAreaChartOptions): CircularInstance;
    Pie(data: CircularChartData[], options?: PieChartOptions): CircularInstance;
    Doughnut(data: CircularChartData[], options?: PieChartOptions): CircularInstance;
}
```

This is the definition for the Chart interface and, as you can see, there are types assigned to each of the parameters. Having these in place ensures that all the required parameters are filled in and that they are all filled in with the appropriate values.

As an added bonus, using TypeScript enables better autocomplete in editors. This is an example from the Visual Studio Code editor showing not just the functions available from the chart object, but also the details of the parameters. This can be seen in Figure 15-4.

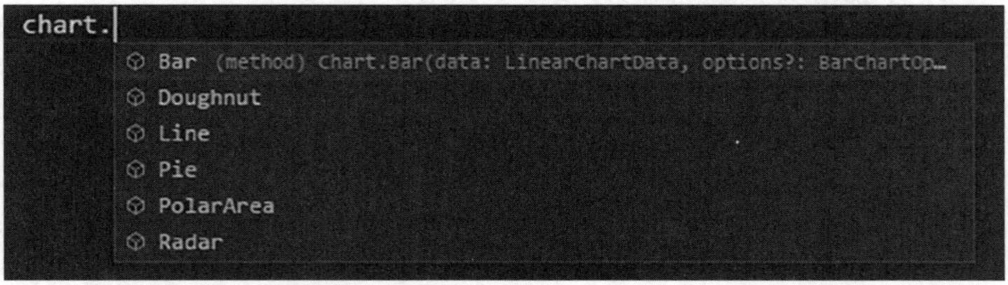

```
chart.
    ⊙ Bar  (method) Chart.Bar(data: LinearChartData, options?: BarChartOp...
    ⊙ Doughnut
    ⊙ Line
    ⊙ Pie
    ⊙ PolarArea
    ⊙ Radar
```

FIGURE 15-4 The drop down menu suggesting completion

Exit Cost

When adopting a new technology, it is important to consider the cost of abandoning the technology if the team decides it isn't the right solution. The beautiful thing about TypeScript is that the exit cost is effectively zero. Simply compile all the .ts files to .js and delete the .ts files. The code generated is quite readable and it is even possible to preserve comments. The cost of implementing TypeScript is also very low. Because all JavaScript is syntactically valid TypeScript, many files can be converted just by renaming them from js to ts.

You might notice that we stressed syntactically valid TypeScript and not simply valid TypeScript. This is because the TypeScript compiler performs type checking on any parts of your JavaScript that it can. The compiler can find bugs in your JavaScript that you didn't even know existed!

TypeScript is as easy to install as running:

```
npm update -g typescript
```

Of course, if you're using one of the build tools mentioned in the previous section, you've already seen how to compile TypeScript. TypeScript is a fantastic addition to JavaScript and provides powerful tooling for any large JavaScript code base.

Module Loading

In the previous section, we mentioned that the TypeScript compiler for Alpine Ski House is set up to produce system.js style modules. This is because the team has settled on using the system.js module loader to bring in appropriate JavaScript files. Module loaders add the ability to pull together a number of individual JavaScript files as needed. Modules, for most purposes, can simply be thought of as the JavaScript equivalent of VB or C#'s classes.

System.js is a library that provides for module loading either from individual files on disk or from a single concatenated file. The loader keeps track of which modules have been retrieved from the server so that importing a module more than once won't incur an additional network request. Getting started with system.js is as simple as including the library and then using it to retrieve files.

```
<script src="~/js/system.js"></script>
<script src="~/js/jspmconfig.js"></script>
<script> System.import("Pages/Home/Index");</script>
```

In this example, the `System.import` reaches out and retrieves `/js/Pags/Home/Index`. The `/js` prefix is provided by the `jspmconfig.js` file. This file is the second part of module loading with system.js.

jspm is a package manager for JavaScript libraries. In many ways it is similar to Bower, however the libraries in jspm tend to be better curated than those in Bower, which frequently requires some tinkering to get it to work. jspm can also pull libraries directly from GitHub or npm, ensuring that you have the very latest libraries available to you. jspm also uses standard module formats where Bower tends to be a wild jumble of different formats.

To get started with jspm, we need to install it, from npm:

```
npm install jspm -g
```

With jspm installed globally, we can follow steps similar to those you might follow when setting up npm for a project.

```
jspm init
```

This asks a number of questions to produce a jspmconfig.js file that contains, among other things, the /js prefix we saw earlier. Installing packages is now as simple as running:

```
jspm install chartjs
```

This outputs:

```
     Updating registry cache...
     Looking up github:chartjs/Chart.js
ok   Installed chart as github:chartjs/Chart.js@^2.2.2 (2.2.2)
ok   Install tree has no forks.

ok   Install complete.
```

jspm found our charting library and installed it from GitHub in a format that can simply be loaded by doing either:

```
<script>System.import("chart").then( function(chart){
//do things with chart
});</script>
```

Or, if you're in a TypeScript file:

```
import {Chart} from "chart";
```

You can use JSPM, or one of the other build tools, to concatenate and bundle the JavaScript resources for the loader into a single file. If your clients and servers both support HTTP 2, however, you might simply be able to allow system.js to download files as it finds that they are required.

System.js and jspm are designed to work well together, but they are, of course, not the only tools in this space. Require.js is also a very popular loader. The Alpine Ski House team decided on the combination of System.js and jspm due to their seamless nature and generally good support.

Picking a Framework

If you think the number of module types or package managers or build tools available in the JavaScript community is intimidating, you might want to sit down for this section. There are literally thousands of JavaScript frameworks to choose from, including Angular, React, Aurelia, Backbone, Meteor, and Ember.js. Making the decision on which one to use is not a simple one by any stretch of the imagination. Even just listing the factors to consider when picking one is difficult to fit within this chapter. You might want to consider adoption rates, availability of skilled help, stability, age, features, speed, maintainability, and cross browser support. Alternately, you could take the approach taken by most startups and pick whichever one shows up the most on the web development subreddit.

For the purposes of Alpine Ski House, the team decided to use the React view library coupled with the RefluxJS unidirectional dataflow library. React is a very popular library that is supported by Facebook and is used heavily on their site. It leverages a virtual DOM to allow for rapid changes to the DOM without excessive reflows or complete redraws of a section of the page. React is a component oriented framework that focuses on composing custom tags. It is a minimalist library, unlike something like AngularJS, so it must be coupled with other tools such as RefluxJS.

React meshes quite nicely with TypeScript because newer versions of TypeScript support .tsx files. "What is a .tsx file?" you might ask. Well, it is simply a TypeScript version of the .jsx file. "What is a .jsx file?" JSX is a rather odd looking mixture of JavaScript and XML that is very popular in the React community. For example, you might define a number entry field in react like:

```
function() {
return (<div>
        <label for={this.state.controlName}>{this.state.label}</label>
        <input type="number" name={this.state.controlName}/>
    </div>);
}
```

The code might look extremely odd, but after you've gotten used to it, React and JSX are highly productive tools. TypeScript understands this syntax and can provide type checking for the properties embedded inside of the HTML.

One thing the Alpine Ski House team decided from the outset was that they would avoid using jQuery. To many, this is a heretical notion. Building a website without jQuery? Shocking. The truth is that jQuery filled a very large gap in functionality in older browsers. JavaScript however, has come a long way in adding such features as querySelector that are vastly more performant versions of the JavaScript functionality.

> **Note** Don't want to use jQuery? Well then *http://youmightnotneedjquery.com/* is certainly for you. The site does not just provide pure JavaScript equivalents to common jQuery functions, but also provides suggestions for smaller, more granular libraries that can be used instead.

Summary

The space in this chapter and, in fact, this entire book is woefully inadequate to fully explore the entirety of the ecosystem that is JavaScript. What is perhaps more concerning is that no book could be written in a timely enough fashion to not be comically out of date as soon as the ink was dry. JavaScript moves faster than any programming language and ecosystem we've ever seen. It is, however, an integral part of any web development effort. Perhaps the best possible advice when dealing with JavaScript is to look to the writings of J. R. R. Tolkien:

"All that is gold does not glitter"

The best JavaScript tools for your project might not be the glittering paragons of JavaScript coolness, but instead might be more solid and well supported libraries and tools. Whatever you do choose, it is comforting to know that ASP.NET Core has taken great strides toward being observant of best practices for JavaScript. No longer do we have runtime compiled bundles of JavaScript or ridiculous abstractions like update panels. JavaScript is, at last, a first class citizen. In the next chapter we will cover dependency injection and the many benefits of using it.

CHAPTER 16

Dependency Management

Development was coming along fast. Builds were shipping to the test environment as many as 20 times a day. The bugs list hovered around two or three issues as the development team knocked off problems as fast as they showed up. Danielle was delighted at all the things she was learning. She even went home at night and read blogs and watched videos. The enthusiasm of people like Marc was infectious. And it wasn't just her. There wasn't a day where she came in that somebody on the team hadn't found some awesome new library, tool, or concept that they felt would make things better.

"Have you seen this GenFu library?" Arjun asked one Wednesday. "It generates realistic testing data by just looking at our class names. Watch!" Arjun refreshed his browser and a list of skiers popped up. "Look, it filled in the name Lionel Penuchot for this skier and that could be a real person's name. The QA team will love this. I'm going to check this package in!"

Danielle thought for a second. Hadn't she read something about checking in dependencies one night last week? "Hold on Arjun, I don't think we need to check that file in. I think we can just list it as a dependency."

"Oh no!" cried Arjun "I did that on one project and then everybody had different versions of the same library and nothing worked and everybody got fired and I ended up living in a van, down by the river... That last part might not have happened, but it is still a terrible idea."

"No, no hear me out. I was just reading about this nougat or nugget or something like that tool the other night. It can handle all of our dependencies and even dependencies of dependencies using transit closures."

"Transit closures? Do you mean 'Transitive Closures'?" asked Arjun. "I didn't know any such tool existed. It would be great to use that. Do you think there are tools like that for JavaScript too?"

"You know what, I bet there are. Let's look into it."

Now more than ever, our applications are composed of a large number of small components. Often, those components are libraries written by other developers and are used by thousands of other applications. In the past, it was common for developers to download libraries and commit those libraries to source control along with the application's source code. This process quickly became tedious, especially when libraries started depending on specific versions of other libraries. Updating to new versions of a particular library became especially difficult because you might accidentally break another library in the chain of dependencies. Package managers are a result of this tedium. They are used to automate the process of installing packages, ensuring any dependent packages are installed and providing a sane method of updating packages when new versions are available.

A typical ASP.NET Core application makes use of at least two package managers: NuGet for .NET packages and another package manager for client side packages like JQuery and Bootstrap. There are a few options for client side package managers that we will discuss in this chapter.

NuGet

NuGet is an open source package manager for .NET that ships with Visual Studio and is deeply integrated into the dotnet command line interface. At the time of writing this book, NuGet has over 60,000 packages and has served over 1.3 billion package downloads. Those numbers are growing daily. Even the assemblies that make up ASP.NET Core ship via NuGet, so you don't need to do anything to start using NuGet because it's already built right in.

Installing packages with NuGet

There are a few different approaches for installing NuGet packages in ASP.NET Core applications. One option is to edit the dependencies section of the application's project.json file. For example, the project.json file for AlpineSkiHouse.Web lists a dependency on version 2.1.0 of the MediatR package.

dependencies from project.json file in AlpineSkiHouse.Web

```
"dependencies": {
    //Other dependencies omitted for brevity

    "MediatR": "2.1.0",
    "MediatR.Extensions.Microsoft.DependencyInjection": "1.0.0"
}
```

To install packages from the command line, execute the dotnet restore command to install all the packages listed in the project.json file. Visual Studio automatically executes a dotnet restore upon saving project.json after modifications.

Visual Studio Tooling

NuGet packages for a project can be seen under the Reference node in Solution Explorer, as shown in Figure 16-1.

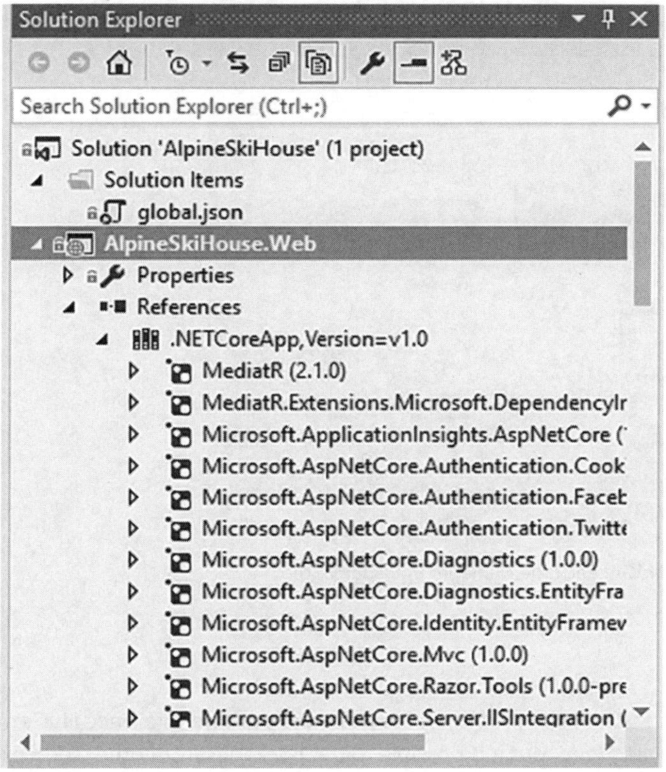

FIGURE 16-1 A screen shot shows NuGet Packages for AlpineSkiHouse.Web

Visual Studio also provides a rich visual interface to manage NuGet packages. You can manage NuGet packages for a single project by right-clicking the project in Solution Explorer and selecting Manage NuGet Packages. To manage NuGet packages for the entire solution, right-click the Solution node in Solution Explorer and select Manage NuGet Packages For Solution.

The NuGet Package Manager tools in Visual Studio, as shown in Figure 16-2, allow you to browse packages from NuGet.org, view installed packages, and update installed packages.

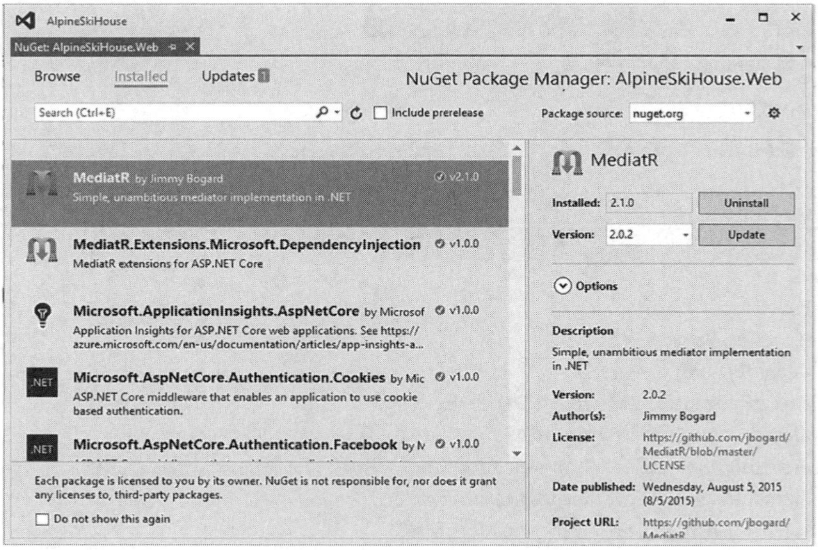

FIGURE 16-2 A screen shot shows the NuGet Package Manager in Visual Studio

NuGet Feeds

A NuGet feed is a location that hosts NuGet packages. For the most part, we reference NuGet packages from the public nuget.org feed, but it is possible to get packages from other sources as well. Some large organizations prefer to limit the set of NuGet packages to a set of pre-approved packages, in which case, it is possible to host an internal NuGet feed that contains only those pre-approved packages. Another common use case is for companies to use a private NuGet feed to distribute proprietary packages within an organization.

Hosting your own NuGet feed might sound like overkill, but in reality it is very easy to do and is often very much worth the effort. Limiting the list of approved packages for an organization can keep developers from downloading a package that is known to causes problems or lack support and proper updates. There is an impressive set of both hosted and on premise solutions available to support these types of scenarios. MyGet, available at *http://myget.org/* is a popular hosted service used by the ASP.NET team to host nightly builds. Refer to *https://docs.nuget.org/Contribute/Ecosystem* for a good overview on some of the more popular products available. Many of the options that the article lists also work with other package managers, such as NPM and Bower.

npm

npm is the package manager for Node.js. You might be asking yourself, "Why are we talking about Node.js in a book dedicated to writing ASP.NET Core applications?" When you look at the broader landscape of web development, a large amount of tooling for web developers is actually written as Node.js packages and is distributed using npm. Some examples of these tools include the TypeScript compiler, the gulp and grunt task runners, and the Jasmine JavaScript unit framework. As you saw in Chapter 15, "The Role of Javascript," JavaScript is an important part of all modern web applications. Having access to the tools that developers use outside of the ASP.NET world is important, because it helps to ensure that you don't lose touch with the greater web development community.

npm is a command line tool. To use npm in our application, start by creating a `package.json` file. You can create the file manually or use the `npm init` command, which asks you a few questions and creates the `package.json` file automatically. Here is a basic `package.json` file that references the Jasmine unit test framework and the Karma unit test runner. We spend more time on configuring Jasmine and Karma in Chapter 19, "Testing."

```
{
    "name": "alpineskihouse",
    "version": "1.0.0",
    "description": "",
    "private": true,
    "main": "gulpfile.js",
    "dependencies": {},
    "devDependencies": {
        "jasmine": "2.5.0",
        "karma": "1.2.0"
    },
    "author": "Alpine Ski House"
}
```

We list the packages we want to use under `devDependencies`, because these are not packages that we want to ship as part of our application, but rather tools that developers are going to use to help them write the application. We also set the `"private": true,` which ensures that the application is not accidentally published to the public npm package registry.

> **Note** Running the `npm install` command restores all of the dependencies listed in the `package.json` file. By default, all the listed dependencies and devDependencies are downloaded in the current project to a folder named node_modules.

Adding Dependencies

New dependencies can be added by directly editing the `package.json` file or by calling the `npm install` command and specifying the package name and the `--save-dev` flag. Note that there is also a `--save` flag that adds packages to the dependencies section of `package.json`. This flag is used to add runtime dependencies.

```
npm install karma --save-dev
```

npm's default behavior is to add a dependency to the latest stable release of the specified package. If your application requires a specific version of a package, either edit the package.json file manually or specify the version by adding the @x.x.x to the package name when calling the npm install command.

```
npm install karma@1.2.0 --save-dev
```

Using npm modules

Many npm modules include command line interfaces so you can use them directly from the command line without having to enter the Node runtime environment. A good example of this is the Karma test runner that includes a command line interface called karma, which can be used to run unit tests. Tools like karma can be made available globally on a developer machine or build server by installing them globally using the –g flag.

```
npm install karma –g
```

Globally installing packages requires more setup than we would like, especially for new developers. Ideally, a new developer would simply run npm install and immediately have access to the necessary commands. npm makes this possible by installing command line tools locally in the /node_modules/.bin/ folder, so while the Karma command line tool might not be available on the developer's global path, she can reference it from ./node_modules/.bin/karma.

```
.\node_modules\.bin\karma start
```

We can make this even easier by defining an npm script in the package.json file:

```
{
    "name": "alpineskihouse",
    "version": "1.0.0",
    "description": "",
    "private": true,
    "main": "gulpfile.js",
    "dependencies": {},
    "devDependencies": {
        "jasmine": "2.5.0",
        "karma": "1.2.0"
    },
    "author": "Alpine Ski House",
    "scripts": {
        "test-js": ".\\node_modules\\.bin\\karma start --single-run"
    }
}
```

After a script has been defined, you can execute the script by calling the npm run-script command:

```
npm run-script test-js
```

Visual Studio Integration

The command line tooling for npm may be familiar to you, but if you use the Visual Studio Integrated Development Environment (IDE), you might be expecting a more integrated experience. Fortunately, the latest versions of Visual Studio have great integration with npm. Visual Studio automatically detects when a project contains a `package.json` file and lists npm under the Dependencies node in Solution Explorer, as shown in Figure 16-3.

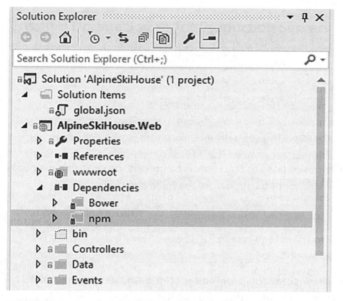

FIGURE 16-3 npm dependencies node in Solution Explorer

Visual Studio automatically detects changes to the `package.json` file and calls `npm install` whenever necessary. You can also manually trigger an `npm install` by right-clicking the npm node in Solution Explorer and selecting the Restore Packages menu option. You can find the output from the npm install command in the Visual Studio output window by selecting the `bower/npm` output option.

> **Note** With the use of a Visual Studio Extension, you can execute NPM scripts directly from Visual Studio by using the Task Runner Explorer. First, follow the directions listed at *https://github.com/madskristensen/NpmTaskRunner* to install the NPM Task Runner extension. Next, open the Task Runner Explorer window in Visual Studio by selecting View | Other Windows | Task Runner Explorer. Task Runner Explorer lists all the npm scripts for the current project. Individual tasks can be executed by right-clicking the task and selecting the Run menu option, as shown in Figure 16-4.

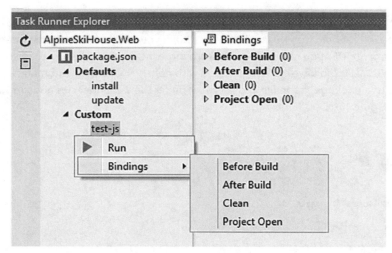

FIGURE 16-4 Add bindings to npm scripts using Task Runner Explorer

Task Runner Explorer also provides options to bind scripts to specific Visual Studio events. For example, you can configure the test-js script to run before the Build event.

Yarn

The de facto package manager for server side JavaScript tools is npm. Some people even make use of it for installing client libraries (keep reading to hear about Bower, the alternative client side library manager). However, npm has its failings. In this section we will cover npm as well as Yarn, a new JavaScript package manager designed to solve any npm failings. Consider the package.json file, which contains versions for each module included as part of npm. If you're concerned that people on your project might end up with incorrect versions of libraries, you can fix packages on a specific version number:

```
"devDependencies": {
    "@types/chartjs": "0.0.28",
    "@types/lodash": "^4.14.34",
}
```

The @type/chartjs package is given a specific version number, which means you'll always get exactly that version of the package installed. @types/lodash on the other hand starts with a ^ character. This character means that npm will install a version of @types/lodash that is compatible with the version number listed in accordance with semver. Running the package restore at the time of publishing actually gives you @types/lodash@4.14.37. Even specifying exact version numbers in the packages.json doesn't guarantee that the install will be the same from one day to another. Packages can have dependencies and the authors of packages may have used non-specific version of packages. For example grabbing a random package.json from the node_modules directory contains:

```
"devDependencies": {
    "chai": "^3.2.0",
    "coveralls": "^2.11.2",
    "graceful-fs": "4.1.4",
    "istanbul": "^0.3.20",
    "mocha": "^2.0.0",
    "rimraf": "^2.4.3",
    "sinon": "^1.10.3",
    "sinon-chai": "^2.6.0"
},
```

Almost all of the packages contain semver restricted packages. npm is also non-deterministic, meaning that the order in which the packages are installed can result in a differ version of modules for each person who runs the install step. This is quite concerning, because a piece of code may work ondeveloper workstation A and not on developer workstation B due to different package versions.

Doing a full restore of a node_modules directory from the Internet can be terribly slow. Literally thousands of packages must be downloaded and unpacked. On a build server this can slow down the build process dramatically. What's worse is that transient failures during the installation, like a network hiccup for instance, will break the build.

Alternately the node_modules directory can be checked in, but that is many thousands of files and updating a package tends to create massive changes in git history which is undesirable. The problem is that npm does not create a local cache of packages, so each build requires a trip out to the package registry.

For years we've pretty much just suffered with these defects in npm, however, those days may be over with the introduction of the new Yarn package manager. This package manager can be slotted in to replace npm pretty much without change. Yarn is a project of Facebook, Exponent, Google and Tilde, and strives to address the shortcomings of npm. The first thing Yarn provides is a deterministic installation of packages for a project. No matter in what order packages are installed, the resulting package tree in node_modules will remain the same. Yarn also runs multiple downloads and installs in parallel, retrying those which fail. This speeds up the installation process while adding a degree of robustness.

To install Yarn you need only run the following:

```
npm install -g yarn
```

Now Yarn can be used on an existing package.json file by deleting the node_modules directory and running:

```
yarn
```

Adding packages no longer requires specifying --save or --save-dev, because they will be saved automatically. A --dev flag may be added to save in the dependencies section:

```
yarn add jquery
yarn add gulp --dev
```

The secret to Yarn's abilities is found in a new file called yarn.lock. This file should be included in version control to ensure that all users get the same versions. An excerpt from the lock file looks like:

```
mkdirp@^0.5.0, mkdirp@^0.5.1, "mkdirp@>=0.5 0", mkdirp@~0.5.0, mkdirp@~0.5.1, mkdirp@0.5:
  version "0.5.1"
  resolved "https://registry.yarnpkg.com/mkdirp/-/mkdirp-0.5.1.tgz#30057438eac6cf7f8c4767f38648
d6697d75c903"
  dependencies:
    minimist "0.0.8"
```

This lists the versions to use for a package called mkdirp. The first line lists a number of versions of mkdirp, and each of these versions is listed somewhere in a package in our package tree. Yarn has seen all of these versions and resolved them to a single version, which can satisfy all of the required versions.

Yarn solves many of the shortcomings of npm. It is, however, too early to tell if Yarn will gain wider acceptance. The ease of upgrading to Yarn from npm, the speed increase, and deterministic package installation are quite compelling, so it is more likely that it will be adopted than not.

Bower

ASP.NET Core uses Bower as the default package manager for client side libraries. Client side libraries are made up of assets that are eventually sent to the client's browser. These assets are typically JavaScript and CSS, as is the case with jQuery and Bootstrap, however they can also include other assets like images, fonts, and icons. It is not uncommon for a large web application to use dozens of client side libraries, so it is important to have a good package manager at your disposal.

Why Bower?

In previous versions of ASP.NET, client side libraries were distributed using NuGet, but unfortunately, NuGet was not well suited to client side package management. One big problem is that client side libraries are created by and consumed by the wider web development community. Because the .NET development community makes up only a small part of the overall community, authors of a client side library might not have any .NET based experience and can't possibly be expected to learn the intricacies of NuGet or maintain NuGet packages specifically for .NET developers. In many cases, a keen developer in the Microsoft community would try to maintain a NuGet package on behalf of the library authors, but this proved to be onerous and error prone. The result was often that NuGet packages for popular client side libraries were either not available or horribly out of date.

Instead of attempting to maintain client side packages in NuGet, the ASP.NET Core and Visual Studio in particular have great support for package managers commonly used by the web developer community. Bower is one such package manager and happens to be the package manager used by the default ASP.NET Core application templates.

Visual Studio has some excellent tooling that helps hide some of Bower's complexities, but let's start by exploring how Bower is used from the command line. Bower is a node based command line tool that is installed via npm. You can install it globally using the following command:

```
npm install bower -g
```

With Bower, packages are defined in a `bower.json` file. This file can be created manually or you can use the `bower init` command.

```
{
  "name": "alpineskihouse",
  "private": true,
  "dependencies": {
    "bootstrap": "3.3.6",
    "jquery": "2.2.0",
    "jquery-validation": "1.14.0",
    "jquery-validation-unobtrusive": "3.2.6"
  }
}
```

The name "alpineskihouse" is used to identify our current package, and the private flag is set to true to ensure that the application is not accidentally published to the Bower package registry. Library authors should set the private flag to false. The libraries that the application uses are listed in the dependencies section. Each library also has an associated version. To install all the packages listed in the `bower.json` file, call the `bower install` command:

```
bower install
```

By default, all of the listed `dependencies` are downloaded to a folder named bower_components in the current project. This location can be overwritten by specifying a different directory in the .bowerrc configuration file. In the Alpine Ski House Web project, we changed the default location to wwwroot/lib:

Contents of .bowerrc file

```
{
  "directory": "wwwroot/lib"
}
```

Adding Dependencies

To add a dependency to a new package, either edit the `bower.json` file manually or call the `bower install` command, specifying the package name and the `--save` option.

```
bower install jquery --save
```

As is the case with npm, Bower adds a dependency on the latest stable version of the specified package. You can use the `--save-exact` option if a specific version is required.

```
bower install jquery --save --save-exact 2.4.1
```

Bower pulls packages from a publicly available git repository, usually GitHub. At times you might need to reference a pre-release version of a library that has yet to make it into a release package; being able to pull packages from github makes this seamless. You can tell Bower to reference a specific git location, or even a specific commit from a git repository. To make these overrides possible, provide a git URL instead of a version number for the dependency in question:

```
"canvg": "https://github.com/gabelerner/canvg.git#f5519bc910ecefe083f636707b27e436386fdeed"
```

Referencing Assets from Bower Packages

After calling `bower install`, the assets you need are available in the bower components directory. In our case, the wwwroot/lib directory. We can reference these scripts in our application just like we would any other script or stylesheet. The location of the relevant files for each bower package varies, but many packages follow the convention of putting the important files in a folder name dist.

```
<html>
   <head>
      ...
      <link rel="stylesheet" href="~/lib/bootstrap/dist/css/bootstrap.css" />
      ...
   </head>
   <body>
      ...

      <script src="~/lib/jquery/dist/jquery.js"></script>
      <script src="~/lib/bootstrap/dist/js/bootstrap.js"></script>

      ...

   </body>

</html>
```

In a production deployment, you might want to reference some of the common client libraries from a Content Delivery Network (CDN), rather than from the versions stored on your web server. ASP.NET Core provides a set of tag helpers that simplifies this process. We explore these tag helpers in Chapter 19, "Reusable Components."

Summary

The web development landscape is constantly evolving. While Bower is popular today as the default ASP.NET package manager for client side libraries, other options are available and might become more popular over time. Some developers are using npm for both developer tools and client side libraries, while JSPM is another alternative to Bower that is gaining popularity. Even in the .NET world where NuGet is well established, alternate package managers like Paket are emerging.

The package manager choices we made for the Alpine Ski House application were based on a combination of the default project templates in ASP.NET Core and the experience of the team members. Ultimately, most package managers offer similar functionality. Pick what works for your team and don't be afraid to investigate alternative options if you think they might simplify the process for your team and your application. In the next chapter we talk about how to use stylesheets to make the application's front end look great.

## CHAPTER 17

Front End with Style

Mark had looped in Danielle on a regression that had reappeared a couple of times. He'd corrected it on his machine and had it working, but after the latest build went out to the staging server, it was like his changes had been reverted.

"See?" started Mark. "This is the commit for my change right here!"

"Yeah, that is unusual," replied Danielle. "Are you sure that your changes made it to the build server?"

"Yes. 100% certain. I checked the SHA and it's an exact match for the changes that were picked up before it built. And yet, look at the CSS that was deployed to…"

"Waaaaaaait a minute!" Adrian interrupted, standing up in the cubical next to Mark. "Are you talking about checking in changes to the stylesheets?"

"Yes," answered Mark. "I swear this is the third time this ticket's come back to me. I make all the changes, it works locally, and after I check it in I verify it's there."

"He's right," added Danielle, "I reviewed his code on his last pull request. He made the changes. But it's like it's being overwritten or something after the PR is merged. I just haven't put my finger on where it's happening."

Adrian smiled broadly. "I know," he said. He plopped back down in his seat and started wheeling over to Mark and Danielle. He sat there with an excited look on his face, waiting for one of them to ask him what was going on.

"Okay Adrian," laughed Danielle. "Wipe that grin off your face and help us out here. What's causing the overwrite?"

"I am so glad you asked." He started to rub his hands together. "Okay, so remember how I was pairing with the other Marc earlier this week? That's what we were doing."

"You were conspiring to overwrite my CSS changes?" asked Mark.

"Well, yes…in a way I guess we were," answered Adrian. "I guess this is our fault because we didn't update the git.ignore, but basically we shouldn't have the CSS in in the repo anymore."

"Yeah, but we version everything," said Danielle. "Our CSS needs to be under source control too, doesn't it? Did I miss a meeting?"

"Well, our CSS doesn't need to be under source control because it's a build artifact now." The grin came back to his face just as broadly as it had before. "Oh, can I just say I'm really going to enjoy this. You guys have taught me a lot here, but in nearly a month, this is the first thing that I get to show you."

"Yeah, yeah, Adrian," said Mark. "I'll make you a medal." They all laughed. "Now out with it. What's going on?"

"Ladies and gentlemen, please allow me to direct your attention to the SCSS file now located in your favorite project's Style folder..."

Building Websites with Style Sheets

When we first set out to write a chapter on style, we assumed that we were going to be writing about the Bootstrap CSS framework. After all, Bootstrap is so prevalent in the .NET world, having been included in the templates by default since 2013. It's a mature framework however and there are already plenty of resources that cover how to incorporate it into your application, so instead we are going to focus this chapter on workflow. We're going to talk about how the Alpine team used CSS and built it into their project. We share some alternate strategies for workflow and even some alternates to Bootstrap. Because of its maturity however, we can also hold Bootstrap up as a familiar beacon to model some of what we're trying to achieve as the team builds out the style for their site.

The idea of a Cascading Style Sheet (CSS) has been around for almost as long as we've had browsers. This chapter is not going to try to persuade you to use CSS, because if you've been doing any web development over the last 20 years you are likely aware of style sheets and how they can impact your development. If you're new to web development, you were likely indoctrinated into using CSS without having to think much about it. And if you're not using style sheets...well, you're likely doing it in a style that is collectively agreed to as wrong, or you're simply just not building websites.

If anything, we hope to affirm what you might already know, shed some light on why we do the things we do, and spread some ideas around about how you can use the tooling that supports CSS in the world of ASP.NET Core MVC.

Digging up the Past

You can trace the roots of CSS back to the marketing industry, where those who were in charge of communications and the success of their campaigns had long ago made some strong realizations. When you work from a style guide or a style book, people tend to accept the message better, form stronger memory about your brand, and recognize elements of your campaign even if they are subtle. It doesn't take long to connect the dots when you think about major cola brands or fast food chains and how over time a simple mark or even just a letter in their well-known font can be associated to the brand as a whole.

On the other end of the spectrum, a series of messages that do not jive visually are harder to relate to a cohesive brand. Even a single page advertisement that struggles visually is not well received. It is the job of the designer to ensure that the way the message is being communicated is not a distraction from the message itself.

The idea behind the style book, style guide, or in web parlance, the style sheet, is to build a cohesive set of rules that can be used to influence content formatting. It is a separation of the content from the presentation in such a way that the visual goals of the design can be demonstrated and then repeated consistently to help with the development of the communication, whether it is for print, television or the web.

Originally put forth as a recommendation by Håkon Wium Lie in 1996, it would take nearly four years before a web browser would achieve full support of the CSS specification. While it removed the need to explicitly style each element to adhere to a design for font, color, size, and border, early implementations were inconsistent and the vision of using this separation of presentation and content had difficulties in coming to fruition.

CSS is made up of only a few, simple concepts. There is a syntax to describe style rules that ultimately need to be understood by the client that is rendering the document to be styled. There are selectors that help you identify target elements of your document and set rules for how those elements are to be displayed. Finally, there is the concept of value assignment, where various types of units can be ascribed to the elements that match the defined rules.

It's hard to fathom that someone in the web development space hasn't worked with CSS in some capacity, although while CSS has been around for nearly two decades, it would be hard to fault someone for saying that it hasn't always been easy. The standard has continued to evolve while businesses have tried to use it in their web applications. Different vendors have interpreted the CSS specifications differently and their implementations render different layouts as a result, leading to revisions of the specification coming forward that has at times broken the visual flow of existing websites. This has improved dramatically over the years, but even when two browsers say that they have implemented a feature you might see different results in the final rendered product. This has been a source of frustration for developers since the second browser to support CSS was released.

The reasons why we use CSS are easy to articulate. If you were going to explain it to someone outside of the web development world, you might say something like this:

> Let's say I'm building this website for you, which you need for your business to stay competitive. You have a look and feel that you want to achieve and so you give me the colors, fonts, and other information that you want to use. You write all the content needed for the site and give me forty pages of text that we end up turning into dozens of webpages. Each page uses the same font, the same set of colors, and spacing that visually mimics the printed documentation you share with your customers. Each of the dozens of pages we create end up having hundreds of elements, including things like paragraphs, columns, buttons, links to other pages, menus, and the like, and each one of those needs to carry that same style you've asked of me. For me to ensure that that all those many

thousands of elements adhere to the guidelines you have laid out, I need a tool to express the rules these elements must follow. That tool is called Cascading Style Sheets. If a month down the road, you choose to move from light-blue borders to cornflower blue borders, I can either change it once in the CSS, or in every instance of every element on every page where the borders must be updated. Also, you pay by the hour. Just sayin'.

Try not to pay too much attention to the version numbers, especially when you see things like CSS3 or CSS4, which both, technically, don't exist[1]. CSS3 is the result of the WC3's CSS working group realizing that the entirety of the CSS specification can't move forward as a whole, and thus nicknamed everything that came after CSS 2.1 as CSS3. Each of the components of CSS are now represented as modules, of which there are now thirty-five and growing. This has been extremely beneficial to the development community for a couple of primary reasons. First, issues around clarification for individual modules like backgrounds and borders have been able to advance at a much quicker pace to disambiguate rules and help make rendering more consistent from browser to browser. Secondly, it allows new modules to be introduced without waiting for a working group to decide on all aspects of CSS as a whole.

> **Note** We wouldn't recommend that anyone try to memorize which browsers support which CSS modules, along with which features within a module are supported. Take a look at *http://caniuse.com* where you can search by browser, version, usage by country, and a variety of other slices to see which features are right for your project.

Listing 17-1 is a basic example of how you can simplify a single element by using a style sheet. The first line of this fictional HTML document contains styling inline, and the second line applies style rules to the `<div>` element through the use of class names.

LISTING 17-1 Simplifying an HTML tag by using CSS

```
<div style="border: 1px solid blue; padding: 10px; color: navy;">hello!</div>
<div class="simple-label victory">hello!</div>
```

While there isn't a ton of difference at first glance, this single-element demonstration allows us to extrapolate the changes that would be required based on the scenario we discussed with our client above. Changes to `simple-label` or `victory` can be centralized and with a change in one location, you can update every element across all pages that use those classes.

Creating Your Own Style Sheet

Style sheets are just text files, much the same as any other source you're going to have in your project. Creating a CSS file is as easy as adding a text document with a .css extension. Visual Studio also supports adding CSS documents through the Add New Item dialog, as you can see in Figure 17-1.

---

[1] http://www.xanthir.com/b4Ko0

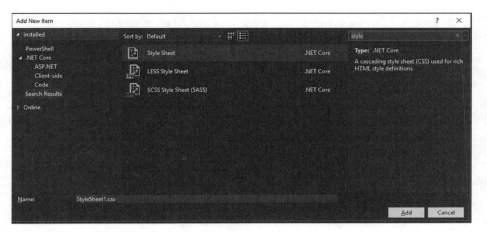

FIGURE 17-1 The Add New Item Dialog while adding a stylesheet

To include a style sheet in a page, you add a line of markup like so:

```
<link rel="stylesheet" href="~/css/site.css" />
```

After you have a CSS document and you have it included in your page, you're going to want to define a few rules so that your page conforms to the design. Rules are composed of two parts, as highlighted in Figure 17-2. You can see the selector block in the larger rectangle and the declaration block in the smaller rectangle.

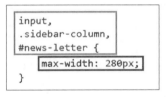

FIGURE 17-2 The selector and declaration blocks

The selector block can contain as many selectors as you like. A selector can be an HTML element, such as the input above, a class name that you define like the .sidebar-column in the example, or the unique ID of an element that exists on a page, like the #newsletter. Selectors can also be based on presence or absence, substring matches, hierarchy and ancestry, or a special case known as pseudo-selectors that describe an element's state or relation to another element, such as a visited link or which element is before or after another. You can include as many selectors as you require. The declaration of the rule contains the property assignments and values that are applied to any elements that match the selectors you've included in the selector block.

All rule applications to elements in your document are performed in a particular fashion. The order that you define rules in, the nesting of an element in the document, and the order in which you apply class styles on elements all affect which style is used. This is a concept called specificity, which goes beyond the scope of this section.

You can read about the entire selector definition, including specificity, on the W3C site at https://www.w3.org/TR/css3-selectors/.

In ASP.NET Core MVC, you're more likely interested in putting your style sheets into a layout so that the style can be shared across multiple views. As discussed in Chapter 11, "Razor Views," you should include different versions of your style sheet for different environments. Using the `environment` tag helper allows you to include a minified version of your CSS in production, while having the human-readable version working locally in your development environment.

```
<environment names="Development">
    <link rel="stylesheet" href="~/css/site.css" />
</environment>
<environment names="Staging,Production">
    <link rel="stylesheet" href="~/css/site.min.css" asp-append-version="true" />
</environment>
```

Again, the beauty of Razor is in play here, so you can go even further by combining things like service injection and conditional statements to determine which style sheet to use. If you have a white label application that allows for styling based on user-specified CSS sources, this presents a powerful opportunity to dynamically modify the appearance of your entire site with as little as a few lines of code.

CSS can become quite cumbersome to build, especially if you're trying to handle the different ways that browsers implement specification features. Creating rule sets that span multiple elements or factor in browser-specific prefixes are tedious and can be error prone. This is especially true because often the overall design you are building is prone to repetition, has blocks of similar rule declarations, and is predicated upon hierarchies in your document intended to build out user experiences.

As with all things in the application development space, when there is friction, someone comes along and builds tooling that helps to alleviate it.

Getting Sassy with Your Style

Over the years it became apparent that writing all of the CSS by hand, given the high level of repetitiveness in it, was a chore that could be simplified. More importantly, CSS documents were being broken down into smaller, more manageable chunks and folks wanted to take away the possibility of an error surfacing in their style rules due to mismatched colors, fonts, and sizes. CSS lacks the ability to compose the documents, define and share variables, apply logic, and import other rules. If the goal is to remove the repetitive, error-prone work from our HTML documents in the first place, why should we stop when we get to the CSS level and allow it to happen there?

It is also apparent that the syntax specification doesn't need to change to facilitate an easier developer workflow. CSS can provide metadata for HTML elements, but it is not a programming language and shouldn't evolve as one. Yet at the same time, CSS doesn't provide enough to work around some of the shortcomings that are present outside of a programming language, and not everyone wants to write 500 lines of code to define styles for buttons by hand.

With those understandings, a set of tooling come out in a class known as "CSS Pre-processors," the goal of which is to extend CSS in a way that allows a programmatic syntax to build styling documents in a 100 percent compatible-to-CSS way. These tools introduced variables, operators, inheritance, and a form of functions to allow designers and developers to treat CSS the same way we treat HTML. You might even say that we no longer have to write CSS because we can write "software" that generates the CSS for us. Table 17-1 shows a few of the more popular pre-processors that have come to market.

TABLE 17-1 Popular CSS pre-processors

Pre-Processor	Advantages	Where it fits for .NET Devs
SASS, SCSS	Arguable the most mature, many samples, great documentation, popular and used by leading CSS frameworks	Can be built from the command line or with tooling built into Visual Studio, good set of features to handle most CSS development requirements
LESS	Allows for use of LESS source with a JS pre-processor in-browser	Can be built from the command line or with tooling built into Visual Studio, mature enough to be trusted, but some CSS frameworks are moving away from it
Stylus	Automatic vendor prefixes, over 60 built-in functions, expansive feature set	Requires node.js and some tweaks to compile in Visual Studio. Potentially higher learning curve, but advantageous if you're building a complex CSS framework of your own

There are many other pre-processors out there as well, some requiring PHP, some with tooling to better support Ruby on Rails developers, and others still in their infancy but that aspire to fill in gaps they feel are missing in the market leaders. All of them use a similar set of constructs to give developers a little more flexibility in how they create their style sheets. It is the compilation of the SCSS file in the Alpine project that is tripping up Mark, because the build server was overwriting the CSS file as part of its process.

SASS, or "Syntactically Awesome Style Sheets" was the predecessor to SCSS, also known as "Sassy CSS." Whereas SASS focused on a terser syntax based on indentation and ignoring curly braces and semi-colons, SCSS is a superset of CSS, meaning that every valid CSS document out there was also a valid SCSS document. Having valid SCSS with every CSS document makes it trivial for development teams to switch to SCSS with little learning curve, and for those teams to immediately benefit from the gaps SCSS fills in native CSS.

Basics of SCSS

Adding a SCSS file to your project is as simple as any other file type. In fact, have a peek back at Figure 17-1. In the new file dialog is an option to create an SCSS file instead of a straight CSS file. You can take that option or even just rename a CSS file that you've been working on.

Variables

Let's start by addressing one of the biggest complaints that we've heard from developers about working with style sheets, which is having to update them. If we consider the scenario where we have a color palette to work from, we might have a list of colors that we get from a designer. Rather than use those colors directly in our rules, what we do instead is create some variables as we have defined in Listing 17-2.

LISTING 17-2 Defining colors as variables in SCSS

```
$dark-border:        #7a7265;
$light-background:   #cecac4;
$main-text-color:    #433e3f;
$primary-border-width: 2px;
```

With those variables in place, we can refer to the colors by their names instead of by hexadecimal value, like we see in Listing 17-3. The advantage of this is obviously that we can alter the variable values without having to root through all the code or try to rely on the Find and Replace features of our editors.

LISTING 17-3 Using variables in CSS rules

```
.banner-text {
    color: $main-text-color;
    background-color: $light-background;
    border: $primary-border-width solid $dark-border;
}
```

All of the code in Listing 17-2 and 17-3 can appear in the same file. After being run through the SCSS pre-processor, we get the resultant CSS shown in Listing 17-4. The variables are replaced with their values, which provide a valid CSS rule.

LISTING 17-4 CSS resulting from pre-processing of Listing 17-2 and 17-3

```
.banner-text {
  color: #433e3f;
  background-color: #cecac4;
  border: 2px solid #7a7265; }
```

Imports and Partials

You can take this example of colors a little further and break out the color palette into its own file. If you assume that all of the code from Listing 17-2 appeared in a file called _color-palette.scss, you can then include it in our main SCSS file, like in Listing 17-5. We prefix the color palette file name with an underscore to mark it as a partial. This way the pre-processor knows that it shouldn't attempt to build a CSS file out of it.

LISTING 17-5 Importing an SCSS partial

```scss
@import 'color-palette';

.banner-text {
    color: $main-text-color;
    background-color: $light-background;
    border: $primary-border-width solid $dark-border;
}
```

This approach shares the color palette with a designer, keeping the colors versioned under source control on their own. We can continue developing our SCSS rules while the color palette is finalized and we can include it in as many sources as we need to while we lean on the variables without having to worry about what the final values are.

Inheritance

When you have a set of rules that are based off of a core set of styles, you might want to leverage SCSS's inheritance capabilities. As illustrated in Listing 17-6, you use `@extend` to pull in the properties from another rule.

LISTING 17-6 Using @extend to inherit from another style rule

```scss
.simple-label {
  border: 1px solid #ccc;
  padding: 10px;
  color: #334;
}

.victory {
  @extend .simple-label;
  border-color: blue;
}

.defeat {
  @extend .simple-label;
  border-color: red;
}
```

SCSS takes the code and combines the rules for output, similar to Listing 17-7. This might not seem like it has many benefits at first, but when you start combining inheritance with variables and importing other SCSS files, it becomes quite a powerful feature.

LISTING 17-7 The result of inheriting from a previously defined rule

```
.simple-label, .victory, .defeat {
  border: 1px solid #ccc;
  padding: 10px;
  color: #334; }

.victory {
  border-color: blue; }

.defeat {
  border-color: red; }
```

Nesting

Nesting is a way to help you simplify your CSS and mimic the HTML structure a little more closely. HTML and CSS don't always align well, but with nesting you can get a little closer. Let's say you have an HTML element structure that looks like this:

```
<div>
    <p>Hello <span>world</span>!</p>
</div>
```

With nesting you can easily target the inner span like so:

```
div {
    p {
        color: $main-text-color;
        span {
            font-weight: bold;
        }
    }
}
```

Nesting can also help us avoid retyping CSS namespaces over and over again. In Listing 17-8 we specify the font namespace one time and then set the inner values of the namespace.

LISTING 17-8 Taking advantage of namespace shorthand in SCSS

```
div {
    p {
        color: $main-text-color;
        span {
            font: {
                weight: bold;
                size: 1.25em;
                style: italic;
            }
        }
    }
}
```

When run through the pre-compiler, we get the output seen in Listing 17-9. SCSS is able to correctly pack the properties of the namespace back into compliance and properly produce two corresponding rules.

LISTING 17-9 Style rules generated from listing 17-8

```
div p {
  color: #433e3f; }
div p span {
    font-weight: bold;
    font-size: 1.25em;
    font-style: italic; }
```

An important point to note is that you can end up over-qualifying the CSS with complex nesting. In the case of Listing 17-9, two rules were generated from the source SCSS, but further nesting or style declarations at any of the selector levels can cause trouble. If you find yourself creating several nested blocks of rules, it might be a bit of a style smell. Nesting is a great way to target a specific element, but if used without caution, it can explode into dozens of unintended and likely unnecessary rules. Often this happens when folks are running into trouble correctly isolating an element. There is usually a simpler, easier to maintain way than building out a deeper level of nesting, such as revisiting the HTML structure, adding a stand-alone class, or favoring inheritance to nesting.

SASS Script Functions

Today there are around 100 different functions that you can use to build your style sheet. The idea of using a function might sound a little absurd at first, at least we though it did, but then you start to see the benefits when you can do things like modify colors.

In Listing 17-10 we revisit the code from Listing 17-2 where we were defining colors, but this time we use one of the dozens of color functions to compute the background color.

LISTING 17-10 Using built-in Sass Script functions

```
$dark-border:          #7a7265;
$light-background:     lighten($dark-border,35%);
$main-text-color:      #433e3f;
$primary-border-width: 2px;
```

Here, we're taking the value of the `$dark-border` and applying a `lighten()` function to it to come up with a lighter shade of the color. There are functions in Sass Script that allow you to work with colors, manipulate strings, perform calculations, define lists and maps, and more.

You can find the complete list of SASS Script functions at http://sass-lang.com/documentation/Sass/Script/Functions.html.

If you've been following along and experimenting with some of the basics, you might want to start to see your SCSS become CSS. In the next section we talk about building up your workflow and some of the tools, but first we have one more powerful feature that we should walk through, mixins.

Creating Mixins

A mixin in many languages is a class in which there are two or more classes mixed together, rather than having one inherit from the other. In SCSS, it is a way to group, or mix attributes and values for reuse across elements. You can almost think of a mixin as a template function that can accept parameters and return the template populated with the values provided. Here, a `label` mixin definition forms such a template for rendering a CSS class that is based off of the provided color:

```
@mixin label($base-color){
    color: $base-color;
    background-color: lighten($base-color,25%);
    border: 1px solid darken($base-color, 10%);
}
```

Then we can use the mixin in a class definition and just pass in the label color we want to generate:

```
.red-label { @include label(red); }
```

And here is the output we get:

```
.red-label {
  color: red;
  background-color: #ff8080;
  border: 1px solid #cc0000; }
```

You are not limited to using only a mixin as the body of the CSS class. In fact, the power of mixins can really start to show when you combine, for example, a `thick-border` mixin, an `oversize` mixin and a `label` mixin together to fuse all their properties into one class.

Mixing Mixins and Directives

We can really start to see the benefit of SCSS when combining all of the features that we've learned so far. We have the ability to store colors in variables, apply functions to those colors, and then define a mixin that allows us to easily generate a relevant class. If you go even further, you can start to make some interesting things happen.

Let's rework the label sample, but now, in Listing 17-11, we introduce one of the directives for working with lists—the @each directive. @each takes a list or a map and iterates over it, generating style rules based on the elements in the list.

LISTING 17-11 Applying a directive to generate style rules

```
@each $label-color in red, green, blue {
  .#{$label-color}-label { @include label($label-color); }
}
```

We're introducing a few things in Listing 17-11, so let's walk through it. red, green, and blue are just items in a list. In this case, they are interpreted as colors when the SCSS is compiled because they are known CSS named colors or we could have just as easily used hex values. When we want to work with the string literal name of an item, we can escape it with `#{..}`, as we've done with `#{$label-color}`. This lets us build the name for the class we're generating. Finally, we call our previously defined mixin and pass in one of the values from the provided list. Our output is quite pleasing, considering that we only have three lines of code in Listing 17-11.

```
.red-label {
  color: red;
  background-color: #ff8080;
  border: 1px solid #cc0000; }

.green-label {
  color: green;
  background-color: #01ff01;
  border: 1px solid #004d00; }

.blue-label {
  color: blue;
  background-color: #8080ff;
  border: 1px solid #0000cc; }
```

Establishing a Development Workflow

There is no single IDE that is going to please every developer on the planet, so naturally different patterns emerge on how folks build out their workflows. A particular developer might even have preferences for working with certain project or file types.

Using Command Line Tools

If you just want the simplicity of building from the command line, you need the tooling for SASS. The sass-lang.org website recommends using Ruby and downloading gems, however .NET developers are becoming more and more familiar with node.js and the npm package manager. npm has a package called `node-sass` that also has a command line interface. It's built in C and runs very quickly. To install `node-sass`, type the following from a command line:

```
npm install node-sass
```

Next, navigate to somewhere in your project structure where you can easily access the SCSS file you want to compile and the target directory where you'd like the final CSS to end up. You can then run `node-sass` to build your CSS file by passing in the source and output file names. Here, we're running the command from the root of the `src` directory in a fictitious project:

```
node-sass style/site.scss wwwroot/css/site.css
```

The CSS file would be generated at `src/wwwroot/css/site.css`.

Working in Visual Studio Code

In 2015, Microsoft unveiled the first release of Visual Studio Code, or VS Code, which is an open source editor that runs across all platforms. Compared to the full version of Visual Studio it is lightweight, customizable, extensible through a fast developing plug-in repository, and supports a wide variety of languages and script types.

Many developers enjoy working in VS Code because it doesn't have any of the chrome of fully-fledged IDEs. It recommends plug-ins that are helpful in their current context and it natively knows about the file extensions that they use most, including SCSS. Developers can pull up a copy of their SCSS and the CSS that is output at the same time to get a good feel for the style rules that they are building. To get that to work, we run the `node-sass` tool again, but we add the optional watch parameter with a `-w`:

```
node-sass -w style/site.scss wwwroot/css/site.css
```

You can see in Figure 17-3 what a typical session looks like for authoring a stylesheet. On the left hand side, there is a console running with node-sass watching for changes. As any changes are made to the SCSS that is being watched or any files that it imports, node-sass runs the pre-processing routines and automatically updates the CSS output file, and VS Code in turn instantly refreshes with the updated file on the right.

FIGURE 17-3 A sample workflow with a console and side-by-side files in VS Code

This workflow is also a great way to help you learn SCSS because you can quickly iterate, watch for compilation errors, and see the results immediately in your editor.

Modifying the Project Build Tasks

For the Alpine team, the priority was to ensure that the build server was aware of the SCSS files and to generate CSS as an artifact of the build. Along with the benefits we've been covering in this chapter, adding the SCSS to the build pipeline allowed the Alpine team to generate one style sheet that would be incorporated into a build. The build that was released to the pre-production environment for verification is the same style sheet that ends up in production.

To include the SCSS file in a pre-existing gulp task, the only required step is to expand the globbing definition for SASS files, adding a wildcard to pick up both .sass and .scss files.

```
sass: "style/**/*.s*ss"
```

If you'd like to refresh your memory, the team previously configured SASS processing, bundling, and minification in Chapter 15, "The Role of JavaScript." And don't worry, we're going to look at how we get the bootstrap.scss file before we close out the chapter.

Using Third Party Frameworks

A third-party CSS framework or library gives you an easy on-ramp to building out the design for your website. Designers are often familiar with one or more frameworks and use them as a point of reference when communicating their design goals to developers. Even when a designer opts to move in a direction that is a complete departure from what a framework has to offer, there can still be value in using one for some of its base constructs.

A couple of examples you might already be familiar with are Bootstrap from getbootstrap.com and Foundation from foundation.zurb.com. These libraries provide facilities for normalizing layouts across browsers and devices, provide flexible grid systems that collapse nicely on different screen sizes, and give us a design language and component set that makes it easy to put together a good looking application. They often have JavaScript libraries that add rich features and enable pre-crafted experiences that are hard to do with CSS alone.

Having said that, there are many reasons to choose a third-party framework, but none of them should be for the stock design they offer lest every website on the Internet start to look the same. Considering what we know about CSS and SCSS, it's not hard to make a design our own.

Extending a CSS Framework

If it turns out that we're okay with what the library has to offer for style after all, where perhaps we have a one-off site to build for a client or an internal application that we need to build, we have two incredibly simple ways to extend a base framework.

First, just edit the stylesheet. Yes, this is okay! Our team was working on a site in the not-so-distant past where we had about four weeks from start to finish. The client approved the use of Bootstrap, but wanted a few of the colors updated and the font changed to better suit their logo. By taking the pre-built CSS and doing a search-and-replace operation, we were able to address the style changes in under an hour and focus on the code.

A second straightforward approach is to use the style language of the framework, but add additional style rules that are based on their implementation. We recently did this for a client that didn't like how Bootstrap's badges only came in one color. By using the same patterns Bootstrap had already defined for buttons, we were able to create a set of rules for badges that fit right into the design.

These light-touch approaches are handy, but also come with certain caveats. If the framework you are starting from has an update or bug fixes along the way, you can't easily get your code updated as well without carefully keeping track of which changes you've made. Working with the native CSS format might also start boxing you in to those same traps we were talking about before, with sprawling files, missed color updates, and hard-to-find display bugs. On top of that, if you're only using a small number of features in the framework, you are forcing your clients to download the entire library for no reason.

Let's look at how we can reduce the size of the style sheets that users must pull down.

Customizing a CSS Framework Footprint

Bootstrap and Foundation both offer an online tool where you can select the elements you want to include in your project and even customize the grid implementation, color selection, fonts, and other aspects of the components as you can see in Figure 17-4. You can then download the source without having to configure tooling and get just the amount of CSS you need.

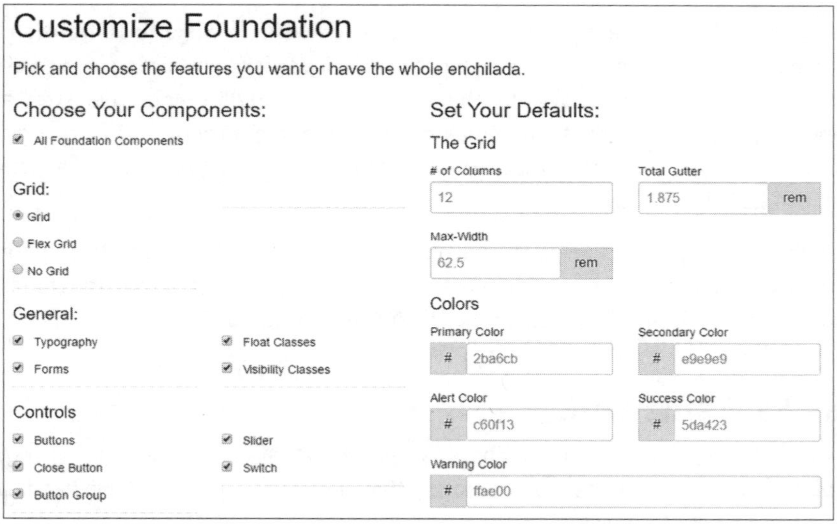

FIGURE 17-4 Customizing Foundation from the Foundation Website

In Bootstrap's case, they even build a JSON file for you that contains the configuration for your CSS output. You can bring that back to the site at a later date to make incremental updates. This is an okay approach, but it doesn't allow you to leverage many of the great features of SCSS and you're unable to build your own components based on the variables, mixins, and functions that a library like Bootstrap can offer.

Leveraging CSS Frameworks for Custom Style Sheets

The limiting factors around customization were what steered the Alpine team in the direction they went. Rather than just downloading a customized CSS, they wanted to use Bootstrap as a base but then enrich the site with their own style rules. The team opted to build a custom version of Bootstrap from the source, which allowed them to pare out any of the parts they didn't need and tailor it to get the style they were after.

This involved a couple of steps. First, they added a bower.json file to the project, which is a known file to Visual Studio 2015. Their file ended up looking like this:

```
{
  "name": "asp.net",
  "private": true,
  "dependencies": {
    "bootstrap": "4.0.0-alpha.4",
    "jquery": "2.2.0",
    "jquery-validation": "1.14.0",
    "jquery-validation-unobtrusive": "3.2.6"
  }
}
```

The IDE recognizes bower.json as a file that declares dependencies and automatically restores those packages for you into a folder called bower_components in your project directory. The next step for the Alpine team was simply to copy the main Bootstrap SCSS build file into their Styles folder, which they renamed bootstrap-alpine.scss. You can find bootstrap.scss in the bower_components\bootstrap\scss directory after Visual Studio has finished restoring your files.

Having moved the SCSS into the Style directory, the Alpine team was essentially done, with the only remaining task being to update the relative file location. Originally the SCSS partials that were used to build Bootstrap were located in the same directory, so the import directives had to be updated from:

```
@import "custom";
```

To include the relative location:

```
@import "../bower_components/bootstrap/scss/custom";
```

The paths are entirely dependent on your project layout. The gulp tasks were previously created and the requisite dependencies wired in, as discussed in Chapter 1 enabling builds of the final CSS on the fly. The CSS also appears in the wwwroot/css folder so that it can be easily incorporated into the layout. This gives you a great way to reduce the amount of CSS that is sent to the browser by removing the un-needed components and to import variables or utilize the pre-built mixins that Bootstrap affords.

Alternatives to CSS Frameworks

Not everyone is in favor of using pre-built CSS frameworks. There are a number of voices with valid concerns not only over websites starting to all look alike, but also over web developers who don't ever fully learn how to write CSS of their own. One of the biggest complaints is where people pull in an entire framework, sometimes inflating the download requirements by hundreds of KB or even into MB territory, all to only use a menu bar, a grid system, or a button.

Because of this, a number of minimalist frameworks have surfaced that exclusively focus on things like typography and layout, but do away with color swatches and components. Again, we are not making any assertions here as to the correct approach for your team. Find the balance that works for your project, remove the pieces you don't need, eliminate the friction, and make it easy for your team to customize and maintain your project's CSS.

Summary

Building your CSS shouldn't involve manually creating every rule you need in your web application. There is no *right* CSS framework to use, nor is there a right tool, workflow, or pre-processor that should be mandated as the right fit for every project, but there certainly exists one that can become the right one for your team. As you become more familiar with the development landscape that is CSS, you build a vase that it is easy to pivot from to other approaches. And with an ever-expanding set of starting points and well-supported frameworks making their way into the hands of .NET developers, many of the complications of developing CSS can be compensated for, allowing you to focus on the more important aspects of your application.

Optimizing the CSS you deliver to the browser is a good way to improve the experience of the end user, but it's not the only way to boost perceived performance. In the next chapter we look at how caching can dramatically reduce the load on your server, while minimizing the time a user ends up waiting for a page to load.

CHAPTER 18

Caching

It was getting close to the deadline for Alpine Ski House to go live. Tim had hauled a bunch of kids in from the local college to act as software testers and everything was going great. Well, everything was going great in that the testers were writing a lot of bug reports, but the bug reports had gone from "Logging in crashes Internet Explorer" to "Color on the buttons is hard to see for red green color blind." Balázs was prioritizing like a human quick sort algorithm. The team was firing on all cylinders, which is why it was weird to see Tim show up in their stand up.

After everybody had reported their status and blockers, Balázs said "You may have noticed Tim is here. It is unusual, but he wanted to bring an issue right to us. What so you have for us Tim?"

Tim stepped forward. "Thanks so much for letting me talk in the stand up, I know it isn't usually permitted for outsiders to talk. Thing is we've been doing really well handling the load our testers are throwing at the site, but the management team has been kicking around the idea of putting on a huge promotion in a couple of weeks. We're going to sell tickets at prices that are so low people will fall out of their chairs. My concern is that the site is going to topple over when we do our marketing push. What can we do to inoculate ourselves against that?"

Chester spoke up first. "We can step up the number of load tests we do. Maybe spend some time tuning the parameters, ramping up the load. It won't save us, but at least we'll know if there is going to be a problem."

"I think there are some query optimizations we could do, since a couple of the queries are pretty heavy on the database server. You can never have too many indexes!" suggested Adrian.

"What about adding in some caching?" asked Candice "I seem to remember reading something about how you can add output caching to ASP.NET MVC."

"How would that help?" asked Tim. "Wouldn't people still be hitting the site?"

"Not necessarily" answered Candice, "and even if they did, the load on the database and web servers would be alleviated by having a layer of caching in there."

"Okay," replied Tim "Let's get some load tests set up for, say 500 simultaneous users, clean up some queries, and add this cache thing."

Reducing the load on web servers to ensure that they can serve pages quickly is never a bad thing. There are a number of techniques to either shift load off the web servers or reduce the number of times a server needs to perform an action. All of these fall under the general heading of caching.

When you think of a computer's storage components, you typically think of the hard drive, memory, USB drives, and 5 ¼ inch floppy drives. Well perhaps not so much the last one, but there are actually quite a few different storage locations that we don't normally think about.

The fastest place to store data on a computer is in the registers on the CPU. On an X86-64 chip, there are 16 64bit registers and a whole collection of other registers that have been added as part of various processor extensions, like SIMD and x87. Beyond the registers, there is L1, L2, and L3 cache. As we move from registers through the three levels of cache, we get more storage but the storage is slower. Main memory is the next largest and is still quite fast, finally hard drive is for large slow storage. You can see the approximate times to access various storage locations in table 18-1.

TABLE 18-1 Timings for accessing various storage locations

Location	Time to Access
L1 Cache	0.5 ns
L2 Cache	7ns
Main memory	100ns
Solid State Hard Drive	150µs

> **Note** If you're interested in learning more about modern processor architecture, Intel published some very interesting documents, including the Intel 64 and IA-32 Architectures Software Developer's Manual at *http://www.intel.com/content/dam/www/public/us/en/documents/manuals/64-ia-32-architectures-software-developer-manual-325462.pdf*. It is really quite an interesting read, if a bit long at 4,670 pages. Be glad that you work at a level of abstraction that doesn't require you to know all of that!

The reason modern processors have all of these cache levels is to speed up access to information. The idea is that if we have accessed a piece of information once, we are likely to want to access that same piece of information again soon. When we do ask for a piece of data a second time, the information might already reside in a cache and we don't need to incur the hit to go all the way out to main memory, or worse, disk.

We use cache on a web server for exactly the same purpose. Often, data on a site updates relatively infrequently. The landing page on a website is a prime example. Landing pages are typically the most visited pages on a website, but they also tend to contain mostly static data. For example, the home page of a site like *http://www.microsoft.com* is the same for one user as it is for another. Updates might happen only a handful of times in a day as new stories surface or as content is moved into focus. Instead of incurring the cost of running the code in a controller, fetching data from a database, and then rendering content in a view, perhaps we could save the output of the page or use parts of the page that are already rendered.

Cache Control Headers

The HTTP protocol is built with caching in mind. There are a number of verbs defined in the specification that you are certain to be familiar with if you've done any work with well build RESTful APIs. The GET verb, which is used whenever you enter a URL in your browser and hit Enter, is meant to simply retrieve a resource. It should not change any data or state on the server. GET requests are typically safe for proxy servers between the client and the server to cache. Verbs like POST and PATCH alter the state on the server, and therefore, of course, are not safe to cache because they must make it back to the server to update the data (see Figure 18-1).

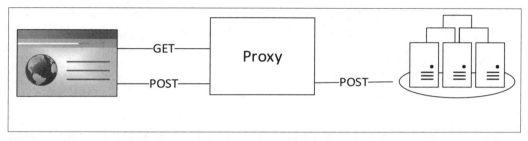

FIGURE 18-1 A proxy server intercepting get requests and passing post requests through to the servers

Sometimes you don't want proxy servers or clients to cache GET requests. Perhaps the data changes rapidly, or the page is part of a list-edit-list loop and users want to see their data updated right away. At other times, we're happy to let the proxy server or client cache our pages for a period of time. To control how proxy servers and clients cache information, you can use cache control headers.

Output Caching

In previous versions of ASP.NET MVC, it was possible to add output cache directives to actions that instructed the framework to save the output and serve it up in the future instead of running the action. The code looked like this:

```
[OutputCache(5)]
public ActionResult Index()
{
    //some expensive operation
}
```

Unfortunately, this flavor of caching is not yet available in ASP.NET Core MVC at the time of writing, but it is on the list of features announced for version 1.1 of the framework. It will be implemented as middleware.

There are some useful attributes that can be added to a controller action to assist in adding cache control headers to responses. Unlike the output cache mentioned above the caching here is not done on the server but on client machines or intermediate proxy server. For instance, if you want to ensure that a page is not cached, you can specify:

```
[ResponseCache(Location = ResponseCacheLocation.None, NoStore = true)]
public IActionResult Index()
{
    //some operation we don't want cached
}
```

This sets `Cache-Control` to `no-store;no-cache`, which actually demands that the proxy not store any content. Simply specifying `no-cache` is, weirdly, not enough because it merely instructs the proxy to revalidate with the HTTP server before serving up content. Adding `no-store` ensures that the proxy actually passes requests back upstream to the HTTP server.

If you actually want to store the content on a proxy server, you need to specify different headers. You can control two aspects of the caching, including how long it is cached and whether the cache content should be individual to a user or generally available. Duration can be specified like so:

```
[ResponseCache(Duration = 60)]
public IActionResult Index()
{
    //some operation we want cached for 60 seconds
}
```

Duration is specified in seconds and unfortunately an *int* is used for this rather than a `TimeStamp`, `which would be clearer.` Even the ASP.NET team can be guilty of an obsession with primitives. The response cache attribute sets a field in the `cache-control` header called max-age. The location can be specified as either Any or `Client` and map to `public` and `private` in the HTTP header. A public setting means that proxy servers on the way to the client machine can cache the content and a private setting means that only the browser on the client machine should save the content. Specify Any in situations where the content is shared, such as a home page, and specify private where the page is specific to a user, like a profile page. Public pages can be served to other users who share the proxy server. It should be noted however that setting the value to `private` doesn't actually add any security because it just requests that public proxy servers don't save the content.

```
[ResponseCache(Duration = 60, Location = ResponseCacheLocation.Client)]
public IActionResult Index()
{
    //some operation we want cached for 60 seconds and is specific to a single user
}
```

It can be somewhat annoying to specify cache control headers on every action. If there is a need to change from 60 seconds to 90 seconds, you don't want to have to change every action that you've set the response cache attribute on. You can alleviate this by cache profiles. When configuring services in the Startup.cs, profiles can be added like so:

```
public void ConfigureServices(IServiceCollection services)
{
    services.AddMvc(options =>
    {
        options.CacheProfiles.Add("Never",
            new CacheProfile()
```

```
        {
            Location = ResponseCacheLocation.None,
            NoStore = true
        });
    });
    options.CacheProfiles.Add("Normal",
        new CacheProfile()
        {
            Duration=90;
            Location = ResponseCacheLocation.Client;
        });

}
```

These profiles can then be applied like so:

```
[ResponseCache(CacheProfileName = "Normal")]
public IActionResult Index()
{
    //some operation we want cached using the normal settings
}
```

Cache control headers are very useful, but they do rely on clients to cache information and we cannot guarantee that they actually do. The headers are also quite coarse because they apply to an entire resource and not just portions of a page. If we want to cache just portions of a page, the headers are not as useful. We need a different approach.

Using the Data-Cache

Expensive operations on the server can be saved off to a cache so that we don't need to run the operation again. An example of this might be a database query to retrieve a collection of records. If the query results don't change all that frequently, they can be cached for several seconds, maybe even several minutes. It is important to consider the impact of stale data on the user however. Data, such as a list of hotels in Vancouver, is unlikely to frequently change and can be cached for a comparatively long time, but a stock quote can change by the second and, as such, should not be cached.

Caching in ASP.NET Core comes in two flavors: in memory and distributed. The in memory cache saves data to memory on the machine, while the distributed cache places data in some sort of data store external to the HTTP server. Let's look at the in-memory version first.

In Memory Cache

To start, we need to pull the in memory caching into our project by adding the nuget package in project.json:

```
"dependencies": {
    ...
    Microsoft.Extensions.Caching.Memory": "1.0.0"
}
```

This service then needs to be added to the service registration in the Startup.cs

```
public void ConfigureServices(IServiceCollection services)
{
    …
    services.AddMemoryCache();
    …
}
```

This adds a service satisfying IMemoryCache to the container. It can be resolved anywhere you can use the DI container, which is most anywhere, like here on the SkiCardController:

```
public SkiCardController(SkiCardContext skiCardContext,
                         UserManager<ApplicationUser> userManager,
                         IAuthorizationService authorizationService,
                         IBlobFileUploadService uploadservice,
                         IMemoryCache memoryCache,
                         ILogger<SkiCardController> logger)
{
    _memoryCache = memoryCache;
```

The usual pattern for using the in memory cache, or any cache, is to check the contents of the cache, use the value if it is there, or if the value is missing, run the operation and populate the cache. IMemoryCache provides TryGetValue, CreateEntry, and Remove operations for working with data. There are also some extension methods that make the interface a bit more pleasant to work with. We can use a memory cache to save a value for a minute time like so:

```
SkiCard skiCard = null;
if(!_memoryCache.TryGetValue($"skicard:{viewModel.Id}", out skiCard))
{
    skiCard = await _skiCardContext.SkiCards
            .SingleOrDefaultAsync(s => s.Id == viewModel.Id);
    _memoryCache.Set($"skicard:{viewModel.Id}", skiCard,
                    new MemoryCacheEntryOptions().SetAbsoluteExpiration(TimeSpan.
FromMinutes(1)));
}
```

> **Tip** It is important to come up with a good scheme for cache keys so you don't end up clobbering keys with unexpected values. One suggestion is to use the name of the object and then an identifier examples might be *skiCard:{id}* or *user:{id}*.

This retrieves the skiCard object either from the cache or from the underlying database. In cases where the value is in cache, there is no need to go out to the database. The cache entry expires in one minute from when it was entered into the cache.

Distributed Cache

If you only have a single web server, caching data in memory is quick and efficient. As soon as you move to multiple web servers however, you need a more central location for your data. It would be nice if cached data on server A could be retrieved on server B. To do this, we need to make use of a distributed cache. The in memory and distributed caches implement different interfaces in ASP.NET Core even though they do very similar things. There are legitimate scenarios where you might want to choose where data is cached and mix and match in memory and distributed cache, so having different interfaces is useful.

Microsoft provides two implementations of the distributed cache: one backed by SQL Server and the other by Redis. Choosing which one is best for your project comes down largely to what your team is comfortable with. The Redis implementation is likely more performant and easier to set up. Cache storage is a perfect application of Redis because Redis is, ostensibly, a key value store. Many organizations, however, aren't comfortable yet in a world of polyglot persistence and would rather use something that they have some familiarity with, in this case, SQL Server. For at least a decade, SQL Server was the answer to every question about storage on the .NET stack. This is a view that's changing now and we are coming to the realization that data storage requirements are not homogenous, so the storage technology shouldn't be either.

No matter what persistence you choose, the distributed cache provides a unified interface so changing persistence stores mid-stream isn't difficult. As with all things in ASP.NET Core, the implementation is open and pluggable so you can create your own persistence. If, for instance, your company is very big on Apache Casandra, you could implement a cache on top of it quite easily.

Again, start by including the appropriate cache implementation in the project.json. Either the Redis or SQL Server implementation can be included:

```
"Microsoft.Extensions.Caching.Redis": "1.0.0",
"Microsoft.Extensions.Caching.SqlServer": "1.0.0"
```

Next, you need to set up and register the implementation in the container. For Redis the configuration looks like:

```
services.AddDistributedRedisCache(options =>
{
    options.Configuration = Configuration.GetValue("redis.host");
    options.InstanceName = Configuration.GetValue("redis.instance");
});
```

For SQL server, the configuration looks like:

```
services.AddDistributedSqlServerCache(options =>
{
    options.ConnectionString = Configuration.GetConnectionString("cache");
    options.SchemaName = Configuration.GetValue("cache.schemaName");
    options.TableName = Configuration.GetValue("cache.tableName");
});
```

In both cases, we pull values from the configuration file to set up connection information.

> **Note** Redis is nice because it is a schemaless database, so it is pretty easy to add whatever information you want to it. SQL Server is more ridged in its schema, so you need to build the schema ahead of time. You can do this by installing the `Microsoft.Extensions.Caching.SqlConfig.Tools` and by including it in your project.json's tool section.

```
"tools": {
    "Microsoft.Extensions.Caching.SqlConfig.Tools": "1.0.0-*",
 }
```

This allows you to run `dotnet sql-cache create` which creates the cache tables for you.

With the distributed cache configured, you now have access in the DI container to `IDistributed-Cache`, which is quite similar to the `IMemoryCache`. It can be used like so:

```
var cachedSkiCard = await _distributedCache.GetAsync($"skicard:{viewModel.Id}");
if(cachedSkiCard != null)
{
    skiCard = Newtonsoft.Json.JsonConvert.DeserializeObject<SkiCard>(cachedSkiCard);
}
else
{
    skiCard = await _skiCardContext.SkiCards
            .SingleOrDefaultAsync(s => s.Id == viewModel.Id);
    await _distributedCache.SetStringAsync($"skicard:{viewModel.Id}", Newtonsoft.Json.
JsonConvert.SerializeObject(skiCard), new DistributedCacheEntryOptions()
                                      .SetAbsoluteExpiration(TimeSpan.FromMinutes(1)));
}
```

There are a couple of things to take note of in this code. The first is that the cache methods are asynchronous so must be awaited using the `await` keyword. There are synchronous versions too, but you're generally better off using the async versions from a code performance perspective. The next is that the distributed cache only takes in byte arrays and strings, so complex objects, like a ski card, must be serialized. In this case we use the Newtonsoft.Json library to do serialization and deserialization, but you can take your pick of other formats.

How Much Cache is Too Much?

On the surface, caching a lot of data seems like a great idea, but there are projects that go too far in caching data. Some argue that the information in drop-down boxes is slow to change, so why not cache it on the client so that there is no need to go back to the server to fetch it? How about looking up a single value in the database? Well that doesn't change frequently, so cache it. It is important however, to recognize that knowing when to invalidate cache data is quite tricky. If the data in a drop-down actually does change, by keeping it on every client we've created a distributed cache invalidation problem.

Caching needs to balance ease of maintenance with the impact of stale data on users. There are also some cases where going to the database is as performant as caching, especially in distributed cache scenarios. Before making a decision to dedicate significant resources to caching, it behooves you to run some benchmarks to see if caching really helps. Take a data driven approach to adding cache.

Summary

ASP.NET MVC provides for a number of methods to cache data, using both proxy servers and client browser caches, and on the server proper. The in memory cache is the simplest implementation of cache available and is suited for single server deploys or for data that doesn't need to be distributed between servers. The distributed cache leverages external storage tools, such as Redis and SQL Server, to hold values. It allows for one server to insert into the cache and another to retrieve it. Caching usually improves performance and takes load off difficult to scale resources, such as relational databases, however it is important to benchmark the cache to ensure it actually serves as a help and not a hindrance.

In the next chapter we'll take a look at reusable components and how they can be leveraged to make writing a site faster and more consistent.

#### PART 4

Sprint Retro: Home Stretch

Danielle couldn't even blink. She had just finished a really weird episode of the X-Files and had been on the edge of her seat all day. Season 4 episode 2. Every time she thought about it she exhaled and shook her head. If she was going to continue to sleep with the lights on, then she should get some of those energy efficient LEDs. Besides, you can get really bright ones that would light up her whole room so nothing can sneak up on her. She was just paying for the express shipping on her phone when Balázs came in.

He had with him a big box. It was a box of shirts. "I bought shirts for the team!" he said excitedly. He pulled one of the white shirts out of the box. On the front was the very familiar Alpine Ski House logo. Danielle was a little disappointed; she would have liked something related to the project. Balázs flipped the shirts around to reveal the back. There was a large caricature of a bunch of parsley giving the thumbs up. Above it was written "Project Parsley" and under the caricature was written "I ate the parsley."

"I know a thing or two about good looking clothing," said Chester "and those shirts are on fleek."

Danielle wasn't sure what fleek was or whether being on it was good, but she loved the shirts. The team seem to agree, there was a lot of happy chattering as Balázs passed the shirts around for everybody.

"Okay, okay" Balázs interrupted, "let's get to this retrospective. You know the drill by now, find your pens and let's see how things are going this week."

Start	Stop	Continue
Reorganizing the application	Having so many bugs reported	Making use of Azure for hosting
Putting more automated tests in place	Adding so much code to controllers, some of them are 300 lines long	Using dependency injection
Reusing some of the code we have in multiple places		Doing awesome stuff with JavaScript
		Wearing cool shirts

"I don't like that testing is still on the start column. Did we not get to that this sprint?" asked Balázs.

"Not quite" said Mark "We had a lunch and learn, and I think a lot of the team is on board now, but we haven't actually pulled the trigger on it yet."

Danielle had been pretty impressed by the test driven development approach. She was sure it would yield better code but there was only one week left before they were shipping. No way was she going to change things up this late in the game. Mark had explained that there were a number of camps around TDD and Danielle was pretty sure that she was closer to a middle of the spectrum point of view, but she certainly wasn't a "zealot" as Mark had described certain people.

"I understand, " said Balázs, "This late in the project we can only take on so much. Folks I'm super proud of you. The major pieces of functionality are all done. We have pages loading. They look good and I think we even have the credit card integration figured out. I know this is a long slog, but we have one week left to really knock the socks off management. We can do it! This next sprint is about filling in the gaps and listening to the testers. "

Tim chimed in, "I was looking at some numbers and yesterday we had 48 deploys to our test environment. I couldn't believe it but that's amazing. The testers are telling me that the time from bugs being found to them being solved is usually just a couple of hours. You should all wear your shirts with pride."

Danielle felt pretty happy about the team's progress, it was almost enough to wipe out that episode... no, she shook her head she was going to get through this.

"Okay, enough patting ourselves on the back," said Balázs "We aren't done yet. There is still work to be done. I see a complaint about the length of some of our controllers—who wrote that?"

"That's me" said Mark, "some of these fellas are over 300 lines long. That isn't maintainable, and we keep running into merge conflicts when more than one person is working on the file at a time. I'd like to see them split up a little."

"I don't like that" piped in Danielle, "I mean, I hate the length as much as the next person, but we're really late in the game to be changing things like URLs. I don't want to move the actions to different controllers."

"I don't think we have to" replied Mark, "There have to be some tools to move code out of the controller without actually changing any of the routes. Perhaps we can update the routing table or something."

"Yeah, or something," agreed Danielle.

"Alright," said Balázs, "I don't want to keep this room of big brains cooped up any longer, get out there and fix anything that's wrong. We're in the home stretch now."

## CHAPTER 19

Reusable Components

The code base was starting to grow when Danielle overheard Mark typing on his mechanical keyboard in the next cubicle. It was one of those really noisy keyboards, but Danielle didn't mind, she worked with headphones on and enjoyed a day full of Enya. This tapping seemed louder than normal however, so she popped her head over the cubicle's wall.

"What's happening, Mark?"

"Oh, hi Danielle. It's this keyboard. The Ctrl, C, and V keys don't work like they used to. You need to really hammer on them to get them to work."

"I thought those mechanical switches were rated to 50 or 60 million keystrokes, you can't have used them all up," joked Danielle.

Mark didn't look amused. "They are rated for that, but I'm just copying and pasting a lot of code between places on the site. It's okay for the back end stuff, I can use classes and hierarchies and all that, but on the front end I have to do Ctrl+C, Ctrl+V."

"You mean," asked Danielle "you can't use inheritance on a Razor view?"

"Not really. I mean how would that look? You would override a section of the page? Would we have polymorphic views? It feels odd."

"I can see how that would be confusing, but inheritance isn't the only form of code reuse. Composition is probably a more applicable pattern for front end code. Here, let me show you how you can save yourself a bunch of copying and pasting."

"That would be great, Danielle. I don't think Tim is going to spring for another keyboard for me."

We've all heard of the Don't Repeat Yourself (DRY) acronym. Adhering to this idea is a constant battle in software development because avoiding duplicating code and application logic can be a challenge. Code duplication comes with an increase in maintenance efforts because changes need to be applied in multiple locations, and even worse, you run the risk of introducing bugs if changes are not applied in all instances of the duplicated code. Unfortunately, the quest to reduce duplication sometimes leads to an equally damaging increase in complexity. There is no benefit to achieving 100 percent code reuse if the resulting implementation is too complicated for any developer to understand.

Fortunately, ASP.NET Core MVC includes some helpful features for encapsulating UI components in a way that, when implemented correctly, is easy to understand and easy to reuse. Let's take a closer look at Tag Helpers, View Components, and Partial Views.

Tag Helpers

Tag helpers, features of the Razor view engine, are a great mechanism for encapsulating small bits of view logic and ensuring consistent generation of HTML. In Chapter 11, "Razor Views," you saw how to use tag helpers to describe forms in a very clear and concise manor. Before we look at some of the other built-in tag helpers and how we can create our own, let's review the makeup of a tag helper.

Anatomy of a Tag Helper

The built-in tag helpers are useful, but things get really interesting when you start building your own tag helpers. Before you can create your own tag helpers, it is important to understand the different pieces that make up a tag helper. Let's take a look at the input tag helper in Figure 19-1 as an example.

FIGURE 19-1 Example usage of the input tag helper

A tag helper targets a particular HTML element called the target element. In the case of the input tag helper, the target element is the input element. The input tag helper, however, is not executed against every input element in the application. It only applies to the input elements that also have the `asp-for` attribute. The `asp-for` attribute is an example of a tag helper attribute. Tag helper attributes are used to provide parameters to a particular tag helper. It is the combination of a target element and the existence of a tag helper attribute that causes Razor to treat an element as a tag helper. Some tag helpers target existing HTML elements, while others target custom elements. The cache tag helper is an example of a custom element.

Tag helper attributes are defined to expect a specific .NET type, such as a `string`, an `int`, or a `TimeSpan`. The `asp-for` attribute is a special attribute of type `ModelExpression`, which tells Razor that the attribute expects an expression mapping to the current model.

A tag helper can also contain any other valid HTML attributes that are applied to the output HTML. Some tag helpers, such as the cache tag helper, also contain child contents. Depending on the tag helper, the child contents might be modified in some way or wrapped by HTML generated by the tag helper.

Scripts, Links, and Environment Tag Helpers

The Environment tag helper provides an easy way to render different sections of HTML depending on the current environment. For example, you might choose to use minified CSS files in Staging and Production environments, but use non-minified versions in Development. The current environment is read from the ASPNET_ENVIRONMENT environment variable, and if the environment variable is not set, ASP.NET assumes it is Production.

```
<environment names="Development">
    <link rel="stylesheet" href="~/css/site1.css" />
    <link rel="stylesheet" href="~/css/site2.css" />
</environment>
<environment names="Staging,Production">
    <link rel="stylesheet" href="~/css/site.min.css"/>
</environment>
```

Only the contents of the environment tag helper are sent to the client, while the environment tag itself is not included in the HTML output. The environment tag helper is most often used with the link and script tag helpers. The link and script tag helpers provide options for globbing, referencing assets from CDNs, and cache busting.

Glob Patterns

Both the link and script tag helpers provide an option to reference files using a wildcard pattern. For example, if you want to reference all of the .js files in the scripts folder, use the ~/scripts/**/*.js pattern by using the script tag's asp-src-include attribute.

```
<script asp-src-include="~/scripts/**/*.js" ></script>
```

The script tag helper renders an individual script tag for each file that matches the specified pattern. You can also use the optional asp-src-exclude attribute to exclude files. The link tag helper works in exactly the same way with the asp-href-include and asp-href-exclude attributes, providing the ability to specify glob patterns.

Cache Busting

Cache busting is the process of appending some form of file version hash to the filename of resources like JavaScript and CSS files. The performance advantage of doing this is so you can tell the browser to cache these files indefinitely without worrying about the client not getting the latest version when the file changes. Because the name of the resource changes when the file contents change, the updated files are always downloaded. To enable cache busting, just set the asp-append-version="true" on the link or script tag helpers.

```
<link rel="stylesheet" href="~/css/site.min.css" asp-append-version="true"/>
```

At runtime, the tag helper generates a version hash and appends it as a query parameter to the URL for the file being referenced.

```
<link rel="stylesheet" href="/css/site.min.css?v=UdxKHVNJ42vb1EsG9O9uURADfEE3j1E3DgwL6NiDFOe" />
```

Cache busting can also be used with image asset by adding the `asp-append-version="true"` attribute to img tags.

CDNs and Fallbacks

It is a common optimization method to reference popular frameworks from hosted Content Delivery Networks (CDNs) to reduce network loads on your server and potentially improve performance for the user. For popular frameworks like jQuery and Bootstrap, there is a good chance that the client's browser already has a cached version of these files.

Referencing files from a CDN can be a bit of a pain because you also need to provide a fallback to a version of the file hosted on your servers. A fallback is necessary because you do not want your application to go down just because the CDN is not currently reachable. While CDNs are generally very reliable, they can suffer from outages just like any other hosted service and some eager network admins have also been known to block access to CDNs using enterprise firewalls.

While configuring a fallback is necessary, it is also a pain. Here is an example of ensuring a proper fallback for the popular Bootstrap JavaScript and CSS assets:

```
<link rel="stylesheet" href="//ajax.aspnetcdn.com/ajax/bootstrap/3.0.0/css/bootstrap.min.css" />
<meta name="x-stylesheet-fallback-test" class="hidden" />
<script>!function(a,b,c){var d,e=document,f=e.getElementsByTagName("SCRIPT"),g=f[f.length-1].
previousElementSibling,h=e.defaultView&amp;&amp;e.defaultView.getComputedStyle?e.defaultView.
getComputedStyle(g):g.currentStyle;if(h&amp;&amp;h[a]!==b)for(d=0;d<c.length;d++)e.write('<link
rel="stylesheet" href="'+c[d]+'"/>')}("visibility","hidden",["\/lib\/bootstrap\/css\/bootstrap.
min.css"]);</script>

<script src="//ajax.aspnetcdn.com/ajax/bootstrap/3.0.0/bootstrap.min.js">
</script>
<script>(typeof($.fn.modal) === 'undefined'||document.write("<script src=\"\/lib\/bootstrap\/
js\/bootstrap.min.js\"><\/script>"));</script>
```

Luckily, the script and link tag helpers make it much easier to specify a fallback test and file location.

```
<link rel="stylesheet" href="//ajax.aspnetcdn.com/ajax/bootstrap/3.0.0/css/bootstrap.min.css"
      asp-fallback-href="~/lib/bootstrap/css/bootstrap.min.css"
      asp-fallback-test-class="hidden"
      asp-fallback-test-property="visibility"
      asp-fallback-test-value="hidden" />

<script src="//ajax.aspnetcdn.com/ajax/bootstrap/3.0.0/bootstrap.min.js"
        asp-fallback-src="~/lib/bootstrap/js/bootstrap.min.js"
        asp-fallback-test="window.jQuery">
</script>
```

Cache Tag Helper

You can use the cache tag helper to cache any HTML fragment to an in-memory store. It provides a number of options for cache expiry and for varying cache keys based on the request context.

For example, the following instance of the cache tag helper caches the contents for a period of 5 minutes. A different instance is cached for each unique user in the system.

```
<cache expires-sliding="@TimeSpan.FromMinutes(5)" vary-by-user="true">
    <!--Any HTML or Razor markup-->
    *last updated  @DateTime.Now.ToLongTimeString()
</cache>
```

In more advanced scenarios, you can use the distributed cache tag helper to store the HTML fragments in a distributed cache. For an in-depth tour of the cache and distributed cache tag helpers, visit *http://bit.ly/CacheTagHelper* and *http://bit.ly/distributedcachetaghelper*.

Creating Tag Helpers

As you start adding more and more features to your application, patterns might start to emerge in the cshtml files. Small repeating sections of Razor / HTML are good candidates for a custom tag helper.

A tag helper is simply a class that inherits from the base TagHelper class and implements either the Process or ProcessAsync method.

```
public virtual void Process(TagHelperContext context, TagHelperOutput output)
public virtual Task ProcessAsync(TagHelperContext context, TagHelperOutput output)
```

Within the Process method, the tag helper is able to inspect the current TagHelperContext and generate some HTML or change the TagHelperOutput in some way.

A very simple example is the button displayed on the login page in Alpine Ski House to log in via external providers. While it is not necessarily something that is used extensively within the application, it does show how we can clean up some rather complex looking Razor code. Tag helpers are great for removing duplicate code, but they are also great for abstracting particularly complex HTML or Razor code. The button described in the following code is bound to a particular external login provider.

```
<button type="submit" class="btn btn-default" name="provider" value="@provider.
AuthenticationScheme" title="Log in using your @provider.DisplayName account">@provider.
AuthenticationScheme</button>
```

Let's extract this to a tag helper class named LoginProviderButtonTagHelper. The target element is the button and it has a single tag helper attribute named ski-login-provider. By convention, tag helper attributes should be prefixed when the tag helper is targeting an existing HTML element. This helps to distinguish the tag helper attributes from regular HTML attributes. The built-in ASP.NET Core tag helpers use the prefix asp-. For Alpine Ski House we use ski-.

```
[HtmlTargetElement("button", Attributes = "ski-login-provider")]
public class LoginProviderButtonTagHelper : TagHelper
{
    [HtmlAttributeName("ski-login-provider")]
    public AuthenticationDescription LoginProvider { get; set; }

    public override void Process(TagHelperContext context, TagHelperOutput output)
    {
```

```
        output.Attributes.SetAttribute("type", "submit");
        output.Attributes.SetAttribute("name", "provider");
        output.Attributes.SetAttribute("value", LoginProvider.AuthenticationScheme);
        output.Attributes.SetAttribute("title", $"Log in using your {LoginProvider.DisplayName}
account");
        output.Attributes.SetAttribute("class", "btn btn-default");
        output.Content.SetContent(LoginProvider.AuthenticationScheme);
    }
}
```

Before you can use this new tag helper, you need to make the tag helpers from this project available in the views. You can do this by using the addTagHelper directive. To apply the addTagHelper directive globally, add it to the Views/_ViewImports.cshtml file.

```
@addTagHelper *, AlpineSkiHouse.Web
```

Now you can simplify the buttons in our login page by using the new tag helper.

```
<button ski-login-provider="provider"></button>
```

Visual Studio provides excellent IntelliSense support for custom tag helpers as shown in Figure 19-2.

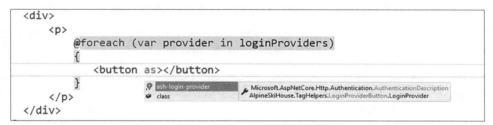

FIGURE 19-2 Visual Studio displaying IntelliSense for a custom tag helper

Handling Existing Attributes and Contents

When creating a tag helper, it is important to consider the context that it is used in. Most tag helpers target existing HTML elements that can have HTML attributes. You should also consider what attributes have been added to the element already. Should those attributes be overwritten or should they be left alone? Another option is to merge the values with your own values. Merging attribute values is most common with the class attribute. In our external login provider example, the tag helper should honor any classes added to the button and only append the "btn btn-default" classes to the value provided by the user. The syntax for merging attributes is a little verbose.

```
string classValue = "btn btn-default";
if (output.Attributes.ContainsName("class"))
{
    classValue = $"{output.Attributes["class"].Value} {classValue}";
}
output.Attributes.SetAttribute("class", classValue);
```

This code is not something you want to write over and over again, so let's extract it to an extension method:

```
public static class TagHelperAttributeListExtensions
{
    public static void MergeClassAttributeValue(this TagHelperAttributeList attributes, string
newClassValue)
    {
        string classValue = newClassValue;
        if (attributes.ContainsName("class"))
        {
            classValue = $"{attributes["class"].Value} {classValue}";
        }
        attributes.SetAttribute("class", classValue);
    }
}
```

Using the `MergeClassAttributeValue` extension method greatly simplifies the code in our tag helper.

```
output.Attributes.MergeClassAttributeValue("btn btn-default");
```

In addition to attributes, you also need to consider the existing HTML content of a tag helper. By default, Razor processes the tag helper contents and the resulting HTML is included in the tag helper output. The tag helper output, however, provides the ability to modify or overwrite the child contents via the Content property. In addition to Content, the tag helper output also provides properties for PreElement, PreContent, PostContent, and PostElement. The one piece of HTML that can't be modified directly from within a tag helper is the parent content.

```
public async override Task ProcessAsync(TagHelperContext context, TagHelperOutput output)
{
    output.PreElement.SetHtmlContent("<div>Pre-Element</div>");
    output.PreContent.SetHtmlContent("<div>Pre-Content</div>");
    output.Content = await output.GetChildContentAsync();
    output.Content.Append("Adding some text after the existing content");
    output.PostContent.SetHtmlContent("<div>Post-Content</div>");
    output.PostElement.SetHtmlContent("<div>Post-Element</div>");
}
```

It is only necessary to call to GetChildContentAsync() if the tag helper is making changes to the Content. If no changes are made to the child content, the Content is automatically set by the framework.

> **Note** Tag helpers are a powerful extension point in the Razor view engine, providing ASP. NET developers with a new way to generate HTML. Take a look at *https://github.com/dpaquette/taghelpersamples* for a variety of real-world examples, including some more complex scenarios that illustrate communicating between parent and child tag helpers.

View Components

A view component is another construct in MVC that allows you to build reusable widgets. In this case, the widgets consist of Razor markup and some backend logic. View components are made up of two parts: a view component class and a Razor view.

To implement the view component class, inherit from the base `ViewComponent` and implement an `Invoke` or `InvokeAsync` method. This class can be placed anywhere in your project, but a common convention is to place it in a folder named `ViewComponents`.

```
Public class MyWidgetViewComponent : ViewComponent
{
    public IviewComponentResult Invoke()
    {
        return View();
    }
}
```

A view component can contain more than one `Invoke` method, with each method containing a unique set of arguments.

```
public class MyWidgetViewComponent : ViewComponent
{
    public IViewComponentResult Invoke()
    {
        return View();
    }
    public IViewComponentResult Invoke(int id)
    {
        return View();
    }
}
```

View components make heavy use of convention over configuration. Unless otherwise specified, the name of the view component is the name of the class with the `ViewComponent` portion removed. A `ViewComponent` name can be explicitly defined by adding the `ViewComponent` attribute to the class.

```
[ViewComponent(Name = "Widget1")]
public class MyWidgetViewComponent : ViewComponent
{
    public IViewComponentResult Invoke()
    {
        return View();
    }
}
```

Much like a controller action, the `Invoke` method of a view component returns a view. At that point, the view engine looks for a matching cshtml file. If no view name is explicitly specified, the default `Views\Shared\Components\ViewComponentName\Default.cshtml` is used, which in this case is `Views\Shared\Components\MyWidget\Default.cshtml`.

The view portion of a view component can be model bound just like Razor views for a controller action.

```
public class MyWidgetViewComponent : ViewComponent
{
    public IViewComponentResult Invoke()
    {
        WidgetModel model = new WidgetModel
         {
                    Name = "My Widget",
                    NumberOfItems = 2
         }
     return View(model);
    }
}
```

Invoking View Components

View components can be included in any Razor view by calling `Component.Invoke` and by specifying the name of the view component.

```
@await Component.InvokeAsync("MyWidget")
```

The view component engine finds the view component with the matching name and maps the invocation to one of the view component's `Invoke` methods. To match a particular overload of the Invoke method, you need to specify the arguments as an anonymous class.

```
@await Component.InvokeAsync("MyWidget", new {id = 5})
```

> ### What happened to child actions?
>
> In previous versions of MVC, we used Child Actions to build reusable components or widgets that consisted of both Razor markup and some backend logic. The backend logic was implemented as a controller action and was typically marked with a `[ChildActionOnly]` attribute. Child Actions were extremely useful, but it was easy to configure them in a way that would have had unintended consequences with the request pipeline.
>
> Child Actions do not exist in ASP.NET Core MVC. Instead, you should use the new View Component feature to support this use case. Conceptually, view components are a lot like child actions, but they are lighter weight and no longer involve the lifecycles and pipelines related to Controllers.

Contact Customer Service View Component

Now that we have covered the basics of view components, let's take a look at a real-world example. Imagine that we want to provide some integration with the customer service representative's app in the Alpine Ski House project. In Chapter 12, "Configuration and Logging," we created the `ICsrInformationService` that provides information about the customer service call center, including the number to call and how many representatives are currently online. We would like to add a small section to the bottom of the website to provide some of this information to the user. Using a view component to implement this gives us a good place to interact with the ICsrInformationService. It also provides us with some flexibility if we want to experiment with placing the Call Center callout in different locations on the site.

The view component class takes a dependency on the ICsrInformationService and implements a single Invoke method. If the call center is online, our view component gets information from the ICsrInformationService and passes it to the Default view. If the call center is closed, it returns the Closed view. Splitting the view into two pieces ensures this logic is in the view component instead of the view, which makes this view component much easier to test.

```
public class CallCenterStatusViewComponent : ViewComponent
{
    private readonly ICsrInformationService _csrInformationService;

    public CallCenterStatusViewComponent(ICsrInformationService csrInformationService)
    {
        _csrInformationService = csrInformationService;
    }

    public IViewComponentResult Invoke()
    {
        if (_csrInformationService.CallCenterOnline)
        {
            var viewModel = new CallCenterStatusViewModel
            {
                OnlineRepresentatives = _csrInformationService.OnlineRepresentatives,
                PhoneNumber = _csrInformationService.CallCenterPhoneNumber
            };
            return View(viewModel);
        }
        else
        {
            return View("Closed");
        }
    }
}
```

The views are simple Razor files. The Default view is bound to the CallCenterStatusViewModel, while the Closed view is not bound to any model.

Views\Shared\Components\CallCenterStatus\Default.cshtml

```
@using AlpineSkiHouse.Models.CallCenterViewModels
@model CallCenterStatusViewModel

<div class="panel panel-success">
    <div class="panel-heading">Having trouble? We're here to help!</div>
    <div class="panel-body">
        We have @Model.OnlineRepresentatives friendly agents available.
        <br/>
        Give us a call at <i class="glyphicon glyphicon-earphone"></i> <a href="tel:@Model.
PhoneNumber">@Model.PhoneNumber</a>
    </div>
</div>
```

Views\Shared\Components\CallCenterStatus\Closed.cshtml

```
<div>The call center is closed</div>
```

Now you can add this view component to any cshtml file in our application. For example, here we added it just above the footer in _Layout.cshtml.

```
<div class="container body-content">
    @RenderBody()
    <hr />
    @await Component.InvokeAsync("CallCenterStatus")
    <footer>
        <p>&copy; @DateTime.Now.Year.ToString() - AlpineSkiHouse</p>
    </footer>
</div>
```

> **Note** In larger organizations, it might be useful to create view components that can be used in a number of different projects. In this case, the view components can be implemented in a separate class library and loaded by each application startup. This only requires a small amount of configuration at startup. For a full tutorial, see: *http://aspnetmonsters.com/2016/07/2016-07-16-loading-view-components-from-a-class-library-in-asp-net-core/*.

Partial Views

A partial view is simply a Razor view that can be rendered within another Razor view. Unlike a view component, there is no class to implement any logic in or interact with services in. While a view component class passes view model data to the view, it is the parent view's responsibility to pass data to the partial view. Partial views are useful when data has already been loaded and all you need to do is display it. Regardless of whether view model data is involved, you can use partial views to break down larger views into more manageable pieces.

The default ASP.NET Core MVC project template includes a partial view that you can use to render validation scripts. You need these scripts to enable client side validation on any pages containing forms.

Views/Shared/_ValidationScriptsPartial.cshtml

```
<environment names="Development">
    <script src="~/lib/jquery-validation/dist/jquery.validate.js"></script>
    <script src="~/lib/jquery-validation-unobtrusive/jquery.validate.unobtrusive.js"></script>
</environment>
<environment names="Staging,Production">
    <script src="https://ajax.aspnetcdn.com/ajax/jquery.validate/1.14.0/jquery.validate.min.js"
            asp-fallback-src="~/lib/jquery-validation/dist/jquery.validate.min.js"
            asp-fallback-test="window.jQuery && window.jQuery.validator">
    </script>
    <script src="https://ajax.aspnetcdn.com/ajax/jquery.validation.unobtrusive/3.2.6/jquery.
validate.unobtrusive.min.js"
```

```
                asp-fallback-src="~/lib/jquery-validation-unobtrusive/jquery.validate.unobtrusive.
min.js"
                asp-fallback-test="window.jQuery && window.jQuery.validator && window.jQuery.
validator.unobtrusive">
    </script>
</environment>
```

Any view that needs these scripts can include them by calling: `@Html.Partial("@_Validation-ScriptsPartial")`.

Snippet from Account/Register.cshtml

```
...
@section Scripts {
    @Html.Partial("_ValidationScriptsPartial")
}
```

Overloads also exist to allow for passing a view model, which means a partial view can also be model bound just like a regular view. For more details on how to use partial views, check out the official ASP. NET Core documentation, located at *https://docs.asp.net/en/latest/mvc/views/partial.html*.

Summary

By using the user interface building blocks that the ASP.NET Core MVC framework provides to you, it is easy to structure applications into reusable components. You can use tag helpers to augment HTML and define HTML elements or attributes that are specific to your application domain, which results in concise and easy to understand Razor files. View components are excellent tools for defining reusable user interface components that contain complex logic or that interact with other application services. Finally, partial views provide a simple mechanism for defining reusable sections of Razor views. As you will see in the next chapter, Chapter 20, "Testing," both view components and tag helpers are designed with testing in mind.

Testing

Balázs punched the hangup button on the expensive Polycom in the conference room.

"So?" he asked. They had just finished a call with some of the testers and they didn't sound happy. "They're constantly running into bugs preventing them from testing. Why are we delivering such poor quality software?"

Danielle bristled at the idea that their software was bad quality. The problem was that they were moving too quickly to do manual testing. That is what the testers are for, right?

"Look, Balázs" said Danielle, "we are pushing out ten builds a day to the testers. Even if they are blocked, they're sure not blocked for very long. We're fixing things at record pace."

"Then why am I seeing the same bugs reoccurring a week after we've fixed them?" asked Balázs.

There was an awkward silence. Danielle knew that she had been caught. There was no excuse for the bugs creeping back in after they had been fixed.

Mark jumped to the rescue. "We could certainly be doing a better job at testing. We're not doing Test Driven Development TDD, not even close. I know everybody here wants to do a good job, but that sort of testing is slowing us down and we have tight deadlines to make."

"I know," sighed Balázs. "But you have to see that we're wasting a lot of the tester's time on this stuff. Can we at least put some automated tests behind some of the places where we keep having recurring bugs?"

"I think that's a great idea" agreed Danielle "Let's do it!"

Automated testing, that is tests written by developers to test their own code, is pretty much universally regarded as a best practice. Many will argue that tests should be written before the application code, following a TDD methodology. We won't get into that debate here, but we will say that any production level software should have at least some form of automated testing. In this chapter, we cover some approaches to testing the various portions of an ASP.NET Core MVC application.

Unit Testing

The first type of testing we will incorporate into our project is automated unit testing. With unit testing, the goal is to execute small parts of the application in isolation, and ensure they are working as expected. The small parts are the unit portion of unit testing. In a C# context, the units are typically methods or classes. The tests are written in a way that they can be easily and quickly executed to ensure changes to the application's source code, and that they have not unintentionally broken some aspect of the application.

A solid suite of unit tests can provide a higher level of confidence that a change to the application's code will not introduce a regression in the application. Well written unit tests can also serve as a form of documentation for the intended behavior of a component.

XUnit

There are a number of test frameworks available for unit testing C# code. The most popular are: nUnit, MSTest, and xUnit.net. Although they have some different features, the basic concept remains the same. Test methods are annotated using attributes. In those tests, you write code to execute the code being tested, and you make assertions regarding the expected outcome. The assertions will either pass or fail, and the results will be reported by the unit test runner. One difference between xUnit and other unit test frameworks is that xUnit does not have a class level attribute used to mark classes that contain test methods. The xUnit documentation includes a handy comparison of xUnit to other test frameworks (*https://xunit.github.io/docs/comparisons.html*).

Alpine Ski House decided to use xUnit.net, primarily because that's the tool used by the ASP.NET team for unit testing the ASP.NET Core framework, but also because it is a great framework and everybody enjoys using it.

To get started, you need to create a new project. There is no requirement to put C# unit tests in a separate assembly, but this it's generally a good idea. One reason for this is that you don't want to ship the unit test code with your application, because it's solely for unit testing purposes. As an example, we created a new project called `AlpineSkiHouse.Web.Test`, which will contain tests for the code located in the `AlpineSkiHouse.Web` project. In the folder structure, the application projects are located in the `src` folder, while the test projects are located in the `test` folder. Again, there is no requirement to follow this convention but it is a common approach used by many .NET applications.

In addition, the test project needs to reference two packages: `xunit` and `dotnet-test-xunit`. The `testRunner` property also needs to be set to `xunit`, and of course we will need a reference to the project we are testing, in this case `AlpineSkiHouse.Web`.

```
"dependencies": {
    "AlpineSkiHouse.Web": "1.0.0-*",
    "dotnet-test-xunit": "1.0.0-rc2-build10025",
    "xunit": "2.1.0"
},
"testRunner": "xunit"
```

xUnit Basics

In xUnit, a unit test is denoted by an attribute on a method. There are two types of attributes that can be used: Fact and Theory. A fact is something that is always true, whereas a theory is a test that should hold true for a set of inputs. A theory can be used to test a number of scenarios using a single test method.

```
public class SimpleTest
{
    [Fact]
    public void SimpleFact()
    {
        var result = Math.Pow(2, 2);
        Assert.Equal(4, result);
    }

    [Theory]
    [InlineData(2, 4)]
    [InlineData(4, 16)]
    [InlineData(8, 64)]
    public void SimpleTheory(int amount, int expected)
    {
        var result = Math.Pow(amount, 2);
        Assert.Equal(expected, result);
    }

}
```

For more complete documentation, visit the official xunit.net documentation at *https://xunit.github.io.*

Running the Tests

The easiest way to run unit tests is using the dotnet command line tool. From the folder containing the test project, run dotnet test, which will compile the test project and run all of the tests as show in Figure 20-1.

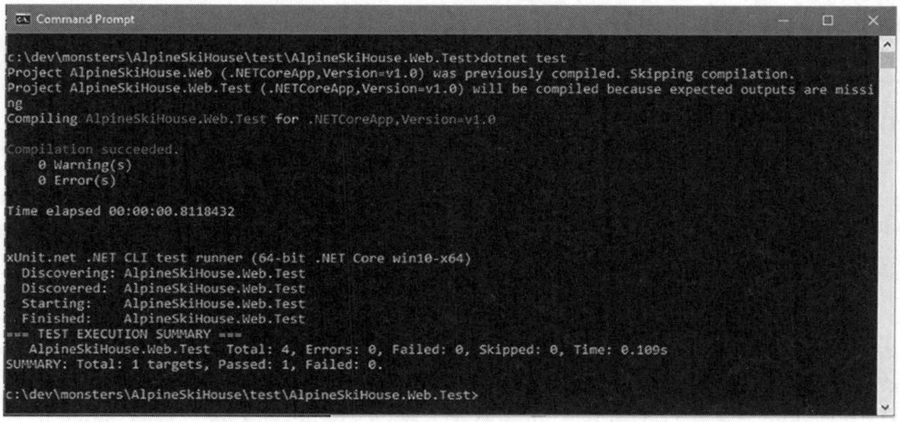

FIGURE 20-1 Running unit tests from the command line using dotnet test

The command line tooling also makes it easy to integrate with the existing build scripts. All you need to do is add a step to run our tests.

Another option is to run unit tests directly from Visual Studio using the built-in Test Explorer. This provides an integrated experience for developers, and provides an option to run tests with the debugger attached.

Open the Test Explorer window in Visual Studio by selecting Test then Windows then Test Explorer from the main menu. The Test Explorer window, shown in Figure 20-2, should display a list of all the tests in your solution. If the tests are not listed, you might need to rebuild the solution while the Test Explorer window is opened.

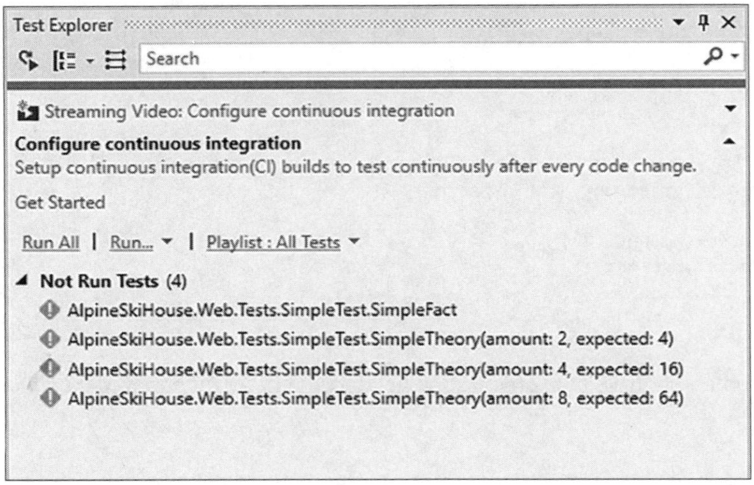

FIGURE 20-2 The Test Explorer in Visual Studio

Click the Run All link to run all of the tests. Tests that pass will be marked with a green checkmark, while tests that fail will be marked with a red x. Clicking on a failed test will display a summary of the failed assertion, including a link to the method that failed and the specific assertion that failed.

Continuous Testing

The test runner explorer has a little known feature to enable continuous testing. There is a toggle button at the top left of the Test Explorer toolbar labeled Run Tests After Build. When this button is toggled on, Visual Studio will automatically rerun tests after a project is built. Using this feature you will get nearly instant feedback if changes you have made happen to break some existing tests.

For those developing in an editor other the Visual Studio the dotnet watch task found at *https://github.com/aspnet/DotNetTools/tree/dev/src/Microsoft.DotNet.Watcher.Tools* might be of interest. The watch task will recompile and run your tests whenever it detects a change to a source file in the project.

East Regional Library
6301 Bridge St
817-392-5550

Borrowed Items 1/4/2020 12:35
XXXXXXXXX7885

Item Title	Due Date
C# programming in easy steps	1/25/2020
ASP.NET core application development : building an application in four sprints (developer reference)	1/25/2020
The C# programming language	1/25/2020
Pro C# 2010 and the .Net 4 platform	1/25/2020

Thank you for using the Self Check
Website: www.fortworthtexas.gov/library
Hours of Operations
Monday: Noon - 8:00 pm
Tuesday - Thursday: 10:00 am - 8:00 pm
Friday and Saturday: 10:00 am - 6:00 pm
Sunday: 12:Noon - 6:00 pm

Organizing Unit Tests

We've talked about the benefits of automated unit tests but it's important to also consider the cost involved in maintaining unit tests. Unit tests are themselves code and need to be treated with the same level of care as any other production code. Without standard naming conventions and coding styles, unit tests can become a nightmare to maintain.

We will try to follow a few rules for naming and organizing our testing. First, the folder structure of the test project should match the folder structure of the assembly being tested. There is more on how to organize project files in Chapter 24, "Organizing the Code."

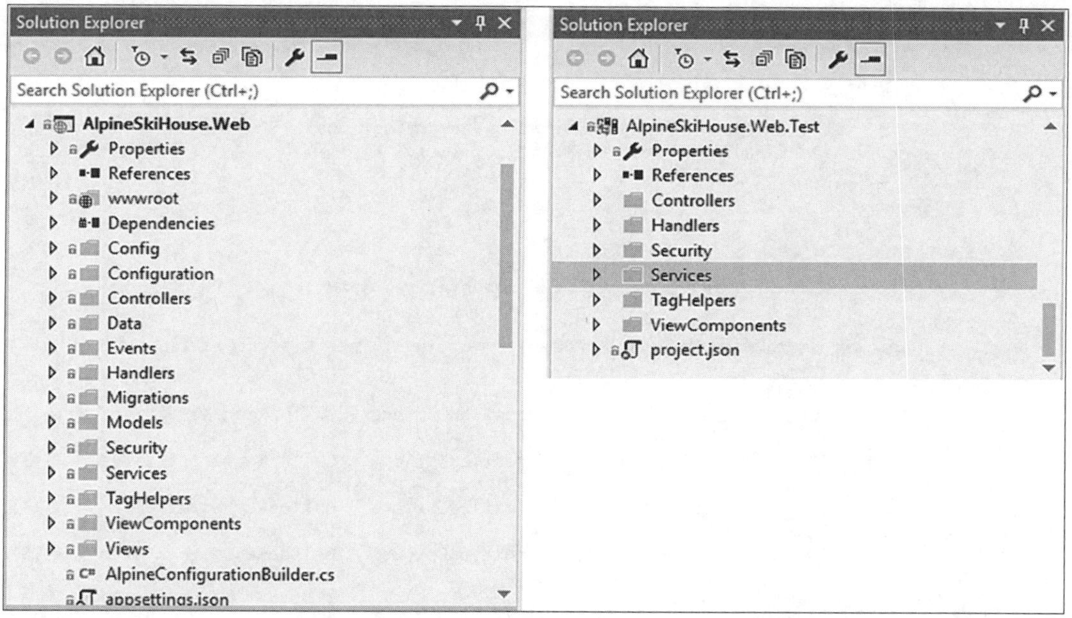

FIGURE 20-3 Comparing the folder structure in the AlpineSkiHouse.Web and AlpineSkiHouse.Web.Test projects

We will also organize all the tests for a particular class within a single file. That is, the tests for CsrInformationService would exist in a file named CsrInformationServiceTests.cs as shown in listing 20-1. Within a test class, tests are organized using nested classes. Each inner class focuses on testing a specific scenario. For example, with the CsrInformationService, we want to test the scenario when there are no representatives online. This scenario is tested in the inner class named GivenThereIsAtLeastOneRepresentativeOnline in Listing 20-1. The CsrInformationService has a dependency on IOptions<CsrInformationOptions>, which is initialized in the constructor for the inner class. Finally, a test method tests the expectations for the current scenario. In this simple scenario, the CallCenterOnline property is expected to be false. The contents of CsrInformationServiceTests.cs can be seen in Listing 20-1.

LISTING 20-1 Unit tests for the CsrInformationService

```
public class CsrInformationServiceTests
{
    public class GivenThereAreNoRepresentativesOnline
    {
        private IOptions<CsrInformationOptions> options;

        public GivenThereAreNoRepresentativesOnline()
        {
            options = Options.Create(new CsrInformationOptions());
            options.Value.OnlineRepresentatives = 0;
        }

        [Fact]
        public void CallCenterOnlineShouldBeFalse()
        {
            var service = new CsrInformationService(options);
            Assert.False(service.CallCenterOnline);
        }
    }


    public class GivenThereIsAtLeastOneRepresentativeOnline
    {
        public static readonly List<object[]> options = new List<object[]>
        {
            new object[]
              {Options.Create(new CsrInformationOptions { OnlineRepresentatives = 1} )},
            new object[]
              {Options.Create(new CsrInformationOptions { OnlineRepresentatives = 2} )},
            new object[]
              {Options.Create(new CsrInformationOptions { OnlineRepresentatives = 3} )},
            new object[]
              {Options.Create(new CsrInformationOptions { OnlineRepresentatives = 1000}
)},
            new object[]
              {Options.Create(new CsrInformationOptions { OnlineRepresentatives = 100000}
)}
        };

        [Theory]
        [MemberData(nameof(options))]
        public void CallCenterOnlineShouldBeTrue(IOptions<CsrInformationOptions> options)
        {
            var service = new CsrInformationService(options);
            Assert.True(service.CallCenterOnline);
        }

        [Theory]
        [MemberData(nameof(options))]
        public void
OnlineRepresentativesShouldMatchOptionsSource(IOptions<CsrInformationOptions> options)
        {
            var service = new CsrInformationService(options);
            Assert.Equal(options.Value.OnlineRepresentatives,
                        service.OnlineRepresentatives);
        }
    }
}
```

Listing 20-1 also tests a second scenario in the `GivenThereIsAtLeastOneRepresentativeOnline` inner class. This scenario tests the `CsrInformationService` when there is at least one representative online. Note the use of the `Theory` and `MemberData` attributes to test with a set of possible inputs mapping to the number of online representatives. The `options` property provides an array of possible values for `CsrInformationOptions`, each with a different number specified for `OnlineRepresentatives`. This scenario includes two tests marked with the `Theory` attribute. The first test checks that the `CallCenterOnline` property returns true while the second test checks that the `OnlineRepresentatives` property is equal to the expected value.

Testing Controllers

Ideally our controllers will contain minimal logic, which means there shouldn't be a lot of testing needed. A controller should really only be responsible for translating between web concepts like HTTP requests and responses and our application concepts. Most of the hard work should be implemented in services, command and event handlers, and other more reusable places in our code. Having said that, there is some value in testing controllers to ensure services are used as expected and that the correct HTTP responses are returned. For example, it is useful to test a controller to ensure that an unauthorized user is not able to access a restricted resource.

Let's take a look at the `SkiCardController` from Chapter 10, "Entity Framework Core." The `SkiCardController` has a dependency on `SkiCardContext`, `UserManager<ApplicationUser>`, and `IAuthorizationService`. The more dependencies there are, the harder the setup will be. In some cases, we will want to use a technique called mocking to pass in a fake version of a dependency and test how the controller interacts with only a portion of that interface. We will use mocking to test the `SkiCardController`'s interaction with `IAuthorizationService`. Some dependencies, like the `SkiCardContext`, might be difficult to mock. In the case of an Entity Framework `DbContext` like the SkiCardContext, it is much easier to create a concrete instance of the context and have it backed by an in memory data store rather than a full-fledged database. The important take away here is that mocking isn't always the answer. Be pragmatic about your testing and do what works best for the situation.

To create a `SkiCardContext` that is backed by an in memory database, you have to pass in different options than those used by the application at runtime. Creating these options is usually handled by the dependency injection framework, but in the unit test project we need to handle this on our own. We created a factory method to avoid a lot of repetitive code, and it can be used for any `DbContext`, as shown here:

```
public static class InMemoryDbContextOptionsFactory
{
    public static DbContextOptions<T> Create<T>() where T : DbContext
    {
        var serviceProvider = new ServiceCollection()
            .AddEntityFrameworkInMemoryDatabase()
            .BuildServiceProvider();

        var builder = new DbContextOptionsBuilder<T>();
        builder.UseInMemoryDatabase()
            .UseInternalServiceProvider(serviceProvider);
```

```
            return builder.Options;
    }
}
```

Let's start by testing a scenario where the `HttpPost Edit` action is called for a `SkiCard` that does not exist in the context. In this case, the action method should return a `NotFoundResult`. The `UserManager` and `IAuthorizationService` are not even used in this scenario, so we can actually get away with passing in null values for this particular test.

```
public class WhenEditingASkiCardThatDoesNotExistInTheContext
{
    [Fact]
    public async Task EditActionShouldReturnNotFound()
    {
        using (SkiCardContext context =
            new SkiCardContext(InMemoryDbContextOptionsFactory.Create<SkiCardContext>()))
        {
            var controller = new SkiCardController(context, null, null);
            var result = await controller.Edit(new EditSkiCardViewModel
            {
                Id = 2,
                CardHolderFirstName = "Dave",
                CardHolderLastName = "Paquette",
                CardHolderBirthDate = DateTime.Now.AddYears(-99),
                CardHolderPhoneNumber = "555-123-1234"
            });
            Assert.IsType<NotFoundResult>(result);
        }
    }
}
```

A slightly more complex scenario is where a malicious user attempts to call the `HttpPost Edit` action method to edit a `SkiCard` that does not belong to them. This scenario is tested in the GivenAHackerTriesToEditSomoneElsesSkiCard class shown in Listing 20-2. It involves two dependencies, and also requires some information to be setup on the `ControllerContext`. Specifically, you have the `User` that is internally pulled from the `HttpContext`. Moving this setup code to the constructor helps keep the test method simple and easy to read. First, create a `SkiCardContext` and add the `SkiCard` that the malicious user will attempt to edit. Next, create a `ControllerContext` with a `DefaultHttpContext` and a new `ClaimsPrincipal`. It is not necessary to set any values on the claims principal because the only thing you want to ensure is that the `ClaimsPrincipal` is properly passed to the `IAuthorizationService`. In the test method, create the controller and setup the expected call to the `IAuthorizationService`. Specifically, expect a call to the `AuthorizeAsync` method with the _badGuyPrincipal and _skiCard passed in, checking for the `EditSkiCardAuthorizationRequirement`. We use Moq, a simple yet powerful mocking library for .NET, to setup and verify the expected interaction between the `SkiCardController` and the `IAuthorizationService`. For more on Moq, visit *https://github.com/Moq/moq4*.

LISTING 20-2 An example of testing the SkiCardController's Edit action method

```
public class GivenAHackerTriesToEditSomeoneElsesSkiCard : IDisposable
{
    SkiCardContext _skiCardContext;
    SkiCard _skiCard;
    ControllerContext _controllerContext;
    ClaimsPrincipal _badGuyPrincipal;
    Mock<IAuthorizationService> _mockAuthorizationService;

    public GivenAHackerTriesToEditSomeoneElsesSkiCard()
    {
        _skiCardContext =
            new SkiCardContext(InMemoryDbContextOptionsFactory.Create<SkiCardContext>());
        _skiCard = new SkiCard
        {
            ApplicationUserId = Guid.NewGuid().ToString(),
            Id = 5,
            CardHolderFirstName = "James",
            CardHolderLastName = "Chambers",
            CardHolderBirthDate = DateTime.Now.AddYears(-150),
            CardHolderPhoneNumber = "555-555-5555",
            CreatedOn = DateTime.UtcNow
        };

        _skiCardContext.SkiCards.Add(_skiCard);
        _skiCardContext.SaveChanges();


        _badGuyPrincipal = new ClaimsPrincipal();
        _controllerContext = new ControllerContext()
        {
            HttpContext = new DefaultHttpContext
            {
                User = _badGuyPrincipal
            }
        };

        _mockAuthorizationService = new Mock<IAuthorizationService>();
    }

    [Fact]
    public async void EditActionShouldReturnChallengeResult()
    {

        var controller = new SkiCardController(_skiCardContext, null, _
mockAuthorizationService.Object)
        {
            ControllerContext = _controllerContext
        };

        _mockAuthorizationService.Setup(
            a => a.AuthorizeAsync(
                    _badGuyPrincipal,
                    _skiCard,
```

```
                        It.Is<IEnumerable<IAuthorizationRequirement>>(
                            r => r.Count() == 1 && r.First() is
    EditSkiCardAuthorizationRequirement)))
              .Returns(Task.FromResult(false));

        var result = await controller.Edit(new EditSkiCardViewModel
        {
            Id = _skiCard.Id,
            CardHolderFirstName = "BadGuy",
            CardHolderLastName = "McHacker",
            CardHolderBirthDate = DateTime.Now.AddYears(-25),
            CardHolderPhoneNumber = "555-555-5555"
        });

        Assert.IsType<ChallengeResult>(result);
        _mockAuthorizationService.VerifyAll();
    }
    public void Dispose()
    {
        _skiCardContext.Dispose();
    }
}
```

xUnit creates a new instance of the test class for every test it runs. When a class is marked as IDis-posable, xUnit will also call the Dispose method after every test. In the scenario shown in Listing 20-2, the class is marked as IDisposable and cleanup logic is added to the Dispose method which ensures the _skiCardContext instance is disposed after the test is executed. There is much more that can and should be tested in Listing 20-2. For example, in the scenario above you should be testing to make sure the ski card was not modified. Better yet, you should move a lot of the interaction with the SkiCardContext out to a command to make this controller easier to test. See Chapter 23, "Refactoring" for more details on refactoring to the command pattern.

Testing Tag Helpers

Unit testing tag helpers provide a chance to test the HTML that is output by the tag helper in different scenarios. Aside from some setup cruft, testing tag helpers is fairly simple. Basically, setup a TagHelperContext, call Process or ProcessAsync on the tag helper and check that the expected changes were made to the TagHelperOutput. The tricky part comes in creating TagHelperContext and TagHelperOutput for testing.

Because ASP.NET Core MVC is open source you can examine the source code if you get stuck. In this case, we checked how the ASP.NET team tested the built-in tag helpers. After a few minutes of digging through the source on GitHub, we found the approach of writing a couple static methods to create the TagHelperContext and TagHelperOutput.

```
private static TagHelperContext GetTagHelperContext(string id = "testid")
{
    return new TagHelperContext(
        allAttributes: new TagHelperAttributeList(),
```

```
            items: new Dictionary<object, object>(),
            uniqueId: id);
}

private static TagHelperOutput GetTagHelperOutput(
    string tagName = "button",
    TagHelperAttributeList attributes = null,
    string childContent = "")
{
    attributes = attributes ?? new TagHelperAttributeList();
    return new TagHelperOutput(
        tagName,
        attributes,
        getChildContentAsync: (useCachedResult, encoder) =>
        {
            var tagHelperContent = new DefaultTagHelperContent();
            tagHelperContent.SetHtmlContent(childContent);
            return Task.FromResult<TagHelperContent>(tagHelperContent);
        });
}
```

These methods are specific to each tag helper being tested. For example, when testing certain tag
helpers, be sure you add default attributes to TagHelperContext and TagHelperOutput. In this
case, we added these static methods to the LoginProviderButtonTagHelperTests class so they
can be used for all of the tag helper scenarios. Listing 20-3 shows one of the scenarios from the Login-
ProviderButtonTagHelperTests class.

LISTING 20-3 Unit tests for the LoginProviderButtonTagHelper

```
public class WhenTargettingAnEmptyButtonTag
{
    TagHelperContext _context;
    TagHelperOutput _output;
    AuthenticationDescription _loginProvider;
    LoginProviderButtonTagHelper _tagHelper;

    public WhenTargettingAnEmptyButtonTag()
    {
        _loginProvider = new AuthenticationDescription
        {
            DisplayName = "This is the display name",
            AuthenticationScheme = "This is the scheme"
        };

        _tagHelper = new LoginProviderButtonTagHelper()
        {
            LoginProvider = _loginProvider
        };

        _context = GetTagHelperContext();
        _output = GetTagHelperOutput();
    }
```

```
[Fact]
public void TheTypeAttributeShouldBeSetToSubmit()
{
    _tagHelper.Process(_context, _output);

    Assert.True(_output.Attributes.ContainsName("type"));
    Assert.Equal("submit", _output.Attributes["type"].Value);
}

[Fact]
public void TheNameAttributeShouldBeSetToProvider()
{
    _tagHelper.Process(_context, _output);

    Assert.True(_output.Attributes.ContainsName("name"));
    Assert.Equal("provider", _output.Attributes["name"].Value);
}

[Fact]
public void TheValueAttributeShouldBeTheAuthenticationScheme()
{
    _tagHelper.Process(_context, _output);

    Assert.True(_output.Attributes.ContainsName("value"));
    Assert.Equal(_loginProvider.AuthenticationScheme, _output.Attributes["value"].
Value);
}

[Fact]
public void TheTitleAttributeShouldContainTheDisplayName()
{
    _tagHelper.Process(_context, _output);

    Assert.True(_output.Attributes.ContainsName("title"));
    Assert.Contains(_loginProvider.DisplayName, _output.Attributes["title"].Value.
ToString());
}

[Fact]
public void TheContentsShouldBeSetToTheAuthenticationScheme()
{
    _tagHelper.Process(_context, _output);

    Assert.Equal(_loginProvider.AuthenticationScheme, _output.Content.GetContent());
}
}
```

The scenario in Listing 20-3 tests the expected output of the LoginProviderButtonTagHelper when targeting a button that does not contain any inner HTML and does not have any HTML attributes set. The TagHelperContext, TagHelperOutput and LoginProviderButtonTagHelper are initialized in the constructor. Each individual test method calls the tag helper's Process method and asserts that a particular attribute has been properly set on the TagHelperOutput. The LoginProviderButtonTagHelper should also be tested in scenarios when there are existing HTML attributes on the button and when the button has some inner HTML. You can see these additional scenarios in the Alpine Ski House GitHub repo: *https://github.com/AspNetMonsters/AlpineSkiHouse/*.

Testing View Components

Testing view components is not much different than testing a controller. You setup or mock any required dependencies, call the Invoke method, and then check the result. Listing 20-4 shows an example that of testing the CallCenterStatusViewComponent.

LISTING 20-4 Unit tests for the CallCenterStatusViewComponent

```
public class CallCenterStatusViewComponentTests
{
    public class GivenTheCallCenterIsClosed
    {
        [Fact]
        public void TheClosedViewShouldBeReturned()
        {
            var _csrInfoServiceMock = new Mock<ICsrInformationService>();
            _csrInfoServiceMock.Setup(c => c.CallCenterOnline).Returns(false);

            var viewComponent = new CallCenterStatusViewComponent(_csrInfoServiceMock.
Object);

            var result = viewComponent.Invoke();

            Assert.IsType<ViewViewComponentResult>(result);
            var viewResult = result as ViewViewComponentResult;
            Assert.Equal("Closed", viewResult.ViewName);
        }
    }

    public class GivenTheCallCenterIsOpen
    {
        [Fact]
        public void TheDefaultViewShouldBeReturned()
        {
            var _csrInfoServiceMock = new Mock<ICsrInformationService>();
            _csrInfoServiceMock.Setup(c => c.CallCenterOnline).Returns(true);

            var viewComponent = new CallCenterStatusViewComponent(_csrInfoServiceMock.
Object);

            var result = viewComponent.Invoke();

            Assert.IsType<ViewViewComponentResult>(result);
            var viewResult = result as ViewViewComponentResult;
            Assert.Null(viewResult.ViewName);
        }
    }
}
```

In Listing 20-4, the `CallCenterStatusViewComponent` is tested using a mock of the `ICsrInformationService`. The first scenario checks that the "Closed" view is returned when the `ICsrInformationService`'s `CallCenterOnline` property is `false`. The second scenario checks that the default view is returned when the `CallCenterOnline` property is `true`.

Unit testing the C# code in an ASP.NET Core application is easy and way easier than explaining to your boss that your application accidentally issued $50,000 of free ski passes.

JavaScript Testing

As you saw in Chapter 15, "The Role of JavaScript," our application contains a significant amount of JavaScript, in addition to C# code. The complexity of the client side code in most applications warrants some testing, but this is often missed in many ASP.NET applications. Fortunately, there is some excellent tooling available for testing the JavaScript using a very similar approach to that used with xUnit.net.

Jasmine

As is the case with all things JavaScript, there are at least a dozen competing unit test frameworks to choose from. An in-depth comparison of these frameworks is outside the scope of this book. For the Apline Ski House project, we settled on using Jasmine, mainly because it was the tool we have the most experience using. Jasmine itself is installed using npm.

```
npm install --save-dev jasmine
npm install -g jasmine
```

The convention with Jasmine is to place these files in a folder named spec. Unlike C# tests, it is better to place JavaScript tests in the same project as the JavaScript source code. In this case, that is the AlpineSkiHouse.Web project. Attempting to place JavaScript tests in a separate project causes unnecessary complexity and makes it much more difficult to run the tests. Since the tests themselves are JavaScript files and not embedded into the assembly, we can easily exclude them from the publishing process. That is, we can make sure we don't accidently ship the test code as part of the application.

Unit tests in Jasmine are implemented by nesting functions. Each file starts with a call to Jasmine's global `describe` function where you pass in some text to describe the scenario being tested and a function implementing that scenario. Within the implementation function, you can implement a number of tests by calling Jasmine's `it` function, passing in a description of the test and a function implementing the test. The `expect` function is used to describe the expectations, which is similar to how you use `Assert` in xUnit.net.

```
describe("The scenario we are testing", function() {
  var someValue;
  it("should be true", function() {
    a = true;
    expect(a).toBe(true);
  });
});
```

The describe functions can be nested, and Jasmine also provides some useful setup and teardown functions: beforeEach, afterEach, beforeAll and afterAll. Jasmine has great documentation over at *http://jasmine.github.io/*.

Organizing JavaScript Tests

As much as possible, we will organize the Jasmine JavaScript tests using the same approach we used for organizing the C# unit tests. Specifically, the folder structure within the specs folder will mirror the folder structure of the Scripts folder where all the application's JavaScript is located. For example, the test for Controls/MetersSkied.js are found in specs/Controls/MetersSkiedTest.js.

Each test file will start by describing a high level scenario and loading the module being tested. In this case, the module is Controls/MetersSkied. The loading happens in Jasmine's beforeAll function. It is important to signal when the import is completed by calling the done() function. The tests or nested scenarios will follow.

```
describe("When viewing the MetersSkied chart", function () {
    var MetersSkied;
    beforeAll(function (done) {
        System.import("Controls/MetersSkied").then(function (m) {
            MetersSkied = m;
            done();
        });
    });
    //Nested Scenarios or Tests
    it("should display data for the ski season", function () {
        var div = document.createElement("div");
        var chart = new MetersSkied.MetersSkied(div);

        expect(chart.labels.length).toBe(6);
        expect(chart.labels).toContain("November");
        expect(chart.labels).toContain("December");
        expect(chart.labels).toContain("January");
        expect(chart.labels).toContain("February");
        expect(chart.labels).toContain("March");
        expect(chart.labels).toContain("April");
    })
});
```

Running the Tests

Jasmine includes a unit test runner but it is mostly geared towards Node.js applications, as opposed to applications that run in the browser. Fortunately, there are other unit test runners designed for executing Jasmine unit tests in a browser. For web applications like AlpineSkiHouse.Web, Karma is a good choice of unit test runners because it can be used to execute tests in the context of several browsers like Chrome, FireFox, Internet Explorer and PhantomJS. Karma takes care or bootstrapping the Jasmine tests. Bootstrapping in this context means creating an HTML page that includes the appropriate JavaScript files and firing up a webserver to serve those pages to the browser. Karma also takes care of executing your tests against your choice of browsers. Karma is easily installed using npm.

```
npm install --save-dev karma
npm install -g karma
npm install --save-dev karma-jasmine
```

Once Karma is installed, run `karma init` from the command line, which will ask a series of questions about the JavaScript files to include and which browsers to test against. After going through the list of questions, Karma will create a `karma.conf.js` file.

```
// Karma configuration
module.exports = function(config) {
  config.set({
    // base path that will be used to resolve all patterns (eg. files, exclude)
    basePath: 'wwwroot',
    frameworks: ['jasmine'],

    // list of files / patterns to load in the browser
    files: [
      'js/system.js',
      'js/system-polyfills.js',
      'js/jspmconfig.js',
      { pattern: 'js/**/*.js', included: false, watched: true, served: true },
      //'js/Controls/MetersSkied.js',
      '../spec/**/*Tests.js'
    ],
    reporters: ['progress'],
    // web server port
    port: 9876,
    colors: true,
    logLevel: config.LOG_INFO,
    // enable / disable watching file and executing tests whenever any file changes
    autoWatch: true,
    browsers: ['Chrome', 'PhantomJS', 'IE'],
    singleRun: false,
    concurrency: Infinity,
    proxies: {
        '/js': '/base/js'
    }
  })
}
```

The `files` property is pretty important. You need to load `system.js` and `system-polyfills.js` first, then `jspmconfig.js`. That provides the initial steps needed for loading modules into our tests. Next, specify a pattern of all `*.js` files in the `js` folder, but tell Karma not to include those files automatically. The Karma web server needs to serve the individual JavaScript files only when they are requested by the System.js module loader.

For starters, we configured Karma to run the tests against Chrome, IE and PhantomJS. PhantomJS is a headless browser which means you can run the tests without launching a browser window. For each browser specified, install the `karma-*-launcher` plugin. There are also plugins for Edge, Firefox and other browsers.

```
npm install --save-dev karma-chrome-launcher
npm install --save-dev karma-phantomjs-launcher
npm install --save-dev karma-ie-launcher
```

Now that Karma is configured, run the unit tests by executing the `karma start` from the command line. Karma will launch the Chrome and Internet Explorer browsers and execute any Jasmine unit tests it finds. The results are reported on the command line as shown in Figure 20-4.

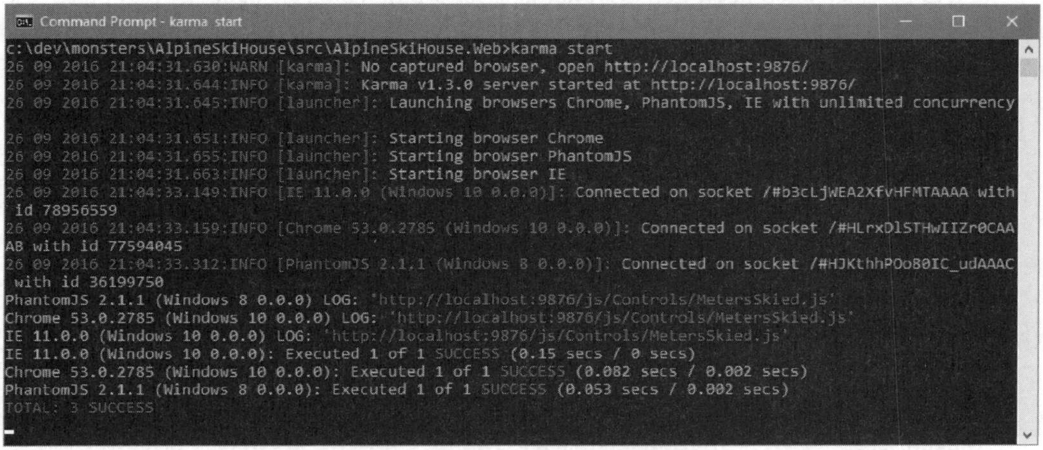

FIGURE 20-4 Running the karma unit tests runner from the command line

With Karma, you get continuous testing for free. Karma will also watch for changes to any of the source or test files and re-run the tests as necessary, giving developers instance feedback.

> **Note** You can also integrate Karma into the existing Gulp based client side build process using the `gulp-karma` plugin. We will stick with the simple command line process for our app, but take a look at *https://github.com/karma-runner/gulp-karma* and *https://github.com/karma-runner/grunt-karma* if you are interested.

Since Karma is a command line tool, it is easy to integrate with a continuous integration build system. However, you probably won't want to run Karma on your build server with the same settings as you do on a developer machine. For example, you will not want Karma to watch for changes to source and test files because that would cause your build to sit in a waiting state forever. Instead you will only want to run the tests once. You might also choose to simplify your build process on the server and only run the tests against PhantomJS. Opening browser windows on a server that doesn't have a user interface session can be problematic and on some servers, the test runner will hang while trying to launch a browser window. Most of those settings you can specify with command line options.

```
karma start --single-run --browsers PhantomJS
```

You might also want to specify a reporter for the build server you are using. Build server integration along with all the other Karma features are well documented at *https://karma-runner.github.io/*.

Other Types of Testing

We have covered C# and JavaScript unit testing in great detail but there are other types of automated testing to consider. Integration testing is another layer of automated testing that attempts to test the applications behavior when all the modules are used together. That is, rather than testing individual pieces in isolation, test how pieces work when they are actually interacting with other real pieces of the application.

For the most part, integration tests can be written using the same tools used for unit testing, yet each test will need more setup. For example, you will probably need a relational database containing some seed data. You might also need to start a web server to host the application.

Another important consideration is whether or not to include the user interface in your integration tests. Some integration tests take the approach of simulating a user interacting with the browser using a browser automation tool such as Selenium's WebDriver (*http://www.seleniumhq.org/projects/webdriver/*). Others will take the approach of simulating only the HTTP requests that a browser would make.

The official ASP.NET Core documentation has a good tutorial on integration testing: *https://docs.asp.net/en/latest/testing/integration-testing.html*.

Another type of testing to consider is load testing. The worst possible time to find out about a performance problem is when your server starts to fail under high load. Luckily, there are some great load testing tools that can simulate high load in your application. Visual Studio has some built in tooling (*https://www.visualstudio.com/en-us/docs/test/performance-testing/getting-started/getting-started-with-performance-testing*). Web Surge is another great option (*http://websurge.west-wind.com/*).

Summary

The ASP.NET Core framework was designed from the ground up with consideration for automated testing. ASP.NET Core's use of constructor injection, as discussed in Chapter 14, "Dependency Injection," simplifies the setup required to test components of your application. Mock objects can be passed in to a class to test the expected interaction with a dependency. In this chapter, we explored some concrete examples of testing services, controllers, view components and tag helpers.

A typically ASP.NET Core application consists of both C# and JavaScript code. Unit testing should span both those sections. In this chapter, we used Jasmine and Karma to achieve automated unit testing of client side JavaScript code. With the right tooling and a little discipline on your team, automated testing doesn't have to be difficult. A solid set of automated tests can help your team move forward more confidence and potentially higher speed.

The unit testing techniques described in this chapter can be applied to other aspects of the ASP.NET Core Framework like the extensibility points discussed in the next chapter, "Extensibility."

## CHAPTER 21

Extensibility

Chester was reading a book in his cubicle as Danielle walked by. Always curious about what people were reading, she started up a conversation. "What are you reading Chester?"

"Oh" said Chester, a bit startled. "It is actually this book on ASP.NET MVC Core called "ASP.NET Core Application Development: Building an application in four sprints". It's kind of interesting. A lot of the stuff in the earlier chapters feels like things we encountered already on this project. But, this chapter on extensibility has a bunch of things I didn't know."

"We've kind of been looking things up as we need them and not learning about the framework as a whole. Are there things in there we could be using?" Danielle asked.

"To tell you the truth, we're using these things, and they just kind of work. If we were doing something slick with different pipelines or writing our own middleware, this chapter would be the place to be. This bit," said Chester tapping the current page", could be useful. It is about isomorphic applications."

"Isomorphic applications? Ones that are triangular and have at least two sides that are the same length?"

"Ha ha," laughed Chester. "I think those might be isosceles applications and I'm not certain, but I think they might not be a real thing. You know how when we load up a page in the single page application it takes a little while to load?"

"Yeah," said Danielle. It was something that annoyed her.

"Okay, so an isomorphic application would run our initial document object model generation on the server and pass down an already-hydrated page. Then the JavaScript on the client could take over and leverage the DOM that was already there. It would be way faster, because the page would already be there rendered, and the JavaScript wouldn't need to really change anything."

"That sounds faster and better all around. It would be nifty to do that on our project."

"The tools are all here and we could get started any time. I'd sure be interested in removing that annoying loading delay. There is no way a webpage should start with a loading graphic, that's just plain silly."

"It sure is," said Danielle. "We might as well have a splash screen. As we add more JavaScript I imagine our page loading is just going to take longer and longer. That's not a solution that is scalene."

> "Was that a triangle joke?" asked Chester.
>
> "It was," admitted Danielle. Perhaps she had been spending a bit too much with the Marks. "I wanted to make sure all my angles were covered."

The ASP.NET Core MVC framework is built for extensibility. There are hooks at almost every level of the framework that allow you to support some advanced scenarios. We've talked about some of these extensibility points already, but we get into them in a little more detail in this chapter.

Conventions

The ASP.NET Core MVC framework is very heavily based on conventions. The location of a view, by convention, is `Views/ControllerName/ActionName.cshtml`. Controllers, by convention, are located in the Controllers folder. These conventions work to remove some of the effort needed to get applications running. By favoring convention over configuration, we can quickly add features and extend an ASP.NET Core MVC application with minimal effort.

The default framework conventions typically work well for most applications, but there can be situations where it would be nice to modify existing conventions or even add our own custom conventions. Table 21-1 lists the types of conventions that can be modified or created in ASP.NET Core MVC.

TABLE 21-1 Types of conventions in ASP.NET Core MVC

Convention	Interface	Description
Application	IApplicationModelConvention	Provides access to application-wide conventions, allowing you to iterate over each of the levels below.
Controller	IControllerModelConvention	Conventions that are specific to a controller, but also allows you to evaluate lower levels.
Action	IActionModelConvention	Changes to action-level conventions can be made here, as well as on any parameters of the actions.
Parameter	IParameterModelConvention	Specific to parameters only.

As an ASP.NET Core application starts, it uses any conventions that you have added, starting at the outer-most field of view, application conventions, then working its way in through controller and action conventions to parameter conventions. In this way, the most specific conventions are applied last. It is important to note that if when you add a parameter convention by using `IControllerModelConvention`, it could be overwritten by `IParameterModelConvention`, regardless of the order that you add the conventions into the project. This is different from middleware because the order of conventions only applies within the same level, and there is a priority on level that you can't adjust.

Creating Custom Conventions

To create a custom convention, create a class that inherits from the appropriately scoped convention. For example, to create a custom convention that applies at the application level, implement the IApplicationModelConvention interface. Each of the interfaces listed in Table 21-1 has a single *Apply* method that is called at runtime. The Apply method accepts a model for the appropriate level. For example, the Apply method for the IApplicationModelConvention accepts an Application-Model argument. Among other things, the ApplicationModel contains a list of the controllers that were discovered at startup time. Also in the Apply method, we can inspect this list and modify the controllers' properties.

An application level custom convention

```
public class CustomApplicationModelConvention : IApplicationModelConvention
{
    public void Apply(ApplicationModel application)
    {
        //Apply custom conventions here
    }
}
```

Conventions are registered with the MVC framework at startup when we call the AddMvc extension method in Startup.ConfigureServices. All we need to do is add an instance of the custom convention to the Conventions list.

Registering custom conventions in Startup.Configure

```
services.AddMvc(mvcOptions =>
{
    mvcOptions.Conventions.Add(new CustomApplicationModelConvention());
});
```

As a simple example, let's create a custom IActionModelConvention. In this convention, we want to automatically add the ValidateAntiForgeryToken filter to any action methods that have the HttpPost attribute and do not have the ValidateAntiForgeryToken explicitly added. In the Apply method, we are able to inspect the attributes of the action method and add the filter only to the action methods where our convention applies.

An Action level convention that automatically adds the ValidateAnitForgeryToken filter

```
public class AutoValidateAntiForgeryTokenModelConvention : IActionModelConvention
{
    public void Apply(ActionModel action)
    {
        if (IsConventionApplicable(action))
        {
            action.Filters.Add(new ValidateAntiForgeryTokenAttribute());
        }
    }
```

```
    public bool IsConventionApplicable(ActionModel action)
    {
        if ( action.Attributes.Any(f => f.GetType() == typeof(HttpPostAttribute)) &&
             !action.Attributes.Any(f => f.GetType() == typeof(ValidateAntiForgeryTokenAttribu
te))){
            return true;
        }
        return false;
    }
}
```

> **Note** Conventions can be used to enable some pretty great scenarios. In MSDN magazine, Steve Smith describes how conventions can be used to structure an application into features folders[1]. The knowledgeable Filip Wojcieszyn also has some great examples on his blog showing how to apply global route prefixes[2] and also has an interesting approach to providing localized routes[3].

Creating custom conventions is easy in ASP.NET Core MVC. Of course, you should take care when making changes to the default ASP.NET Core MVC conventions. Any changes to the default conventions makes it more difficult for new developers to understand the application, because it doesn't look the same as other ASP.NET Core MVC applications.

Middleware

As we saw in Chapter 3, "Models, Views and Controllers," ASP.NET Core applications are configured as a series of middleware components that process incoming requests and manipulate outgoing responses. Architecturally, the pattern used by ASP.NET Core is a well-known reference architecture known as Pipes and Filters, which is further explained in a separate MSDN article located at *https://msdn.microsoft.com/en-us/library/dn568100.aspx*. One of the underlying benefits of this type of architecture is just how easy it is to extend. Middleware can easily be added to an application without requiring large scale changes to other middleware modules.

---

[1] *https://msdn.microsoft.com/magazine/mt763233*

[2] *http://www.strathweb.com/2016/06/global-route-prefix-with-asp-net-core-mvc-revisited/*

[3] *http://www.strathweb.com/2015/11/localized-routes-with-asp-net-5-and-mvc-6/*

Configuring the pipeline

In an ASP.NET Core application, the pipeline is configured in the `Startup.Configure` method. It is common to include a number of the built-in middleware components that can be easily added by calling the appropriate extension methods on `IApplicationBuilder`. The following code example shows a simplified version of the pipeline configured in AlpineSkiHouse.Web, which is shown in Figure 21-1.

Abbreviated version of Startup.Configure from AlpineSkiHouse.Web

```
public void Configure(IApplicationBuilder app, IHostingEnvironment env)
{
    app.UseExceptionHandler("/Home/Error");
    app.UseStaticFiles();
    app.UseIdentity();
    app.UseMvc(routes =>
    {
        routes.MapRoute(
            name: "default",
            template: "{controller=Home}/{action=Index}/{id?}");
    });
}
```

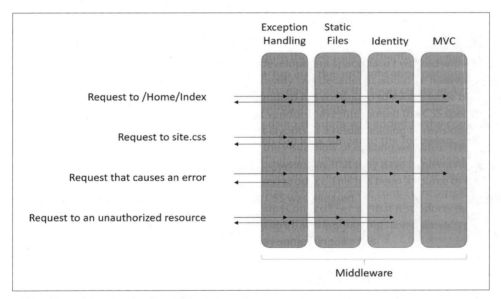

FIGURE 21-1 A simplified request pipeline for AlpineSkiHouse.Web

The beauty of middleware in ASP.NET Core is just how easy it is to make changes to the request pipeline. A great example of this is turning on special exception and error handling pages only when the application is running in a development environment.

Example of configuring middleware for development environments

```
if (env.IsDevelopment())
{
```

```
    app.UseDeveloperExceptionPage();
    app.UseDatabaseErrorPage();
}
else
{
    app.UseExceptionHandler("/Home/Error");
}
```

With that one simple change to the pipeline, you have access to special error diagnostics pages in your local development environments. An example of the database error page can be seen in Figure 21-2.

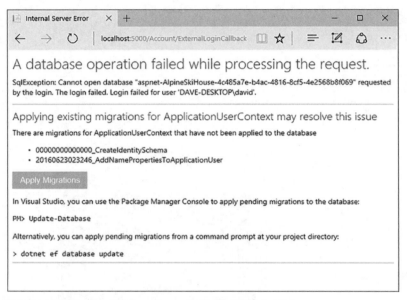

FIGURE 21-2 The database error page in AlpineSkiHouse.Web

In addition to making use of the built-in middleware components, it is also easy to write custom middleware or bring in additional middleware components via NuGet. Any custom middleware is added to the pipeline by calling the Use method on the IApplicationBuilder instance.

Writing your own Middleware

For basic applications, there is no need to implement custom middleware because there likely is middleware either built-in or available from third parties that solves for the most common use cases. It is, however, worth understanding how middleware is implemented. If nothing else, it helps to demystify the concept.

Middleware, in simple terms, is a delegate that acts on a request, and then passes the request on to the next delegate in the pipeline.

Let's take a look at a simple example of middleware that adds the `Content-Security-Policy` header to the response. You can implement this behavior by declaring an anonymous method in the `Startup.Configure` method.

> **Note** The Content Security Policy Header is an important tool for protecting your website against cross site scripting attacks. You can learn more about how this header works and why it is important by watching the related episode on the ASP.NET Monsters on Channel 9[4].

Example of middleware implemented as an anonymous method

```
app.Use(async (context, next) =>
{
    context.Response.Headers.Add("Content-Security-Policy", "default-src 'self'");
    await next.Invoke();
});
```

Anonymous methods, however, are not very testable or reusable. It is usually a better choice to implement middleware as a class. A middleware class is a class that implements an async `Invoke` method and accepts a `RequestDelegate` via constructor injection. Note that middleware classes take part in dependency injection just like any other service in ASP.NET Core. After the class is created, the middleware is configured in `Startup.Configure`.

Middleware for adding the Content-Security-Policy header

```
public class CSPMiddleware
{
    private readonly RequestDelegate _next;

    public CSPMiddleware(RequestDelegate next)
    {
        _next = next;
    }

    public async Task Invoke(HttpContext context)
    {
        context.Response.Headers.Add("Content-Security-Policy", "default-src 'self'");
        await _next.Invoke(context);
    }
}
```

Configuring the CSPMiddleware in Startup.Configure

```
app.UseMiddleware<CSPMiddleware>();
```

With the middleware created and implemented, any request to the Alpine Ski House website now has the Content-Security-Policy header added, as shown in Figure 21-3

---

[4] https://channel9.msdn.com/Series/aspnetmonsters/ASP-NET-Monsters-66-Content-Security-Policy-Headers

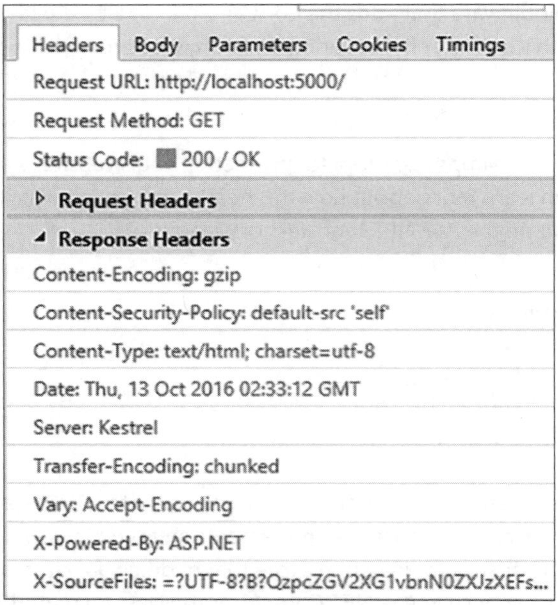

Headers	Body	Parameters	Cookies	Timings

Request URL: http://localhost:5000/

Request Method: GET

Status Code: ■ 200 / OK

▷ **Request Headers**

◢ **Response Headers**

Content-Encoding: gzip

Content-Security-Policy: default-src 'self'

Content-Type: text/html; charset=utf-8

Date: Thu, 13 Oct 2016 02:33:12 GMT

Server: Kestrel

Transfer-Encoding: chunked

Vary: Accept-Encoding

X-Powered-By: ASP.NET

X-SourceFiles: =?UTF-8?B?QzpcZGV22XG1vbnN0ZXJcJzXEFs...

FIGURE 21-3 Content-Security-Policy response header

This is of course a very simple example. It is also possible to add some logic after the call to `await _next.Invoke(context)` that executes after any middleware components have finished running. Any request in the pipeline also has the option to not invoke the next middleware component. This technique is called short-circuiting the request pipeline. An example of short-circuiting by the static files module can be seen with the request for site.css in Figure 21-1.

> **Note** In previous versions of ASP.NET, modules and handlers were used to implement custom request processing logic. Handlers were used to handle requests with a given filename or extension, while modules were invoked for every request and had the ability to short-circuit requests or modify the HTTP response. Both modules and handlers were hooks into the request pipeline in older versions of ASP.NET and both have been replaced by middleware in ASP.NET Core. Visit the official ASP.NET Core documentation, located at *https://docs.asp.net/en/latest/migration/http-modules.html*, for guidance on migrating from handlers and modules to middleware.

Pipeline Branching

ASP.NET Core middleware can be configured in such a way as to branch the pipeline based on the criteria you choose. The easiest option is to branch based on the request path by using the Map extension method on IApplicationBuilder. In the following example, any requests that start with the path /

download would use the `CustomFileDownloadMiddleware` instead of using the middleware configured for the regular MVC pipeline. This branched pipeline is illustrated in Figure 21-4.

Example of pipeline branching using Map

```
public void Configure(IApplicationBuilder app, IHostingEnvironment env)
{
    app.UseExceptionHandler("/Home/Error");
    app.Map("/download", appBuilder =>
    {
        appBuilder.UseMiddleware<CustomFileDownloadMiddleware>();
    });
    app.UseStaticFiles();
    app.UseIdentity();
    app.UseMvc(routes =>
    {
        routes.MapRoute(
            name: "default",
            template: "{controller=Home}/{action=Index}/{id?}");
    });
}
```

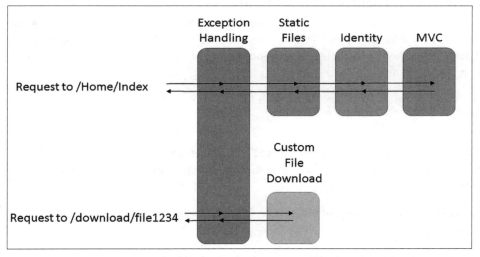

FIGURE 21-4 A simple example of pipeline branching

More complex branching strategies can be implemented by using the `MapWhen` function, which allows branching based on a predicate of type `Func<HttpContext, bool>`. This means that a function can be used to inspect the current `HttpContext` and decide whether or not to branch based on the current request.

Loading External Controller and Views

Out of the box, ASP.NET Core MVC discovers controllers from any assemblies that are referenced by the application. We can place all of our controllers in a separate project named AlpineSkiHouse.Web. Controllers, and as long as AlpineSkiHouse.Web has a reference to the AlpineSkiHouse.Web. Controllers project, everything works as expected. In the case of AlpineSkiHouse.Web, moving controllers to a separate project serves no useful purpose and needlessly increases the complexity of the solution. Loading controllers and other application components from external assemblies can be useful in some situations however. Consider, for example, that a fully featured content management system would likely want to provide some plug-in style extensibility.

While controllers are automatically discovered for projects that are directly referenced, there are a couple of caveats. First, Razor views are not automatically discovered from external projects. Second, controllers are not automatically discovered for assemblies that are loaded at runtime. Fortunately, ASP.NET Core MVC provides extension points to support both of those scenarios.

Loading Views from External Projects

To load views from an external project, those views first need to be stored directly in the assembly as embedded resources. Assuming the views are all located in a Views folder, you can specify that all cshtml files in the Views folder should be embedded into the assembly by adding the following to the project's project.json file:

```
"buildOptions": {
   "embed": "Views/**/*.cshtml"
}
```

Next, in the main Web project you need to add a reference to the Microsoft.Extensions. FileProviders NuGet package and configure Razor to look for views as embedded files in the referenced project.

Configuring Razor to load views from embedded resources

```
services.AddMvc();

//Get a reference to the assembly that contains the embedded views
var assembly = typeof(AlpineSkiHouse.Web.Controllers.ExternalController).GetTypeInfo().Assembly;

//Create an EmbeddedFileProvider for that assembly
var embeddedFileProvider = new EmbeddedFileProvider(
    assembly
);

//Add the file provider to the Razor view engine
services.Configure<RazorViewEngineOptions>(options =>
{
    options.FileProviders.Add(embeddedFileProvider);
});
```

With that small change, both Views and Controllers are loaded from the external project.

Loading Controllers from External Assemblies

In the case of a plug-in framework, the external project would not likely be known at compile time. Instead, the plug-in assemblies would be loaded at runtime and in this case, those dynamically loaded assemblies need to be explicitly added to the `IMvcBuilder` by calling the `AddApplicationPart` method.

Dynamically load an assembly and add it to the IMvcBuilder

```
var assembly = AssemblyLoadContext.Default.LoadFromAssemblyPath("fullpathtoassembly.dll");

services.AddMvc()
    .AddApplicationPart(assembly);
```

By combining these two approaches, it is relatively easy to create a custom plug-in architecture for an ASP.NET Core MVC application. Of course, a fully-fledged plug-in architecture requires much more consideration in terms of application security, configuration of which assemblies to load dynamically, and error handling.

Routing

Routing in ASP.NET Core is the process of mapping an incoming request's URL to a route handler. When we think of routing in ASP.NET Core, we typically think of MVC routing, which routes an incoming request to a particular action method on a controller.

Routing in MVC is configured by defining routes on the `IRouteBuilder` when calling the `UseMvc` method in `Startup.Configure`. A typical ASP.NET Core MVC application makes use of the default routing behavior that is configured by the File then New Project template in Visual Studio.

Default routing as configured in AlpineSkiHouse

```
app.UseMvc(routes =>
{
    routes.MapRoute(
        name: "default",
        template: "{controller=Home}/{action=Index}/{id?}");
});
```

Routes are created by calling `MapRoute` on the `IRouteBuilder`. Each route is composed of a name and a template. The routing middleware uses the specified template to match an incoming request's URL to a particular route. A template consists of a number of route parameters, each wrapped by curly braces. The default route previously mentioned is made up of three route parameters: the *{controller}*, the *{action}*, and an *{id}*. For the controller and action parameters, default values have been specified. For example, if the path does not include a section that maps to the Action portion of the template, the Index action is used. Likewise, if the controller is also not specified, the Home controller is used. The id portion is also optional, but no default value is specified. If an id is matched in the URL, the value of the id maps to an `id` argument of the action method. Table 21-2 shows some example URLs and the resulting controller/action method mapping.

TABLE 21-2 Example URLs with resulting controller and action method routing

Request URL	Controller	Action Method
Home/Index/	HomeController	Index()
Home/	HomeController	Index()
/	HomeController	Index()
SkiCard/	SkiCardController	Index()
SkiCard/Create/	SkiCardController	Create()
SkiCard/Edit/1	SkiCardController	Edit(int id) with id = 1

The default route is an example of convention based, or conventional, routing. Conventional routing allows you to add more controllers and action methods without having to think explicitly about mapping new URLs. It is also possible to define multiple routes with conventional routing.

Example of mapping multiple routes

```
app.UseMvc(routes =>
{
    routes.MapRoute(
        name: "cards",
        template: "Cards/{action=Index}/{id?}",
        defaults: new { controller = "SkiCard" });
    routes.MapRoute(
        name: "default",
        template: "{controller=Home}/{action=Index}/{id?}");
});
```

In this example, we defined a route that would map requests starting with `Cards` to the `SkiCardcontroller`. Using multiple routes can help to define more specific or more user-friendly URLs, but it comes at the cost of increased complexity. The more routes you define, the harder it is to determine how request URLs get mapped to a controller and action method. Routes are processed in the order they are added and are considered to be greedy. Any incoming requests are first matched against the cards route. If the URL cannot be processed by the cards route, the default route is used.

Attribute Routing

An alternative to conventional routing is Attribute based routing. With attribute routing, route templates are defined directly on the controllers and action methods by using the `Route` attribute.

Simple example of attribute based routing

```
public class HomeController : Controller
{

    [Route("/")]
    public IActionResult Index()
    {
        return View();
    }

    [Route("/about")]
```

```
        public IActionResult About()
        {
            return View();
        }

        [Route("/contact")]
        public IActionResult Contact()
        {
            return View();
        }
    }
}
```

The sample `HomeController` uses the `Route` attribute on each action method to route incoming requests to a specific action method. For example, the */contact* URL is routed to the `Contact` action method.

Advanced Routing

Routing in ASP.NET Core MVC is very flexible. For more details on advanced usage of both conventional and attribute based routing, take a look at the official ASP.NET Core documentation, located at *https://docs.asp.net/en/latest/mvc/controllers/routing.html*.

Routing middleware can also be used more generically outside the context of the MVC framework. By configuring routing middleware outside of MVC, it is possible to map URLs to a route handler that directly handles the HTTP request. Take a look at the official ASP.NET Core documentation, located at *https://docs.asp.net/en/latest/fundamentals/routing.html* for a complete overview of advanced routing in ASP.NET Core.

Dotnet tools

The command line tooling for `dotnet` is another great extensibility point in the framework. In addition to the built-in command for `dotnet`, tools can be brought in via NuGet at the project level. In Chapter 10, "Entity Framework Core," we explored the `dotnet ef` command line tooling, which simplifies the process of creating and executing database migrations scripts. The `dotnet ef` tool is actually brought into the project by adding a reference to `Microsoft.EntityFrameworkCore.Tools` to the tools section in `project.json`. This makes it very easy to pull in additional tools provided by Microsoft or other third parties in a repeatable way. Because the tooling is installed locally by NuGet, we can be sure that every developer has access to the same tooling.

Adding dotnet command line tools via Nuget
```
"tools": {
  "Microsoft.EntityFrameworkCore.Tools": "1.0.0-preview2-final"
}
```

It is also possible to create your own `dotnet` CLI tooling. Visit *https://docs.microsoft.com/en-us/dotnet/articles/core/tools/extensibility* for a full overview of the `dotnet` CLI extensibility.

JavaScript Services and Isomorphic Applications

We have seen a few examples of how ASP.NET Core has great integration with Node.js. The Visual Studio tooling has built-in support for npm and other package managers, giving ASP.NET Core developers access to the rich node.js ecosystem, at least for client side development. The one area so far that is lacking is in executing JavaScript on the server at runtime.

Okay, the idea of running JavaScript on the server seems natural in the context of a Node.js application, but it probably sounds a little unbelievable within the context of a .NET application. Let's take a step back and first talk about why we would even consider this in the first place, starting with a concept called isomorphic applications.

Isomorphic Applications

An isomorphic application is an application whose code is capable of running in both the client and the server. The concept of isomorphic applications has become popular in part as a solution to some of the commonly cited disadvantages of single page applications (SPAs). When the client loads the initial page in a SPA, the HTML is basically an empty shell containing references to some scripts. An empty page is displayed in the client until additional JavaScript files are downloaded and executed. In most cases, several other requests are needed to load data. This architecture can lead to slow initial page loads and a potentially sub-optimal user experience. It is difficult to create a SPA that doesn't involve at least some flashing as the page redraws or some spinning loading indicators as requests are made to retrieve scripts and data.

Aside from the user experience, a request that returns an empty HTML shell can also be a big negative for search engine optimization (SEO). Ideally, a request from a search engine crawler contains the same HTML that is eventually displayed in the client.

Both the user experience and SEO problems can be solved if you pre-render the HTML on the server side. On the server, you have the benefit of being able to cache the page output, which can make subsequent requests much faster.

The `Microsoft.AspNetCore.SpaServices` package enables server side pre-rendering of SPA components. SpaServices is used in combination with your favorite SPA framework to pre-render HTML on the server-side, and then transfer the results to the client side where execution continues.

Rather than being tied to a particular SPA framework like Angular or React, SpaServices provides a set of ASP.NET Core APIs that know how to invoke a JavaScript function for server-side pre-rendering and inject the resulting HTML into the HTML that is sent to the client. The method of pre-rendering is different for each SPA framework. For example, Angular 2 uses the angular-universal package[5] to support server-side page rendering.

---

[5] *https://github.com/angular/universal*

For more details on the SpaServices package and examples using both Angular 2 and React, visit *https://github.com/aspnet/JavaScriptServices/tree/dev/src/Microsoft.AspNetCore.SpaServices*.

Node Services

In addition to the excellent support for isomorphic applications, ASP.NET Core also has support for invoking Node.js code at runtime in an ASP.NET Core application. While it is typically preferred to use .NET code and NuGet packages to implement features, there are times when you might need to use a Node.js package to perform specific tasks. As an example, some third-party services might not provide .NET APIs, but do provide Node.js APIs. The ability to invoke Node.js packages at runtime provides a new level of extensibility to ASP.NET Core applications. In addition to packages available within the rich .NET ecosystem, ASP.NET Core developers now also have access to the broad set of packages available within the Node.js community.

Runtime Node.js functionality is provided by the `Microsoft.AspNetCore.NodeServices` package. More details on the NodeServices package, including examples and common use cases, can be found at *https://github.com/aspnet/JavaScriptServices/tree/dev/src/Microsoft.AspNetCore.NodeServices*.

Summary

The MVC framework has always been very extensible, but the architectural changes made in ASP.NET Core MVC have taken the extensibility to a new level. Middleware represents the biggest change from previous versions and provides you with a request pipeline that is easy to understand, configure, and extend for any conceivable scenario.

In addition to middleware, ASP.NET Core MVC exposes interfaces for customizing and extending framework conventions. Routing can be used to support complex request routing within an application. JavaScript services can be used to bridge the gap between the .NET and JavaScript/Node.js ecosystem. Even the dotnet command line tooling provides extensibility points that allow for custom cross platform command line tooling. We would be hard pressed to find a scenario that could not be supported by using some combination of the extension points built into the ASP.NET Core MVC framework.

In the next chapter, Chapter 22, "Internationalization," we explore the extension points in ASP.NET Core that allow you to build applications that target multiple languages and regions across the globe.

Internationalization

"... and that's why there are so many French speaking people around these parts." Danielle was explaining to Balázs about the cultural history of the land around Alpine Ski House.

"I'm amazed," said Balázs, "that so many people would move from France just because a few truffles were found in the woods."

"It wasn't just a few, these woods are just full of them. I understand that they're pretty high quality truffles too. We actually export a lot of them back to France where they're sold as the real thing. Consumers really can't tell the difference after they're cooked. Did you know a truffle can go for $3,000 a pound?"

"That's outrageous. But then I suppose around my home town we spend as much for fish eggs, so I can't really point fingers. So, you hear a lot of French on the ski hill?"

"Yeah, tons. We usually hire a bunch of bilingual ski instructors to do lessons in French as well as in English."

"The market is big enough to support that? Don't most people around here speak English too?"

"They do, but they have relatives from France or Quebec who don't. We did some analysis on it a few years back and it was absolutely worth the money to have both languages on the hill."

"Do you think it might be worthwhile to have Alpine Ski House in French and English?"

"Hmm, I'd never thought about it. We should check with marketing. They have a bunch of statistics on our target market. I think they sent out mailers last year in French. Come on over, I'll introduce you to some people there who will have a better idea."

"Before I get into it, will it even be possible to add another language to the application?"

"Technically it is pretty easy for our scenario since the app is still fairly small. We'll have to extract our existing strings into a resource file and call out to a resource manager or something to pull the strings into the application. I haven't done it in a few years, so I'd have to get into it a little to see how it is actually done. The tricky part is getting it translated—that's going to take a few weeks. We would have to launch in English and pull in other languages as we decide they're needed."

"Thanks so much, Danielle" said Balázs. "I've got a few things to think about here. I'm going to put this on our backlog for after launch."

For many public web applications, it is important to provide a version of the application in a different language. At this time, the Alpine Ski House website only supports the English language. For a web application to reach the widest possible audience, the application should be set up to support as many locales as possible. Think of a locale as a grouping of a region and a language. The combination of region and language is important for a couple reasons. A particular language can vary from region to region. For example, the English language spoken in Ireland is slightly different than the English language spoken in Canada. The second reason is that formatting for dates and numbers can vary from region to region. There has been no shortage of confusion around the word due to some regions formatting dates as MM-dd-yyyy and others as dd-MM-yyyy. Does 09-10-2016 refer to September 10th or October 9th? The answer is, it depends on the region.

Some large websites like the Microsoft website shown in Figure 22-1 can go as far as supporting dozens of locales. Most websites start out by supporting a much smaller set of locales.

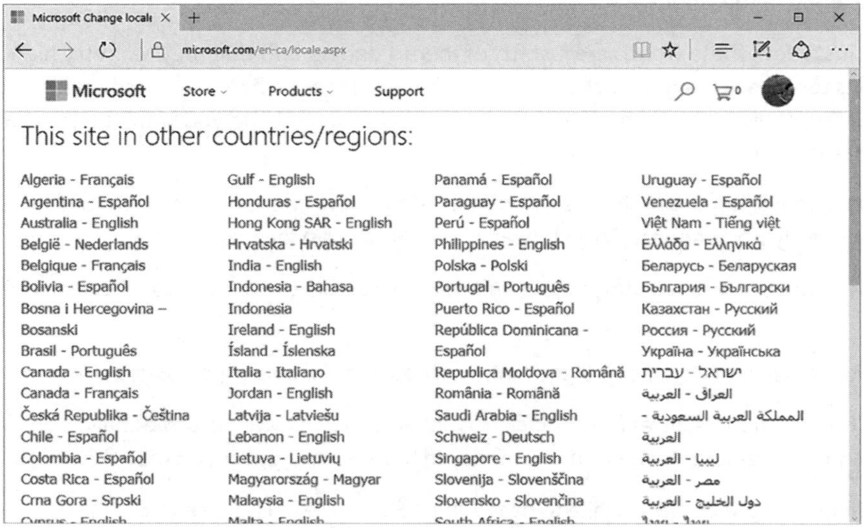

FIGURE 22-1 Selecting a region and language on the Microsoft website

While the task of supporting multiple locales might seem daunting, you can take some comfort that ASP.NET Core provides some middleware and services that alleviate some of the technical barriers.

Before we dive in to the implementation details, let's begin by reviewing some important terms. A *locale* is a language and a region and a locale is often referred to as a *culture*. A culture is uniquely identified by a culture name, which is the two-letter language code followed by the two-letter region or sub-culture code. For example, "en-CA" for English Canada and "en-IE" for English Ireland. A culture that specifies the language and region is called a *specific culture*. A culture that specifies only a language, for example "en," is called a *neutral culture*. Finally, the long words that sometimes get mixed up. *Globalization* is the process of making an app support different cultures. *Localization* is the process of customizing an app for a given culture. *Internationalization* is the process of customizing an app for a given language and region.

.NET has always had rich support for internationalization. In .NET, a culture is represented by the `CultureInfo` class, which among other things includes information about how to format dates and numbers. Every thread in .NET has two `CultureInfo` properties: `CurrentCulture` and `CurrentUICulture`. Typically, the `CurrentCulture` and `CurrentUICulture` is set to the same culture. At runtime, the thread's `CultureInfo` property is used to determine the default formats for dates, numbers, currency values, the sorting order of text, and other culture specific formatting features. The `CurrentUICulture` on the other hand is used look up culture-specific resources at runtime, which brings us to the topic of resources.

A resource file is simply a file containing key value pairs. Typically, the value is text, but the value could also be other binary content such as images. Resource files are important because they allow you to separate the localizable strings from your code. Culture specific resource files can be loaded at runtime, providing language and region specific translations.

Globalizing Existing Applications

We once worked on a fairly large WinForms based .NET application where the sales team landed international sale. This sale represented a potentially significant windfall for the company and had the potential of opening the product to a much larger client base. The problem was, the app was in no way ready to be localized. Text that was displayed in the user interface was hard coded in every layer of the application, including the database.

So we began the painful process of first extracting text to resource files. This process alone took two full time developers several months to complete. After the strings were extracted, we were able to hire translators to begin translating all the strings to the target language. At this point we thought the project was largely complete until we loaded the resource files into the application. In some cases, buttons were too narrow to contain the translated text. In other cases, labels were overlapping with text boxes because the form layouts had assumed the text was a specific width. The UI looked like a mess. We spent another several months reworking layouts to make the app look reasonable with the translated resources.

The moral of the story is that retrofitting globalizations into a large, existing app is a time consuming process. If there is a good chance that the app needs to be localized, consider incorporating the necessary features early on.

Localizable Text

To support localization, you need to make sure that any text that is displayed to the user is not hard coded in the application code. As we mentioned already, we need to set up the application to pull localized values from resource files. ASP.NET Core provides a set of services that makes this process relatively straight forward. Localization services are enabled by adding localization in `Startup.ConfigureServices`.

```
services.AddLocalization(options => options.ResourcesPath = "Resources");
services.AddMvc()
    .AddViewLocalization()
    .AddDataAnnotationsLocalization();
```

String Localization

Typically, most of the localizable text in an application is located in the view, but some text is also located in a controller or perhaps in a service. The Login action of the Account controller for example adds the "Invalid login attempt." text that is eventually displayed to the user as a validation error when the view is rendered.

Section of Login action from the AccountController

```
ModelState.AddModelError(string.Empty, "Invalid login attempt.");
return View(model);
```

When these strings are hard coded, it is not possible for a localized version of the text to be loaded at runtime. ASP.NET Core provides the IStringLocalizer service to solve this problem. You can inject the IStringLocalizer service into the controller just like any other service.

Injecting the IStringLocalizer in a controller

```
[Authorize]
public class AccountController : Controller
{
    private readonly UserManager<ApplicationUser> _userManager;
    private readonly SignInManager<ApplicationUser> _signInManager;
    private readonly IEmailSender _emailSender;
    private readonly ISmsSender _smsSender;
    private readonly ILogger _logger;
    private readonly IStringLocalizer<AccountController> _stringLocalizer;

    public AccountController(
        UserManager<ApplicationUser> userManager,
        SignInManager<ApplicationUser> signInManager,
        IEmailSender emailSender,
        ISmsSender smsSender,
        ILoggerFactory loggerFactory,
        IStringLocalizer<AccountController> stringLocalizer)
    {
        _userManager = userManager;
        _signInManager = signInManager;
        _emailSender = emailSender;
        _smsSender = smsSender;
        _logger = loggerFactory.CreateLogger<AccountController>();
        _stringLocalizer = stringLocalizer;
    }
    //Action methods…
}
```

Now the account controller can load localized strings at runtime by calling the `IStringLocal-izer`'s `GetString` method and passing in a unique key identifying the string to be retrieved. An alternative syntax is to use the default indexer, like we do in the following code sample. The `IStringLocalizer` looks for a localized version of the string matching the current culture by using the .NET framework's `ResourceManager`. One of the nice things about the `IStringLocalizer` is that it doesn't require you to create a resource file for the default language. If the unique key is not found, the `IStringLocalizer` simply returns the key.

Section of Login action from the AccountController using the IStringLocalizer

```
ModelState.AddModelError(string.Empty, _stringLocalizer["Invalid login attempt."]);
return View(model);
```

Creating Culture-Specific Resource Files

The string localizer loads resource files based on the current request culture by using naming conventions. The convention you use for resource file names is `ContainerNamespace.Culture-Name.resx`, where `ContainerNamespace` is the namespace of the type parameter specified in `IStringLocalizer<T>` minus the application's default namespace. In the case of `AlpineSkiHouse.Web.Controllers.AccountController`, the `ContainerNamespace` is `Controllers.Account-Controller`. When we added localization services to the AlpineSkiHouse.Web application, we specified that resources would be located in the Resources folder.

For example, we could provide French Canadian localized strings by adding a new resource file named `Controllers.AccountController.fr-CA.resx` to the Resources folder. To add a resource file in Visual Studio, right-click the Resources folder in Solution Explorer and select Add, then New Item. In the Add New Item dialog box, select Code and Resource File. The resource file editor in Visual Studio provides a table including Name and Value columns. In Figure 22-2 you can see the entry with a localized French Canadian value for the "Invalid login attempt." string.

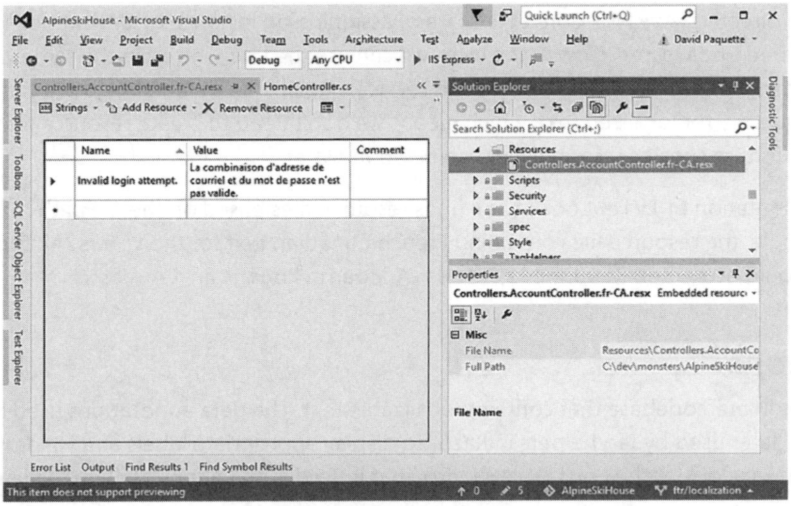

FIGURE 22-2 Editing resources files in Visual Studio

You can edit resource files in any text editor because they are actually XML Files. After you get past the schema and versioning portion of the file, the individual entries are easy to work with.

Entry from a resource file

```
<data name="Invalid login attempt." xml:space="preserve">
  <value>La combinaison d'adresse de courriel et du mot de passe n'est pas valide.</value>
</data>
```

View Localization

You can use the IViewLocalizer to provide localized text to a Razor view. Access the IViewLocalizer by injecting it into the view.

Using the IViewLocalizer in Views/Account/Login.cshtml

```
@using Microsoft.AspNetCore.Mvc.Localization
@model LoginViewModel
@inject IViewLocalizer Localizer

@{
    ViewData["Title"] = Localizer["Log in"];
}

<h2>@ViewData["Title"].</h2>
<div class="row">
    <div class="col-md-8">
        <section>
                <h4>@Localizer["Use a local account to log in."]</h4>
          <!-- … -->
            </section>
    </div>
</div>
<!-- … -->
```

Using the @inject directive, ASP.NET Core takes care of assigning an instance of IViewLocalizer to a local property named Localizer. Now in the view, we can use the Localizer in the same way that we used the IStringLocalizer in controllers and services. Again, the default language can be used inline as the unique key for localized text, which means we don't need to create resource files for the default language. Culture specific resource files can be added later.

The default implementation of IViewLocalizer finds resource files based on the file path for the current view. For example, the resource file containing French Canadian text for the Views/Account/Login.chtml view would be named Resources/Views.Account.Login.fr-CA.resx.

Data Annotations

There is one final place in our codebase that contains localizable text. The data annotations used in view model classes are later used by tag helpers in Razor to display appropriate labels and validation error messages. Let's take a look at the LoginViewModel that is used in the Account/Login view.

```
public class LoginViewModel
{
    [Required(ErrorMessage = "Email is required")]
    [EmailAddress(ErrorMessage = "Not a valid email address")]
    [Display(Name= "Email")]
    public string Email { get; set; }

    [Required(ErrorMessage = "Password is required")]
    [DataType(DataType.Password)]
    [Display(Name="Password")]
    public string Password { get; set; }

    [Display(Name = "Remember me?")]
    public bool RememberMe { get; set; }
}
```

Localized versions of data annotation error messages are loaded at runtime from resource files using a similar naming convention that the IStringLocalizer uses. The French Canadian text can be loaded from the resource file named Resources/Models.AccountViewModels.LoginViewModel. fr-CA.resx.

Note at the time of writing, the Name values specified in the Display attribute are not localized. ASP.NET Core MVC 1.1 will support localization of display names when it is released.

Sharing Resource Files

In the examples so far, each different piece of the application has its own resource file. While this approach does help to keep each section of the app separate, it can lead to a large number of resource files. It can be helpful to at least store some resources in a shared location.

First, we need to create an empty class to use as a placeholder for all shared resources. Cultural specific resources for the shared resources follow the naming convention Resources/ SharedResources.CutureName.resx.

SharedResources.cs

```
/// <summary>
/// An empty class used as a placeholder for shared resources
/// </summary>
public class SharedResources
{
}
```

You can access shared resources in controllers and services by injecting an instance of IStringLocalizer<SharedResources>. Likewise, you can also access shared resources in views by injecting an instance of IHtmlLocalizer<SharedResources>.

Using shared resources in a view

```
@using Microsoft.AspNetCore.Mvc.Localization
@inject IHtmlLocalizer<SharedResources> SharedLocalizer
```

```
<!DOCTYPE html>
<html>
<head>
    <meta charset="utf-8" />
    <meta name="viewport" content="width=device-width, initial-scale=1.0" />
    <title>@ViewData["Title"] - @SharedLocalizer["AlpineSkiHouse"]</title>
    <!-- … -->
</head>
        <!-- … -->
</html>
```

Now that the application is set up to read culture specific resources at runtime, we need to provide a mechanism for the user to select the right culture.

Setting the Current Culture

In a web application, you can't just set the current culture at startup and use that for all requests. To support users from multiple regions, the culture needs to be set at the request level. In ASP.NET Core, the current request culture is set using the localization middleware.

When adding the localization middleware to the pipeline, we need to specify the cultures that are supported and the default culture. Note, there is an option to specify a different list of support cultures versus supported UI cultures. Remember that the UI Culture is used to look up resources, while the Culture is used to control the formatting of numbers, dates, and *for* string comparisons. For AlpineSki-House, the list of support cultures and supported UI cultures are the same.

Section of Startup.Configure method adding request localization middleware.

```
var supportedCultures = new[]
    {
        new CultureInfo("en-CA"),
        new CultureInfo("fr-CA")
    };

var requestLocalizationOptions = new RequestLocalizationOptions
{
    DefaultRequestCulture = new RequestCulture("en-CA"),
    SupportedCultures = supportedCultures,
    SupportedUICultures = supportedCultures
};
app.UseRequestLocalization(requestLocalizationOptions);


app.UseMvc(routes =>
{
    routes.MapRoute(
        name: "default",
        template: "{controller=Home}/{action=Index}/{id?}");
});
```

The localization middleware provides a few built-in options for setting the culture of every request. Specifically, there are options to use query strings, cookies, or request headers. In AlpineSkiHouse we rely on the cookie provided, which is implemented in `CookiRequestCultureProvider`. Using the cookie method, the current culture is set via a cookie named `.AspNetCore.Culture`. If the cookie is not set, the default request culture is used.

We need to provide a way for the user to see both what language/region is currently selected and an option to select from the list of supported cultures. As seems to be common for many websites, we are displaying the current language/region as a link in the footer.

Footer section in Views/Shared/_Layout.cshtml

```
<footer>
    @await Html.PartialAsync("_CurrentLanguage")
    <p>&copy; @DateTime.Now.Year.ToString() - AlpineSkiHouse</p>
</footer>
```

In the _CurrentLanguage partial, we can access the current culture by requesting the `IRequest-CultureFeature` from the view context.

Views/Shared/_CurrentLanguage.cshtml

```
@using Microsoft.AspNetCore.Http.Features
@using Microsoft.AspNetCore.Localization

@{
    var requestCulture = Context.Features.Get<IRequestCultureFeature>();
}
<div class="pull-left">
    <a asp-controller="SelectLanguage"
       asp-action="Index"
       asp-route-returnUrl="@Context.Request.Path">
         @requestCulture.RequestCulture.Culture.DisplayName
       </a>
    <span> | </span>
</div>
```

The `SelectLanguageController` is able to get a list of the supported cultures from the `Request-LocalizationOptions`. The Index action passes the list of supported cultures to the view, which presents each option as a small form. When the user selects one of the available options, an `HttpPost` is made to the `SetLanguage` action method, which then adds the cookie to the response, setting the current culture. Any future requests that user makes has the current culture set to the culture that was previously selected.

Controllers/SelectLanguageController

```
public class SelectLanguageController : Controller
{
    private readonly RequestLocalizationOptions _requestLocalizationOptions;

    public SelectLanguageController(IOptions<RequestLocalizationOptions>
requestLocalizationOptions)
    {
```

```
            _requestLocalizationOptions = requestLocalizationOptions.Value;
        }

        public IActionResult Index(string returnUrl = null)
        {
            ViewData["ReturnUrl"] = returnUrl;
            return View(_requestLocalizationOptions.SupportedUICultures);
        }

        [HttpPost]
        [ValidateAntiForgeryToken]
        public IActionResult SetLanguage(string cultureName, string returnUrl = null)
        {
            Response.Cookies.Append(
                CookieRequestCultureProvider.DefaultCookieName,
                CookieRequestCultureProvider.MakeCookieValue(new RequestCulture(cultureName)),
                new CookieOptions { Expires = DateTimeOffset.UtcNow.AddYears(1) }
                );

            if (returnUrl != null)
            {
                return LocalRedirect(returnUrl);
            }
            else
            {
                return RedirectToAction("Index", "Home");
            }

        }
    }
}
```

The SetLanguage action method uses the CookieRequestCultureProvider to generate a
cookie value for the selected culture. The cookie is added to the Response using the default cookie
name from the CookieRequestProvider and an expiry of one year.

The Index view displays a simple form and button for each supported culture. Clicking one of these
buttons initiates an HttpPost to the SetLanguage action method with the appropriate cultureName
route value set.

Views/SelectLanguage/Index.cshtml

```
@using System.Globalization
@using Microsoft.AspNetCore.Mvc.Localization

@model IEnumerable<CultureInfo>
@inject IViewLocalizer Localizer

<h2>@Localizer["Select your language"]</h2>

<div class="row">
    @foreach(var culture in Model)
    {
        <div class="col-md-3">
            <form asp-action="SetLanguage" method="post"
```

```
            asp-route-cultureName="@culture.Name"
             asp-route-returnUrl="@ViewData["ReturnUrl"]">
            <button class="btn btn-link" type="submit">
               @culture.DisplayName
            </button>
        </form>
      </div>

    }
  </div>
```

Summary

Now our application is fully globalized and can be easily set up to support new cultures. Adding support for additional cultures requires new culture specific resources files, and some minor modifications to the list of supported cultures in `Startup.cs`. For all but the smallest applications, the globalization process is time consuming and costly when done late in the product development lifecycle. Consider globalizing your application early on if there is any chance your application will require support for multiple cultures.

Another important consideration is the cost of fully translating the resources for an application. Translation is time consuming and requires a specialized skill-set that might be difficult to find. Once translated resources have been created, a significant amount of testing is also required to ensure the application behaves correctly and that all text has been translated appropriately.

In the next chapter, we tackle some of the complexity that has crept into the Alpine Ski House application by exploring some refactoring techniques to improve code quality.

## CHAPTER 23

Refactoring and Improving Code Quality

"Ugly!" Marc was on the warpath.

"UGLY!" He was storming around the office yelling and stomping as only Marc could.

Danielle took out her headphones, checked the date on her computer, sighed, and moved to intercept Marc. Thursdays were her designated day to calm Marc down. If only this were a Wednesday it would be Chester's job. "What's up, Marc?"

As she knew he would, Marc wheeled around and walked over to Danielle. "I hate this code, Danielle. I hate every line, every semicolon, every whitespace character. Tabs and spaces, Danielle, I'm an equal opportunity hater."

"What's wrong with it?"

"Well just look at it, the methods are long, there are unused variables, and what is this? A string called stringybob?"

"There is not a string called stringybob," laughed Danielle.

"Okay that one I made up, but the rest are true."

"Do you know about refactoring, Marc?"

"Nope, is it a Buick?"

"Not at all" replied Danielle. "It is a way to improve code quality incrementally and safely. I have a book on it right here. Why don't you read it and come back in a couple of hours?"

"You know what, Danielle I think I will. Thanks a lot." Placated, Marc went back to his desk and sat down. As soon as he was gone, Chester came over to see Danielle.

"I'm sorry Danielle," he said sheepishly.

"What are you sorry for?" asked Danielle.

"I saw Marc on the warpath and I sort of changed the date on your computer. It is only Wednesday."

Few are ever satisfied with the code they wrote a year ago. The running joke in many programming shops is the frequency of situations where somebody exclaims "Who wrote this garbage?" only to find in looking at the history, that it was them. This is a great position to be in. When we write code for the first time, we're often struggling with understanding the domain, the programming problem, and the shape of an application that has yet to be written. There is only so much at a time that one mind can contain and all these moving parts frequently lead to mistakes being made in the structure or function of code. It is the greatest of luxuries to be able to go back and fix old code months later after your understanding of the application has improved.

In this chapter, we explore the idea of refactoring and how we can improve the application functions without breaking everything.

What is refactoring?

Refactoring is a term that was coined in the early 1990's by William Opdyke and Ralph Johnson. Yes, there is a book written by the Gang of Four. Refactoring means changing the internal structure of a chunk of code to be more understandable, testable, adaptable, or performant, while not changing the outward facing functionality. If you think of a function as a black box that you can feed input into and gather outputs from, changing the internal wiring of the black box shouldn't matter so long as the inputs and outputs remain unchanged, as shown in Figure 23-1.

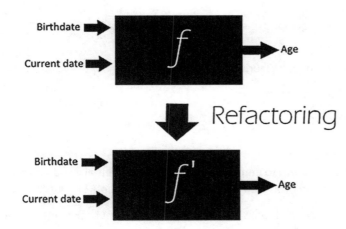

FIGURE 23-1 Refactoring takes a function f and replaces it with f' which yields the same inputs and outputs

This observation allows you to replace or substitute different code into your application, while maintaining the same functionality and improving the overall quality of the application. Although we've used the term function here as a unit of code, refactoring does not need to be limited in its scope to the internals of a function. Object oriented programming is all about introducing abstractions where possible as protection against leaking implementation details. There are plenty of constructs that you can consider as a black box for the purposes of refactoring. Classes are a prime candidate. The implementation of a class is not a matter of great importance, and as long as the inputs and outputs remain the same, we can feel free to alter how it works to our heart's content. Namespaces do not enforce quite the same level of protection as classes, and can be considered as replaceable units also. Finally, in a world of microservices, an entire application can be swapped out for a different application as part of a refactoring.

Consider a service whose responsibility is to send emails to a mailing list. The inputs might be a list of recipients and an email to send. The output is not so much an output, but rather an outcome, which is when all the addresses on the recipient list have received an email, as shown in Figure 23-2

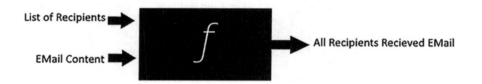

FIGURE 23-2 A larger refactoring of an entire microservice

It doesn't really matter if the microservice sends emails using Sendgrid or its own mail server. In either case, the result is the same. In this case, swapping microservices can be considered refactoring.

Programmers commonly refer to anything that makes improvements to code as refactoring. Removed an extra parameter on a method? Added logging around a tricky method to better support devops? While both of those improve code quality or application quality, neither of them are technically refactorings because they change the functionality of the application. Strictly adhering to the definition of refactoring requires that there is *no* change to inputs, including extra parameters, nor outputs, including extra log messages.

Measuring Quality

If refactorings are embarked upon to improve code quality, we must surely have some form of measuring code quality. It would be wonderful to place in your laps, the solution to measuring code quality—a metric so perfect that it can represent all aspects of code quality in a single number. Unfortunately, no such metric exists. A myriad of code quality metrics have been suggested over the years from measuring afferent and efferent coupling, to estimating the number of errors in a line of code, to code coverage by tests. Deciding on a suite of code quality metrics to use is likely a book onto itself.

It is useful to focus on a few simple metrics to measure code quality:

- **Does the code do what it is supposed to?** It seems simple, but often this is an overlooked metric. This can be measured by the number of bugs reported per thousand lines of code or bugs per class. Some developers use this metric in a global way by examining the comparative code quality of two projects by the number of defects found. This is counterproductive, however, because no two projects solve the same problem. Would you expect a system for creating and delivering online birthday cards to have the same level of complexity or number of bugs as a system for controlling an insulin pump? Of course not. This metric, and most others, should simply be used as a way to see if the team and the product is improving over time.

- **Does the code meet its non-functional requirements?** These requirements are things that are not related to the inputs and outputs of the function. An example might be the performance of a piece of code or whether or not the code is secure.

- **Is the code understandable?** No piece of code is perfect and somebody, inevitably, needs to update it due to a bug or a changing requirement. That somebody might, in fact, be the original author: you! Look at this code:

```
for (var i = 1; i < parts.length; i++) {
        root[parts[i]] = root[parts[i]] || (root[parts[i]] = {});
        root = root[parts[i]];
}
```

This code might be efficient and smart, but it's almost incomprehensible. An objective metric for readability or understandability is difficult to achieve. The metric here is less of a number and more of a consensus of maintainability by the developers. It is unusual for a team of modest individuals to greatly disagree on the understandability of a section of code. Code reviews are dynamite for finding parts of code with poor understandability.

Another lightweight metric you can use is the cyclometric complexity, which measures the complexity of functions by looking at the number of code paths through the method. A method with a single *if* statement has two possible code paths and therefore has a cyclomatic complexity of two, as shown in Figure 23-3.

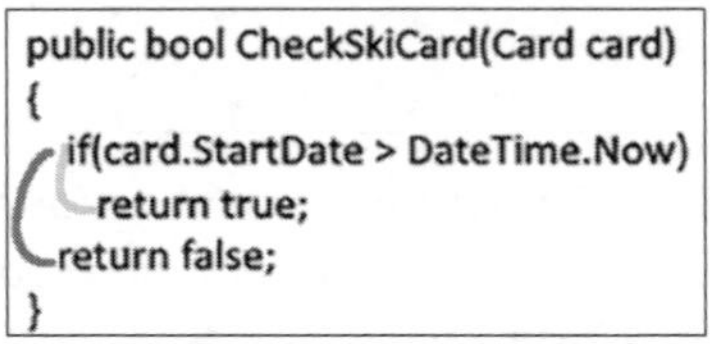

```
public bool CheckSkiCard(Card card)
{
    if(card.StartDate > DateTime.Now)
        return true;
    return false;
}
```

FIGURE 23-3 There are two possible code paths through this function

- **Can the code react to changes in requirements easily?** Again, this is not a metric that finds itself in a position to be expressed with a simple numeric value. Instead, it is a feeling a mature team develops. The look of pain on developers' faces when a large change is suggested should be enough of an indication on whether the goal has been reached.

> ### Showing Cyclomatic Complexity in Visual Studio
>
> There are a bunch of tools for showing code complexity metrics in Visual Studio. A good free one is the Code Metrics Viewer from: *https://visualstudiogallery.msdn.microsoft.com/03de6710-4573-460c-aded-96588572dc19*. The CodeRush tool from DevExpress goes one step further and includes code metric numbers next to every method. It is a great visual aide for reminding developers that a function should not be expanded further.

These four simple metrics should be a good starting point to decide what areas of the application are ripe for some refactoring help. As the application matures and grows, it is likely that new metrics will be identified and included.

With all of these metrics, it is important to ensure that you're not optimizing for the wrong metric. People have a tendency to game the system, knowingly or not. If a metric for performance is put into place to ensure that a function returns as quickly as possible but no metric is put into place to ensure that its memory footprint is reasonable, there is a huge incentive to optimize the function to trade memory for clock cycles. Consider if that is really what you want to achieve or if a balance is really the end goal. It pays to review the metrics to ensure that they aren't optimizing for the wrong things and then you should update them if they are.

Finding Time to Refactor

Frequently, developers complain that the business allocates no time to do refactorings and improve code quality. The business sees little value in improving code quality until it becomes a major problem and starts costing the company measurable quantities of money. You might be reminded of the previous warning about selecting incorrect metrics and that can certainly be the truth.

Refactoring does not need to be something you take on as a discrete activity. Instead, refactoring should be the natural offshoot of working in a code base. Notice a method that is too long for its own good? Refactor it while you are in the file, even if it was for other purposes. Perhaps a variable with a confusing name has slowed you down while changing some code. Rename it and save yourself from wasting time next time you're in the code. Refactoring should be approached like Robert Baden Powell, founder of the Scouting movement, suggests the way that boys approach the world:

"Try and leave this world a little better than you found it and when your turn comes to die, you can die happy in feeling that at any rate you have not wasted your time but have done your best. 'Be Prepared' in this way, to live happy and to die happy — stick to your Scout Promise always — even after you have ceased to be a boy — and God help you to do it."

—Robert Baden Powell

Do not perform a commit unless it improves the quality of code. In a legacy code base, fixing all the code by doing only minor, small-scale improvements might seem futile, but small changes add up over time. Unmaintainable code was not written in a single day and it is not fixed in a single day either, but just as you can pay down a mortgage over the years by paying off a tiny percentage, you can also pay down technical debt in much the same way. Paying down debt, either technical or fiscal, is interesting because paying down just slightly more in the early years can have a massive impact on the lifetime of the debt. As the principle is reduced, the amount of money going to the principle instead of the interest increases. Similarly, with technical debt the more you pay off, the more time you free up to pay down more debt. Start today, do not delay!

Refactoring with a Safety Net

Changing code that has been working for years is not without risk. Subtle differences in how the old code and the new code works might be responsible for introducing a terrible bug. Before making changes to an existing piece of code, be sure that it is well tested.

If you're lucky, you find that the method is indeed under test and no further work is required before making changes. In most cases, however, you aren't so lucky. Legacy code bases tend to be characterized by not being well covered by automated tests. In fact, the lack of automated testing is exactly how some people define legacy code.

> **Note** The de facto book for learning how to maintain and update legacy code is certainly Michael Feather's book "Working Effectively with Legacy Code." It presents a number of fantastic approaches to decoupling code and getting it under test. If you're looking for something more specific to ASP.NET there is "Evolving Legacy ASP.NET Web Applications" by Simon Timms and David Paquette.

Before starting on the refactoring, we need to write tests to test what the function currently does. These tests are called Characterization Tests and they act as living documentation of what the method actually does. It might be that the code under test is actually incorrect in which case the characterization tests we write are enforcing that incorrectness. Frequently in legacy code bases incorrect behavior is relied upon so correcting the underlying code will break the application. Characterization tests are different from most of the tests you would normally write, because of this. Testing incorrect functionality can be a disturbing switch for developers, but it helps to think of the tests as preventing future bugs rather than addressing existing bugs. Often, some other piece of code relies on the broken functionality and fixing the "broken" behavior actually breaks things.

> **Tip** IntelliTest has been under development at Microsoft for years and was finally included in Visual Studio 2015 Enterprise. It is a tool that examines the execution paths for a function and provides inputs that execute every possible code path. These inputs can then be used to create unit tests that act as perfect characterization tests. The tool is not without limits however, because it doesn't work on 64-bit code and cannot generate XUnit tests, but it does find boundary cases that you might not otherwise find.

With the method under tests, we can continue to refactor without fear of breaking things.

Let's take a look at some code from Alpine Ski House to wrap with characterization tests to ensure future refactorings don't break. The Handle method of AddSkiPassOnPurchaseCompleted.cs is a prime candidate. It is a fairly long method at 30 lines and isn't currently covered by any tests. The cyclomatic complexly is fairly low at three, so other than the length, there may be little enough reason to refactor it from the perspective of complexity (see Listing 23-1).

LISTING 23-1 The current handler function for the purchased compled notification

```
public void Handle(PurchaseCompleted notification)
{
    var newPasses = new List<Pass>();
    foreach (var passPurchase in notification.Passes)
    {
        Pass pass = new Pass
        {
            CardId = passPurchase.CardId,
            CreatedOn = DateTime.UtcNow,
            PassTypeId = passPurchase.PassTypeId
        };
        newPasses.Add(pass);
    }

    _passContext.Passes.AddRange(newPasses);
    _passContext.SaveChanges();

    foreach (var newPass in newPasses)
    {
        var passAddedEvent = new PassAdded
        {
            PassId = newPass.Id,
            PassTypeId = newPass.PassTypeId,
            CardId = newPass.CardId,
            CreatedOn = newPass.CreatedOn
        };
        _bus.Publish(passAddedEvent);
    }

}
```

At first glance, the inputs and outputs are minimal. The method takes a single notification and returns void. Digging a little deeper, however, reveals that the method writes to the database and publishes events. These events also count as outputs. It seems like we need a test to check that passes are added to the database and another to test that publishing happens. We might also need to test what happens if there are no passes in the notification.Passes collection.

To start, let's put in place test skeletons for how we think things in this function work (see Listing 23-2).

LISTING 23-2 A testing skeleton for the purchase completed event handler

```
public class AddSkiPassOnPurchaseCompletedTests
{
    public class When_handling_purchase_completed
    {
        [Fact]
        public void Pass_is_saved_to_the_database_for_each_pass()
        {
            throw new NotImplementedException();
        }

        [Fact]
        public void PassesAddedEvents_is_published_for_each_pass()
        {
            throw new NotImplementedException();
        }

        [Fact]
        public void Empty_passes_collection_saves_nothing_to_the_database()
        {
            throw new NotImplementedException();
        }
    }
}
```

The test skeletons, shown in Listing 23-2, are useful placeholders to remind you to implement a test. Often while writing one test, you discover other behaviors that you want to get under tests. Instead of changing gears to write a whole new test, just put in a skeleton as a reminder to come back later. Implementing the first test is probably the most difficult. We need to make use of an in memory EF context, as discussed in Chapter 20, "Testing," as well as a mock object for the bus. The test shown in Listing 23-3 builds a PassPurchased event then passes it to the handler to be acted upon. The properties expected in the data base are then asserted.

LISTING 23-3 The filled in test skeleton testing the data in the context is as expected

```
[Fact]
public void Pass_is_saved_to_the_database_for_each_pass()
{
    using (PassContext context =
            new PassContext(InMemoryDbContextOptionsFactory.Create<PassContext>()))
    {
        var mediator = new Mock<IMediator>();
        var sut = new AddSkiPassOnPurchaseCompleted(context, mediator.Object);
        var passPurchased = new PassPurchased
        {
            CardId = 1,
            PassTypeId = 2,
            DiscountCode = "2016springpromotion",
            PricePaid = 200m
        };
        sut.Handle(new Events.PurchaseCompleted
        {
            Passes = new List<PassPurchased>
                    {
                            passPurchased
                    }
        });

        Assert.Equal(1, context.Passes.Count());
        Assert.Equal(passPurchased.CardId, context.Passes.Single().CardId);
        Assert.Equal(passPurchased.PassTypeId, context.Passes.Single().PassTypeId);
    }
}
```

Particularly astute readers might notice in Listing 23-3 that we test two properties on the created Pass from the database, but that in the original code, we set three properties. The missing piece is the CreateOn date, which is set to UTCNow. Dates are always troublesome to test because time moves on between creating the date and testing it. Often you see intricate logic in place to do fuzzy matching on the dates, but instead we can inject an object to get dates for us (see Listing 23-4).

LISTING 23-4 A date service which simply wraps UtcNow for purposes of injecting

```
public class DateService : IDateService
{
    public DateTime Now()
    {
        return DateTime.UtcNow;
    }
}
```

This can be injected into the AddSkiPAssOnPurchaseCompleted class via the constructor, and the code can be updated to use it (see Listing 23-5).

LISTING 23-5 Leveraging the date service

```
Pass pass = new Pass
{
    CardId = passPurchase.CardId,
    CreatedOn = _dateService.Now(),
    PassTypeId = passPurchase.PassTypeId
};
```

There is some risk to changing the implementation, but the risk is likely less than the risk of leaving the object only partly tested. You have to use your best judgement to tell if this change requires additional tests. The updated test look like Listing 23-6.

LISTING 23-6 The updated test using the date service

```
[Fact]
public void Pass_is_saved_to_the_database_for_each_pass()
{
    using (PassContext context =
            new PassContext(InMemoryDbContextOptionsFactory.Create<PassContext>()))
    {
        var mediator = new Mock<IMediator>();
        var dateService = new Mock<IDateService>();
        var currentDate = DateTime.UtcNow;
        dateService.Setup(x => x.Now()).Returns(currentDate);
        var sut = new AddSkiPassOnPurchaseCompleted(context, mediator.Object, dateService.
Object);
        var passPurchased = new PassPurchased
        {
            CardId = 1,
            PassTypeId = 2,
            DiscountCode = "2016springpromotion",
            PricePaid = 200m
        };
        sut.Handle(new Events.PurchaseCompleted
        {
            Passes = new List<PassPurchased>
                    {
                        passPurchased
                    }
        });

        Assert.Equal(1, context.Passes.Count());
        Assert.Equal(passPurchased.CardId, context.Passes.Single().CardId);
        Assert.Equal(passPurchased.PassTypeId, context.Passes.Single().PassTypeId);
        Assert.Equal(currentDate, context.Passes.Single().CreatedOn);
    }
}
```

This approach to extracting the date logic can be useful for testing dates in the future as well as in the past. We can now implement the remaining test methods, shown in Listing 23-7.

```
[Fact]
public void PassesAddedEvents_is_published_for_each_pass()
{
    using (PassContext context =
            new PassContext(InMemoryDbContextOptionsFactory.Create<PassContext>()))
    {
        var mediator = new Mock<IMediator>();
        var dateService = new Mock<IDateService>();
        var currentDate = DateTime.UtcNow;
        dateService.Setup(x => x.Now()).Returns(currentDate);
        var sut = new AddSkiPassOnPurchaseCompleted(context, mediator.Object, dateService.
Object);
        var passPurchased = new PassPurchased
        {
            CardId = 1,
            PassTypeId = 2,
            DiscountCode = "2016springpromotion",
            PricePaid = 200m
        };
        sut.Handle(new Events.PurchaseCompleted
        {
            Passes = new List<PassPurchased>
            {
                passPurchased
            }
        });
        var dbPass = context.Passes.Single();
        mediator.Verify(x => x.Publish(It.Is<PassAdded>(y => y.CardId == passPurchased.
CardId &&
                                        y.CreatedOn == currentDate
&&
                                        y.PassId == dbPass.Id &&
                                        y.PassTypeId ==
passPurchased.PassTypeId)));
    }
}
```

This test performs the set up of the handler, and then leverages the mock object presented by the Moq library to verify that events were fired. The lambda passed to It.Is checks each property on the event.

You may notice that there is a great deal of similarity between this test and the previous test. Certainly there are some commonalities we can refactor out of the tests to make future tests easier. Even in test code, it is important to maintain good readability. Our final test looks like Listing 23-8.

LISTING 23-8 Testing the case where an empty collection is passed to the handler

```
[Fact]
public void Empty_passes_collection_saves_nothing_to_the_database()
{
    using (PassContext context = GetContext())
    {
        var mediator = new Mock<IMediator>();
        var dateService = new Mock<IDateService>();
        var currentDate = DateTime.UtcNow;
        dateService.Setup(x => x.Now()).Returns(currentDate);
        var sut = new AddSkiPassOnPurchaseCompleted(context, mediator.Object, dateService.
Object);
        sut.Handle(new Events.PurchaseCompleted { Passes = new List<PassPurchased>() });

        Assert.Equal(0, context.Passes.Count());
    }
}
```

This test checks to make sure that passing in an empty collection doesn't save anything to the database. We don't really expect anything to be saved to the database even if the underlying code is broken, but there is a good chance that there will be exceptions thrown due to empty collections. It is always a good idea to test negative cases such as these.

While writing this test, however, it became obvious that another test had been missed, which is the equivalent test for publishing messages when the passes collection is empty (see Listing 23-9).

LISTING 23-9 A test ensuring that no messages are published

```
[Fact]
public void Empty_passes_collection_publishes_no_messages()
{
    using (PassContext context = GetContext())
    {
        var mediator = new Mock<IMediator>();
        var dateService = new Mock<IDateService>();
        var currentDate = DateTime.UtcNow;
        dateService.Setup(x => x.Now()).Returns(currentDate);
        var sut = new AddSkiPassOnPurchaseCompleted(context, mediator.Object, dateService.
Object);

        sut.Handle(new Events.PurchaseCompleted { Passes = new List<PassPurchased>() });

        mediator.Verify(x => x.Publish(It.IsAny<PassAdded>()), Times.Never);
    }
}
```

This final test mirrors the one in Listing 23-8, but checks that there are no messages published by the mediator.

These four tests serve to characterize the function we're refactoring. None of them focus on the internal structure of the function, but they do check all the inputs and outputs from the function. Now we can change whatever we want about the internals of the function and know that as long as the four tests pass, we aren't breaking any of the code that relies on the function.

Refactoring without a safety net in place can be done, but it should make you feel uncomfortable and you should worry about the unintended side effects of the changes. The best part about adding these sorts of tests is that they become general tests that help build the integrity of your test suite. If you like, you can annotate your characterization tests so that they don't become confused with regular tests.

Data Driven Changes

In Chapter 12, "Configuration and Logging" we talked about the importance of logging and how it can be useful in production scenarios. Well now that is becoming important. During their initial roll out to the testing group, the Alpine Ski team found that some areas of the site were throwing exceptions. They were able to look into their logs and analyze the thrown exceptions over the history of the project to see which areas were particularly problematic. This sort of analysis is better known as heat mapping and is used to find hotspots in the application.

Knowing where problems frequently arise in the application gives us a solid hint for where to start refactoring. You might want to overlay the error heat map with another map that shows which areas of the application are most frequently visited.

Imagine that you have these number for errors per request and for number of requests daily, as shown in Table 23-1.

TABLE 23-1 Errors per request and number of requests daily

Area	# errors per request	# of requests daily
Login	0.002	123
Landing Page	0.0003	50000
Register	0.1	10
Purchase Pass	0.2	50

At first glance it might seem that the high error rate on Purchase Pass would be the greatest concern, but there are actually more users affected by the landing page errors.

Many engineering organizations like GitLabs, Etsy, and the Windows product group, gather extensive metrics about how their applications work and how people interact with them. They would not move forward with doing refactoring without having metrics around the existing code. Characterization unit tests are great for measuring the functional properties of methods, but often we're also interested in making sure that we haven't introduced regressions in performance. Being able to see real world data on the performance of our refactoring is invaluable. Data driven development is a larger discussion than simply refactoring or code quality and is certainly worthwhile.

A Code Cleanup Example

Learning to do effective code cleanup is a long process and certainly one that can take years to learn properly. Taking a look at a code example is instructive. Fortunately, like any project of any complexity, there are plenty of candidates in Alpine Ski House to refactor. A good candidate is the Create action in `SkiCardController` (see Listing 23-10).

LISTING 23-10 The create action in the `SkiCardController`

```
public async Task<ActionResult> Create(CreateSkiCardViewModel viewModel)
{
    // return to view if the modelstate is invalid
    if (!ModelState.IsValid)
        return View(viewModel);

    // create and save the card
    string userId = _userManager.GetUserId(User);
    _logger.LogDebug("Creating ski card for " + userId);

    using (_logger.BeginScope("CreateSkiCard:" + userId))
    {
        var createImage = viewModel.CardImage != null;
        Guid? imageId = null;

        if (createImage)
        {
            _logger.LogInformation("Uploading ski card image for " + userId);
            imageId = Guid.NewGuid();
            string imageUri = await _uploadservice.UploadFileFromStream("cardimages",
imageId + ".jpg", viewModel.CardImage.OpenReadStream());
        }

        _logger.LogInformation("Saving ski card to DB for " + userId);
        SkiCard s = new SkiCard
        {
            ApplicationUserId = userId,
            CreatedOn = DateTime.UtcNow,
            CardHolderFirstName = viewModel.CardHolderFirstName,
            CardHolderLastName = viewModel.CardHolderLastName,
            CardHolderBirthDate = viewModel.CardHolderBirthDate.Value.Date,
            CardHolderPhoneNumber = viewModel.CardHolderPhoneNumber,
            CardImageId = imageId
        };
        _skiCardContext.SkiCards.Add(s);
        await _skiCardContext.SaveChangesAsync();

        _logger.LogInformation("Ski card created for " + userId);
    }

    _logger.LogDebug("Ski card for " + userId + " created successfully, redirecting to
Index...");
    return RedirectToAction(nameof(Index));
}
```

This method performs validation, and saves a record to the database. At first glance, the method looks quite long, and indeed it is, clocking in at 42 lines long and with a maintenance complexity of 206.

> **Note** The maintenance complexity we use here is a CodeRush specific measure. Its goal is to reduce the signal-to-noise ratio of many existing code metrics. Maintenance complexity assigns a point score to various code constructs, like locks and comments and try/catch blocks. These scores are added up to give an idea of how complex the methods are. Ideally we'd like the numbers to be under 100. The original blog post detailing the logic behind the calculation has been lost, but Mark Miller's post has been republished at *http://www.skorkin. com/2010/11/code-metrics-heres-your-new-code-metric/#.V_8P__ArKUk*.

FIGURE 23-4 Screenshot of the lines of code annotated by CodeRush. The 42 in the left gutter is the maintenance complexity

Let's first address a number of code quality issues before we attempt to break the method out to make it easier to understand and have fewer lines. An easy win is the use of + to concatenate strings. Modern versions of C# support string interpolation, which allows you to replace the concatenation.

```
//before
_logger.LogDebug("Ski card for " + userId + " created successfully, redirecting to Index...");
//after
_logger.LogDebug($"Ski card for {userId} created successfully, redirecting to Index...");
```

Next, there is a variable `imageUri` that is created, but never written. Here, the variable can be removed completely and we can just ignore the return value. While we're looking at variables, let's take a look at some of the variable names. A SkiCard called *s* is confusing because *s* doesn't really tell us anything about what the variable is or does. A common convention is to name the variable after the type when there is only a single instance of it (see Listing 23-11).

LISTING 23-11 Creating a ski card

```
var skiCard = new SkiCard
{
    ApplicationUserId = userId,
    CreatedOn = DateTime.UtcNow,
    CardHolderFirstName = viewModel.CardHolderFirstName,
    CardHolderLastName = viewModel.CardHolderLastName,
    CardHolderBirthDate = viewModel.CardHolderBirthDate.Value.Date,
    CardHolderPhoneNumber = viewModel.CardHolderPhoneNumber,
    CardImageId = imageId
};
_skiCardContext.SkiCards.Add(skiCard);
```

At the same time, we make the variable implicit using var. This is a stylistic choice, but if languages like F# can infer types everywhere, there is no reason that C# can't do this type inference for us.

Next is the null check for card image, which is done as a distinct step with a temporary variable called createImage. Temporary variables are useful if you need to do a resource intensive operation and save the result to use in a number of places in your function. That doesn't appear to be the case here however, because the variable is only used once and it is a simple null check so it is not at all intensive. We can inline the variable as seen here:

```
if (viewModel.CardImage != null)
{ ...
```

Our method is down to 40 lines and a maintenance complexity of 165, but there is still opportunity to further reduce the complexity. A good hint about things that can be extracted is the location of comments. The debate about the utility of comments in source code is ongoing, but the majority now seem to be in the camp of self-documenting code being sufficient. Comments should be reserved for the why rather than the how. For example, look at this comment:

```
//What's this a lock? Do you not care about performance? Do you hate everybody?
//Calm down, there is a good reason: when we request a new key from SBT they invalidate
//the previous key so if we ask for two it automatically invalidates one of them. We
//need the lock to ensure that we're not invalidating our own keys.
```

This gives some insight into why an unusual block of code exists. The comment in our example, method // create and save the card, does nothing to help with the why. All it does is suggest the start of a block of code that is better as a function. We can extract a few functions from our code and then remove the comments. In the end, our code cleanup looks like Listing 23-12.

```
private async Task<Guid> UploadImage(CreateSkiCardViewModel viewModel, string userId)
{
    Guid imageId;
    _logger.LogInformation("Uploading ski card image for " + userId);
    imageId = Guid.NewGuid();
    await _uploadservice.UploadFileFromStream("cardimages", $"{imageId}.jpg", viewModel.
CardImage.OpenReadStream());
    return imageId;
}
private bool HasCardImage(CreateSkiCardViewModel viewModel)
{
    return viewModel.CardImage != null;
}
private async Task CreateAndSaveCard(CreateSkiCardViewModel viewModel)
{
    var userId = _userManager.GetUserId(User);
    _logger.LogDebug($"Creating ski card for {userId}");

    using (_logger.BeginScope($"CreateSkiCard: {userId}"))
    {
        Guid? imageId = null;
        if (HasCardImage(viewModel))
        {
            imageId = await UploadImage(viewModel, userId);
        }

        _logger.LogInformation($"Saving ski card to DB for {userId}");
        var skiCard = new SkiCard
        {
            ApplicationUserId = userId,
            CreatedOn = DateTime.UtcNow,
            CardHolderFirstName = viewModel.CardHolderFirstName,
            CardHolderLastName = viewModel.CardHolderLastName,
            CardHolderBirthDate = viewModel.CardHolderBirthDate.Value.Date,
            CardHolderPhoneNumber = viewModel.CardHolderPhoneNumber,
            CardImageId = imageId
        };
        _skiCardContext.SkiCards.Add(skiCard);
        await _skiCardContext.SaveChangesAsync();

        _logger.LogInformation("Ski card created for " + userId);
    }
}
// POST: SkiCard/Create
[HttpPost]
[ValidateAntiForgeryToken]
public async Task<ActionResult> Create(CreateSkiCardViewModel viewModel)
{
    if (!ModelState.IsValid)
        return View(viewModel);

    await CreateAndSaveCard(viewModel);

    _logger.LogDebug($"Ski card for {_userManager.GetUserId(User)} created successfully,
redirecting to Index...");
    return RedirectToAction(nameof(Index));
}
```

The code is broken up into a number of functions, each of which has a single purpose. No method here has a maintenance complexity over 100 or a line count over 30. The code is cleaner and, thanks to extracting methods like HasCardImage, it's easier to read.

Tools That Want to Help

Some fantastic tools exist for analyzing code and suggesting solutions. We've already talked a little bit about CodeRush, but Resharper, or R# as it is commonly known, is another popular tool. Both Code-Rush and R# are more than code analysis tools, they also provide refactoring and productivity tools.

StyleCop and NDepend are code analysis tools that apply rules to your code to enforce good practices. For example, NDepend can be set up to throw errors whenever a method is too long or too complex, which prevents this code from ever making it into the product in the first place.

The cheapest and easiest tool is one you already have: the compiler. Simply switching on Warnings as Errors in the project configuration forces you to fix compiler warnings. Warnings are there for a reason and in almost every case, they are highlighting some subtle problem with your code.

Getting to Quality

Improving code quality in an application needs to be a concerted effort by the entire team. The single most important thing you need to improve code quality is not a swish tool like CodeRush or NDepend, it is a sense of shared code ownership inside the team. There should never be a time when you look at a piece of code and think, "Oh Leonids wrote this, so I had best not change it." Code reviews and pair programming can go a long way to improving the culture of a team and pulling them away from feeling a strong sense of attachment to a piece of code.

> **Note** It is all too easy to fall prey to having negative code reviews like: "Why did you do this?" and "This looks inefficient" and so forth. These comments don't help anybody and can tear a team apart. Lori Lalonde talks about the culture of code reviews in her blog post The Code Review Blues, located at *http://www.westerndevs.com/the-code-review-blues/*.

Summary

Refactoring and code cleanup is like paying down a mortgage: The quicker you pay it down, the easier the payments become. To paraphrase a Chinese proverb, "The best time to improve quality was six months ago, the second best time is now." By simply improving one thing, each commit to your code becomes easier to maintain and more enjoyable to work with.

Making changes to untested code can be dangerous. It is best to build a suite of tests around your code before going too deep into cleaning it up. As a rule, clean code that doesn't work properly is worse than messy code that works.

Finally, try to foster a sense of shared code ownership. The entire team should be outraged by messy, difficult to maintain code. Messy code tends to beget messy code, while clean code encourages developers to write more clean code. It is the broken windows theory of software development.

In the final chapter, next, we'll take a look at how we can keep the code in our application organized in way that is scalable and easy to maintain.

## CHAPTER 24

Organizing the Code

Everything was going well and Danielle was looking forward to some time off after implementation. She thought perhaps she would go somewhere that had no skiing, no ski passes and certainly no Entity Framework. In the last retrospective Mark had been complaining about the size of some of the controllers. Today she was feeling that pain.

This was the third time she had been forced to rebase her changes while working on this controller. Other people were making changes to the code at the same time and they kept beating her to the check in. Danielle was convinced the situation can be improved and she was pretty sure that she knew how to fix it. She called Mark and Balázs over to her cubicle, giving up on ever getting this file committed.

"Balázs, this code is getting out of hand. We need to fix it," she said

"You'll get no argument from me," chimed in Mark.

"Well," said Balázs, "It looks like we all agree that we have some technical debt related to the structure of the project. In my home country we have a saying Без муки нет науки. It means that we build character from adversity. Let's talk about how we can address this problem because after all Вода□ ка□мень то□чит."

Danielle wasn't sure what any of that meant but it sounded like she had some political will to make the required changes. Now she just had to find some way to get her current change set in before somebody else swooped in on her files.

There are standards for most everything in computers, including standards for networking, standards for plugs, and standards for languages. There are even standards for writing standards (RFC 2119). The standards in computing are a huge triumph. For example, consider the fact that you can buy any video card for your computer. There is no need to buy a Dell video card for your Dell computer because the interface between motherboard and video card is standard. Of course, it hasn't always been this way. In the earlier days of computers, you really did have to buy Compaq components for your Compaq computer. If this same level of standardization that exists in computing existed in other fields, car parts would be interchangeable between manufactures and dishwasher parts would be cheaper, because they could be mass produced to a single standard.

Despite all of this, there really isn't a formalized standard for the directory structure of an ASP.NET MVC project. Oh certainly, there is the structure that exists when you create a new project, but this structure is just a suggestion and it can become a confusing mess quite quickly. The lack of standards is likely a carry-over from the days of WebForms where the lack of formalized structure was a selling point. Every WebForm application ended up as a snowflake application, where different naming conventions and folder structures kept things very interesting. Since that time, we have gained an appreciation for convention over configuration.

In this chapter we'll look at some of the shortcomings of the current directory structure of our project and suggest how you can improve the structure for medium and large projects.

Repository Structure

Before we even get to the project structure, we should visit the structure of the source code repository. It is unusual for a project to have no resources except source code. There are frequently other bits and pieces that need a home, including project logos, build scripts, maintenance scripts, and so forth. Therefore, you should keep source code away from the root directory of the project so it does not mix with these other resources. A simple /src directory is sufficient to achieve this goal.

Moving the source down a directory could be a little confusing for somebody just coming into the project, so you should also include a build script at the top level named something obvious like build. bat. This script can be anything from a simple batch file that calls the solution file in the source directory, to a complete Make file of some sort. In addition, it is often helpful to have a readme file at this level describing what the project does. It doesn't take many projects before people forget what each one does. A readme file at this level provides a place to describe the application.

The rest of the folders at this level are dependent on your project. Experience suggests that when running the application in production that there is a need for scripts and tools. Frequently there is also a need to back fill data, or manipulate messages in error queues. Devops scripts like these need a place to live, somewhere like /tools or /scripts. It is very useful to keep these scripts and tools around. While the very same problem might not, and should not, reappear similar problems might crop up and the ability to modify an existing script is a huge time saver, especially when the scripts all perform boiler plate actions like editing messages in a queue. Waste not, want not!

Speaking of devops scripts, in a world of infrastructure as code, there needs to be somewhere to keep these scripts. There is little point to being able to reproduce your environment from scripts unless they are well versioned and their history is tracked.

Another thing you might want to keep at this level is documentation.

Inside the Source

There is a great temptation to click File | New Project, but most of the time that temptation should be ignored. Adding new projects to the solution makes the build take longer and just produces a large number of DLLs. The belief is that keeping code in different projects provides a degree of isolation. For instance, many people keep interfaces in a Core or Common project and then the implementation in a parallel location in another project, as shown in Figure 24-1. The Blob directory inside the Completions.Common project is mirrored in the `Completions.DataProject`.

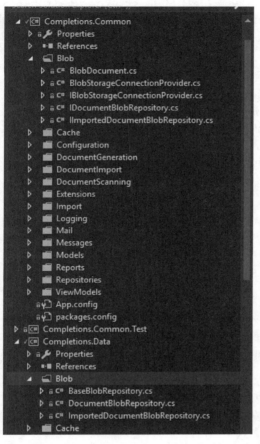

FIGURE 24-1 The project structure of a sample solution that uses several projects

Also, in this screenshot, you can see the Completions.Common.Test project that contains tests for things found inside the Completions.Common project. As you can imagine, taking this approach leads to a proliferation of projects inside a solution. This solution actually contains 22 projects. In most cases, the advantages of creating new projects can be achieved just by using namespaces. Splitting implementations and their interfaces allows you to easily put in new interface implementations. In most cases however, like in Highlander, there is only one implementation. Splitting files into different projects is a premature optimization. Instead of assuming that we will need multiple projects and structuring our applications that way, we should assume the opposite and only split the projects when the need arises.

Another useful thing this screenshot shows is an example of parallel structure.

Parallel Structure

Web applications traditionally split resources by file type. The HTML lives in its own folder, the CSS in another, and the JavaScript in yet another folder. When working on a component there is frequently a need to bounce around between these folders. To make things easier, it is helpful to keep a parallel structure for each directory.

> **Note** Tools such as ReactJS suggest a different organization by component, but for most projects that would be a bridge too far. For instance, in a react project the CSS, JavaScript, and markup are located in the same file, which eliminates the need to keep resources in their own directory. In many ways, this structure makes more sense from a code reuse perspective. We'd rather reuse an entire, encapsulated component than reuse just the CSS or just the JavaScript.

This approach is applicable all over the application. As well as keeping web resources in a parallel structure, unit and integration tests should also be kept in this structure. The default template uses this approach where the views directory parallels the names of the controllers.

MediatR

Organizing the code within a project can be done in any number of ways, but one of the more scalable approaches is to leverage a pattern called Mediator, which decouples the communication between components.

In a mediator pattern the responsibility for communicating is moved into a mediator class. Let's look at an example of how it might work. Whenever riders scan their passes at Alpine Ski House, there is a need to check and see if that scan is valid. At the same time the scan should be saved in the database to gather metrics on whether the pass is valid. To do this right now, the code looks like:

```
[HttpPost]
public async Task<IActionResult> Post([FromBody]Scan scan)
{
  _context.Scans.Add(scan);
  await _context.SaveChangesAsync();

  if(_cardValidator.IsValid(scan.CardId, scan.LocationId))
    return StatusCode((int)HttpStatusCode.Created);
  return StatusCode((int)HttpStatusCode.Unauthorized);
}
```

The problem here is that this method is doing a couple of different things at once. It would be better to keep the single responsibility principle intact and reduce it to one thing, meaning that you should extract some of this functionality and decouple the communication between the classes. You can create two new services: one that just logs scans and one that is responsible for checking to see if the card is valid. The controller retains responsibility for converting the response from the card validator into an HTTP status code. The return from the controller method is predicated on the return from the card validator but we always save the scan information to the database. This sounds a bit like a messaging pattern.

A Brief Introduction to the Messaging Pattern

Messaging is an old pattern and, some say, it was how object oriented programming was originally supposed to work. A message is simply a collection of fields together that provide information. If you have a method that takes a few parameters then you can think of the culmination of the parameters as a message, in this case id, date, and numberOfSkiers.

```
public ValidationResult(int id, DateTime date, int numberOfSkiers)
```

There is a lot of overhead to build messages for each and every method in an application, so we allow this deconstructed form as a shortcut. In a distributed system, messages are frequently more formal and are what is sent over the wire between two services, sometimes even with a messaging bus serving as a reliable transport mechanism.

Messages come in two forms: commands and events. A command is an order to do something and you see these named in the imperative, such as LogSkiCardSwipe, DeleteUser, and AddLocation. As with all orders they might be refused if they are not legal. You probably don't want to show this part of the book to your commanding officer. Events on the other hand are notifications that something has happened and are named using past tense. SkiCardSwipeLogged, UserDeleted, and LocationAdded are the equivalent events for the commands previously mentioned. The command is handled by some sort of a service, typically called a command handler. After the command has been successfully completed, the handler might publish a notification or event stating that it has completed the action.

Any number of other services can subscribe to the event. An event is sent from one place after the command has been handled and is received in many places. While a command can be sent from many places, for example a user can be deleted by an admin or the user can delete himself, the command is only handled in the singular command handler.

Implementing a Mediator

There are many ways to implement a mediator. The easiest and least robust is to simply list all the components that might be interested in handling a specific message type in one giant mediator class. You could even split up the mediator class by message type. However, that still leaves you in pretty much the same position that you were in before, which is shown in Figure 24-2.

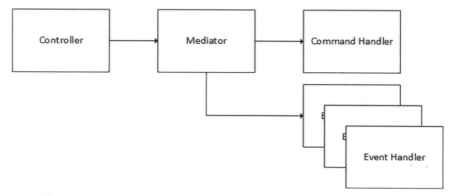

FIGURE 24-2 The naïve implementation of mediator

There remains a class that knows about the command handler and the event handlers and this is what we'd like to avoid. Not wanting classes to know about concrete implementations seems like a problem that was mostly solved in Chapter 14, "Dependency Injection." What we need now is a way of registering command and event handlers in the container and having them wire themselves up.

Fortunately, there is a great implementation of the mediator pattern available called MediatR. It handles the wiring of handlers and of events. The first step in implementing it on Alpine Ski House is to register it with the dependency injection framework. The nugget package you need is called Mediatr. Next, this code must be added to the container configuration:

```
services.AddScoped<SingleInstanceFactory>(p => t => p.GetRequiredService(t));
services.AddScoped<MultiInstanceFactory>(p => t => p.GetServices(t));
services.AddMediatR(typeof(Startup).GetTypeInfo().Assembly);
```

This code registers the mediator as well as two factories that build the command and event handlers. Next, you need to craft a command to send. Start by creating a new directory at the root of the project called `features`. Inside this folder you want to build a sensible directory structure. What's sensible depends on what your project is dealing with. You might want to split up your handlers by bounded context or by entity. You can see how we have set up a features directory for Alpine Ski House in Figure 24-3. Alpine Ski House has already started down the road of dealing in bounded contexts with the separation of the data contexts and we'll continue with that approach to organize the features.

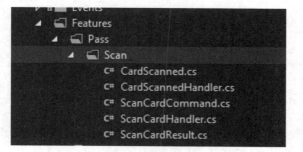

FIGURE 24-3 A screenshot of the feature directory

Let's look at the classes involved. The first one is the ScanCardCommand.

```
public class ScanCardCommand : IAsyncRequest<ScanCardResult>
{
    public int CardId { get; set; }
    public int LocationId { get; set; }
    public DateTime DateTime { get; set; }
}
```

The command contains all the fields that are bound from the client. Commands implement the IAsyncRequest interface and take in a generic parameter, which is the result from the command. In this case, the result is a ScanCardResult, which is a very simple DTO.

```
public class ScanCardResult
    {
        public bool CardIsValid { get; set; }
    }
```

The command handler is perhaps the most interesting part of this command flow.

```
public class ScanCardHandler : IAsyncRequestHandler<ScanCardCommand, ScanCardResult>
{
    private readonly ICardValidator _validator;
    private readonly IMediator _mediator;
    public ScanCardHandler(ICardValidator validator, IMediator mediator)
    {
        _mediator = mediator;
        _validator = validator;
    }

    public async Task<ScanCardResult> Handle(ScanCardCommand message)
    {
        await _mediator.PublishAsync(new CardScanned { CardId = message.CardId, LocationId =
message.LocationId, DateTime = message.DateTime });
        return await Task.FromResult(new ScanCardResult { CardIsValid = _validator.
IsValid(message.CardId, message.LocationId) });
    }
}
```

The constructor here takes advantage of being a participant in dependency injection to pull in the card validator and mediator itself. Ideally, the application should be asynchronous from top to bottom, so the asynchronous interfaces of MediatR are used. Within the asynchronous Handle method, the CardScanned event, or as MediatR calls it "notification," is published and then the validation is run and the ScanCardResult is returned to the caller.

The mediator is responsible for routing the publish event to any event handlers that are interested. In the example here there is but one interested party, the CardScannedHandler:

```
public class CardScannedHandler : IAsyncNotificationHandler<CardScanned>
{
    private readonly PassContext _context;
    public CardScannedHandler(PassContext context)
    {
        _context = context;
```

```
    }

    public async Task Handle(CardScanned notification)
    {
        var scan = new Models.Scan
        {
            CardId = notification.CardId,
            DateTime = notification.DateTime,
            LocationId = notification.LocationId
        };
        _context.Scans.Add(scan);
        await _context.SaveChangesAsync();
    }
}
```

This class implements the IAsyncNotificationHandler for the CardScanned event. This is how MediatR knows to wire it up. Within the Handle method, the notification is used to save data to the database. There can be multiple handlers if you want to do multiple things and each handler should have a very narrow purpose that is easily testable.

This implementation has a few places you might consider putting in improvements. First is the name of the CardScannedHandler. The name tells us nothing about what it does, and if you have many different handlers interested in the same event, there is little to distinguish between them. A better name might be LogCardScanToDatabase. Next, the order of the code in the command handler is questionable. Should the CardScannedEvent be fired before you know if the card is valid? Perhaps. Maybe there is a missing event such as ValidCardScannedEvent or InvalidCardScannedEvent. MediatR observes polymorphism, so if both the ValidCardScannedEvent and InvalidCardScannedEvent extend CardScannedEvent, any subscribers to the base event are also called when a descendant event is fired.

You might be wondering what happened to the controller now that all the logic has been moved inside a couple of handlers and we're glad that you've remained curious. The action method in the controller has shrunk significantly and now only contains:

```
[HttpPost]
public async Task<IActionResult> Post([FromBody]ScanCardCommand scan)
{
    if ((await _mediator.SendAsync(scan)).CardIsValid)
        return StatusCode((int)HttpStatusCode.Created);
    return StatusCode((int)HttpStatusCode.Unauthorized);
}
```

As you can see, the method is highly anemic. It is trivial to write tests around this method and it has but a single responsibility, to translate the ScanCardResult into an HTTP status code.

Leveraging the mediator pattern encourages separation of concerns and allows you to group actions together. Some might consider taking things a step further and locate the controllers and views for the feature in the same directory as the commands and events. Because this is a non-standard location for these items, you need to override some ASP.NET Core MVC conventions to get it to work.

Note ASP.NET MVC is a convention driven framework, so if you follow the conventions, things fall into place nicely. Not every project however, needs to follow the same conventions. In these scenarios, the IApplicationModelConvention interface might be something that you want to look into. The ASP.NET Monsters have a video on it, located at *https://channel9.msdn.com/ Series/aspnetmonsters/ASPNET-Monsters-Ep-68-Creating-Custom-Conventions-for-ASPNET-Core-MVC.*

Areas

Particularly large applications might need to be subdivided into smaller chunks to maintain a semblance of order. Areas are built into ASP.NET MVC and provide a Russian doll like approach to organization. At the root level of the project is an Areas folder that contains one or more different areas. Inside of each area is a Controllers folder, a Views folder, and a Models folder just as there are at the root level (see Figure 24-4).

FIGURE 24-4 The folder structure within an area

Through the magic of routing, these controllers can be accessed after they are annotated with the Area attribute. For instance, a UserController inside of the Admin area would look like:

```
[Area("Admin")]
public class UserController
```

The routing table that comes in the default template should also be updated to include a route for the new areas.

```
app.UseMvc(routes =>
        {
            routes.MapRoute(
                name: "default",
                template: "{controller=Home}/{action=Index}/{id?}");
            routes.MapAreaRoute("defaultArea", "Admin", "{area}/{controller}/{action=Index}/
{id?}");
        });
```

With the new route in place, you can now route to controllers inside of the area.

How does this fit with the idea of feature folders? They can both be used at once for large applications. The need to use both, however, should emerge organically during the construction of the application. You generally don't want to set out from day one to use both.

> **Note** The ever interesting Steve Smith wrote a great MSDN Magazine article on much of what we've covered in this chapter. If you're intrigued and want to see more code, his article located at *https://msdn.microsoft.com/magazine/mt763233* should be your first stop.

Summary

Code organization is difficult. Chances are that the exact approaches presented in this chapter won't be perfect for your needs. It's important to constantly hold moments of introspection to see where the points of pain are in your application and how the structure can be improved to solve these. While modern Integrated Development Environments and even good text editors provide fabulous search and code navigation tools, it is still easier and more intuitive to be able to find the path through code yourself. Consider while you're building the code that the next person who has to navigate the code in six months' time might be you.

Postfix

There was an air of excited exhaustion in the room. Danielle hadn't felt anything like it in years, except maybe back when she was doing competitive skiing. The team had pulled out all the stops in the last week and the application looked amazing. It did everything it was supposed to do, and it did it with style. Danielle couldn't be prouder of what they had accomplished in four weeks if she had fallen into a vat of liquid proudness when she was a baby.

The team sat at one end of the table while the management team wandered in. There was quite the dichotomy between the bedraggled development team and the golf loving management team. They looked relaxed and cool, while a couple of the developers hadn't shaved. Danielle knew the company didn't like this sort of project, which resulted in people not going home on time to their families, and Tim had really gone to bat for them with upper management making it clear that this wasn't going to be a thing that continued after today.

"If 40 hours a week was enough for Henry Ford, then it should be good enough for Alpine Ski House," he had said.

Balázs stood at the front of the room with a computer, some RFID cards and a scanner. He waited for all the golfers to quiet down and listen to the presentation.

"Four weeks ago," he began, "we set out on an impossible project. To build an entire system and get it into production in four short weeks. I'll tell you the truth, at the beginning Tim and I worked pretty hard on strategies to manage expectations and explain why we didn't hit our goals. That was before I knew the team and what they could accomplish."

"They really pulled together on this and, using a brand new technology stack, came up with an application which checks all the boxes we had laid out originally. I wasted that time I spent managing expectations."

With that said Balázs started taking the golfers though how users would log into the application, how they could buy a variety of different types of passes. The golfers looked pretty impressed, they asked a couple of questions but for the most part they sat quietly. Perhaps they were looking to get through the meeting and get back out for a tee time.

It was frosty in the morning now and ski season was probably only a month or so out. The HR people were already sorting through huge piles of resumes of applicants who would become lift operators or ski instructors.

Danielle's ears perked up as she heard Balázs talking about localization "Yes, Frank," he was saying "we've thought of that. I understand that there are a lot of people skiing here who only speak French. We don't have support for multiple languages, but it's something we're planning to do pretty soon. See, Frank, a project like this is never done, since there are always going to be improvements we can make. I've been busy talking to the business, and many of you even," Balázs gestured towards the golfers "to see what other features you'd like in the application. I've compiled a pretty exhaustive list and we'll need to spend some time prioritizing them. I'd say we have enough work here for months to come."

"That," piped up Tim, never one to keep quiet, "is only the start of things too. We have a bunch of other applications we've been thinking about replacing with off the shelf software. The thing is that the off the shelf software is only going to make us as good as our competitors, we think this development team, writing us custom software, will give us a competitive advantage. In this day and age the truth is that every company is a technology company. We have to innovate or perish," Tim looked like he was ready to keep talking about this for quite a while but he was interrupted by one of the golfers that Danielle recognized as the chairman of the board.

"Thanks Tim, based on what we've seen here today I think we probably agree with you." Heads around him nodded in agreement. "This Project Parsley initiative is exactly what we wanted and I can see the path do doing a lot more development in house. Please continue, Balázs."

The developers exchanged nods. Danielle hadn't really been thinking much about finding a new job over the last few weeks. She has been too busy just getting things done. She did know that she didn't want to work for the FBI but that probably wasn't a major revelation.

Balázs continued on through the demo. Everybody was really excited at the RFID readers. "People just ski up?" the golfers asked.

"Yep," replied Balázs, "it is actually a pretty robust system. We can really scale back on checking lift passes, and it should save us money and the skiers should get on the hill much faster."

The demo finally wrapped up and all at once the golfers started asking for features. "Could we have it so you can buy gift cards for people? Could we accept payments in the cafeteria using these same cards? Wouldn't it be cool if an LED sign could greet everybody by name as they came through?"

This was a good sign. The golfers had already accepted that the application was a success and were anxious to add more things to it. Balázs fielded a lot of questions and eventually just told them to come see him the next week. It was going to be quite the task to figure out what the team was going to work on next. The cost of being successful, Danielle supposed. Eventually the golfers gave up on trying to get Balázs to agree to new features on the spot and headed out, half an hour late, their tee time forgotten in the excitement.

Balázs turned to the team and said "I think that went quite well. So it looks pretty good for us being able to continue on the project. I never doubted you all."

"Never?" asked Mark "Didn't you just tell them you doubted us in the beginning?"

"Umm, well mostly never doubted you," squirmed Balázs. "I mean I didn't know any of you yet."

"Okay, okay" said Tim, copying Balázs normal line "I think we're done here. All of you get out of here. I don't want to see any of your faces around here until we launch on Monday morning."

"Okay everybody, be sure to keep your Monday afternoon open too so we can talk about the second phase of the project. I think we're calling it Project Mustard," called Balázs as they filed out. "I call it that because it is going to be so hot! Guys? Guys?" But everybody was already tarragon.

Index

G

H

I

X

Y

About the Authors

 JAMES CHAMBERS, a five-time Microsoft MVP in Developer Technologies, currently develops with ASP.NET Core and the MVC Framework running on Azure and AWS. He is an independent consultant, mentor and active blogger and contributes to several open source projects.

 DAVID PAQUETTE, a four-time Microsoft MVP, is a software developer and independent consultant. He has extensive experience using .NET to build both web-based and Windows applications; deep software engineering knowledge, and a passion for quality user experiences.

 SIMON TIMMS is a multi-year Microsoft MVP, community builder, blogger, developer and independent consultant. His technological interests are varied and he enjoys everything from distributed systems to hot new JavaScript frameworks. He has a strong background in both development as well as operations, and so drives his teams crazy by being involved in everything from builds to development to server provisioning.

Visit us today at

microsoftpressstore.com

- **Hundreds of titles available** – Books, eBooks, and online resources from industry experts

- **Free U.S. shipping**

- **eBooks in multiple formats** – Read on your computer, tablet, mobile device, or e-reader

- **Print & eBook Best Value Packs**

- **eBook Deal of the Week** – Save up to 60% on featured titles

- **Newsletter and special offers** – Be the first to hear about new releases, specials, and more

- **Register your book** – Get additional benefits

From technical overviews to drilldowns on special topics, get *free* ebooks from Microsoft Press at:

www.microsoftvirtualacademy.com/ebooks

Download your free ebooks in PDF, EPUB, and/or Mobi for Kindle formats.

Look for other great resources at Microsoft Virtual Academy, where you can learn new skills and help advance your career with free Microsoft training delivered by experts.

Microsoft Press

Now that you've read the book...

Tell us what you think!

Was it useful?
Did it teach you what you wanted to learn?
Was there room for improvement?

Let us know at http://aka.ms/tellpress

Your feedback goes directly to the staff at Microsoft Press,
and we read every one of your responses. Thanks in advance!